Cost-Benefit Analysis

Cost—Benefit Analysis

A Symposium held in The Hague in July, 1969
under the aegis of the NATO Scientific Affairs Committee

Edited by M.G. Kendall, Sc.D.
Chairman, Scientific Control Systems Ltd.

AMERICAN ELSEVIER PUBLISHING COMPANY, INC.
New York, 1971

Published in the United States by
AMERICAN ELSEVIER PUBLISHING COMPANY, INC.
52 Vanderbilt Avenue, New York, N.Y. 10017

First printed 1971

Library of Congress Catalog Card Number: 75-130759
International Standard Book Number: 0-444-19641-2

Printed and bound in Great Britain

CONTENTS

SECTION 1

OPENING CEREMONY AND HISTORICAL REVIEW

Chairman: **M.G. Kendall**

**Conference Director and
Chairman, Scientific Control Systems Ltd, U.K.**

Speaker: R. Turvey
National Board for Prices and Incomes, U.K.

OPENING CEREMONY

Dr. M.G. Kendall opened the Symposium by welcoming the participants. He then introduced Prof. Dr. H.W. Julius, the Head of Centrale Organisatie TNO — the Dutch scientific research organisation — who had been kind enough to make available TNO Conference Hall and its facilities in which the Symposium could be held.

Prof. Julius welcomed the participants on behalf of the Dutch Government and stressed the importance of cost-benefit analysis.

Dr. Kendall thanked Prof. Julius for his kind words and then introduced Dr. G.R. Lindsey, Chief of the Defence Research Analysis Establishment in Ottawa, Canada, and also a member for the NATO Advisory Panel on Operational Research who said a few words on behalf of the Scientific Affairs Division of NATO.

Mr. R. Turvey started the Symposium proper by presenting the first, and the main paper, on the development of cost-benefit analysis.

ON THE DEVELOPMENT OF COST BENEFIT ANALYSIS

Ralph Turvey

1. INTRODUCTION

Most of the papers to be presented at this conference deal with particular applications of cost-benefit analysis. In this introductory paper, I had better keep on general ground. So I started by re-reading the general part of the survey of cost-benefit analysis which Professor Prest and I published in 1965 [6] and picking up four topics where subsequent reading and reflection suggest, with the wisdom of hindsight, that we should have said something more or something different. As you will see, I am not sure what that something should be; in other words I am posing problems rather than solving them. But at least it gives us something to discuss.

Cost-benefit analysis can be understood in two senses. In one it consists simply of the work necessary to present a decision-taker with the information which he requires in order to make a decision. In the other sense it goes further and includes the task of taking the decision.

The distinction is not, of course, completely clear cut. In some cases the cost-benefit analyst may reject some alternatives even though he is not the decision-taker, because he is able to predict that the decision-taker himself would reject them. But all the same, there are two different topics for discussion. There is firstly, the formulation of alternatives and the enumeration, quantification and (where possible) valuation of the relevant costs and benefits of each. Secondly, there is the topic of decision algorithms and preference functions.

I propose to restrict myself to the first topic, the provision of information. Ideally, this should be given by constructing a mutually exclusive list of all costs and benefits and a mutually exclusive list of all the sectors into which the economy can be divided for the purpose of the analysis. If the first list is written vertically and the second horizontally, then any cell will show the amount of a particular benefit gained or cost incurred by a particular sector. A final total column for the economy as a whole will show economy-wide net totals for each cost and benefit and a final total row will show the algebraic sum of benefits and cost for each sector. The bottom-right cell of the whole matrix will then show the algebraic sum of benefits and costs for the alternative in question for the economy as a whole. Where some costs or benefits are quantifiable but not measurable in terms of money the entries will naturally be more complicated, as they will also be if, on account of uncertainty, the entries are not given as single values. Where costs and benefits are not quantifiable at all the entry will contain (or refer to) some prose.

2. UNCERTAINTY

I start with the question of whether a decision-taker should only be presented with single-valued estimates of costs and benefits or whether he should be given a range or probability distribution of answers. A formal answer is that this depends on his utility function. If a decision-taker's utility function is linear, then his utility of the expected net benefit is the same as his expected utility of net benefits. He is then neither averse nor attracted to risk and need only know the single figure of expected net benefit to make his choice.

It has been argued that in most cases the decision-taker's utility function will be approximately linear because the range of possible net benefits afforded by a single project will be minutely small in relation to the size of the economy. Thus it is plausible to suggest that in an economy with eight million cars each driven on average five hundred hours a year, the Minister of Transport will regard an annual saving of one million car-hours as worth exactly twice as much as a saving of half a million car-hours.

An additional consideration strengthens the argument. Presumably the decision-taker's utility is a function of the sum of the net benefits of all the projects undertaken. Thus even if his utility function is not linear, the risk which matters to him is not that of each individual project but that attaching to the whole set of projects. Where the number of projects is large and where their net benefits are uncorrelated, his choice between individual project can then be made without knowing their individual risks.

These two arguments against a need to provide anything more than expected values are naturally appealing to cost-benefit analysts because they make life easy for them. But, as stated above, they are both formal arguments. If the job of cost-benefit analysts is to present decision-takers with useful information, the relevant criterion of usefulness is surely what decision-takers actually want to know and not what economic theorists think they ought to want to know!

Now it seems to me that decision-takers will actually want to know something about risk quite often. One reason for this is that they care about the distribution of net benefits as well as their national total, and a variability of net benefits which is trivially small from a national point of view may be very large from the point of view of the group of people directly affected by a project. If their utility functions are non-linear, the decision-taker's will be non-linear too. Thus coastal works to protect a village from sea flooding which occurs on average only four times each century may be favoured even though 4% of the damage is low in relation to annuitised costs.

There is another reason. Decision-takers are often politicians, and politicians hate having to admit that they were wrong. Hence the disutility of negative net benefits may exceed the utility of equal positive net benefits. The Minister responsible for a dam which silts up within three years is made to feel a fool whether or not the best civil engineers rated the probability of its happening at only 5%.

I therefore suggest that decision-takers are quite often averse to risk and consequently that the cost-benefit analysts who serve them ought to provide some range or probability distribution of possible outcomes or, alternatively, a sensitivity analysis.

The trouble with sensitivity analysis is that its results are too voluminous to be of any practical help to a decision-taker if there are more than, say, two stochastic parameters in the calculation of net benefits. But if sensitivity analysis is possible so, apart from the extra arithmetic effort, is a Monte Carlo analysis. Both involve picking a set of particular values of the stochastic parameters, calculating the answer and then repeating the process. The Monte Carlo analysis merely picks values according to probabilities and repeats the process sufficiently often to generate a probability distribution of net benefits.

If this is done, care must be taken in dealing with stochastic parameters which are correlated. Thus suppose that the net benefits of a river project depend partly upon the amount of generated barge traffic and partly upon the system marginal cost of steam electric power output displaced by the project's output of hydro-electricity. Neither can be estimated with certainty, but in both cases we can assume that they are increasing functions of the general level of economic activity. Consequently they are positively correlated in that one factor causing a large volume of barge traffic will also raise the system marginal cost of steam power. If this correlation is neglected, the variability of net benefits will be underestimated.

To avoid such underestimations it is necessary to bring correlations explicitly into the calculations.* In terms of the example, both benefits must be calculated as functions of (inter alia) some indicator of the general level of activity. The parameters of these functions, which may themselves be stochastic, and a forecast probability distribution of the economic activity indicator then constitute inputs to the analysis.

If all the probability distributions involved in a cost-benefit analysis have the same form, a more analytical calculation may be possible. But this is likely to be difficult or impossible when some of the probability distributions are skewed. I am now going to argue that this will frequently be the case with project construction costs. If my argument is correct the point is one of some importance. Not only may it render analytical calculation more difficult, but it may also require the cost benefit calculation to be done in probability terms in order to obtain expected net benefit even when the decision-taker has a neutral attitude to risk and does not want to know anything about it.

My assertion rests upon two ideas. The first is that when people are asked to give a single-valued estimate of anything, they normally think of its most likely value and not of its expected value. In other words they estimate the mode and not the mean. The second is that construction cost probability distributions are usually positively skewed, the mean exceeding the mode. Taken together, these two ideas mean that people normally underestimate project construction costs.

The basis of the first idea is really nothing more than introspection. One can readily think about what is most likely to happen, while one cannot guess at an expected value without going through the process of attributing probabilities to a whole set of different possible outcomes. So if one starts with the idea that one is going to state just one single outcome it is natural to avoid bothering to think about the whole set. In addition, it is often difficult to distinguish targets from expectations; the confusion of hope with belief (wishful thinking) is a common failing. When a shopkeeper promises to deliver a carpet next Tuesday he "most probably" means that Tuesday is the most probable day, even though he is aware that there is a one in ten chance that the manufacturer will not be able to deliver to him for three weeks!

---

* I owe my understanding of this, and several other of the technical points above to an admirable report by Shlomo Reutlinger [7]

The second idea, positive skewness, is nothing but one aspect of the apparent malevolence of the inanimate universe! In building a bridge there are, let us say, one hundred separate stages. In nearly all of them are quite a few things which could go wrong and few things which could go right. Somewhere or other, some of the things which could go wrong will do so. Hence the expected cost of the bridge exceeds the sum of the modal costs of each of the stages.

Everyday experience supports my idea. I sometimes say that I will go to the kitchen and make a cup of coffee. I never say (or think) that I will go to the kitchen and make 0.99 of a cup of coffee. Yet there is roughly a one per cent chance that I will drop the pot and/or the cup.

To sum up, then, I have suggested that decision-makers may want to know about risk and that even if they do not, the cost-benefit analysts who serve them may need to deal with it in order to avoid an important source of systematic error.

3.   INFLATION

My second topic relates to the valuation of costs and benefits. It seems to be generally agreed that the expectation of future inflation should not be allowed to bias choice in favour of projects where costs occur early relative to benefits. There are two ways of avoiding this. The first is to allow for expected inflation both in the estimation of future costs and benefits and in the discount rate. The second is to allow for it in neither, using constant prices in all the estimates and using a discount rate which does not reflect the estimation of inflation.

The first of these possibilities seems to me to be either inferior to the second or else to reduce to an arithmetically equivalent but more complicated version of it. It clearly requires a forecast of the future development of the general price level, thus adding a particularly difficult item to the list of things which have to be forecast in making a cost-benefit analysis. In addition, it is natural to require that the expectation of inflation which is embodied in the cost and benefit estimates should be consistent with the expectation implicit in the discount rate which is used. The most obvious way of securing this is for the cost-benefit analyst himself to choose both. Thus, for example, he might assume a 4% annual increase in the price level and pick a 12% discount rate or he might assume 3% as the probable rate of inflation and use a discount rate of 11%. But it would be just as good to assume no inflation and use an 8% discount rate. This, of course, is nothing but the second alternative of constant prices and an inflation-free discount rate. This is simpler arithmetically, guarantees consistency and avoids any need to forecast future inflation.

There remains, however, the problem of allowing for anticipated future changes in *relative* prices. Such changes may be just as difficult to forecast as changes in the general price level; the point is, however, that their forecast cannot be avoided in order to produce useful results. The most general and important relative price change to be expected is presumably a rise in the cost of labour as a consequence of economic growth. Let us accordingly suppose that in the economy as a whole labour productivity and real wages and salaries are expected to rise at an annual rate of 3% and consider how to deal with this in a single project evaluation. We suppose that the estimates of labour inputs for the project allow for any productivity growth within it and that no other relative price changes are expected.

The way in which the 3% change is allowed for creates a problem.* Either the price of labour can be assumed to rise 3% a year or the price of all other domestic inputs and the unit value of outputs can be assumed to fall by 3% per annum. From the point of view of introducing the relative rise in the price of labour, these alternatives are equally good. Nonetheless they are not equivalent, as an absurdly simple example will show

Consider a project with a capital cost in 1969 of C which yields benefits of B only in 1979 and whose only other input is the use of n units of labour in 1979. Let the discount rate be 8% and the 1969 price of a unit of labour be w. Then if we let the price of labour rise at 3% per annum, the present worth of benefits minus costs is:

$$\frac{B}{(1.08)^{10}} - C - \frac{nw\,(1.03)^{10}}{(1.08)^{10}}$$

Alternatively, if we assume the value of benefits to fall, we get:

$$\frac{B}{(1.03)^{10}\,(1.08)^{10}} - C - \frac{nw}{(1.08)^{10}}$$

which is not identical.

Both these formulations get the correct change in relative prices but neither of them can be said to involve a constant price level. The first implies a rising price-level, since some items are rising and none are falling, while the second implies a falling price-level, since some items are falling and none are rising. This suggests a compromise where all outputs are measured at constant prices and inputs are measured at prices whose weighted average is constant. Thus wages could be assumed to rise and other input prices could be assumed to fall through time so as to secure a 3% annual rise in wages compared with other input prices within a constant average.

The difficulty here lies in choosing the weights. I would suggest that a rough and ready choice of weights might produce a practical answer but have to admit that I cannot see what is the correct answer in principle. The rise in wages relative to other prices will change the composition of costs through time so that base-year weighting will differ from current-year weighting as time passes. Here, then, is an interesting theoretical problem which requires solution.

4. UNEMPLOYMENT

In our survey of cost-benefit analysis [6] Prest and I set out the argument that where unused resources are employed in a project their market prices overstate their social costs. This suggests that the costs of such a project should be adjusted downwards. We then listed three arguments against making such a correction.

(a) It is easier to allow for the overpricing of labour which is to be used in constructing or operating a project than to allow for the overpricing of equipment, fuel, materials, etc., which are overpriced because they, too, include

---

*I am indebted to Mr H. Christie for bringing this to my attention.

in their costs some overpriced labour. Yet if correction is made for project labour costs only, the relative social costs of project labour and of other inputs may be more poorly estimated than if no correction at all is made.

(b)   Correcting future costs requires estimates of future employment. Government agencies are not usually equipped to make such forecasts, and governments may be reluctant to provide them on a realistic basis in view of the difficulty of keeping them out of public notice.

(c)   The effect of a project upon unemployment depends not only upon the expenditure which it involves but also upon the way it is financed, and this may not be known to the people doing the cost-benefit analysis (e.g. in the case of an agency financed by government grants).

A recent book by Haveman and Krutilla [4] meets the first of these three arguments by using input-output analysis. Taking as their examples a sample of water-resource projects, they use the following sets of data:

i)   A breakdown of project construction inputs of equipment and materials by supplying industry and a breakdown of direct labour inputs by occupation;

ii)   A national input-output matrix and a regional breakdown of each industry's output;

iii)   An occupational breakdown of the labour input of all industries;

iv)   Assumptions as to the fraction of an increase in final demand arising in any region which is supplied by each of the ten regions.

For each of their sample projects undertaken in each of the ten regions they are then able to calculate the distribution between regions of, first, the gross output of each industry arising from the project and, second, the labour requirement in each occupation.

These findings are of considerable interest. Let me cite the first six from their own summary on page 63:

"1)   With the exception of Regions II and III (Mid-Atlantic and East North Central), the industrial demands placed on the region in which the water resource projects are built are primarily in the categories of trade, transportation, and services.

2)   A substantial proportion of total industrial demands (more particularly, demands for durable goods) and off-site labor costs accrue to the Mid-Atlantic and East North Central regions, irrespective of the region wherein the water resource project is constructed.

3)   Except for Regions II and III, a relatively small percentage of total industrial and off-site labor demands is retained within the region of demand imposition in spite of the local preference shown the region where the project is located in the model.

4) Water projects vary greatly in the demands they create for local output and off-site labor demands; while some project types are regionally oriented, others register their demands far from the construction site.

5) While an estimate of the percentage of total labor costs retained in the region of project construction is significant in assessing the local impact of the expenditure, the occupational demands imposed on the project region vary significantly among regions. Likewise, the pattern of occupational demands retained within the region in which the demand is imposed varies significantly among project types.

6) The labor demand for the operatives and kindred workers and the laborers—both of them occupational categories marked by low incomes and high unemployment—which is retained in the region of project construction seldom exceeds 15 per cent to 20 per cent of the total dollar construction cost."

The authors are commendably frank about the assumptions in their analysis. Two deserve particular mention. The first is common to most input-output analysis, namely the assumption that average and marginal co-efficients are the same. It means, for example, that a 1% increase in the output of any industry requires a 1% increase in its employment of accountants and night watchmen. The second is the way in which the authors allocate an increase in final demand for the output of any industry arising in a particular region between that region and the other nine regions. For "national" industries they allocate proportionately to each region's share of national output and for "local" industries (such as automobile repair) they allocate all the demand to the region of origin. They also have two intermediate categories. This is all done very intelligently, but it is nevertheless necessarily guessing rather than estimating. Furthermore, it seems a little odd that this is done only for direct demands; all indirect demands are allocated in the same way as direct demands for the output of "national" industries.

Far from relaxing after these herculean efforts, the authors go on to use a value-added breakdown of their results to correct project construction costs for the zero opportunity costs of idle resources. Thus suppose that a project involves a total increase in expenditure on labourers in a particular region of 100. If they estimate that half of the extra labourers employed there were previously employed then they calculate the shadow cost as only 50. They proceed similarly with corporate profits + depreciation + net interest in relation to idle industrial capacity.

Without going into a more detailed description of their approach, it is clear that the key question is how they estimate the probability that idle resources will be used as a function of, respectively, the percentages of unemployed labour and of idle capacity. What they do is to put this probability at zero for the 1953 unemployment rate and for zero idle capacity and at unity for their 1933 levels. They then fit various alternative sine curves between these extreme points, calling one an upper-bound and another a lower-bound. Many of their results are then given as ranges.

Once again, the authors are engaging in intelligent guessing. It is fun and it is plausible. Nevertheless, even on the plane of principle I have some doubts which I can best express in terms of an example. Suppose that a given increase of 1,000 tons in the output of cement in a particular region is one (of the many) output requirements calculated to result from a particular project. The authors' procedure is to use the cement industry's input co-efficients to determine the labour and production capacity needed for that 1,000 ton increase in cement output. They then examine the question of how much of the labour and how much of the productive capacity thus needed will have been previously idle and therefore costless.

This seems to me to be a curious way round. Surely the first question to ask is whether the additional demand for 1,000 tons of cement will be wholly met by a 1,000 ton increase in cement output, or whether it will partly be met by a reduction in the supply of cement to other consumers of cement. Let us say that 500 tons extra will be produced and 500 tons will be bid away from other consumers. The social cost of the second 500 tons is presumably measured by the amount these other consumers would have paid for it. What is the social cost of the first 500 tons, the net increase in output? Taking first the labour cost of this increase, the answer is that part of the extra labour which was not previously unemployed and which has to be bid away from other employers. The capital cost part of the social cost, on the other hand, will simply be the extra wear and tear of equipment if the cement producers have sufficient idle capacity to raise output by 500 tons.

Now of course the supply response of the cement producers will be a function of their labour supply position and of the amount of idle capacity they have. But to wrap everything up into a labour response function and a separate and independent capital response function, which is what the authors do, does seem to me to miss out some important relationships which are shown by my example to be relevant.

In the end, therefore, I do not know whether Haveman and Krutilla's type of analysis can be regarded as helpful. But it was certainly a good try. It would be interesting to hear whether anyone else has tackled the same problem.

5.   CHOICE OF DISCOUNT RATE

Finally, I propose to take up certain conundrums concerning the choice of the discount rate in cost benefit analysis. These arise when the marginal rate of return on private investment exceeds the social rate of time preference, i.e. when the share of national income devoted to investment is considered to be too low. There are a number of reasons why such misallocation should exist, one of them recently stressed by Harberger in an unpublished paper on the social opportunity cost of capital and by Baumol [1] being the existence of corporation taxes. But the reasons for such misallocation will not be discussed here; it is simply assumed to exist.

The line of argument culminating in Feldstein's paper [3] still seems to me formally correct. I shall describe it briefly and informally. It starts with the notion that what matters is consumption, so that the costs of a project consist of consumption sacrificed elsewhere and its benefits consist of the consumption it provides, directly or indirectly.

Where the resources used by a project are taken entirely from consumption and its benefits are entirely consumed, no problem arises. Both have to be discounted at the social rate of time preference which, by definition, expresses the decision-taker's attitude to consumption now versus consumption in the future.

But if part of the resources used by the project are taken from investment, the consumption foregone is the stream of consumption to which that foregone investment would have given rise. Similarly, if part of the output of the project is used to increase investment in the future, the benefit consists not of the output itself but of the subsequent increases in consumption to which that increased investment will give rise. So in order to ascertain the effects of a project on consumption it is necessary to know, in the first place, how much investment it displaces, what that investment would have yielded, how much of its yield would have been reinvested, and so on ad infinitum. In the second place it is necessary to know how much of the output of the project will be reinvested, what this will yield, how its yield is used, and so on ad infinitum. All this is necessary in order to discover the outcome of the project purely in terms of consumption, an outcome which is then turned into a present value by using the social rate of time preference.

I believe that this approach is logically correct. Unfortunately it is quite impossible to apply; the necessary knowledge is too difficult to obtain. Consequently any criticisms of this approach which suggest a simpler answer are attractive.

One such criticism has been put forward by Mishan [5] and Carr [2]. Their papers have in common the assertion that the postulated excess of the marginal rate of return over the rate of social time preference means that:

a)   Resources used for the project *ought* otherwise to have been invested;

b)   Gains from the project *should* be reinvested to the maximum extent possible.

Thus both costs and (reinvestible) benefits can be compounded forward at the marginal rate of return on investment to yield a terminal value at some computationally convenient date. The alternative with the highest terminal value is the best one. If, as Carr implicitly assumes and Mishan explains, all benefits are reinvestible and all investment opportunities carry the same marginal rate of return, this rate can just as well be used for discounting back to the present as for compounding forward to a terminal date. Thus in this simple case the conclusion is that costs and benefits should all be discounted at the marginal rate of return on investment, *not* at the social time preference rate.

Now this argument does not deny that it is consumption that matters. The point is simply that, in the postulated circumstances, investing rather than consuming raises the present worth of future consumption. The project whose benefits and costs cumulate forward to give the highest terminal value is the project which adds most to the present worth of all future consumption.

Where then does the difference lie between Feldstein and his predecessors on the one hand and such authors as Carr and Mishan on the other? The answer is that the former argue in terms of what *will* happen while the latter argue in terms of what *should* happen. Thus Feldstein is concerned to forecast the proportion of benefits which will be reinvested, while Carr and Mishan require this proportion to be maximised. Similarly Feldstein asks what alternative use would have been made of resources taken by the project while they measure cost by the use that ought to have been made of them.

My sympathies lie with the line represented by Feldstein. We are considering a state of affairs where there is general resource misallocation and examining how to decide on a project against this background. To assume that what should be done will be done or would have been done in the particular case of the resources provided and used by the project seems contradictory. The decision-maker concerned with the project must surely consider things as they are and will be except when they lie within his control. Thus it is his predictions and his plans which matter, not his ideas about what ought to be done in matters beyond his control.

Reluctantly, therefore, I conclude that the impracticable answer is the right one. This is distressing. Perhaps some member of the conference can see a way out.

REFERENCES

1. Baumol, W.J. (Sept. 1968) 'On the Social Rate of Discount' *The American Economic Review*, Vol. LVIII, No. 4, pp. 788-802.

2. Carr, J.L. (Dec. 1966) 'Social Time Preference Versus Social Opportunity Cost in Investment Criteria', *The Economic Journal*, Vol. LXXVI, No. 304, pp. 933-934.

3. Feldstein, M.S. (March 1964) 'Net Social Benefit Calculation and the Public Investment Decision', *Oxford Economic Papers, New Series*, Vol. 16, No. 1, pp. 114-131.

4. Haveman, R.H. & Krutilla, J.V. (1968) *'Unemployment, Idle Capacity, and the Evaluation of Public Expenditure'*, John Hopkins Press.

5. Mishan, E.J. (Dec. 1967) 'A Proposed Normalisation Procedure for Public Investment Criteria', *The Economic Journal*, Vol. LXXVII, No. 308, pp. 777-796.

6. Prest, A.R. & Turvey, R. (1965 & 1966) 'Cost Benefit Analysis: A Survey', *The Economic Journal*, Dec. 1965, reprinted in *Surveys of Economic Theory*, Vol. III, Macmillan, London, Melbourne & Toronto. St. Martin's Press, New York, 1966. pp. 153-207.

7. Reutlinger, S. (1968) *'Techniques for Project Appraisal Under Uncertainty'* International Bank for Reconstruction and Development.

SECTION 2

HEALTH and COMMUNITY SERVICES

Chairman: **A. B. Weiss**
Secretary, Cost Effectiveness Branch,
Operational Research Society of America.

Speakers: R. N. Grosse
School of Public Health, University of Michigan.
and Resource Management Corporation, Bethesda, U.S.A.

W. H. Kirby
Director, Administrative Research Staff,
Veteran's Administration, U.S.A.

J. J. Warford
Department of Economics, University of Manchester, U.K.
and The Brookings Insitution, U.S.A.

A. Williams
Professor of Economics, University of York, U.K.

A. H. Pascal
RAND Corporation, U.S.A.

A. Blumstein
Carnegie-Mellon University
and Office of Urban Research, Institute for Defense
Analysis, U.S.A.

F. Perret
Ministère de l'Economie et des Finances, France

A.D.J. Flowerdew
Third London Airport Enquiry, U.K.

C. Bozon and
A. Maugard
Ministère de l'Equipement et du Logement, France.

COST-BENEFIT ANALYSIS IN DISEASE CONTROL PROGRAMS

Robert N. Grosse

1. INTRODUCTION

In the area of social welfare, one of the first applications of cost-benefit analyses by the government of the United States was to disease control programs. Considerable work had been done during the last ten years in estimating the economic costs of particular diseases. Among the best known of these are Rashi Fein's *Economics of Mental Illness* [1], Burton Weisbrod's *Economics of Public Health* [2] in which he estimated the costs of cancer, tuberculosis, and poliomyelitis, Herbert Klarman's paper on syphilis control programs [3], and Dorothy Rice's studies covering the International Classification of Diseases [4]. A generation earlier Dublin and Lotka's classic explored the impact of disease and disability and their relation to changes in earning power [5]. The economic implications of disability were, of course, a matter of central interest in the area of workmen's compensation insurance [6]. It was not surprising, then, that when systematic quantitative analysis of government programs and policies began to spread from defense to civilian applications, one of the first analytical studies was a study of disease control programs [7].

The basic concept of the study was a simple one. The Department of Health, Education, and Welfare supports (or could support) a number of categorical disease control programs, whose objectives are to save lives or to prevent disability by controlling specific diseases. The study was an attempt to answer the question: If additional money were to be allocated to disease control programs, which programs would show the highest pay off in terms of lives saved and disability prevented per dollar spent?

I'm talking here not about research, but where a technology exists and the problem is whether to put the same, more or less, Federal funds behind these control programs to support activities in hospitals, States and communities. The question we address is where should we allocate the resources available for this purpose. The Department of Health, Education, and Welfare studied five programs, cancer, arthritis, tuberculosis, syphilis and motor vehicle injury. After discussing these studies concerned with allocations among disease programs, I will describe a later study addressed to the proper mix of approaches to kidney disease.

2. FACTORS INFLUENCING CONTROL PROGRAMS

The effectiveness of the Department's disease control programs is influenced by a number of factors. Of most significance is the ability of medical technology to provide the scientific knowledge to prevent the disease, to diagnose disease early enough so that the impact on health can be minimized and to treat the disease to cure the patient. In order to determine the relative emphasis on the Department's disease control programs we addressed such questions as:

Does the knowledge exist for disease prevention?

How can the knowledge be applied?

Does the knowledge exist for disease diagnosis and treatment?

What are the more productive methods for applying this knowledge?

What are the costs involved in applying the knowledge?

What benefits in terms of lives saved, disability prevented and other economic and social losses averted can be achieved?

For each of the diseases discussed in this memorandum, medical knowledge exists for some measure of disease control. However, for such diseases as head and neck cancer and colon-rectum cancer, techniques of diagnosis have not yet been developed to make it economical to screen the large number of people that would be necessary in order to identify a relatively small number of these cancers. Although primitive technology exists, the cost of a control program may be too high measured by benefits foregone in programs with higher potential for saving of lives and decreasing the impact of illness.

3.   THE FEDERAL ROLE

The Federal interest in disease control programs stems from two concerns:

1.   Those diseases which may be communicated across State boundaries.

2.   Those diseases where people are not getting adequate medical care because either personnel, knowledge or facilities may not be available, or because they cannot afford health care.

Tuberculosis and syphilis control have been of concern to the Public Health Service for many years. The national spread of these communicable diseases through personal contacts has been a key reason for the Federal role in these programs. In addition, the technology (drugs and diagnostic procedures) for effective control of these diseases has been in existence for many years; penicillin and blood tests for syphilis, isoniazid and x-rays for tuberculosis.

Technology for effective control of the selected cancer sites has only recently become available and in most cases is still under development. Although the Papanicolaou test for uterine cervix cancer disease dates back to 1928, its general acceptance dates to 1943 and as late as 1960 fewer than 5 million tests were reported by national laboratories. With Public Health Service support for case finding and demonstration projects, including the training of technologists, utilization of this technique reached almost 15 million tests by 1965.

Arthritis includes a number of specific diseases where knowledge does not exist to permit prevention, control or even effective amelioration of crippling and/or disabling symptoms in a large number of patients. The limited knowledge that is available is not widely disseminated and only a small portion of the estimated 10 to 13 million people suffering from arthritis have access to good quality diagnosis and care. The Federal concern here is to assure that more people receive better care. The method of approach is similar to that applied to the cancer programs—demonstration projects, that have a major component of training physicians and technicians and developing and testing diagnostic and treatment methods.

Public Health Service programs in motor vehicle injury prevention are in their initial stages. The magnitude of this problem would indicate a major interest for all health agencies.

4.   SELECTED DISEASE ALTERNATIVE ANALYSIS

The Department of Health, Education, and Welfare task groups were established to develop detailed analyses of the individual selected disease control programs. Each of these studied and analyzed a number of alternative programs. Program cost and anticipated benefits were compared for the alternatives within each of the programs.

Two principal criteria were used as a basis for recommending funding allocation among the programs within each disease category as well as among the different diseases analyzed.

1.   The cost per death averted.

2.   The benefit cost ratio.

4.1   Cost Per Death Averted

The cost per death averted is the five-year program costs, divided by the deaths averted due to the programs. These costs range from an estimated $87 per death averted for the seat belt use program to over $40,000 for such programs as head and neck cancer control increasing driver skills, and emergency medical services.

The cost per death averted for each of the programs is an average cost figure. It would be expected that some of the costs would actually be many times the average cost. For example, the uterine cervix program recommended has an average cost per death averted of $3,470. However, of the 34,000 lives expected to be saved due to the programs through 1972, 30,000 of these have an average cost of about $2,000; 2,300 have an average cost of over $3,500 and 400 have an average cost of over $7,000. While it is possible to add additional lives saved at the lower figure, any significant investment of funds in this program would probably be oriented toward the more expensive cases thus averaging over $7,000.

4.2   The Benefit Cost Ratio

There are two problems with cost per death averted as a sole criteria for evaluating program effectiveness.

1.   There is no distinction made regarding the age at which the death is averted and

2.   There is no way to rank those diseases which are not primarily killers.

The benefit cost ratio includes both morbidity and mortality implications of the disease. The benefit cost ratio simply stated is the relationship between the amount of dollars invested in relation to dollars saved.

The economic savings for these diseases are composed of direct savings of dollars that would have been spent on medical care cost including physician's fees, hospital services, drugs, etc., and indirect savings such as the earnings saved because the patient did not die or was not incapacitated due to illness or injury. The average lifetime earnings for different age groups is related to the age at which death occurs and a calculation of the present value of lost lifetime earnings. For example, if a twenty-seven year old man died this year of one of the diseases, his aggregate earnings would have been estimated at $245,000 had he lived a full life. However, discounting this at 4 percent to the current year, the economic loss is actually closer to $125,000. Included in this analysis are economic losses based on future earnings discounted to present value.

For the purpose of estimating benefits among diseases, it is recognized that economic loss or even death do not completely state the damage and harm caused by disease. Pain and the impact on family relationships are among the more obvious additional items. We do not know how to bring such items into this kind of analysis as yet, but it seems likely that these additional considerations argue in the same direction as the other benefits. The pain of arthritis is still another reason beyond incapacitation to support the program as recommended. We have no reason at this moment to believe that such considerations would have changed the relative preferences among programs.

Some of the programs are designed to have an effect beyond the directly supported Federal operations. For example, the uterine cervix program and the proposed arthritis program have major demonstration and training objectives. The training of specialists who will take the newly learned or developed technology outside the public sector is a major benefit of these programs. This analysis does not credit these programs with such benefits since data is not currently available. Such benefits added to these programs which already have high benefit cost ratios would strengthen the conclusions of this analysis.

4.3 Non-Health, Education, and Welfare Costs

The costs attributed to the programs are primarily the direct Health, Education and Welfare program costs. In the Syphilis and Uterine Cervix programs there are additional direct costs; serological screening costs for the syphilis program and early treatment cost of the uterine cervix program. These costs are directly related to the Federal decision about the size and scope of the programs. There are other expenses, costs, and benefits that may be indirectly attributed to the other programs, but since there is not a direct link between the Federal decision and these costs, they have not been charged to the program. For example, the seat belt use educational program will probably cause an increased consumption of these devices. However, the program attempts to encourage people to use the belts that are already installed in the vehicle. The cost of the belts is not attributed to this program. The benefits of a successful injury prevention program could result in lower auto insurance rates, these are not credited to the programs in this analysis.

4.4 Some Results

Table 1 illustrates one set of diseases, cancer. We looked at cancer of the uterine cervix, breast, head and neck and colon-rectum. We estimated cost per examination, the number of examinations that would be required before a case would probably be

TABLE 1 – CANCER CONTROL PROGRAM: 1968-1972

	Uterine cervix	*Breast*	*Head and neck*	*Colon-rectum*
Grant costs ($000)	97,750	17,750	13,250	13,300
Number of examinations (000)	9,363	2,280	609	662
Cost per examination	$10.44	$7.79	$21.76	$20.10
Examinations per case found	87.5	167.3	620.2	496.0
Cancer cases found	107,045	13,628	982	1,334
Cost per case found	$913	$1,302	$13,493	$9,970
Cancer deaths averted	44,084	2,936	303	288
Cost per death averted	$2,217	$6,046	$43,729	$46,181

found. From this was derived the number of cases that would be found, and estimates of the cost per case found. An estimate was made of the number of deaths that could be averted by the treatment following the detection of the cancers and then we calculated the cost per death averted which ranged from about $2,200 in the case of cervical cancer up to $40,000 to $45,000 in the case of head and neck and colon-rectum cancer.

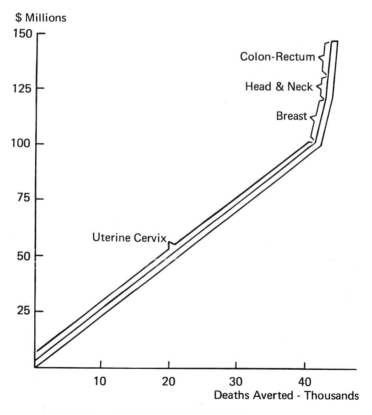

FIGURE 1 – PROGRAMS FOR CONTROL OF CANCER

On the vertical axis of Figure 1 we have plotted the program costs; this includes the cost of the treatment in addition to the Federal detection program. On the horizontal axis estimates of death averted are ordered by increase in cost per death averted in each program. Segments of the curve identified to each disease cover the extent of the program which it was estimated could be mounted in the years 1968–72 before running into sharply increasing costs. In concept, the cervical cancer curve is cut off where costs become higher than the breast cancer program, etc. From this analysis one might say that if there is only available $50 million, cervical cancer should get all the funds. If we have $115 million, then breast cancer control programs look quite competitive. Head and neck and colon-rectum cancer detection programs as major control programs did not look attractive when viewed in this context. The analysts recommended that they concentrate on research and development.

We did the same kind of analysis for each of the five programs studied (Figure 2). There seemed to be a very high potential payoff for certain educational programs in motor vehicle injury prevention. Trying to persuade people that the lump you're sitting on is a seat belt, use it, don't walk in front of a car, and so on. And then as we move up this curve, again ordered by cost of averting death we begin adding the others. This particular criterion, deaths averted, was not completely satisfactory. The number of fatalities attributed to arthritis weren't very impressive. Secondly, we had returned to the question, did it matter who died? Did it matter whether it was a thirty year old mother or a forty year old father of a family or a seventy-five year old grandfather? In Figure 3 I have used dollar savings counting the avoidance or use of lower cost treatment, and a crude estimate of the average (discounted) lifetime earnings saved as a criterion in place of deaths averted. You'll notice two changes in results: cervical cancer and syphilis change places in priority order, and we are able to introduce arthritis.

The way we developed programs from such analyses was to use information such as this and the preceding charts as another insight to give us an additional feel for what

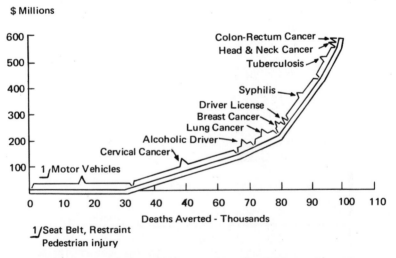

FIGURE 2 – ANALYSIS OF PROGRAMS FOR SELECTED DISEASES :
COST OF PROGRAMS AND DEATHS AVERTED 1968-1972.

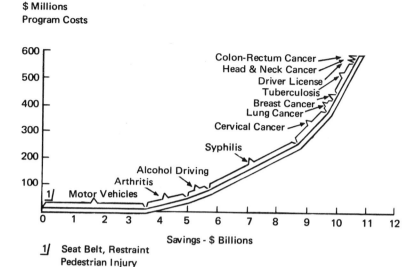

$ Millions
Program Costs

1/   Seat Belt, Restraint
Pedestrian Injury

FIGURE 3 – COST OF BENEFIT : SELECTED DISEASES, 1968-1972.

were relatively high priority and what were relatively low priority programs, and then to feed these insights into the decision making process which also considers the existing commitments, political situation, the rate of spending, the ability to get people moving on programs, and so on.

4.5   Some Criticisms

These studies were not greeted with universal acclaim. Criticisms focused a number of problems. First, with almost no exception the conclusions were based on average relationships. That is, the total benefits were divided by the total costs. There was little evidence of what the actual impact of increasing or decreasing programs by small amounts might be.

Let me illustrate with a hypothetical example how such marginal information might be used to determine the preferred mix of disease control programs. Assume that we can determine as in the following tables the number of lives saved by different expenditures on disease A and disease B:

Disease A

Expenditures	Lives Saved
$ 500,000	360
1,000,000	465

Disease B

$ 500,000	200
1,000,000	270

If we only knew the effect of spending $1,000,000, we might opt for a program where all our money was spent on controlling disease A, as we could save 465 lives instead of 270 if we spent it all on disease B. Similarly, if we only knew the effects of programs of a half million dollars, we would probably prefer A, as we'd save 360 rather than only 200 lives.

But if we knew the results for expenditures of both half a million and one million dollars in each program, we would quickly see that spending half our money in each program was better than putting it all in one assuming we have one million dollars available:

Our calculations would be:

Expenditures	Lives Saved
$1,000,000 on A	465
$1,000,000 on B	270
$ 500 000 on A	360
500,000 on B	200
$1,000,000	560

But suppose we had still more discrete data, as in the following tables which give us the effects of each hundred thousand dollars spent on each control program:

Disease A

Expenditures	Lives Saved
$ 100,000	100
200,000	180
300,000	250
400,000	310
500,000	360
600,000	400
700 000	430
800,000	450
900,000	460
1,000,000	465

Disease B

$ 100,000	50
200,000	95
300,000	135
400,000	170
500,000	200
600,000	225
700,000	240
800,000	255
900,000	265
1,000,000	270

we could then spend the million dollars even more effectively:

	Lives Saved
$ 600,000 on A	400
400,000 on B	170
$1,000,000	570

The lack of marginal data resulted from both a lack of such data for most programs, together with a lack of economic sophistication on the part of the Public Health Service analysts who performed the studies. Despite the theoretical shortcomings, some common sense was used in applying the results.

Practical obstacles of existing commitments made it almost impossible to recommend *reductions* in any program. So the decisions dealt with the allocation of modest increments.

In the case of oral and colon-rectum cancers, the average cost per death averted seemed so high that the Department recommended emphasis on research and development, rather than a control program to demonstrate and extend current technology.

In cervical cancer, investigation indicated a sizeable number of hospitals in low socio-economic areas without detection programs which would establish these if supported by Federal funds. The unit costs of increasing the number of hospitals seemed to be the same as that of those already in the program. Shifting the approach to reach out for additional women in the community would increase costs per examination, but not so high as to change the relative position of this program. At most, it raised costs to about those of the breast cancer control program.

Despite the seeming high potential pay-off of some of the motor vehicle programs there was considerable uncertainty about the success. As a consequence recommendations were for small programs with a large emphasis on evaluation for use in future decisions. The same philosophy was applied to the arthritis program.

What resulted then, was a setting of priorities for additional funding, based on the analytical results, judgement about their reliability, and practical considerations.

A second type of criticism was concerned with the criteria, especially the calculation of benefits. [7a]. They were considered inadequate in that they paid attention to economic productivity alone, and omitted other considerations. In particular, they were thought to discriminate against the old who might be past employment years, and women whose earnings were relatively low. It was also feared that the logic, if vigorously pursued, would penalize not only health programs for the aged such as the newly launched Medicare, but also programs aimed at assisting the poor whose relative earning power is low by definition.

In actual practice on the programs studied these concerns were only hypothetical. The programs for cervical and breast cancer looked to be good despite their being for women. As for the poor, most of the programs considered, especially cervical cancer, syphilis, and tuberculosis were aimed primarily at them, and projects were usually located to serve low income residents.

Another type of objection was raised not against the technique of analysis, but against its being done at all. Choices among diseases to be controlled and concern with costs of saving lives can be viewed as contrary to physicians' attitudes in the care of an individual patient. Prior decisions on allocations to various health problems (and such decisions are made, analysis or no) rested upon a combination of perception of the magnitude of the problem and the political strength organized to secure funding, e.g. the National Tuberculosis Association.

The disease control cost-benefit analyses suggest that additional considerations are very relevant. Given scarce resources (and if they are not, there is no allocation problem), one ought to estimate the costs of achieving improvements in health. If we can save more lives by applying resources to a small (in numbers affected) problem than a large one, we ought to consider doing so.

A somewhat separate issue is that of the disease control approach to personal health. This is too large an issue to deal with in this paper, but if it may make more sense to develop programs of delivering comprehensive health care, including preventive services, than to maintain categorical disease programs. But that is another cost-benefit analysis.

5.   KIDNEY DISEASE PROGRAM ANALYSIS

The following year a number of additional disease control studies were performed. One of the most interesting and important was on kidney diseases [8] . This analysis was launched at a time when the public was becoming conscious of a new technique, the artificial kidney (chronic dialysis), which could preserve the life and productivity of individuals who would otherwise die of end-stage kidney disease. About 50,000 persons a year do so die. It is estimated that about 7.500 of these were "suited" by criteria of age, temperament, and the absence of other damaging illnesses for dialysis treatment. The national capacity could handle only about 900, who would remain on intermittent dialysis the rest of their lives. About 90% would survive from one year to the next. The operating cost of dialysis treatment in hospitals was estimated at about $15,000 per patient per year. A home treatment approach might reduce this to about $5,000 per year.

The Federal government was under great pressure to expand the national capacity, which was limited not only by the large money costs, but also by shortages of trained personnel and supplies of blood. Indeed, at the same time as this analysis was being performed, an advisory group to the U.S. Bureau of the Budget was studying the problem of end-stage kidney disease. This group came in with the recommendation for a massive national dialysis program [9] .

The HEW program analysis was somewhat more broadly charged, and took a more systems oriented approach. It concerned itself not only about the 7,500 annual candidates for dialysis, but also about the other 40,000 or so who would suffer the end-stage disease, but were unsuited to dialysis. If some way could be found to reduce the numbers falling into the pool of end-stage patients, perhaps a larger number of

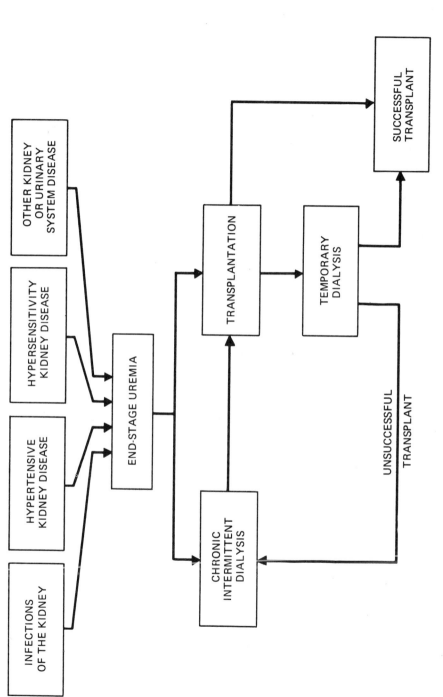

FIGURE 4 — SCHEMATIC OF TRANSPLANT AND DIALYSIS PATIENTS

people could be helped. Figure 4 illustrates the classes of kidney diseases leading to end-stage disease. If these could be better prevented or treated we might keep down the number of patients requiring dialysis or transplantation.

The analysis group, therefore, examined a number of mechanisms or program components. Among these were:

1. Expanded use of existing preventive techniques.

2. Expanded use of existing diagnostic techniques.

3. Expanded use of existing treatments, including chronic dialysis, kidney transplantation and conservative management (drugs, diets, etc.).

4. Laboratory and clinical research to produce new preventive, diagnostic, therapeutic and rehabilitative methods.

5. Increased specialized scientific medical and paramedical training to provide the manpower needed for the research and treatment attack on the kidney disease problem. This also includes continued postgraduate education to train practicing physicians in the use of the latest diagnostic and treatment modalities.

6. Increased public education to alert potential victims of kidney disease to seek medical help at the earliest possible emergence of warning signs.

7. Provision of specialized facilities not currently in existence which are essential for the execution of any of the above programs.

It must be understood from the outset that these program components are interdependent in most cases. For example, preventive techniques exist that need further research to make them maximally effective for broad application. New treatment methods are useless if existing diagnostic techniques are not being applied in medical practice. Because of the present inadequacies of existing treatments, be they dialysis, transplantation, or conservative management, a considerable research effort is called for to increase their efficacy and economy to make them more broadly useful.

Time does not permit a detailed description of the analysis. Costs were estimated for relevant public and private expenditures for the nationwide treatment of kidney disease. The latter includes cost of physician care, hospital care, nursing home care, and other professional services for diagnosis and therapy of kidney diseases, as well as the cost of drugs and net insurance costs. In addition, the cost was estimated for ongoing research efforts, for demonstration, screening and detection programs, for education and training efforts and for that portion of the cost of construction of hospital and medical facilities which can be prorated to the use of patients with kidney disease.

Based on the substantive information obtained and statistical and economic data collected, estimates were made of the benefits to be gained by different approaches to the solution or amelioration of the overall national kidney disease problem at different expenditure levels of HEW funds.

Several different funding levels were assumed, and estimates were made assuming both the current state-of-art and an expected advanced state-of-art in 1975.

Each program consisted of a hypothetical situation where a specific level of HEW program funding was divided among a rational mix of program components (screening, diagnosis and treatment, research, training, etc.) based on the particular characteristics of the specific disease group involved, and was applied to specifically involved or particularly vulnerable groups or, as the case may be, to the entire population. The benefits accruable from these programs were then estimated and stated in terms of overall reduction of mortality, prevalence, and morbidity due to kidney disease.

Benefit indices were quantified in terms of the reduction in annual mortality, the reduction in annual morbidity (number of sick days per year) and in terms of the disease prevalence in the total population due to the specific type of kidney disorder analyzed, which would accrue thanks to the impact of the various program components—such as research advances, disease prevention and improved treatment.

The analysis group avoided estimates of the impact on economic productivity in their results although such calculations have been made independently [10].

The HEW study concluded that concentration in future programs merely on the treatment of end-stage kidney disease is not likely to solve the problem of annual deaths due to irreversible uremia unless unlimited funds are available for an indefinite continuation of such a program, Thus, steps must be taken to decrease the number of people who enter the irreversible fatal stage each year by a systematic prevention or treatment of the primary kidney diseases which initiate their progressive downhill course. It is obvious from the analyses in the three major kidney disease groups—infectious, hypersensitive and hypertensive—that the otherwise inevitable annual reservoir of patients with irreversible kidney failure can be diminished considerably through vigorous programs activated to deal with each of these groups. The application of relatively minor funds in the group of infectious kidney diseases to stimulate systematic screening of high-risk groups followed by diagnosis and treatment, even within the current state-of-art and without awaiting additional advances due to ongoing or future research, can bring about a significant future reduction in the number of end-stage patients. Continued and expanded research activities will be necessary to increase the percentage of patients ultimately benefited by this approach.

In the area of hypersensitivity diseases involving the kidney there appears to be no promising mode of attack in sight except for the launching of a systematic research effort intended to increase our knowledge of the disease mechanisms involved. Here, the sooner this effort is started the greater the likelihood of a reduction of the number of end-stage victims in the near future. The promise for benefits to be derived from this type of research effort is such that it should not be postponed—particularly since any new effective treatment or prevention modality would produce major benefits in the entire field of hypersensitivity diseases, such as rheumatic heart disease, rheumatoid arthritis and others.

In the group of hypertensive diseases of the kidney an immediate start, within the current state-of-the-art, of screening, diagnosis and treatment can begin to diminish the number of patients who will eventually require end-stage treatment because of their progressive renal involvement. Simultaneous research efforts are likely to make this particular portion of the overall program more effective as time goes by, in the same fashion in which the new antihypertensive drugs developed during the last ten years have succeeded in decreasing by about 50 percent the mortality due to malignant hypertension.

Thus, a meaningful Federal program to reduce the annual mortality due to kidney disease and aimed at a general reduction of the prevalence of the various kidney diseases must perforce be a multifactorial one which brings into play all of the program components—research, prevention, treatment and education—available in our armamentarium. An optimally proportioned mix of these program components must be present to yield maximum benefits in overall number of lives saved. This last concept includes not only deaths avoided today but deaths to be prevented in the years to come. Needless to say such a total program, to be meaningful and productive, must be aimed at all three major primary kidney diseases, as well as at end-stage kidney failure.

Figure 5 shows a hypothetical program mix that might come from such conclusions.

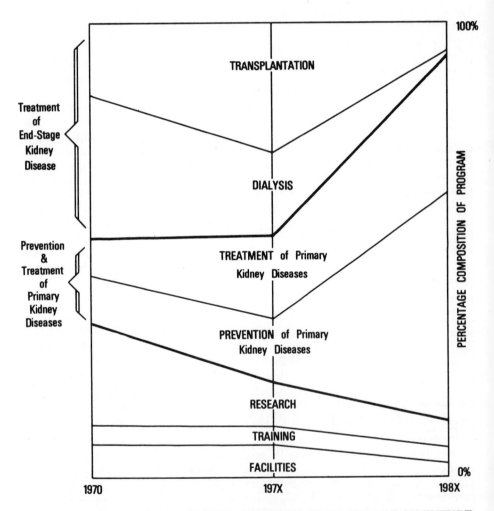

FIGURE 5 – EFFECT OF ADVANCING STATE OF THE ART ON FUTURE
PROGRAM COMPOSITION
(Percentages are wholly arbitrary and merely serve to illustrate shifting trends.)

Note the early emphasis on research to offset the state-of-the-art, and the growth in allocations to the prevention and treatment of primary kidney diseases as relative allocations to dialysis are diminished.

To illustrate some of the cost and benefit calculations developed in the study, Tables 2, 3 and 4 are appended. Table 2 summarizes Federal HEW costs, Table 3 includes all costs, and Table 4 estimates impacts of these programs on deaths, number of cases of each disease, and days of illness.

TABLE 2
HEW COST SUMMARY
($1,000)

Program Level	Kidney Disease Categories				Total	
	Infectious	Hypersensitivity	Hypertensive[***]	End-Stage	Cost	Percent
Current Expenditure Level*						
Diagnosis, Prevention, Treatment						
Prevention (including education & administration)	3,803	1,500	4,000		9,303	19.92
Diagnosis and Treatment	–	–	–	7,240	7,240	15.50
Sub-Total	3,803	1,500	4,000	7,240	16,543	35.42
Research	4,000	5,250	3,800	12,100	25,150	53.85
Training	400	560	380	1,000	2,340	5.01
Facilities	1,000	170	1,000	500	2,670	5.72
TOTAL	9,203	7,480	9,180	20,840	46,703	100.00
Intermediate Expenditure Level*						
Diagnosis, Prevention, Treatment						
Prevention (including education & administration)	5,929	3,000	8,057	–	16,986	14.47
Diagnosis and Treatment	–	–	–	30,000	30,000	25.56
Sub-Total	5,929	3,000	8,057	30,000	46,986	40.03
Research	5,500	8,250	4,650	18,000	36,400	31.01
Training	750	750	500	5,500	7,500	6.39
Facilities	8,000	8,000	8,000	2,500	26,500	22.57
TOTAL	20,179	20,000	21,207	56,000	117,386	100.00
Accelerated Expenditure Level*						
Diagnosis, Prevention, Treatment						
Prevention (including education & administration)	9,919	3,000	10,114	–	23,033	7.94
Diagnosis and Treatment	–	–	–	171,000	171,000	58.98
Sub-Total	9,919	3,000	10,114	171,000	194,033	66,92
Research	6,500	10,125	5,500	24,000	46,125	15.91
Training	975	750	1,425	10,000	13,150	4.54
Facilities	10,000	10,000	11,600	5,000	36,600	12.63
TOTAL	27,394	23,875	28,639	210,000	289,908	100.00
Accelerated Expenditure Level – 1975**						
Diagnosis, Prevention, Treatment						
Prevention (including education & administration)	11,308	{ 43,000-Vaccine { 13,000	11,732	–	76,040	25.94
Diagnosis and Treatment	–	–	–	132,225	132,225	45.11
Sub-Total	11,308	56,000	11,732	132,225	208.265	71.05
Research	7,410	12,450	9,500	1,500	30,860	10.53
Training	1,110	1,870	3,000	5,000	10,980	3.75
Facilities	11,400	10,000	11,600	10,000	43,000	14.67
TOTAL	31,228	77,320	35,832	148,725	293,105	100.00

*   Current State of the Art
**   Advanced State of the Art
***   Attributable to renal disease associated with hypertension.

TABLE 3   TOTAL COST SUMMARY
($1,000)

Program Level	Kidney Disease Categories				Total	
	Infectious	Hypersensitivity	Hypertensive***	End-Stage	Cost	Percent
Current Expenditure Level*						
Diagnosis, Prevention, Treatment						
Prevention (including education & administration)	11,687	2,000	5,330	–	19,017	7.88
Diagnosis and Treatment	139,388	–	28,032	17,825	185,245	76.73
Sub-Total	151,075	2,000	33,362	17,825	204,262	84.61
Research	5,330	7,000	5,070	12,800	30,200	12.50
Training	530	750	510	1,000	2,790	1.16
Facilities	1,330	225	1,330	1,300	4,185	1.73
TOTAL	158,265	9,975	40,272	32,925	241,437	100.00
Intermediate Expenditure Level*						
Diagnosis, Prevention, Treatment						
Prevention (including education & administration)	14,977	4,000	10,954	–	29,931	9.00
Diagnosis and Treatment	140,275	–	32,442	43,200	215,917	64.93
Sub-Total	155,252	4,000	43,396	43,200	245,848	73.93
Research	7,330	11,000	6,200	18,700	43,230	12.99
Training	1,000	1,000	670	5,500	8,170	2.46
Facilities	10,670	10,670	10,670	3,300	35,310	10.62
TOTAL	174,252	26,670	60,936	70,700	332,558	100.00
Accelerated Expenditure Level*						
Diagnosis, Prevention, Treatment						
Prevention (including education & administration)	22,097	4,000	13,899	–	39,996	7.60
Diagnosis and Treatment	143,616	–	36,852	189,375	369,843	70.29
Sub-Total	165,713	4,000	50,751	189,375	409,839	77.89
Research	8,670	13,500	7,330	24,700	54,200	10.30
Training	1,300	1,000	1,900	10,000	14,200	2.70
Facilities	13,330	13,330	15,460	5,800	47,920	9.11
TOTAL	189,013	31,830	75,441	229,875	526,159	100.00
Accelerated Expenditure Level-1975**						
Diagnosis, Prevention, Treatment.		{ 200,000 - Vaccine				
Prevention (including education & administration)	25,190	{ 34,000	16,120	–	275,310	33.84
Diagnosis and Treatment	103,721	68,000	53,858	144,875	430,454	52.91
Sub-Total	188,911	302,000	69,978	144,875	705,764	86.75
Research	9,880	16,600	12,000	1,500	39,980	4.91
Training	1,480	2,490	4,000	5,000	12,970	1.60
Facilities	15,200	13,330	15,460	10,800	54,790	6.74
TOTAL	215,471	334,420	101,438	162,175	813,504	100.00

*   Current State of the Art
**   Advanced State of the Art
***   Attributable to renal disease associated with hypertension.

6.   A FINAL WORD

These highly condensed discussions of HEW's applications of cost-benefit analysis to disease control programs illustrate both the usefulness and limitations of such analyses for decision-making. Issues are sharpened, and quantitative estimates are developed to reduce the decision-makers' uncertainty about costs and effects. Nevertheless the multiplicity of dimensions of output, and their basic incommensurabilities both with costs and the outputs of other claimants for public expenditure still requires the use of value judgements and political consensus.

TABLE 4 – PROGRAM BENEFITS

Program Level	Kidney Disease Categories				Total
	Infectious	Hypersensitivity	Hypertensive ***	End-Stage	
Current Expenditure Level*					
Short-Term Benefit-Reductions:					
Mortality	70 Deaths	610 Deaths	2,190 Deaths	690 Deaths	3,560 Deaths
Prevalence	3,231,260 Cases	–	27,000 Cases	–	3,258,260 Cases
Morbid Days	15,962,420 Days	–	1,802,000 Days	–	17,764,420 Days
Long-Term Benefit-Reductions:					
Annual	1,750 Deaths	–	4,330 Deaths	–	6,080 Deaths
Cumulative	25,850 Deaths	–	86,560 Deaths	–	112,410 Deaths
Intermediate Expenditure Level*					
Short-Term Benefit-Reductions:					
Mortality	70 Deaths	610 Deaths	2,270 Deaths	1,560 Deaths	4,520 Deaths
Prevalence	3,243,860 Cases	–	34,880 Cases	–	3,278,740 Cases
Morbid Days	16,273,640 Days	–	2,056,820 Days	–	18,330,460 Days
Long-Term Benefit-Reductions:					
Annual	1,770 Deaths	–	4,820 Deaths	–	6,590 Deaths
Cumulative	26,190 Deaths	–	96,300 Deaths	–	122,490 Deaths
Accelerated Expenditure Level*					
Short-Term Benefit-Reductions:					
Mortality	70 Deaths	610 Deaths	2,380 Deaths	7,675 Deaths	10,735 Deaths
Prevalence	3,292,860 Cases	–	42,750 Cases	–	3,335,610 Cases
Morbid Days	17,483,880 Days	–	2,311,340 Days	–	19,795,220 Days
Long-Term Benefit-Reductions:					
Annual	1,870 Deaths	–	4,820 Deaths	–	6,690 Deaths
Cumulative	27,480 Deaths	–	96,300 Deaths	–	123,780 Deaths
Accelerated Expenditure Level-1975**					
Short-Term Benefit-Reductions:					
Mortality	80 Deaths	770 Deaths	9,300 Deaths	27,399 Deaths	37,549 Deaths
Prevalence	5,630,700 Cases	62,250 Cases	289,690 Cases	–	5,991,723 Cases
Morbid Days	26,064,430 Days	2,610,000 Days	5,578,860 Days	–	34,253,290 Days
Long-Term Benefit-Reductions:					
Annual	4,125 Deaths	8,610 Deaths	9,480 Deaths	–	21,090 Deaths
Cumulative	76,500 Deaths	320,000 Deaths	189,660 Deaths	–	586,160 Deaths

*   Current State of the Art
**   Advanced State of the Art
***   Renal disease associated with hypertension.

Source: See Chapter 6.

Short-term benefits - reduction in *annual* mortality, etc., when program is fully operative.

Long-term annual benefits - eventual *annual* reduction in number of cases reaching end-stage kidney disease.

Long-term cumulative benefits - sum total of long-term annual benefits.

REFERENCES

1. Rashi Fein, *Economics of Mental Illness*. Basic Books, Inc., New York, 1958. For later study using a new conceptual framework resulting in cost estimates almost 10 times higher see Ronald Conley, Margaret Cromwell, and Mildred Arrill, "An Approach to Measuring the Cost of Mental Illness", *American Journal of Psychiatry*, 12416, December 1967, pp. 63-70.

2. Burton A. Weisbrod, *Economics of Public Health: Measuring the Economic Impact of Diseases*. University of Pennsylvania Press, Philadelphia, 1961.

3. Herbert E. Klarman, "Syphilis Control Programs", *Measuring Benefits of Government Investments*, edited by Robert Dorfman. The Brookings Institution, Washington, D.C., 1965, pp. 367-410.

4. U.S. Department of Health, Education, and Welfare, *Economic Costs of Cardiovascular Diseases and Cancer, 1962.* Public Health Service Publication 947-5, Washington, D.C. May 1965, and Dorothy P. Rice, *Estimating the Cost of Illness*, Public Health Service Publication 947-6, Washington, D.C., May 1966. Jacob Cohen, "Routine Morbidity Statistics as a Tool for Defining Public Health Priorities", *Israel Journal of Medical Sciences*, May 1965, pp. 457-460, estimated the weighted impact of 25 mass diseases on deaths, loss of life years under 65, hospitalization, days of hospitalization and cases in Workers' Sick Fund. Earlier literature for many countries is summarized in C.–E.A. Winslow, *The Cost of Sickness and the Price of Health*, World Health Organization, 1951.

5. Louis I. Dublin and Alfred J. Latka, *The Money Value of a Man*, Ronald Press, New York, 1930.

6. See, for example, Earl F. Cheit, *Injury and Recovery in the Course of Employment*.

7. U.S. Department of Health, Education, and Welfare, Office of Assistant Secretary for Program Coordination, *Motor Vehicle Injury Prevention Program*, August 1966; *Arthritis*, September 1966; *Selected Disease Control Programs*, September 1966; *Cancer*, October 1966. Studies of the tuberculosis and syphilis control programs have not been published.

7a. For discussion of some of these issues see Dorothy P. Rice "Measurement and Application of Illness Costs", *Public Health Reports*, February 1969, pp. 95-101; T.C. Schelling, "The Life You Save May Be Your Own", *Problems in Public Expenditure Analysis*, edited by Samuel B. Chase, Jr., The Brookings Institution, 1968, pp. 127-176; and Pan American Health Organization, *Health Planning: Problems of Concept and Method*, Scientific Publication No. 111, April 1965, esp. pp. 4-6.

8. U.S. Department of Health, Education, and Welfare, Office of the Assistant Secretary (Planning and Evaluation), *Kidney Disease,* December 1967.

9. The Bureau of the Budget convened by an expert Committee on Chronic Kidney Disease. See *Report* by this Committee, Carl W. Gottschalk, Chairman, Washington, September 1967. Herbert E. Klarman, John O.S. Francis, and Gerald D. Rosenthal, "Cost Effectiveness Analysis Applied to the Treatment of Chronic Renal Disease", *Medical Care*, Vol. VI, No. 1, Jan.–Feb. 1968, pp. 48-54, analyzed the Committee's data to explore what is the best mix of center dialysis, home dialysis, and kidney transplantations. The authors restricted their beneficiaries to those in end-stage kidney disease, and concluded that transplantation is economically the most effective way to increase life expectancy of persons with chronic kidney disease, although they recognize the factors that constrain the expansion of transplantation capability.

10. Jerome B. Hallan and Benjamin S.H. Harris, III, "The Economic Cost of End-Stage Uremia", *Inquiry*, Volume V, Number 4, December 1968, pp. 20-25, and J.B. Hallan, B.S.H. Harris, III, and A.V. Alhadeff, *The Economic Costs of Kidney Disease*, Research Triangle Institute, North Carolina, 1967.

COST-BENEFIT ANALYSIS IN A LARGE HEALTH CARE SYSTEM

William H. Kirby

1. INTRODUCTORY REMARKS

Nearly three years ago the Chief Medical Director of the Department of Medicine and Surgery (DM&S) of the Veterans Administration took steps tp bring management science techniques to bear on his medical care operations. The DM&S has 166 hospitals located throughout the United States. They range in size from 50 to 2500 beds and care for approximately 100,000 patients. Thus, the Veterans Administration (VA) offers an unparalled opportunity for management research in the health services field.

I wish to describe very briefly our management or administrative research role, structure and operating characteristics. I also wish to call attention to the challenge which we have in bringing a new kind of interdisciplinary relationship into an operational health care system. I mention this inasmuch as our responsibility does not terminate at the point at which a cost-benefit study is completed. We are concerned with the realization of cost-effectiveness or cost-benefit outcomes. Some examples of this will be given later in the presentation. This means, of course, that we share a large responsibility for implementing our own recommendations. Therefore, the knowledge and experience of introducing new techniques or modifications of on-going practices are an integral part of our staff operation.

1.1 The Administrative Research Staff

It was proposed and accepted by management that our basic organizational structure be composed of a management sciences staff and a projects staff. In this way it was believed that our mission could be supported in the most effective manner.

Our current version of the mission is as follows:

> The mission of this executive staff function is to study, develop, recommend and implement courses of action by which the Department of Medicine and Surgery may maximize the utilization of its resources in meeting its objectives.

> These studies encompass physical, medical, economic and organizational systems analyses leading to the identification of sensitive criteria by which alternative courses of action may be defined for management decision making.

Such studies are concerned with the development of predictive techniques, often phrased in mathematical and statistical form, which permit an evaluation of physical, medical, economic and organizational factors associated with effective management of health systems. These procedures allow for a more systematic approach to complex problems such as those associated with programming, planning and budgeting, and cost benefit studies, among others. Furthermore, it is directed at a better understanding of the relationships among components of medical care. These components include, among others, medical and nursing services, equipment, facilities and logistical services. In brief, these techniques are being used to assist in evaluating present and future medical care from both the medical and management points of view. Management strategies, operational planning techniques and cost control measures are among the principal activities involved in the execution of this function.

Our organizational structure is shown in Figure 1.

The following is a listing of the line and staff activities which we serve:

Line: Chief Medical Director
Deputy Chief Medical Director
Regional Medical Directors
Hospital Directors

Professional Staff: Medical
Surgical
Dental
Pathology
Nursing
Dietetics
Pharmacy
Physical Medicine & Rehabilitation
Psychiatry
Radiology
Prosthetics
Social
Research

Administrative Staff: Management Control
Program Planning & Budgeting
Hospital Construction
Management Systems
Medical Administration
Engineering
Supply
Management & Evaluation.

1.2   Program

Our present program consists of 35-40 short and long term projects scheduled over the next three to five years. This program was generated through discussions with key officials by asking them to specify their most important problems or problem areas. It should be pointed out that while these projects form the basis of our current program, we have a task force composed of certain members of our management sciences staff taking a more funadmental look at our system in order to try and identify more useful approaches for us to use in making the most effective contribution.

1.3   Studies Completed

Our completed studies to-date are more of the short-term, ad-hoc type. They are

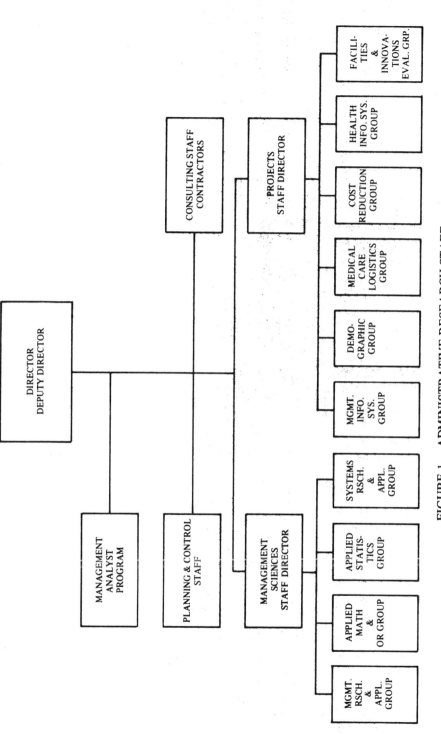

FIGURE 1 – ADMINISTRATIVE RESEARCH STAFF

characterized more in terms of industrial or management engineering methodologies than those in operations research or mathematical statistics. These studies are presented in some detail. Several others are only identified and summarized. They are presented as follows:

2.   CONVEYING SYSTEM

2.1   The Problem

The Administrative Research Staff was asked to respond to a management request to do a generalized economics study of mechanical conveying systems in the Veterans Administration hospitals. After a brief review it was apparent that no such studies had been done before in any of the VA hospitals which meant that even unique or individual case results did not exist. Thus, a study approach was developed which included the need to perform sufficient unique cases on which economic generalizations could be made. Naturally this would amount to a reasonably long term effort particularly with our available resources.

After further consideration management altered its requirements and the result was a request to study the mechanical conveying systems at a given near-by hospital. It was further decided that an effort would be made to measure the annual operating costs; i.e., labor, power, and maintenance; and annual capital costs; i.e., amortization and interest on investment.

2.2   Method of Approach

After some consideration it was believed desirable to see if it were possible to obtain our cost measures on similar VA hospitals which did not contain these conveying systems. If we could accomplish this for hospital sizes above and below that of the test hospital, we could derive a non-conveying system cost line against which the cost outcome of the test hospital could be compared. Specifically, it would fall above, below, or on this cost line. The test hospital bed capacity was approximately 700.

We were quite fortunate to find that there were several such VA hospitals which were similar in configuration, were all general medical and surgical in type and in which patient mix might reasonably be assumed as similar. Due to time and human resources available to perform the study, comprehensive measures of material handling labor were limited to three days for each system in each hospital. All hospitals were surveyed in advance by Administrative Research Staff personnel in order to determine the detailed method needed to obtain reliable data. Data collection teams were then instructed in the procedures to be followed and assigned particular material handling areas to gather the required data.

2.3   General Material Handling System

At the hospitals studied, "general" material includes those materials and supplies (excluding food) used for patient care and "paper" that is too large to be transported by the pneumatic tube system. Areas assigned not related to patient care were excluded from this study.

Elements in each hospital were identified as dispatchers (originators) and receivers of these materials. The costs measured were the total costs associated with the assembling of this material, the dispatching and/or the transport to a central point in the receiving area and the receiving or unloading.

2.4   Labor Costs

At each hospital, only three days of general material handling labor data were collected. However, it is known that some materials move on a two week or monthly cycle at some locations while at others there is a steady flow of materials. For this study, it has been assumed that the average labor content for the three days studied is representative, when in fact this might not be true.

No attempt was made to "tune-up" any part of the handling system by improving methods or the efficiency of personnel. The labor measured was on an "as is" basis and was assumed not to have been influenced by observation and measurement.

The average actual man-minutes measured during the three day sample were extrapolated to an annual basis by assuming that all material is moved Mondays through Fridays only.

The estimated annual labor cost at each hospital was calculated by using the same hourly labor rate based on same intermediate step of each grade plus 7½ per cent for fringe benefits and applying these against the estimated annual man-hours of labor content for each grade for each element observed.

The summary of the labor costs for the hospitals concerned is shown in Table 1.

TABLE 1 – TOTAL ANNUAL GENERAL MATERIAL HANDLING COSTS

	VA Hospitals: Conventional Systems			VA Hospital with Automatic Conveying System
	Hospital # 1	Hospital # 2	Hospital # 3	
Beds:	500 *	500 *	800 *	702 *
Cost Factors $				
Labor	37,925	43,766	51,579	56,445
Capital	25,106	26,855	38,544	86,405
Power & Maint.	7,590	7,945	6,786	26,984
TOTAL:	70,621	78,566	96,909	169,834

* At the time of the study, occupancies were as follows:
      Hospital No. 1   –   448
      Hospital No. 2   – 477
      Hospital No. 3   –   729
      Test Hospital   –   645

It should be noted that the overall average hourly labor rates for labor vary between hospitals. This is caused by variation in the labor grade mix for the different jobs at the hospitals. Therefore, in order that a direct, yet fair, comparison of labor costs created by each separate system could be made among the hospitals, the overall average hourly labor rates for the test hospital were applied to the labor contents at the three other hospitals.

It appears that the automated mechanical conveyor system at the test hospital does not show any economies in labor. Instead, the labor cost is about 14 per cent more. If a projected rate of increase in labor rates (approximately 4 per cent per year) were taken into account, the differences between a manual system and the mechanical system would become even more pronounced as time progressed.

2.5   Capital

The capital investment associated with general material handling includes the investment of fixed or installed material handling equipment—conveyors, service elevators, dumbwaiters and chutes; mobile material handling equipment—carts and trucks, and building construction related to material handling.

Start-up costs are also a part of capital costs. These would include development of procedures, debugging of the system and the initial required training of personnel. However, since reliable records of these costs were not available, start-up costs were not included in this analysis.

The amortization periods for mobile equipment vary from 10 to 20 years depending on the type of equipment and its construction. The General Services Administration advised the use of 20 years for the expected life of all installed equipment. The amortization period for building construction associated with materials handling was also set at 20 years. This is in line with a plan to do a major modernization rebuilding every 15 to 20 years.

A 4 per cent rate of interest was used on the average investment over the life of the capital item in calculating the annual interest cost that should be charged against a given system.

The total capital costs for the hospitals studied are shown in Figure 2. The installed equipment and building construction costs at the test hospital are much higher because of the automated mechanical conveyor system.

2.6   Maintenance and Power

As more equipment is added, or as equipment becomes more sophisticated, maintenance costs generally rise. This is borne out by experience at the test hospital.

Similarly, as powered equipment is added to a system, the power costs rise. Table 1 shows the estimated annual power and maintance costs for general material handling at the 4 hospitals studied. In order to make the data directly comparable, costs were also calculated using the test hospital electric power rate per kilowatt-hour.

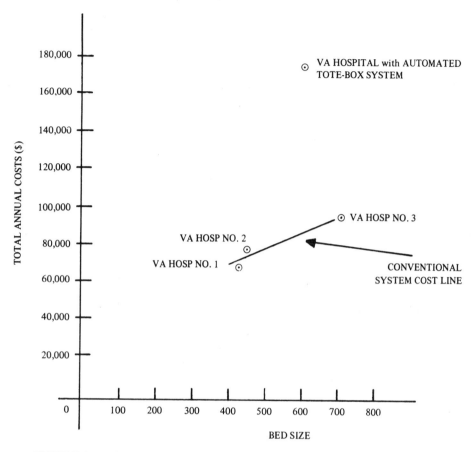

FIGURE 2 – TOTAL ANNUAL GENERAL MATERIAL HANDLING COSTS
AUTOMATED TOTE-BOX vs. "CONVENTIONAL" SYSTEMS

2.7 Summary

The total annual general material handling costs for the 4 hospitals studied are shown
in Table 1. Figure 2 shows the total annual cost line for the non-conveyorized
hospitals. The test hospital costs shown in Table 1 are noted also in Figure 2. As can
be seen from these, the automated hospital is approximately 80 per cent more
expensive to operate.

2.8 Conclusions

Since the automated mechanical conveyor system at the test hospital was superimposed on the designed building, construction costs were probably higher than normal. Also, all conveyor systems should not be judged by this one system. However, it appears that with the present mechanical system at the test hospital even neglecting capital and operating costs, the labor costs would make it uneconomical.

3.   PNEUMATIC TUBE SYSTEM

In order to determine the economic benefits, if any, of the 4" x 7" pneumatic tube system at the test hospital, a method different than that used for the economic evaluation of the general material system was necessary. Since there was no directly comparable manual system and since only one function was involved, the approach used was based primarily on time studies (by an industrial engineer) of the tube handling operations at the test hospital including the mail room messenger operations and a VA hospital without a pneumatic tube system. In addition, other information and data regarding the tube operation were collected, e.g., total tube load between each station, number of items per tube sent, kinds of items, system reject rate, and senders notation of urgency of delivery.

These data regarding labor and flow together with other operating data—power and maintenance—and capital costs were used to evaluate the pneumatic tube system.

3.1   Discussion

Approximately 450-550 "full" tubes were sent daily; the number of tubes returned empty was usually considerably less, only about 28 per cent of the total number transported. Between 15-24 per cent of the "full" tubes originated in the mail room with the balance coming from 64 other stations. The tubes from the mail room carry an average of approximately 11 pieces while the tubes from the other stations average only about 3 pieces.

During the survey, the question was asked as each tube was dispatched whether or not its delivery was urgent or whether it might wait 2 hours for the present mail messenger pick up and delivery. Thirty-seven per cent of the deliveries were classified urgent. The following is the breakdown of the items considered urgent.

Item	Per Cent
Mail and Memos	16.9
Medical Records	13.5
Requisitions	18.7
Drugs	3.5
Equipment and Supplies	2.8
Reports	33.6
Other (TWXs, Cards, Stencils, Vouchers, Worksheets, Evaluations, Overtime, etc,)	11.0
TOTAL	100.0

However, when the medical items classified as urgent were discussed with the Chief of Staff, it was learned that immediate urgency did not really exist and that practically all items could wait 1 or 2 hours for delivery by messenger.

Taking as an average 450 "full" tubes that originate at stations other than the mail room and the 3.2 pieces per tube, the average number of pieces that would have to be sorted and delivered additionally per day would be about 1440 pieces. At a measured time for sorting of approximately 0.03 minutes per piece, the additional sorting time would be about 40 minutes per day.

However, it takes about 0.5 minutes to fill and dial the destination of a tube. Therefore, if the pneumatic tube system was not available, the mail room would not dispatch its 75-125 tubes each day and its workload would be reduced to a minimum of 40 minutes per day. Thus, the additional mail room sorting time would be countered by the reduction in the tube handling time.

The major difference in the pick-up and delivery operation of the mail messenger would be the additional workload required to service the 20 wards which are not covered presently by the messenger service. The time measured to provide this service is 0.92 minutes for travel and 0.50 minutes for delivery and pick-up per ward wing. Thus, this additional workload would amount to about 14 minutes per trip.

The mail messenger service currently takes about 70-90 minutes per fun. With the addition of one other messenger, pick-up and delivery could be hourly or 8 times each day instead of the present 4 deliveries per day. In addition, the extra time could be used to provide additional service to specific areas or stations to handle some "urgent" items or could be used to deliver those "large" items currently delivered by the mechanical conveying system. Thus labor cost would be approximately $5,500 per year more.

3.2   Operating Expenses Pneumatic Tube System

The estimated annual maintenance cost for the 4" x 7" penumatic tube system at the test hospital is $6,160,–$5,460 for labor and $700 for parts. Annual power costs are estimated to be $3,717.

3.3   Capital

The tube system cost $250,000 and $2,900 of spare parts are inventoried. The building construction costs associated with this system are estimated to have been $5,000. The estimated annual capital charges against these investments are $17,908.

3.4   Summary

The estimated total annual costs to operate the pneumatic tube system at the test hospital was $33,820. Contrasted to this is the estimated cost for using only a mail messenger service to provide 8 deliveries per day, of approximately $11,500 per year. These are shown in Figure 3.

3.5   Conclusions

Since only the costs associated with the "mail" or small "paper" load at the test hospital were investigated, no inferences could be drawn for other loadings. However, it is apparent that the pneumatic tube system operation at the test hospital is more costly than a manual mail messenger service that would provide 8 hourly deliveries.

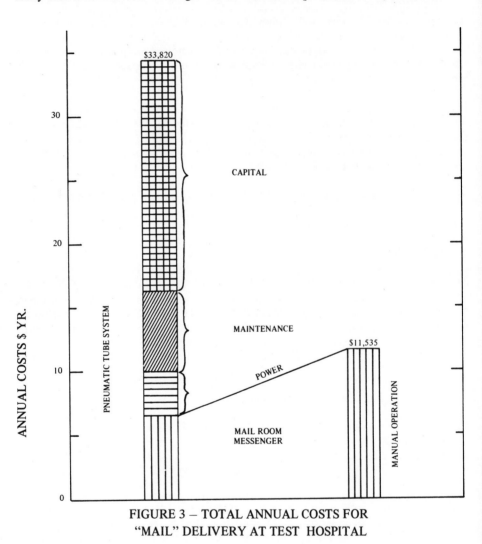

FIGURE 3 – TOTAL ANNUAL COSTS FOR
"MAIL" DELIVERY AT TEST HOSPITAL

4.   FOLLOW-ON COST STUDY OF PNEUMATIC TUBE SYSTEM OPERATIONS

4.1   The Problem

A follow-up study was undertaken to re-examine the cost problem for a selected group of hospitals having operational pneumatic tube systems in order to answer the following questions:

1. If capital costs are taken as "sunk" costs; i.e. not considered in the cost analysis, does it cost more or less to continue using the operating pneumatic tube systems as compared to substitute manual messenger service?
2. Is it more economical to operate only those pneumatic tube stations which have frequency use than the full system?
3. Should proposed new hospitals be equipped with pneumatic tube systems serving only areas which have high frequency use?

4.2   Discussion

The size of a pneumatic tube system is usually expressed in terms of the size of its cross-section. The VA uses two sizes namely, (a) the 4" diameter and (b) the 4" x 7". It was decided to limit the study to four cases due to time and resource limitations. Two hospitals were chosen having the 4" diameter tube system and are known as

TABLE 2 – HOSPITAL AND PNEUMATIC TUBE SYSTEMS CHARACTERISTICS

Characteristics	Hospital A	Hospital B	Hospital C	Hospital D
Type of Hospital	GM&S *	GM&S	GM&S	GM&S
Number of Approved Beds	528	501	794	1340
Number of Operating Beds	441	501	758	1204
Type of Tube System	Non-Auto.	Non-Auto.	Auto.	Auto.
Age of System (Years)	17	17	1	5
Size of Tubes	4"	4"	4" x 7"	4" x 7"
Total Tube Stations	30	39	51	89
Number Operating PTS Stations	28	32	47	80
Number Buildings Served by PTS **	1	1	2	19
Number Floors Served by PTS	10	12	7	56
Number Days/Week PTS Operates	5	5	5	5
Number Hours/Day PTS Operates	8½	8½	8½	8

*   GM&S (General Medical and Surgical)
**   PTS (Pneumatic Tube System)

Hospital A and Hospital B. The other two hospitals, Hospital C and Hospital D, have the 4" x 7" tube systems. Hospital D differs from Hospital C inasmuch as its tube system serves several separate buildings. Table 2 shows certain descriptive factors associated with the sample hospitals.

Costs were developed with the pneumatic tube systems in operation and again after shutting them down. The materials ordinarily sent through the tube system were handled by the messenger service during shut-down. A messenger service was already in existence in each case inasmuch as there were delivery points which did not have tube stations and a significant amount of material was either too large for the tubes or was of such a nature which prevented its transport in a tube system.

4.3   Results

In general it was found that if capital costs for the tube systems were not considered, the total annual operating costs for handling tubed material plus the supplementary messenger service required for handling materials not amenable for tube transport as compared with manual messenger service for handling all such materials were more in the marginal region. According to the observations made in this study the total annual handling costs for hospitals using the 4" diameter tubes (Hospital A and Hospital B) were approximately 2-3 thousand dollars less than the complete manual messenger service. On the other hand the total annual handling costs for hospitals using the 4" x 7" tubes (Hospital C and Hospital D) were approximately 3-6 thousand dollars more than the complete manual messenger service. See Table 3.

If capital costs are included in the analysis as shown in Table 4 then total handling costs are greater for all hospitals using pneumatic tube systems.

The original questions are answered as follows:

Question 1:   *If capital costs are taken as "sunk costs, i.e., not considered in the cost analysis, does it cost more or less to continue using the operating pneumatic tube systems as compared to substitute manual messenger service?*

Answer: *For hospitals using the 4" diameter tube system it costs less (Table 3).*

Question 2:   *Is it more economical to operate only those pneumatic tube stations which have high frequency use than the full system?*

Answer: *For existing 4" (manual systems) a $200 savings in tube operating cost and a $1250 increase in mail room and messenger labor resulting in a $1050 smaller savings per year if only the high activity tube stations were operated.*

For 4" x 7" systems, the use of existing high activity stations only would increase the total annual cost from $17,500 for all tube stations to $18,200 using only high activity tube stations.

Question 3:   *Should proposed new hospitals be equipped with pneumatic tube systems serving only areas which have high frequency use?*

Answer: *For proposed 4" tube systems, $2500 could be saved in amortization and interest costs. However, the use of messengers only would still be $600 per year more economical than the use of high activity tube stations.*

For proposed 4" x 7" systems, $6000 could be saved annually by installing only high activity stations. However, the annual cost would still be $13,500 greater than using messengers only.

TABLE 3 – ANNUAL COST EXCLUDING CAPITAL CHARGES*

| | 4" Manual | | 4" x 7" Automatic | |
	Hospital A	Hospital B	Hospital C	Hospital D
EXISTING SYSTEM:				
(Operation of pneumatic tube system plus a supplemental messenger service)				
1. Mail room activities and supplemental messenger service.	$10,051	$ 6,771	$ 8,405	$25,650
2. Pneumatic tube system operating cost.	1,207	1,777	9,093	22,612
Total	$11,258	$ 8,548	$17,498	$48,262
SUBSTITUTE MESSENGER SERVICE				
1. Mail room activities and substitute messenger service	$14,877	$10,858	$10,944	$45,138
Annual Savings using messengers only	–	–	$ 6,554	$ 3,124
Annual savings using tube system	$ 3,169	$ 2,310		

* These costs are conservative inasmuch as carrier handling costs by clerical personnel at tube stations other than the mail room have been excluded. More time is required to pick up, unload, load, and dispatch mail in carriers† than to receive and dispatch mail by messengers. 4" manual carriers require about 1/8 minute longer per carrier and 4" x 7" automatic carriers require about 1/4 minute longer per carrier. Based on an average of the number of carriers used in Hospitals A and B, the additional annual cost per hospital is $600. For Hospitals C and D the additional annual cost per hospital is $800.

† A carrier is the mail container that travels through the pneumatic tubes.

TABLE 4 – ANNUAL COST INCLUDING CAPITAL CHARGES

| | 4″ Manual | | 4″ x 7″ Automatic | |
	Hospital A	Hospital B	Hospital C	Hospital D
EXISTING SYSTEM:				
(Operation of pneumatic tube system plus a supplemental messenger service)				
1. Mail room activities & supplemental messenger service.	$10,051	$ 6,771	$ 8,405	$25,650
2. Pneumatic tube system operating cost.	1,207	1,777	9,093	22,612
Sub-total	11,258	8,548	17,498	48,262
3. Capital Charges Amortization * (based on 20 years)	3,000	3,900	12,750	22,250
Interest at 4% *	1,200	1,560	5,100	8,900
Annual Capital Cost	4,200	5,460	17,850	31,150
Total Cost	$15,458	$14,008	$35,348	$79,412
SUBSTITUTE MESSENGER SERVICE				
Mail room activities and substitute messenger service	14,877	10,858	10,944	45,138
Annual Loss	$ 581	$ 3,150	$24,404	$34,274

* Based on the following costs in 1968 dollars:

	$60,000	$78,000	$255,000	$445,000

Frequently the question of "tuning up" a system (making it more efficient), manual or automatic, comes up. In a purely manual system the tune up possibility exists in terms of work methods improvements, minimization of delays, and higher individual performance. In the cases studied here the magnitude of the workload required two manual messengers and it did not appear likely that either of them could be completely eliminated even if methods and performance were improved. Therefore, making the operation more efficient would mean increasing the idle time of one or both messengers unless they were specifically assigned other duties at just the right times within their schedules. Savings in terms of personnel (RNs, LPNs, etc) for the tube systems are judged to be very small.

Drugs, blood and other fluids are not transported in the Veterans Administration hospitals by pneumatic tubes. In considering the possibility for doing so one is confronted with a problem similar to paper and record transport, i.e., only certain small items would fit in the tubes. There would still be a need for a parallel system—elevators, dumbwaiters, to handle the larger items at all times and to handle all such items during emergency shut downs of the automated system.

While no experimental exercise was developed as a part of this study concerning the question of operating the tube systems over the 24 hour period and 7 days a week, consideration is given to the idea. To begin with the high frequency users—clinical laboratory and pharmacy and medical administration personnel—do not work those hours. Hence the high volume generating elements are not available. An estimate was made of the additional operating costs for the smaller 4″ tube system in terms of power and maintenance. This came out to be about double of the present costs, or approximately $4500/year. This does not consider the effect of less down time on the life of the system. Night time and week end demands by patients are, of course, decreased thereby reducing the magnitude of the logistics problems especially as they relate to tubable materials.

4.4 Recommendations

1. Due to the marginal nature of annual operating costs when capitalization is ignored for systems already installed, it is recommended that each hospital director examine the operational cost of his own pneumatic tube system, providing he is in a position to carry out an approved plan. (He may not have a qualified analyst available).

   Inasmuch as the 4″ tube systems seem to be characterized by minimum power and maintenance requirements, low noise levels, reasonably favorable labor costs and the possibility of unidentified intangibles, there is no apparent basis for recommending their discontination as a result of this report.

   On the other hand, since the 4″ x 7″ tube systems are characterized by considerably higher maintenance and power requirements, resulting in increased annual costs, there is some basis for considering their discontinuation. High noise level is frequently considered as a negative benefit. However, each station management analyst or other qualified individual should re-examine his own 4″ x 7″ situation closely as mentioned above. There may be other identifiable positive benefits which should be considered in the examination process but which limited resources did not permit in this study.

2.   In considering new hospital construction it is *not* recommended that limited pneumatic tube systems (high frequency use stations) be installed for either size.

3.   If capital costs are to be amortized, then neither of the pneumatic tube systems should be considered for installation unless some as yet unidentifiable benefits develop.

4.5   Background Remarks

The tube systems carry mail and other small items from one area to another within the major hospital buildigs. Tubes seldom service outlying buildings. Hospital D covered by this study was an exception with 19 buildings. In many hospitals the tube systems operate about 40 hours per week but in a few hospitals they operate 24 hours per day seven days per week. In all hospitals it is still necessary to operate a supplemental messenger service to deliver items which are too large to fit into the carriers or are too likely to be damaged. Messengers must also serve areas not reached by the tube system. In addition, messengers must serve all areas during those time when a tube system is shut down according to schedule or because of a breakdown.

For this study 4″ pneumatic tube systems were chosen which required the manual transfer of carriers (Hospitals A and B) and 4″ x 7″ tube systems which had automatic transfer of carriers (Hospitals C & D). A pilot study was conducted at Hospital C, during which period study procedures, scheduling, data collection and analysis forms, and time study forms were designed for use at all hospitals to be studied. data for each of the four hospitals appear in Table 2.

4.6   Methodology

The study was designed to make a direct comparison between the cost of operating the pneumatic tube system and the cost to delivery, by messenger, the material now being carried by the pneumatic tube system.

The costs of the delivery of communications materials in the presence of a pneumatic tube system were divided into three basic categories:

1.   Cost of operating the tube system itself including electric power, carrier repair and replacement, maintenance labor and repair parts for the system.
2.   Supplemental messenger service required to deliver materials which, for varying reasons, were not sent through the tube system and to serve offices not served by the tube system.
3.   Those mail room activities directly related to the delivery of this material, including sorting, loading and unloading mail carts and transfer of carriers in the non-automatic system.

The costs of the delivery of communications materials in the presence of a substitute messenger service include the following activities:

1.   Messenger Service to handle all material which was being handled by the pneumatic tube system and supplemental messenger service.
2.   Mail room activities required to support the supplemental messenger service; loading and unloading mail carts and sorting.

The study required three weeks each at Hospitals A, B, and C and four weeks at Hospital D. There was a considerably larger physical layout with an increased number of tube stations at Hospital D.

The total time spent at each hospital was divided into the following basic phases:

1.   Orientation—Informing hospital personnel of the purpose of the study and the method by which it would be conducted.
2.   Preparation—Tubes operating—Preparation for the collection of tube traffic data to be used in determining messenger routes and schedules for the substitute system.
3.   Data Collection—Tubes operating—Period during which personnel at each tube station recorded the time of dispatch and destination of each loaded carrier sent out.
4.   Data Analysis—Tubes operating—Manual delivery preparations—Period for analyzing the data collected, preparation of messenger schedules and the training of messengers to accomplish these schedules.
5.   Data Collection—Manual messenger service—Pneumatic tube shut down period in which the substitute messenger service was studied.

During the entire period of the study at each hospital, time studies were made on the handling of carriers, loading and unloading of mail carts, sorting of mail and of the messenger runs themselves. Volume counts were also made of the material handled in these various operations.

Messenger Rounds—A time study observer accompanied the messenger on his rounds and recorded the stops that he made and the time required. Delays not related to the job were excluded from the computations. The messenger's time was adjusted to allow credit for his performance and was then increased by a percentage to cover personal time, fatigue, and necessary delays.

Mail Room—Conventional stop watch time studies were taken on sorting mail, loading and unloading carriers, transferring and dispatching carriers, loading and unloading mail carts and other mail room activities. All mail room activities were also timed using GTT (Group-Timing Technique) studies. These studies revealed how each mail room employee utilized every minute of his day. These data indicate when peak load and slack periods occur, the degree of understaffing or overstaffing, and possible rearrangements of duties.

4.7   Findings

The pilot study conducted at Hospital C indicated the noise level of the newer and larger 4″ x 7″ system was of some concern to many of the people. Most of this noise occurred while the carrier traveled through the tube. The noise, plus the constant attention demanded by the tube station, was disruptive to the secretaries and, in some cases, to the supervisors. The receiving stations of the 4″ x 7″ automatic system were unloaded each time a carrier arrived, to prevent jamming of the tube station, the secretary was required to leave her desk, remove the carrier, unload and return the empty carrier to the owning station. This did not seem to be a significant matter of concern at hospitals having the 4″ manual system which was generally much quieter and which had the facility to collect several carriers in the incoming station before it became necessary to remove them. During the test period while the tubes were shutdown the messenger routes and frequency of the runs were based on careful study of data collected on the number of carriers sent and received daily by each tube station. Generally speaking, this provided the administrative offices with a pick up and delivery approximately every hour with specific times set up to meet the expressed requirements of the ward and laboratory personnel.

In each test hospital the pneumatic tube system was turned off for four or five consecutive days and all deliveries were made by messengers. Careful records were kept of the messenger needs of each idle tube station location. After two or three days the substitute messenger service was "tuned up" by improving the substitute messenger schedule. The messenger schedules were so satisfactory that in Hospital B, for example, only three telephone calls per day were received requesting a pick up or delivery by a special messenger provided for the study. Employees in each office, ward, and other location had been instructed verbally and in writing to telephone for the messenger if their mail service was not satisfactory.

4.8 Summary

This brief discussion concerning cost analyses associated with mechanical and pneumatic tube conveying systems in hospitals is presented as a first order or gross approach. More comprehensive studies could and, perhaps, should be made. We are the first to admit that they leave a lot to be desired. In addition to more refined measures, further identification of so-called intangibles is certainly in order.

We have recently initiated a fundamental internal logistic study. In addition to a more basic understanding of the various forms of logistical needs, we are interested in their various interrelationships and, of course, their respective costs.

5. AUTOMATIC DATA PROCESSING APPLICATION TO A CLINICAL LABORATORY

5.1 Purpose

This study was conducted in order to assess the economic feasibility and to identify potential benefits associated with the installation of an automated clinical laboratory information processing system at one of the VA's General Medical and Surgical hospitals.

5.2 Study Design

The study was designed to measure the operational and economic consequences of the existing and the proposed clinical laboratory systems through the complete laboratory processing cycle. An effort was made to observe, record, organize, and analyze all available data regarding the ordering, processing, reporting, and the eventual synthesis of results performed by the clinical laboratory. The study design encompassed activities in (1) automated chemistry, (2) general chemistry, (3) special chemistry, (4) hematology, (5) microbiology, and (6) serology. In addition, activities closely related to the performance of tests (the ward collection of specimens, the delivery and assimilation of laboratory information outputs, etc.) were included within the study design. Activities in histopathology and the blood bank were excluded from the study design since the proposed system innovation does not pertain to these activities at this time.

The study was also designed to include appropriate one-time costs for equipment, system conversion, personnel services, travel, etc.

5.3   Study Methods

To achieve the study objectives, a variety of industrial engineering data collection techniques were adapted to meet VA requirements. The Group-Timing Technique (GTT) was employed as the principal means of obtaining data regarding existing laboratory operations and the extent to which these activities are susceptible to improvement by the proposed automated system. The GTT procedure permitted an observer to document the time spent on productive and non-productive activities and to evaluate the performance of a group of laboratory technologists and technicians. Other pertinent data were obtained in order to establish the most complete and accurate foundation for subsequent analysis. The resulting distribution of expended time by work elements was then subjected to the application of appropriate standard formulas.

Similarly, standard work-measurement techniques were employed to obtain measurements of man-hour requirements for new tasks introduced by the proposed system. These techniques were used to ascertain (1) the time required for a laboratory technologist to enter and transmit test data using various system CRT visual display station formats, and (2) the time required to process varying numbers of requisitions using the system's optical mark reading document processor. These observations were made using the proposed system equipment under simulated conditions. A second principal technique employed was the use of industrial engineering Methods–Time Measurement (MTM) standards for establishing system console monitoring requirements, the affixing and transferring of specimen container labels, etc. These and other techniques, plus an intensive review of the proposed system design, provided adequate data to identify (1) the differing man-hour requirements; and (2) the differing operational capabilities, etc., between the existing and proposed systems.

5.4   Outcome

Assuming a reasonable authenticity of system costs, an essentially uneventful technological installation, a seven-year amortization period, reasonable accuracy in the Clinical Laboratory's workload growth curves, and an effective reduction in laboratory staff resulting from the transfer of clerical and computational processes from the technician staff to the ADP system, a break-even point for the investment could be expected in approximately two years following successful installation, as shown in Table 5.

5.5   Other Benefits

A.   Physicians' Review of Laboratory Test Results

Internal laboratory costs represent only a portion of the overall hospital costs

TABLE 5 – MANPOWER REQUIREMENTS AND SAVINGS TO BE REALIZED

Prescribed for ADP System

1	2	3	4	5	6
	Employees Required		Cumulative Reduction in No. of Employees	Cumulative Dollar Savings	
Fiscal Year	Present Method	ADP System			Remarks
1968	25.3				
1969	30.4			(60,000)	FY 1969 only
1970	36.5	31.9	4.6	(83,370)	Implementation Started
1971	41.9	31.4	10.5	(59,770)	Implementation Complet
1972	48.2	36.2	12.0	(24,190)	The breakeven point will occur about the 3rd Quarter of FY 1972
1973	53.0	39.8	12.2	20,940	
1974	58.3	43.8	14.5	76,430	
1975	64.1	48.1	16.0	143.870	

which are directly related to the current mode of laboratory operations. Accordingly, the study design provided for capturing certain external data which would indicate potential savings when compared with current laboratory information outputs. Specifically, as current outputs are now fragmented on a daily basis, the reviewing physicians presently are required to search a "shingled" chart to identify relevant test result data spread over a period of time. As he turns from sheet to sheet, the physician must assimilate the data in order to identify day-to-day trends, abberations, and/or correlations.

To ascertain the medico/economic significance of this mode of laboratory information output, an analysis of 175 patient charts was undertaken by Hospital personnel under the immediate direction of the Associate Chief of Staff for Research. The 175 charts were categorized in terms of the complexity of pertinent data to be reviewed and the actual expenditure of time for review purposes was systematically recorded by participating physicians. The total expended physician time to review the 175 charts amounted to about 15 hours daily. By projecting this to a review of a station total of 525 charts daily, it is estimated that 44 hours of physician time are expended per day in searching and assimilating laboratory test result data. This represents in one sense an equivalent six man-days of physician time per day for this hospital's physician staff. With the ADP type print-out, more than one-half of this time would be saved for improving patient care and other medical functions.

B.   The following benefits have not been quantified during the study period but should result in significant operational advantages following the installation of the proposed system:

> *Daily Digest of "Out of Normal Range" Results*—will facilitate regular review by professional personnel of all abnormal findings. This information will be most useful in determining data validity, incorrect testing procedures, instrument malfunctions, etc.

> *Outstanding Workload Status Reports*—will provide a powerful supervisory tool for daily manpower distribution within the clinical laboratory. This will further facilitate the timely processing of tests.

> *Delinquent Test Result Listings*—will provide systematic monitoring or tests and regularly identify action necessary to ensure the timely completion and reporting of results.

> *Quality Control Reports*—will permit automated adjustment for instrumentation drifts, verification of existing norms, detection of equipment malfunctions and/or incorrect calibrations, inappropriate specimen controls, etc. The overall consequences of this particular system advantage are vastly important in clinical laboratory operations.

> *Statistical and Research Reports*—will permit the regular assimilation of statistical data and the rapid generation of reports; or with servicing routines, the ability to perform a diversity of research functions.

> *Service to Clinics, Reference Labs and Other Institutions*—will be possible as the system can provide centralized service to remote users via telecommunications media.

> *Automated Bacteriological Monitoring*—will be soon incorporated within the system by means of the frequent automated readings of specimen. This innovation will permit the recognition of minute specimen changes, and reports will be made accordingly. Consequently, significantly more rapid medical determinations will be possible.

In order to assess the common assumption of reduced reporting errors in an ADP process, an acceptable error analysis using a prescribed statistical experimental design procedure is recommended which will show error rate in the present on-going system and in the ADP system to be installed for comparison purposes. This should be in the protocol and actions for the next phase of this effort.

Inasmuch as this is an important user-test-effort which could influence Department-wide decisions especially in terms of: (a) the general usefulness of these hybrid clinical laboratory ADP applications, (b) identifying compatible data systems which are complementary with other available and proposed data systems (AMIS, PTF, AHIS, —VAH Minneapolis acute care system), and (c) station cost-effectiveness, it is recommended that a new protocol and action plan be prepared. The plan should show the detailed installation and implementation tasks including the error analysis and procedures for transferring the specified laboratory staff (see Column 4, Table 1), time schedules, and resources needed to insure successful installation and implementation. It is also recommended that plans be included to accommodate user needs in neighboring clinical laboratories (VAH West Roxbury).

In order to insure that the anticipated gains are realized and retained, the action plan should contain appropriate management review procedures. The Administrative Research Staff would be available to assist in their development.

6. STANDARD COST MANAGEMENT FEASIBILITY STUDY

6.1 Purpose

The general purpose of this study was to determine the feasibility of applying industrial budgeting and standard cost techniques and procedures in Veterans Administration hospitals.

Such procedures were desired for the purpose of: (1) improving the effectiveness of each individual VA hospital facility, (2) providing a better basis for overall station comparisons and (3) assisting in the allocation of funds by the VA Central Management. More specifically, the objectives were:

1. To devise a basis for relating or allocating service and treatment costs to patients, based on an analysis of patient requirements.

2. To determine the suitability and applicability of establishing standard elemental time values and costs for key areas of hospital service and treatments.

3. To estimate the usefulness of a standard cost system based on measured standards as:
    a. A basis for forecasting requirements for facilities and personnel.
    b. A means of accumulating and allocating actual cost to meet requirements of the Bureau of the Budget.
    c. A step towards establishing standards for each hospital against which actual costs can be compared to determine operational efficiency.

6.2 Conclusions

1. It is believed that standard costs could be developed which would be useful for:
    a. Budgeting, allocation of funds and appraisal of relative performance by Central Management.
    b. More effective management and control at each hospital.

2. Many variables in addition to relative efficiency affect cost and performance. Among these are:
    a. Size of hospital
    b. Type of facility
    c. Mix of patients
    d. Local wage rates
    e. Mission of the hospital
    f. Affiliation with a university medical school

g. Provision for handling special types of illness
h. Extent to which difficult cases are referred to one hospital from other Veterans Administration hospitals
i. Centralized scheduling of patients' requirements.

3. Individual hospital budgets could be derived with consideration for the size and type of the facility, local wage rates and the hospital's unique mission.

4. Variable (flexible) budgets should be devised to permit readjustment of the basic budget in response to changes in occupancy rate or patient mix.

5. Such variable budgets could provide a more effective means of control through the separation of budget variances arising from inefficiency from those attributable to uncontrollable factors.

6.3 Probable Savings in Utilization of Resources

While it is impossible to predict on the basis of such a limited study the extent of savings that might be effected by the development of local standards and local standard costs, based upon similar experience with these techniques in industry, the savings in efficiency could be substantial, conservatively estimated at 5% to 8%.

7. OTHER COMPLETED STUDIES

I will call your attention to several other completed studies only in terms of their highlights. They are as follows:

Multi-purpose Space Planning

Question:	Can multi-purpose planning of Chapel and other Hospital space reduce construction costs?
Status:	Completed 7/68.
Findings:	For Chapels under 100 seats—No.
	For larger Chapels and other space—maybe, depending on the case.
Implementation:	Development of techniques for judging each case deferred for higher priority subjects.

Multiple Laboratory Test

Question:	What is effect on patient care and lab operation of multiphase blood test on admission?
Status:	Completed 1/68.
Findings:	No effect on length of stay.
	Little contribution to diagnosis.
	Increased laboratory productivity.
Implementation:	Field investigator requested to write up project for publication.

Prosthetic Distribution Center

Question:	Should the PDC, Denver be moved to the Supply Depot, Hines?
Status:	Completed 6/68.

Findings: Moving PDC would save money.
                   Tuning-up operation would save almost as much ($22,000/year).
Implementation: PDC being tuned-up to reassign 4 positions to expanded mission.

Plastic Eye Clinics

Question: Can VA save money by buying plastic eyes from commercial
                   suppliers?
Status: Completed 7/68.
Findings:

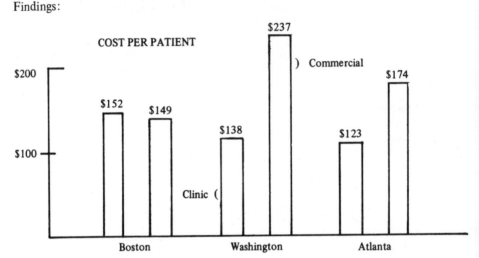

Implementation: Continue VA Clinics in Operation.

8.   ON-GOING STUDIES

Among our on-going projects are the following in terms of their highlights:

VA Hospital Atlanta Innovations

Question: Should the innovations in the design of VAH Atlanta be adopted
                   for future construction?
                   Drug distribution
                   Supply PAD
                   NURSERVER
Status: Begun 7/68; estimated completion 12/69.
Objectives: Evaluate costs vs. savings in nursing service time and patient
                   benefits.
Results to Date: Interim report covering drug distribution system about completed.

Veteran Demand for Medical Care

Question: What are VA's future bed requirements and estimated patient
                   loads?
Status: Begun 1/68; estimated completion: long term.
Objectives: Review existing data on veterans.
                   Develop models for projecting veteran patient loads and bed
                   requirements.

Determine what additional data, if collected, would improve precision of projections.

Results to Date: All available data on veterans' medical care identified.
Additional data needs defined.
Several projection models tested.

Optimum Internal Hospital Transportation

Question: What are the most effective in-hospital transportation systems?
Status: Begun 1/69; estimated completion 6/71.
Objectives: Determine effectiveness of alternative transportation systems.
Relate effectiveness to cost.
Develop a model to select transportation systems with maximum cost effectiveness for specific hospital situations.
Results to Date: Protocol approved.
Background literature reviewed.

Automated Management Information System (AMIS)

Question: What are the facts about VA Hospital operations needed by Central Office management?
Hospital management?
Status: CO System   Begun 1/68
Implementation begun 7/68
Refinement under way
Field System   Begun 4/68
Implementation begins 1/70 using 7/69 data
Objectives: Improved decision making, based on pertinent information that is
accurate
timely
organized
Results to Date: Improved CO System in operation.
Field System designed and being refined.

Patient Treatment File

Question: What is the VA medical history of each veteran?
Status: Initial System—Begun 6/68; implementation begins 7/69
Expanded System—Begin development 7/69
Objectives: Install initial system (Replacing IDDS) covering admission, diagnostic, surgery, & discharge data.
Expand system to provide needed patient-oriented data for Administrative clinical & research uses.
Results to Date: User specifications developed; computer system design and programming in process.

Use of Disposables

Question: What use of disposables in VA hospitals will provide the best patient care at the least cost?
Status: Begun 10/68; estimated completion 4/70.

Objectives:	Test use of disposables to evaluate costs and efficacy.
	Determine effect on space and equipment requirements in hospital construction projects of greater use of disposables.
Results to Date:	Protocol developed and under review.
	Background literature reviewed and orientation field visits made.

Supply Consolidation

Question:	Is it worthwhile to consolidate supply support for hospitals located near one another?
Status:	Begun 9/68; ECD 7/69.
Objectives:	Develop methodologies to determine:
	Feasibility of possible supply consolidations.
	Relative cost advantages of alternative arrangements for consolidation.
Results to Date:	Two of three field studies completed.

Model Laundry

Question:	Are there acceptable, economical disposable linens whose use will reduce laundry workloads?
	Will the latest laundry and dry cleaning equipment reduce laundry costs?
Status:	Begun 10/68; Estimated Completion 3/70.
Objectives:	Evaluate medical and personal acceptability of disposable and synthetic linens.
	Compare cost/effectiveness of new and existing laundry equipment.
	Develop methodology for determining, for a given hospital, the most economic laundry service.
Results to Date:	Existing Louisville laundry tuned up and costed; testing of disposable linens getting under way.

Summary

In summary, we in the Veterans Administration have been busy during the past two years or so reshaping our resources and expanding our techniques in order to increase our capability in the areas of management research and technology.

During this period we have performed a variety of studies, ranging from the short-range, ad hoc to the long-range and more fundamental type. We are trying to apply precision of definition and objective to these problem areas using the tools and techniques of operations research, industrial engineering and statistical analysis in a system frame of reference in order to insure meaningful results. We believe that this effort has been and is productive in this health care system.

RURAL WATER SUPPLIES AND THE ECONOMIC EVALUATION OF ALTERNATIVE LOCATION PATTERNS

J.J. Warford

Alan Williams

1. THE PROBLEM

The construction of water mains to serve rural communities is heavily subsidised in Britain by central and county authorities. It has been observed that as successive rural water schemes are implemented, the areas remaining unserved tend to be the most remote and sparsely populated, and in recent years this has been reflected in a sharp increase in project costs—and subsidies—per potential consumer. This trend has cast doubts on the merits of the existing policy; in other words, the question that has arisen is whether or not the benefits of the policy are now outweighed by its costs.

To answer this question properly requires knowledge of the benefits of providing access to mains water in a given area, as compared to a situation in which supplies from private wells, streams, and roof catchments have to be relied upon. The benefits may accrue partly to business (normally agricultural) activities, and partly to households. For the former the chief benefit is that ample water of good quality sometimes makes possible certain kinds of agricultural activity that would otherwise be precluded, while for the latter the chief benefit may be improved hygiene and health. In the present study, benefits to business presented no problem, but benefits to households proved quite intractable, because we could obtain no satisfactory evidence to indicate that the health record of rural areas without mains water was significantly different from those with such water.

Because of this, it was tempting to conclude that the benefits must be negligible, so the policy should be abandoned. Against this, it was argued that with increased population mobility, there was a growing risk of a serious outbreak of waterborne disease due to the drinking of contaminated water by those unused to it, and therefore the historical data (even if available) would understate the potential benefits. Without necessarily accepting the truth of this assertion, we therefore agreed to tackle the following reformulated problem: Assuming (i) that meeting the health hazard is an absolute constraint, and (ii) that it can only be met by giving people access to a mains water supply, what is the least-cost method of so doing?

Before describing the way in which we approached this problem, assumption (ii) calls for some comment. First, there is at least a *prima facie* case for thinking that improvements in the quality of existing local supplies might be an equally acceptable solution on health grounds and be much cheaper in some areas than providing a mains supply. This possibility was not in our terms of reference, however, and is not included in our study. Secondly, it is important to note that existing policy is to provide the mains supply, but not invariably to compel people to link up to it, although this is done on occasion. To be accurate, then, the objective should be described as "giving people *access* to a mains water supply." It will be noted that there is some illogicality in building water mains because of the health hazard associated with consumption of existing supplies, and at the same time allowing people to please themselves whether or not they connect to the mains once the latter have been built.

We now turn to the specification of the alternatives to be evaluated. Some severe restrictions upon our freedom of choice in this regard have already been mentioned, and within them we decided that the only real alternative to taking mains water to people would be taking people to mains water! Put rather less dramatically, the alternatives would be (i) an extensive scheme to provide access to mains water to people in their existing locations; (ii) at the other extreme a severely restricted scheme which would involve relocating people near the source of the water; and (iii) a series of intermediate arrangements involving various combinations of sizes of water scheme and amounts of relocation.

Once the possibility of relocation is considered, it is clearly necessary to take account of the impact of such a radical change on other public services and on business and private activities in the area. Thus the study became an economic evaluation of alternative location patterns, with water supply problems at its heart, but requiring consideration of matters lying well outside the normal ambit of investment appraisal in the water supply field.

The study was conducted using one actual proposed scheme as a "guinea pig", and the area it was planned to serve (South Atcham, near Shrewsbury, in Shropshire, England) was investigated intensively to provide empirical data to test out the method and to see what kinds of conclusions would emerge. The full results have been published elsewhere [1] and what follows is a digest concentrating upon some methodological issues that arose.

2.   THE METHOD

It might be objected that our reformulation of the problem turns it into a cost-effectiveness study rather than a cost-benefit study. In order not to offend anyone's sensibilities on this point, we have used the neutral term "economic evaluation" to describe what we have done. But we would observe that although the major benefit to households (reduction of the health hazard) is kept constant, and a least-cost method of achievement sought, we include as "negative costs" certain *other benefits* accruing to households or to agriculture, as well as cost-savings to various public services. It is therefore little more than a matter of terminology whether one chooses to regard it as a piece of "cost-benefit analysis" or as a "cost-effectiveness study".

2.1   Some General Conceptual Issues

Our first general conceptual issue concerned the question "costs and benefits *to whom?*". The existing financial arrangements entail contributions from local householders by way of connection charges, all local water users (via water rates), all local householders and occupiers of business premises (via local taxes), and taxpayers in the country at large (via the central government's contribution). We therefore selected the community as a whole as our frame of reference, and restricted our calculations to items having a net effect (positive or negative) on the community as a whole, ignoring any "transfer payments" which simply raised the welfare of one group at the expense of another. We also neglected repercussions outside the study area itslef, e.g. we assumed that the severe local impact on agriculture would be too small in relation to the whole U.K. situation to affect the price of agricultural products.

A second issue concerned the time period over which costs and benefits should be calculated. Since we had rejected the financing arrangements as not relevant to our study, there was no merit in using any particular loan period. The physical life of actual water supply assets varies considerably by type of asset, some of them lasting a century or more. Moreover, our study ranged far more widely than water supply, into housing, agriculture and a wide range of public services. Since no obviously appropriate time period emerged, we arbitrarily selected a period of 30 years for appraisal purposes. Clearly the discounting process makes the exact cut-off date relatively unimportant once it is that far off into the future.

A third conceptual issue related to the choice of a discount rate. We have not here entered into the controversy as to whether it should reflect society's time preference for real income at different points in time, or whether it should reflect the opportunity cost to society of using resources at different points in time. Nor have we attempted to estimate empirically what actual discount rate either of these approaches would generate for the U.K. Our approach has been much more pragmatic. The Treasury has stated that a "test rate of discount" of 8% should be used by nationalised industries in all real investment appraisal. There are clearly strong grounds for using the same rate for all public sector investment, since different cut-off rates would imply the rejection of projects in some fields which (with the same rate of return) would be accepted in others. However, the rate was designed for industrial-type investment subjected to a financial appraisal, not for broader cost-benefit analyses of the kind conducted here. Moreover, the rate has not been changed since it was first promulgated [2] in 1967, and there is no reason to suppose that it will (or should) be the one element in the economic system which is invariant to all changing circumstances. We therefore discounted the various streams of costs and benefits to present value using not only the 8% rate, but also rates of 6%, 10% and 12%, so that the decision-makers might see how sensitive the results are to changes in the discount rate.

The fourth general issue was to decide on the principles which should guide the selection of alternative location patterns. Ideally one would wish to consider all possible patterns, but as that would give us millions of possibilities, it was clearly not feasible. We therefore placed some prior restrictions on the scope of choice, which were (i) that the entire population of the study area would stay in the study area; (ii) that the larger villages in the area which were already local centres of population and commercial activity should be designated "relocation sites" for the displaced residential population within their economic "hinterland"; (iii) that these "hinterlands" were not to be so large that it would be unreasonable to expect a person, after relocation, to continue to work where he did before. We realised that these rules, in particular the last, prejudged some of the issues we were trying to resolve, but as a matter of practical necessity some such initial screening device was unavoidable.

Another general principle followed was that where possible, estimates should be made on the basis that the services and facilities available at the relocation sites would be of an equivalent standard to those that would have been enjoyed in the absence of relocation. It was not possible to adhere to this principle throughout the analysis; special difficulties were encountered in respect of housing, these being discussed below.

The sixth general issue was whether to concentrate on the *difference* between the costs of providing services in alternative locations, or to attempt an estimate of *total* costs. Because of the way the problem was reformulated, only the former was necessary, but it was usually more convenient to estimate the totals in each case in order to arrive at the differences. Sometimes however it was more efficient to adopt the shortened procedure; this applied, for example, to most estimates of transport costs.

The seventh and final general issue concerned the extent to which market prices could be accepted as reflecting social costs and benefits. Where possible we estimated the *factor cost* of resources being used, by eliminating indirect taxes and subsidies. In practice we were only able to make this adjustment where the impact of such measures was immediately recognizable, e.g. the fuel tax element of journey-to-work costs, and the subsidy element of the value of agricultural inputs and outputs. Possible movements in the general level of prices and costs were ignored, since these are irrelevant in a real resource calculation. Possible future changes in relative prices and costs, which would be relevant in principle, were also ignored, their estimation being beyond the scope of this study.

2.2   The Alternatives to be Appraised

The physical, economic and demographic characteristics of the study area in relation to the proposed water supply scheme were such that it could usefully be divided into four sub-areas, these being designated A, B, C and D. The precise attributes of each sub-area are not of sufficient importance to warrant further consideration here, but it is important to note that the borehole and principal storage reservoir for the whole study area would be located in sub-area A. Consequently, if any one sub-area were to be served with mains supplies, it would have to be A. One extreme solution would therefore be the depopulation of sub-areas B, C and D, and relocation of their inhabitants somewhere in A. At the other extreme would be no relocation at all. Intermediate solutions would be relocation of the inhabitants of individual sub-areas B, C or D, and the remaining possible combinations of those sub-areas. We therefore appraised eight possible patterns of relocation, namely (i) none; (ii) from B alone; (iii) from C alone; (iv) from D alone; (v) from B + C; (vi) from B + D; (vii) from C + D; and (viii) from B + C + D.

Estimates for alternatives (v) to (viii) were not obtained by simple addition of the appropriate items for (ii), (iii), or (iv), because of the possibility of interdependence in the location of some important activities. Each alternative was therefore treated as a separate exercise in estimation, and appraised with respect to each of the following variables:

> Water Supply
> Sewage Disposal
> Telephones
> Postal Services
> Electricity
> Schools
> Housing
> Agriculture
> Travel to Work
> Miscellaneous Transport Effects (including effects on mobile libraries, health and welfare services, refuse collection, school transport, mobile shops and other deliveries, and road costs)

The three most important variables turned out to be water supply, housing and agriculture, with schools, sewage disposal and travel to work some way behind, and the rest relatively unimportant. Since the three most important variables between them also raise the most interesting conceptual issues, the others will not be discussed further here, though they are included in the numerical results in Section 3.

2.3 Water Supply

The initial capital outlay on water supply for each of the alternative relocation patterns (in £.000) was:

None	B	C	D	B + C	B + D	C + D	B + C + D
669.2	503.7	629.8	592.1	464.4	426.6	552.7	387.2

Relocation (particularly of B + C + D) would therefore yield substantial initial savings when compared with the no-relocation alternative. Also to be taken into account were connection costs, ranging from £30,000 to £50,000 for the various alternatives, and renewal and running costs during the 30 year period. Converting these to present value terms, and adding them to the capital costs above (the latter being assumed to occur in year 0), we obtained total water supply costs as follows:

PRESENT VALUE OF WATER SUPPLY COSTS
£000

Discount Rate	Sub-Area Relocated							
	None	B	C	D	B + C	B + D	C + D	B + C + D
6%	852.4	654.9	804.1	754.6	606.6	557.1	706.3	508.8
8%	825.4	632.0	778.4	731.0	585.0	537.6	684.0	490.7
10%	806.1	615.6	760.1	714.2	569.6	523.7	668.2	477.7
12%	792.0	603.7	746.7	701.9	558.4	513.6	656.6	468.3

The only conceptual difficulty here concerned the assumption to be made about the connection of individual households to the mains. Of approximately 1,450 households in the study area, 356 already had access to mains supplies. Of these, 93 had not in fact connected. We could have used evidence of this kind to make some assumption regarding connection rates for the scheme under appraisal, but decided that this would not be consistent with treating the health hazard as an overriding consideration. We therefore assumed that *all* properties would be connected (whether at the householders' own expense or not being left an open question).

2.4 Housing

It would have been desirable to estimate the costs of maintaining previous standards of accommodation following relocation, but since people were currently living in houses varying widely in size, age, structure, location, and quality, strict adherence to this principle would have required the replication of existing dwellings on similar sites. This clearly was not a feasible proposition, so we had to abandon the notion. This led us to the following formulation for the treatment of housing in this study.

Let $V_0 =$ the market value of properties as they are currently (i.e. without water supply or, in some cases, adequate sewage disposal facilities);

Let $V_1 =$ the market value of properties when mains water is supplied and adequate sewage disposal facilities exist.

All of the alternatives which leave people where they are will generate the benefits valued at $(V_1 - V_0)$. In addition, householders will spend varying sums (X_1) on internal improvements to plumbing, etc., which will increase the market values of their properties still further, let us say to V_2. $(V_2 - V_1)$ may be greater than, equal to, or less than, X_1. If W_1 represents the water (and sewage disposal) costs, then the net cost to the community of supplying water to people in their existing locations is:

$$W_1 + X_1 - (V_1 - V_0) - (V_2 - V_1) \; or \; W_1 + X_1 + V_0 - V_2$$

If we turn to the relocation alternatives, we have the cost of providing water, etc. at the relocation sites, (W_2), the costs of new housing (Y) and the market value of the new housing (V_3). Clearly, the value of the property which is abandoned is represented by V_0, so the cost of rehousing is:

$$V_0 + W_2 + Y - V_3$$

To discover whether rehousing shows a net benefit or a net cost, we therefore need to compute (1)–(2), which simplifies to:

$$(W_1 - W_2) + X_1 - V_2 + (V_3 - Y)$$

Lack of data forced us to make two simplifying assumptions. The first was that $V_3 = Y$, i.e. the market value of new housing is equal to its cost of construction; this removes the last two terms from expression (3). The second assumption was that $X_1 = V_2 - V_1$, i.e. the market value of housing increases by precisely the amount which householders spend on internal plumbing improvement. Substituting $(V_2 - V_1)$ for X_1 in equation (3), the only housing variable left to estimate was V_1 (the market value of *existing* houses if water were supplied and adequate sewage disposal facilities provided).

The weakness of the first assumption lies in the implied assertion that value-in-use is equal to market value. It is probable that the market value of many existing properties understates their value to the current occupants, and the turnover rate of property in these areas is typically rather low. The existence of this "consumers' surplus" would suggest that all the V expressions are too low as estimates of occupants' valuation of the stream of services provided by their homes. The second assumption postulates a zero net outcome to two influences, one of which is positive and the other negative. Households do not pay the full cost of home improvements, since these are (within limits) grant-aided. Hence if X_1 is *total* expenditure on home improvements (including the grant-aided element) it will tend to exceed $(V_2 - V_1)$. On the other hand, consumers' surplus arguments enter once more, suggesting that even though $X_1 K (V_2 - V_1)$ *at the margin*, it may still be true that X_1 is less than the value of the *total* benefits derived from such improvements.

The actual estimation of houses values V_1 was conducted by direct valuation of a sample of one-third of all residential properties in sub-areas B, C and D. The results are presented below, in net terms for the varying patterns of relocation under two alternative assumptions: (i) that the value of all properties is best reflected at the lower bound of the 95% confidence limit for the sample, and (ii) that it is best reflected at the upper bound thereof, thereby displaying the range of sensitivity of results to estimation procedures. The discount rate chosen is of little consequence here, so only the calculations at an 8% rate are shown:

PRESENT VALUE OF NET COST OF ABANDONED HOUSING

(£000; at 8% discount rate)

Alternative Estimate	B	C	D	B + C	B + D	C + D	B + C + D
(i)	366.4	121.2	204.6	487.6	570.9	325.8	692.1
(ii)	465.6	154.4	287.5	620.0	753.1	441.9	907.5

2.5 Agriculture

The abandonment of farms as residences did not imply the abandonment of farming, because relocation sites were chosen so that farmers and farm workers could commute to their existing places of employment. However, the type of farming that would be possible under these conditions would be limited. In particular, any product dependent on constant attention to livestock would be ruled out; relocation would therefore tend to bring about the replacement of pig, poultry and dairy farming by arable farming and the raising of beef cattle and sheep. The problem was to estimate the value of such changes resulting from each of the possible relocation alternatives.

The first task was to determine what would actually happen if mains water were made available to existing farms. We were advised that it would not make a significant difference, as existing supplies were considered adequate for agricultural purposes. We therefore had to estimate the value of *current* agricultural output, and then make a similar estimate for each of the relocation possibilities.

The abandonment of dairying, pigs and poultry would mean the end of small scale farming. We identified those farms which would cease to be viable under the new conditions, and estimates of output were made on the assumption that such holdings would be absorbed into larger units. As will be shown below, relocation in every case produced a net gain fro the existing farming community, suggesting that a radical change of this sort may be necessary to induce farmers to abandon unprofitable holdings, when 'normal' market forces fail to do so. The post-relocation farming situations postulated were in fact the outcome of the minimum amount of amalgamation necessary for the absorption of all non-viable holdings, and by no means represented an optimal agricultural pattern, privately or socially.

Although amalgamation would be brought about by a dramatic change in market conditions facing farmers in the area, profitability was not our measure of social gain; rather, we needed to estimate the *net social value* of each pattern of output. This entailed removing the subsidy element from the value of inputs and outputs, and pricing farmers' own services at their social opportunity cost (taken to be the cost of hiring a farm manager).

One example of the complications that were encountered in this part of the study concerns the value of milk output. Farmers are paid a "pool" price, which is a weighted average of (a) the price of milk bottled for ordinary domestic consumption, and (b) the price of milk for industrial processing, the "weights" being the proportions of national milk output going to the two users. The pool price can be used to estimate farmers' profits, but the *social value* of the milk is to be found by answering the question: what value is placed by consumers on milk output *at the margin*? "Marginal" milk output goes for industrial processing, so the social value of milk is represented by this figure (which is about 60% of the pool price). Clearly the validity of this approach is conditional upon the change in milk supply having no significant effect upon the price of milk, which is a reasonable assumption in the context of this study, but which might need to be reconsidered if it were broadened to cover a larger area of dairying country.

Another complication concerned the redundancy, caused by relocation and the subsequent change in the pattern of farming, of over half the total agricultural labour force in the study area. Since alternative employment opportunities in the area were virtually limited to vacancies in other types of employment in towns outside the study area, it was likely that the redundant farm workers would experience some difficulty in becoming re-employed. In the absence of any reliable data on what these prospects actually were, we postulated that one-third would be re-employed immediately, one-third a year later, and one-third two years later. This implies that for these periods such workers have no true opportunity cost to society in their existing employments, so that the costs of the existing pattern of agriculture were correspondingly reduced. This involved an adjustment of about £60,000 in present value terms for the whole study area.

The following table shows that all discount rates and in each sub-area, relocation would result in a net private gain to the *existing* farming community:

PRESENT VALUE OF NET PRIVATE GAIN TO FARMERS FROM RELOCATION

(£000)

Discount Rate	B	C	D
6%	171.0	26.2	212.1
8%	133.5	19.2	170.1
10%	106.1	14.1	139.5
12%	85.5	10.3	116.5

Changes in the social value of farm output due to relocation would be *reductions in its net social cost*, i.e. the social value of agricultural output was currently less than the social opportunity cost of the resources going into it, but relocation would reduce the excess of the latter over the former. The figures are as follows:

PRESENT VALUE OF NET SOCIAL COST OF AGRICULTURAL OUTPUT

(£000)

Discount Rate	None	B	C	D	B + C	B + D	C + D	B + C + D
6%	1,830.0	1,379.9	1,704.1	1,501.6	1,253.9	1,051.5	1,375.7	925.5
8%	1,509.9	1,149.1	1,408.4	1,247.6	1,047.6	886.8	1,146.1	785.3
10%	1,275.9	980.4	1,192.3	1,062.0	896.8	766.6	978.4	683.0
12%	1,100.7	854.1	1,030.5	923.1	783.9	676.5	852.8	606.3

It might be argued that the above table shows that agriculture should be abandoned altogether in the area. This raises questions beyond the scope of this exercise, and would require consideration of overall governmental policy towards agriculture. We therefore indicate only that both in terms of private profitability and of our interpretation of social costs and benefits, agriculture would more advantageously be maintained in the area under our relocation alternatives than with the existing location pattern.

3. THE RESULTS

We have had to be selective in our discussion of the important variables affecting the relocation decision, and various alternative assumptions that were used in the exercise have not been explained. However, the results given below are comprehensive in their coverage of variables, and the main sources of variation in valuation are included. The tables show the net benefits from relocation (if positive) or net costs (if negative).

PRESENT VALUE OF NET BENEFITS FROM RELOCATION: ABANDONED HOUSING VALUED AT UPPER ESTIMATE

(£000)

Discount Rate	Sub-Area Relocated						
	B	C	D	B + C	B + D	C + D	B + C + D
6%	197.6	51.5	75.9	252.2	345.5	130.2	393.9
8%	99.8	20.9	19.3	123.8	181.3	42.5	200.0
10%	28.3	− 1.5	−22.1	29.9	61.2	−21.6	58.4
12%	−25.2	−18.2	−53.0	−40.4	−28.5	−69.5	−47.5

PRESENT VALUE OF NET BENEFITS FROM RELOCATION:
ABANDONED HOUSING VALUED AT LOWER ESTIMATE

(£000)

Discount Rate	Sub-Area Relocated						
	B	C	D	B + C	B + D	C + D	B + C + D
6%	296.9	84.6	158.8	384.7	527.8	246.3	609.2
8%	199.1	54.0	102.2	256.2	363.5	158.6	415.4
10%	127.6	31.7	60.9	162.3	243.4	94.5	273.8
12%	74.1	14.9	30.0	92.1	153.7	46.6	167.8

Clearly, the assumptions about house values and the appropriate discount rate are major elements in determining the outcome of the study. The importance of the discount rate is largely in its impact on the agriculture element, and is due to the fact that the agricultural changes would involve sizeable initial capital outlays to make possible the adaptation to a new pattern of output, the benefits from which would then flow steadily over the time period considered. Hence a high discount rate reduces the value of the returns sharply in relation to the initial outlays.

Except for the case where the discount rate is over 10% *and* housing is valued at the upper bound of the 95% confidence limit, the relocation alternatives show a positive net benefit. But the decision-maker would also have to consider the likely margin of error in the estimates, and also the intangible factors not quantified in the analysis, such as the impact on visual amenity and on "the rural way of life". It is quite possible that relocation would not then show a net social benefit of sufficient magnitude to warrant any dramatic change of policy as far as South Atcham itself was concerned.

4.   THE IMPLICATIONS

South Atcham is more densely populated and less remote than many areas as yet unserved by mains supplies. It is therefore likely that if the foregoing analysis were applied in other areas the results would indicate quite clearly that the costs of maintaining the existing settlement pattern would exceed those incurred in providing similar facilities by relocation.

We have noted that the objective of current policy is to give people the *opportunity* to connect to mains supplies. If this objective is accepted as a worthy one, and can clearly be achieved at least cost by relocation, one solution might be to encourage people to move by offering compensation equal to the market value of their homes plus a removal grant. (Compulsion is clearly not a feasible proposition). The size of the grant would be partly a matter of equity, but an upper limit could be set by the net savings to society resulting from the cheaper alternative. By this means the opportunity to connect would be retained, and would in fact become more real for those otherwise unable to afford the cost of connection. The health hazard would remain for those opting to stay in their current locations, unserved by mains supplies. Although a radical change in approach, this solution would therefore involve little departure from the general principles governing existing water supply policy.

REFERENCES

1. Warford, J.J. (1969), *The South Atcham Scheme: An Economic Appraisal*, H.M.S.O., London.

2. Warford, J.J. (1967), *Nationalised Industries: A Review of Economic and Financial Objectives*, (Cmnd. 3437) H.M.S.O., London.

A SYSTEMS ANALYTIC APPROACH TO THE EMPLOYMENT PROBLEMS OF DISADVANTAGED YOUTH

A.H. Pascal

1. INTRODUCTION

The analysis described in this paper is the result of a collaboration between Stephen J. Carroll and Anthony H. Pascal, both economists on the staff of the RAND Corporation. The authors were aided very substantially by the ideas and suggestions of a group of experts, from various disciplines and institutions, who were assembled by RAND under a contract from the Office of Economic Opportunity, Executive Offices of the President (commonly referred to as the "War on Poverty"). While grateful for the advice of the experts and the financial and technical support of OEO, the authors accept full responsibility for any errors or failings which remain in this paper.

2. JOBS AND YOUNG WORKERS: DIMENSIONS OF THE PROBLEM*

The population of the United States has passed the 200 million mark. Young men and women in the 16 to 24 age bracket account for approximately 15 percent of the total. The role of youth in the American labor market is large, and it is growing. In 1960, 17.5 percent of the labor force consisted of men and women between the ages of 16 and 24. By 1965 the youth component of the national labor force was slightly larger than 20 percent. And, before the end of 1970, it is expected that over 22 percent of the working population of the United States will be youth. During the period 1965-1970 the number of persons 20 to 24 years in the job market is expected to grow at a rate 2½ times that of the labor force as a whole.

The problems that these young people will face as they enter the labor force are substantial. Despite continued growth and declining overall unemployment rates since 1961, the unemployment rates among youths have remained persistently high. In 1967 the annual average unemployment rate for males 16 and 17 years old was over 4 times as large as the annual average unemployment rate among all males. The unemployment rate among men in the 18 and 19 year old category was more than three times the size of the overall male unemployment rate.

Many of the young men and women who attempt to enter the labor force in coming years will encounter difficulties surpassing those suggested by the statistics cited above. They will find the normal problems of youth exacerbated by racial discrimination, poverty, insufficient education, and the pressures of an urbanized society. For instance, the annual average unemployment rate among whites in the 16 to 19 year-old age group was 11 percent in 1967; non-whites in the same age category faced an unemployment rate of 26.5 percent in the same year.

---

*The references for the statistics on employment are from the *1967 and 1968 Manpower Reports* and those on education are from *Profile of Youth - 1966,* both published by United States Government Printing Office, Washington D.C

Individuals who live in the officially defined poverty areas in the U.S. bear a disproportionate share of unemployment and the youth from these areas suffer correspondingly from unemployment and sub-employment. In November of 1966 approximately 10 percent of the workers living in the slums of 13 major cities were unemployed. At that time the overall unemployment rate was 3.7 percent. As might be expected, even in urban slums the burden of unemployment falls more heavily upon youth. Individuals in the 14 to 19-year-old bracket from families with incomes less than $3000 had unemployment rates of 17.4 percent, 1½ times the size of the overall teenage unemployment rate.

Unemployment statistics fail to completely describe the road-blocks met by low-income youth in the search for productive work. There are, for instance, many young men and women who are employed only part-time, although they would have preferred full-time work. Others, who have full-time jobs, earn wages which are under the poverty level. Nonparticipation in the labour force is sometimes the response to rejection by the labor market. Finally, significant fractions of the population are not reached in labor force surveys.

A related problem of many low income youth is inadequate education. It is estimated that nearly 30 percent of the young people who will enter the American labor force during the decade of the 1960's will not have completed high school. This exceeds the estimated number of men and women entering the labor force during the 1960's who will have attended (though not necessarily graduated from) college. Labor force entrants who lack education credentials are at a severe disadvantage. The results of a February 1963 survey showed that among 16 to 21-year-old out-of-school youth in their first full-time job, about two-fifths of the male graduates earned at least $60 per week compared with only one-fifth of the dropouts. The education-specific unemployment rates for young workers (16-21) ranged from 7.9 percent for those who had spent at least one year in college to over 27 percent for high school dropouts.

3.   THE PUBLIC CONCERN WITH YOUTH PROBLEMS

The statistics cited above are believed to be indicators of the extent and depth of the social problem represented by low income youth in cities. Public action has thus focused on improving the indicators for disadvantaged youth. But why should the job problems of youth be an issue of public concern? What justifies the mounting of public programs to help alleviate these problems?

The answers to these questions are not entirely obvious. For example, it is rather unlikely that the United States is seriously affected by the sacrifice of current national output entailed by the relatively high youth unemployment and underemployment rates we have reviewed. Nor does the inequality in material condition for youth vis-a-vis the adult population seem a matter of pressing interest.

The connection between youth employment disadvantage and the delinquency and disorder ascribed to youth has often received emphasis. However, the nature of the causal connection here is still far from clear.

Yet public concern is real enough. Its genesis, we believe, lies in the general acceptance of greater equality of opportunity as a national goal. The employment problems of youth are important mainly because of what they portend with respect to the adult welfare of a sizeable fraction of American youth. Unemployment, lack of education, contact with the police on the part of a youth bode ill for his later prospects. The problems evidenced by these indicators are much more likely to apply to poor youth and black youth than they are to youth in general.

We have thus tended to conceptualize the appropriate public objective as the reduction of certain of the inequalities in economic opportunity which confront the young. (In general, we have restricted our view of opportunity to employment performance and have neglected inequalities resulting from the inheritance of tangible wealth.)

We say certain inequalities because there are obviously some differences in employment performance among people which are not viewed as matters requiring governmental intervention. For example, it is clear that people will have differential economic success to the degree that they place different values on goods and leisure, on prestige and income, on consumption now and consumption later, on risk and security, and in general on the many non-pecuniary aspects of work. Nor, do we believe that American society has as yet indicated much interest in ironing out inequalities due to intrinsic differences in ability among people.

Rather, the major part of public attention has been directed at the reduction of those long term inequalities which are a consequence of what, by a growing social consensus, are unacceptable criteria. Most prominent among these unacceptable criteria are race and class origin. Thus, in the most elementary terms, the public objective with respect to the economic performance of youth can be expressed as an attempt to increase the degree to which a youth's expected lifetime economic prospects are a function of his tastes, preferences and innate abilities, and to decrease the degree to which his economic future is dependent on the color and the income of his parents.

We have stressed economic outcomes here for two reasons. First, it seems obvious that most of the dimensions by which we would measure satisfactory outcomes in other spheres—e.g., political power, social acceptance, psychological health—are in fact highly correlated with economic success. Second, economic criteria are relatively tractable from the standpoint of measurement.

That we have chosen to concentrate on a view of the problem which stresses reduction in the inequalities of lifetime economic performance does not mean that we have eschewed all concern with current youth behavior however. It does mean that we consider that behavior important mainly because it affects the future. But the model we present below also has considerable relevance for those whose main concerns are shorter range—e.g., reduction of youth delinquency, prevention of early school leaving, and the immediate raising of youth income (because of its effects on family welfare, for example).

Public concern, then, has spawned a variety of public programs. These range from compensatory education through anti-delinquency and anti-dropout, to skill training and job placement programs. Each is championed by its advocates as the chief solution. More sophisticated observers admit the need for a broader spectrum package of programs but have difficulty in specifying the composition of the package required. Until we understand the complex, dynamic interrelationships that underlie youth behavior and youth opportunities, with all of the manifold feedback loops, we cannot hope to conduct the sorts of project evaluations and the cost/benefit analyses necessary for the design of effective program packages. We hope that the model described in this paper is a first step in gaining that understanding.

4.   A MODEL OF YOUTH EMPLOYMENT PROSPECTS

The conceptual model of the youth employment situation consists of a set of simultaneous equations. In general, this model predicts the economic prospects for an individual on the basis of his experiences, tastes, abilities, perceptions and opportunities. The unit of analysis then is the person. We realize that for ease in data assembly and manipulation and often for policy purposes it is preferable to treat various aggregates of individuals. Modifications of the model which will permit analysis of the behavior of cohorts based on age, race, class, neighbourhood, or other characteristics are possible and are being explored.

4.1 Lifetime Earnings

The first equation in the model is the definition of the present value of lifetime earnings at time t:

$$LE_t = \sum_{j=0}^{\infty} E_{t+j} (1+i)^{-j} \tag{1}$$

where LE_t is the discounted present value of expected lifetime earnings at time t, E_t is expected earnings over any period t, and i is the discount rate. The interpretation of this equation is straightforward. The total amount of an individual's expected income over his lifetime is, of course, equal to the sum of his expected earnings in each period. However, the precise time at which these earnings arise is important. In general, an individual's economic prospects are defined not only by the amount of income he is able to earn in each period of his life, but also by the time profile of these earnings. The use of the discount factor $(1+i)$ reflects this notion.

The essential element in equation (1) is the term E_t. What determines the expected earnings of an individual at each point in his life? In the model the answer to that question is embodied in equation (2).

$$E_t = \sum_{\iota} TV (A_t = A^{\iota}) W_t^{\iota} \tag{2}$$

TV stands for "truth value." It is 1 if the statement in parenthesis is true; 0 otherwise. A_t is the activity in which the individual is actually engaged during period t. A^i is the ιth possible activity. The set of activities in which he may involve himself include, in our schema, five mutually exclusive and exhaustive alternatives; attending school, working, attending a vocational training program, serving in the Armed Forces, or "other," a residual category. An individual's activity over any period in time is determined by his dominant decision. For example, he may attend school and take an after-school, part-time job as well. The primary decision made by this individual is assumed to be school attendance. The decision to work part-time is neglected in the model as being of secondary importance.

The last variable in equation (2) denotes the wage rate associated with each of the possible activities. Thus W_t^σ is the wage rate for students (typically zero), W_t^ω the wage rate to the individual who works. W_t^τ the wage rate (or stipend) paid to trainees, W_t^α the wage rate received by members of the Armed Forces (which would include wages in kind as well as in cash), and W_t^φ the income which the individual will receive should be participate in none of the above activities.

Equation (2) says that we know what earnings an individual will receive in any given period if we know in what activity he is engaged during that period and what wages he receives as a consequence of that choice.

4.2 Youth Behavior

The process by which youth chooses among the alternative activities is described by a behavior equation, (3a), and a set of stochastic assignment relations (3b).

$$\overline{A}_t = f_{3a} (F_t^\sigma, F_t^\omega, F_t^\tau, F_t^\alpha, F_t^\varphi, S_t, C, t) \tag{3a}$$

$$\text{Prob} (A_t = A^\iota) = f_{3b}^\iota (\overline{A}_t, C, S_t, \ldots) \qquad \iota = \sigma, \omega, \tau, \alpha, \varphi \tag{3b}$$

Equation (3a) states that the individual's choice. A_t, among the five alternatives available to him depends upon the anticipated lifetime rewards resulting from choosing activity ι in period t, as perceived by him at time t. These anticipated future returns, $F_t^\iota (\iota = \sigma, \omega, \tau, \alpha, \varphi)$ are associated with the activities school (σ), work (ω), training (τ), Armed Forces (α), and other (φ), respectively.

The next term (S_t) designates the state in which the individual is found at the beginning of period t. This variable is designed to capture the sequential nature of many decisions. That is to say, the youth's choice among activities in any period depends upon the activities that he has chosen in one or more previous periods. S_t may be viewed as a vector of acquired attributes such as: the number of years of school completed, the number of years of work experience acquired, possession of a high school diploma, completion of a training program, possession of a felony conviction record, etc.

The following term, C in equation (3a) denotes the characteristics of the individual. These include factors such as race and IQ, the nature of the family and neighborhood life he experienced, etc. They reflect as well the preferences of the individual.

Clearly, choosing to enlist in an activity does not guarantee the ability to implement the choice. Those who choose to work are sometimes unable to find employment. Those who did not choose to join the Armed Forces are often drafted. Meanwhile, others, who sought to enter the Armed Forces, are rejected. The list of such deviations between activity choice and reality could easily be expanded.

The relationship between the activity chosen by an individual, $\overline{A}_t$, and the activity in which he actually takes part, A_t, is, from the individual's point of view, stochastic. Equations (3b) state that the probability that the individual in question actually engages in activity ι during period t is a function of the activity in which he chose to engage during that period ($\bar{A}_t$), his characteristics, and his state at the beginning of the period. This relationship is expressed in a system of five equations, one for each possible activity.

The concepts embodied in system (3b) can easily be discussed in the context of a set, P_b, of twenty-five elements $p_{\iota\lambda}$ where $p_{\iota\lambda}$ is the probability that an individual who chooses to engage in activity ι in period t actually engages in activity λ during that period. Thus, the system (3b) incorporates twenty-five equations of the form*:

$$p_{\iota\lambda} = g_{\iota\lambda} (\ldots) \qquad \iota\lambda = \sigma, \omega, \tau, \alpha, \varphi$$

The induction standards of the Armed Services, the enrollment qualifications of training programs, job market opportunities, the nature of various kinds of "outreach" programs will all be reflected in the probabilities, $p_{\iota\lambda}$.

4.3 Perceptions and Anticipations

A system of five equations specify the F_t.

$$F_t^\iota = P_t^\iota + rF_{t+1}^\iota \tag{4}$$

Here P_t^ι denotes the earnings that are expected in period t if activity ι is chosen at time t. These earnings are net of all costs of employment; transportation costs, union dues, etc. The psychological discount factor** that the youth applies to income in the future is represented by r.

The term F_{t+1}^ι in (4) is, essentially, a subjective aggregate of the individual's anticipations for all periods beyond the present. The use of this formulation is suggested by the difficulty of obtaining more specific information on individual expectations. Ideally, we should like to define F_t^ι as the discounted sum of the youth's earnings expectations for each period in the future. In practice, such data will be unobtainable. Hence we assume that his anticipations can be obtained by summing his expectations for the present period and his aggregate expectations of the future†.

---

* The system also implies five constraints:

$$\sum_\lambda p_{\iota\lambda} = 1 \qquad \iota = \sigma,\omega,\tau,\alpha,\varphi$$

** There is no necessity that this factor be consistent with the special rate of time discount used by a government agency, i, in equation (1).

† Note that this relation embodies the intuitively appealing notion that the expected discounted present value of lifetime income is equal to the discounted present sum of expected income over each future period. If equation (4) holds for all t:

$$F_t^\iota = P_t^\iota + rF_{t+1}^\iota = P_t^\iota + r[P_{t+1}^\iota + rF_{t+2}^\iota]$$

$$= P_t^\iota + rP_{t+1}^\iota + r^\iota [P_{t+2}^\iota + rF_{t+3}^\iota]$$

$$= \sum_{k=t} r^{k-t} P_k$$

The variables, F_{t+1}^i, are estimates of future earnings which result from the entrance into an activity. The estimates derive from many sources. A youth can obtain information on the potential implications of his behavior from personal experience and experimentation. But he gains much of this knowledge from sources exterior to himself. The experiences of family members, relatives, friends, neighbors, the advice of teachers, counselors, and the mass media, all contribute to his estimation of the outcomes to be expected from each of the choices available to him.

4.4 The Returns from Alternative Activities

We simplify, for most of the activities, the determination of returns.

Thus,

$$P_t^\sigma = W_0^\sigma \tag{5a}$$

$$P_t^\omega = f_{5b}(W_t^\omega, T_t, L_t, C) \tag{5b}$$

$$P_t^\tau = W_0^\tau \tag{5c}$$

$$P_t^\alpha = W_0^\alpha \tag{5d}$$

$$P_t^\varphi = f_{5e}(\ldots) \tag{5e}$$

Equations (5a), (5c), and (5d) are straightforward. We assume that the individual's perception of the returns offered to those who engage in states σ, τ, and α are given and fixed by public policy. In this formulation, the government has determined the returns to individuals who attend school on a full-time basis, W_0^σ. Similarly, those who enroll in training programs or join the Armed Forces receive returns of W_0^τ and W_0^α, respectively, which also are set by public policy. In any case, these returns are assumed to be known.

Equation (5b) specifies the returns which an individual believes he can command on the labor market. It expresses the hypothesis that perceived returns from work are a function of the actual wage rate (W_t^ω), the cost of transportation (T_t), local labor market conditions (L_t), and the individual's personal characteristics C. Since commuting costs are often large relative to the wage for slum and ghetto job seekers, the return which is relevant to the individual's decision to work is net of these costs. Furthermore, the return which he could receive were he to apply for a job signifies only to the extent that he is aware of the return. His knowledge of the opportunities available to him are largely a function of the local labor market conditions and of his characteristics. The degree of unemployment among his friends and neighbors, for example, is expected to influence his perceptions regarding his own chances since it gives him an indication of how difficult and costly job search is likely to be. Similarly, certain personal characteristics may influence his perception of returns, causing either optimistic or pessimistic expectations.

Equation (5d) is not specified in the model. Its specification would present the manner by which an individual forms perceptions of the returns he can expect to receive should he engage in some activity other than school, work, training, or the Armed Forces. It includes such factors as the returns from engaging in criminal activities, or remaining dependent on the resources of family or friends. Thus, it is related to neighborhood and family conditions, but in a way difficult to specify at present. The basic problem encountered in a discussion of equation (5e) is the almost total absence of relevant data.

4.5   Labor Market Opportunities

The next substantive equation of the model, equation (6), defines a demand curve for the individual's services on the labor market

$$W_t^\omega = f_6 (S_t, C, G_t, D_t) \tag{6}$$

The employer would offer W_t^ω to the individual based upon the sequence of his experience, schooling, and training (S_t), his personal characteristics, C, general economic conditions, G_t, and the prices of other factors of production, D_t. The role of the vectors of variables G_t and D_t has been the subject of extensive research by economists and needs little discussion here. The role of S_t is also obvious. Personal characteristics enter the offer equation insofar as employees discriminate on the basis of the personal attributes of job applicants, such as for example, ability or race.

4.6   The State of the Individual

The last two equations of the model serve to define the state in which an individual finds himself at the beginning of period t.

$$S_t = f_{7a} (S_{t-1}, A_{t-1}) \qquad t > t_0 \tag{7a}$$
$$S_{t_0} = f_{7b} (C) \tag{7b}$$

Equation (7a) shows that the state in which an individual is found at the beginning of period t depends upon the state in which he was found at the beginning of the previous period and his activity during the previous period.

The final equation of the model, (7b), is required mathematically to close the system. Its interpretation is that there exists a "starting point" for each individual which is independent of his personal choice, but which depends upon his personal characteristics. For our purposes, given contemporary U.S. age requirements on school attendance, the relevant age might be 16. Essentially, the equation states that his behavior (characterized by the activity in which he is found at any point in time) is dependent only upon personal characteristics (such as his age, race, class, family income,) up to some point t_0. Thereafter, considerations other than personal characteristics (as expressed in the system of equations (3) play a role in predicting his behavior.

4.7   Simultaneity

One aspect of the model described above is particularly susceptible to misinterpretation. The entire model consists of a set of simultaneous structural equations. None of the equations are presented in reduced form. However, the simultaneous nature of the system is particularly apparent in the systems of equations (3) and (4). Note that $\bar{A}_t$ is determined in (3a) and may enter (4) by influencing the

P_t^i. Similarly, F_t^i is determined in (4) and enters (3) as a variable. Intuitively, this relation is as follows. How an individual will choose among alternative activities depends upon how he believes his choice of activity will affect his future. He is assumed to decide between σ, ω, τ, etc. on the basis of his estimates of the future prospects each offers. In short, he takes account of the impact of his present behavior upon his future prospects when he engages in present behavior.

Of course, his future prospects are not the only considerations in his current decisions. The impact of his behavior, i.e., his choice among alternative activities, upon his immediate position is also important. This aspect of his choice formation is reflected in the inclusion of the present returns (P_t^i's) of alternative choices in (4).

4.8   Personal Characteristics

One set of variables, C (personal characteristics), appears in most of the equations of the model. A model which fully describes behavior must incorporate those aspects of personality which influence and affect behavior. While this end is clearly desirable, little is known as to the means by which it may be reached. Such aspects of personality, as motivation, aspiration, ambitions, have yet to be successfully introduced into a general decision model. Probably the most fruitful approach to these problems involves the assumption that personality characteristics are essentially functions of environment. To the extent that this assumption is valid, observations on environmental characteristics can be used as proxies for observations on individual personality characteristics. This approach has often been used successfully. The inclusion of environmental "control variables" in analyses is a case in point.

5.   USING THE MODEL TO PREDICT ACTIVITY PAIRS

Suppose that we use the knowledge accumulated by social scientists to generate measures of the exogenous variables, C, G_t, D_t, L_t. Given C we are able to predict S_{t_0}. Given all the exogenous variables for period t_0+1 and S_{t_0} we can predict A_{t_0} and the distribution of A_{t_0}. By a similar sequence of operations we can generate the entire sequence of activities and earnings which are relevant to the youth over his lifetime. We can thus predict his LE_{t_0}. We refer to this sequence as an activity path.

From the above we see that the most interesting output of the analysis is not the prediction of the state in which the individual will be found at any point in time; nor is it the prediction of LE_t (though that is probably the most reasonable criterion for policy purposes). Rather the essential output of the model is the activity path. This is the true indicator or economic opportunity in any long-run sense.

For example, we might ask whether the relationship between lifetime employability and the acquisition of work habits, skills and experience which was implied earlier, justifies a public concern with youth unemployment. To answer such a question we would need to examine, say, the lifetime activity path of individual 1 who suffered unemployment at t ($A_t^1 = \varphi$) and compare it with the path of a second youth who, otherwise identical with 1, suffered no unemployment. (i.e., $A_t^2 = \omega$, or α, or τ). The larger is the quantity ($LE_t^1 - LE_t^2$), the more justified an intervention which will reduce the probability that $A_t^1 = \varphi$.

5.1   Data Requirements and Data Availability

Ideally, the model should be estimated using data obtained by an extensive longitudinal survey. Such a survey is not currently available. However, there now exist many data which can be used to estimate portions of the model.

One, potentially quite useful, source of information is the Project Talent longitudinal survey. These data consist of an extensive series of tests applied to a 5 percent random sample of all four U.S. high-school cohorts in 1960, and a sequence of follow-up surveys on the sampled population. The sequence of tests provide data on anticipations and characteristics, potentially useful in estimating system (4). The propensities to drop out of high school or to go on to college have also been studied, using the Project Talent information. These studies should be useful in estimating system (3) with respect to the school, work, and military choices. The wealth of data on the characteristics of interviewees which are contained in the files makes them particularly useful.

The Bureau of the Census, the Bureau of Labor Statistics, the Bureau of Employment Security all collect statistics on employment and wages. Much of this information can be utilized in estimating equation (6). The basic problem encountered in utilizing these data is that they are aggregative. Typically it is impossible to obtain data on individuals from these sources. The Survey of Economic Opportunity conducted in 1966 and followed up in 1967 contains most of the data required to estimate equation (5b). It should also be useful in estimating those elements of system (3b.1) which involve ω. Various Armed Forces records can be used to estimate those elements of Pb which involve α. Similarly, training programs' records, to the extent that they are available, would help in fitting those elements of Pb involving τ.

An upcoming OEO Survey of Manpower Programs should provide an opportunity to fill many information gaps. The survey is aimed, primarily, at providing data for evaluation of various skill training and work experience programs. Obviously, it will be most helpful in estimating those elements of system (3) which involve τ. This is no reason, however, to assume that its usefulness need be limited to the elements of the system which address the training activity. In particular, the control group, if properly chosen, should provide information on individuals who have never engaged in activity τ.

5.2   Testing Hypotheses

We have described a general model by means of which the economic prospects of low income urban youth can be appraised. On the conceptual level, the model facilitates the comparison of a number of phenomena which have been offered as explanations of the unsatisfactory economic futures which confront poor youth. Better understanding of the relative power of these various hypotheses and the ways in which they interact will aid in the search for program remedies.

As an example, cultural deprivation and like explanations of poverty seem to imply, with respect to youth problems, that social forces which are channelled through the family, the neighborhood, and the peer group so constrict experiences and attitudes of youth as to substantially inhibit possibilities for emergence from poverty. In the model presented here such a hypothesis would be validated by finding that those components of C which reflect the effects of these institutions have an important influence on the choice of activity. Such would be the case where the coefficients of variables measuring family structure, neighborhood condition, and peer attitudes are significant and large in the activity choice equation (3a), implying that poverty induces peculiar "tastes" such as for early gratification, high values on leisure, a tolerance for low status occupations, etc.

Another frequently offered explanation is that low income or slum residence constitutes an obstacle to the receipt of information necessary for the making of optimal, future-oriented decisions. To the extent this explanation is accurate, family-and neighborhood-based characteristics will be important in the anticipation and perception equations but not in the activity choice equation.

In the same fashion, a number of hypotheses which feature unequal opportunities can be investigated. If a variable measuring a characteristic such as skin color or social class is important in the wage offer equation we can trace through its implication for wage perceptions, activity choice, and ultimately for lifetime earnings. We have then learned something about the real effects of discrimination on the part of employers or unions.

The reader will note that each of the three hypotheses mentioned above argues that youth behavior is a function of personal characteristics. But in the absence of a general model such as the one presented in this report it would be impossible to operationally differentiate among them.

Along quite similar lines, we note that the majority of research into youth behavior has been directed toward estimating the relationship between observed behavior and acquired and innate characteristics, i.e. A_t as a function of S_t and C. As can be seen from examination of system (3) this involves a convolution of two completely independent concepts. On the one hand, there are the questions of what choices a youth will make in varying circumstances, and what factors induced these choices. On the other hand, there is the question of whether the youth actually finds an opportunity to engage in the activity chosen.

Specifically, consider the so-called "discouraged worker effect." In terms of the model such an effect occurs when an individual's lack of success on the labor market causes him to reduce F_t^ω which, in turn, tends to induce the choice of activity ϕ. An alternative hypothesis would be to assume that F_t^ω is unaffected, but that lack of success in the labor market signifies lack of experience to an employer which induces him to reduce $\overline{W}_t^\omega$. This reduction in W_t^ω, unaccompanied by any reduction in F_t^ω, increases $P_{\omega\phi}$.

The hypothesis sketched out above would explain the downward employment spiral as well as would the "discouraged worker's effect." Yet the policy implications of the alternative hypotheses are quite different.

5.3   The Economic Prospects Model and Policy Analysis

We have noted that we believe equality of economic opportunity to be, essentially, a long run concept. This belief is reflected, in this paper, in a concern with career, or activity paths. We do not mean to imply that activity choices, or behavior, in the short run are of no import. The inclusion of the state variable, S_t, in many of the equations demonstrates the role of current behavior as one of the major determinants of future behavior. Rather, the model reflects a desire to place current behavior in its proper perspective.

Programs designed to remedy inequities in economic opportunity are approached from the same point of view. The efficacy of such programs should be measured in terms of their ability to produce desired changes in activity paths, not merely in terms of their ability to induce certain activity choices in the short run. Of course, if we have reason to believe that certain forms of short run behavior have, in general, desirable implications in terms of the long run path, then encouragement of this behavior may become the proximate target of remedial programs. But, we emphasize, the choice of targets crucially depends upon the relationship between the short run activity choice and the long run activity path.

Clearly, the model is conducive to testing these program remedies in a fairly direct fashion. Take vocational training programs as an example. Whether or not an individual enters a training program is seen to be dependent on his preferences (as reflected in his characteristics), his experience (as indicated by the state he is in), on the immediate returns in the program as compared to his perceptions of returns available from other activities, and his anticipations of the future benefits the receipt of training will bring. The last two are functions, in part, of the way employers view training in making wage offers to potential employees.

Thus, we can explore the multiplicity of ways in which a training program affects the ultimate objective, which, to repeat, is the lifetime prospects of disadvantaged youth. The net effects of this set of impacts and the costs incurred in mounting the program can be compared to the results of analyses with respect to other kinds of interventions.

A fair employment law, if successful, decreases the degree to which an employer (or perhaps a union) can use characteristics such as race or class origin in offering employment (or membership). The change will affect perception of opportunities by the potential employee, his choice of state, and thus his earnings, but also his experience and therefore his future wage offers, and so on. Less direct attacks on the effects of prejudice, such as commuting subsidies, housing integration programs, and encouragement of ghetto locations for industry, will have similar, and similarly complicated, effects, all of which can be explored only in the context of a general model of this kind.

School stipend and wage subsidy programs aim directly at the activity choice and thus their impacts should be relatively easy to assess. It is a fundamental question, however, as to how much each might contribute, per dollar of transfer cost, to achieve a given upward lift in the lifetime earnings of disadvantaged youth. The model, when estimated, allows us to compare the costs and benefits of such direct schemes to the more complex consequences of skill training and job development programs.

There are potentially a large number of other policy options one could explore with this model. They include the easing of minimum wage laws and Armed Forces induction standards, the raising of family income status through programs of income maintenance, the provision of more accurate market information to job seekers, and the denial of information to employers on (some aspects of) the police records of job applicants.

So long as budgets are limited, the implications of one program can only be evaluated by comparing them with the implications of alternative uses of funds. But comparisons among the implications of various programs cannot be made until the proximate goals of the programs have been clearly specified and related to one another. This is one of the major attributes of the general model of youth employment prospects presented in this paper. The impact of virtually any program or policy upon an individual can be examined on a common ground. Diverse and seemingly unrelated programs can be interpreted in a manner which facilitates making choices among them.

COST-EFFECTIVENESS ANALYSIS IN THE ALLOCATION OF POLICE RESOURCES

Alfred Blumstein

1. INTRODUCTION

The principal objective of this paper is to present and illustrate an approach to cost-effectiveness analysis of social services and systems. This approach is characterized by an initial focus on the larger system problems, and then a successive closing in on the smaller problems with which one can reasonable deal through cost-effectiveness analysis. Typically, one finds studies that treat only one of these aspects. In the general formulation of a cost-effectiveness problem, one seeks models of the form:

$$\underline{E} = f(\underline{X}, \underline{Y})$$

where:

$\underline{E}$ = measure of effectiveness, typically a vector with at least two components, cost (E_c), and one or more effectiveness components

$\underline{X}$ = set of alternative systems

$\underline{Y}$ = set of uncontrollable or exogenuous variables affecting the effectiveness measures associated with the system alternatives

If one tries to reflect global considerations in the effectiveness measures (say total social costs or public welfare), then one cannot relate the system alternatives to these measures. These measures are difficult to define, even more difficult to measure, and often impossible to incorporate into a model.

On the other hand, if one begins by reducing the problem to that which *is* measurable, (say, response time of a police system or travel time of a public transportation system) then he can be fairly accused of ignoring the most important parts of the problem.

The approach presented here tries to start with these global considerations from a broad social-costs perspective, and then to focus successively on the narrower and more manageable parts. Ideally, a sequence of rigorous steps would be involved in peeling away the outer layers to reach the manageable crux of the problem. In the real case, however, problems are never that neat. The chain of logic, therefore, must involve a number of relatively weak links. These must be covered by assumption or hypothesis, issues to which one must later return but which must be accepted for the present. These issues, of course, represent limitations on the applicability of the final conclusions. But this is no more the case here than if one focuses immediately on the small, manageable problem as is normally done. Instead, by treating these issues explicitly, one gains a clearer insight into the specific limitations of the results in terms of the broader issues which dominate the considerations in the application.

Furthermore, by going through this process, a major set of critical research questions are raised, to be explored in a research program. Thus, the process serves both to indicate the bounds on the validity of the conclusions and to identify the means for exploring the nature of those bounds.

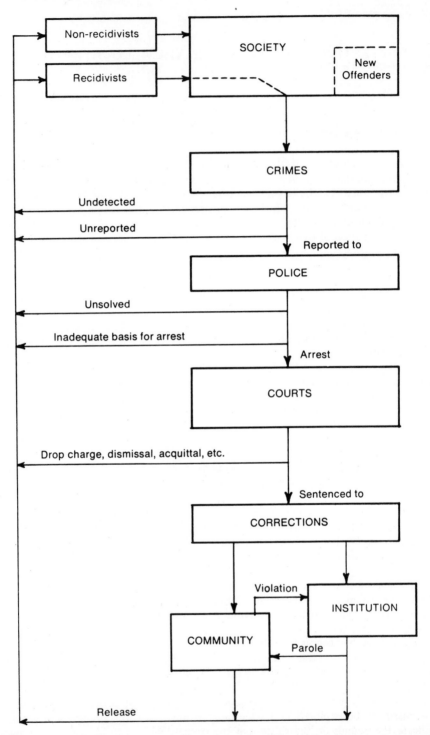

FIGURE 1 – A SIMPLIFIED SCHEMATIC OF THE CRIMINAL JUSTICE SYSTEM

In this paper, this approach is applied to an analysis of the allocation of police resources directed at reducing crime*. Here we begin with an examination of the larger criminal justice system (depicted in Figure 1) which society charges with the responsibility of controlling crime within constraints of due process and individual liberty. The criminal justice system includes the agencies of *police*, which investigate reports of crime and apprehend suspects; *courts* which prosecute arrested suspects, adjudicate their guilt, and sentence convicted offenders to an appropriate punishment of treatment process; and *corrections* which treat suspects within the constraints imposed by the sentencing judge.

Obviously, one could go still further back and examine the social and psychological bases of crime, but part of the art is knowing where the water becomes too deep. Here, since the system alternatives to be considered are allocations of police resources, we stop at the criminal justice system. The larger issue of how best to reduce crime by general means is much larger and is unquestionably intractable at this time.

The first step to be discussed here is an examination of the measure of effectiveness of the criminal justice system; then we shall successively examine the means by which that system controls crime, the role of police in that process, attributes of police performance that relate to crime control, and finally, how police resources can be allocated in a cost-effective way to optimize one of those attributes.

2. MEASURE OF EFFECTIVENESS

As in any cost-effectiveness study, the first question to be addressed is the measure of effectiveness associated with the system being examined. A first impulse, of course, is to use "number of crimes" as the measure of effectiveness. This has important difficulties. Crime is a very heterogeneous phenomenon: murder, shoplifting, drunkeness, and joy-riding are all crimes, and all are not equally serious. Some attempts have been made to achieve commensuration among types of crimes by attaching seriousness values to the various crimes. Such seriousness scores were derived by Sellin and Wolfgang [2] by asking people to attach a seriousness score of arbitrary scale units to various kinds of crimes. These weights are not fully satisfactory because the scaling tends to be logarithmic, and so the indexes are not additive. The index number reported annually by the FBI [3] simply adds the reported number of the seven "index crimes" (willful homocide, forcible rape, aggravated assault, robbery, burglary, larceny of $50 or over, and auto theft). This approach has been widely criticized, partly because it attaches *no* seriousness weights to the individual crimes. Some of these problems have been addressed by Christensen [4] by translating the Sellin-Wolfgang weights to a linear scale, thereby providing for additivity.

Even if one could deal with commensurated crimes, "weighted number of crimes" is insufficient as a measure of effectiveness. One would like to consider a higher-level measure of effectiveness which might be called "social disruption." Such a measure would bring together the total social costs resulting from crime control as well as those

---

* The specific studies conducted here are summarized in the Science and Technology Task Force Report of the President's Commission on Law Enforcement and Administration of Justice [1].

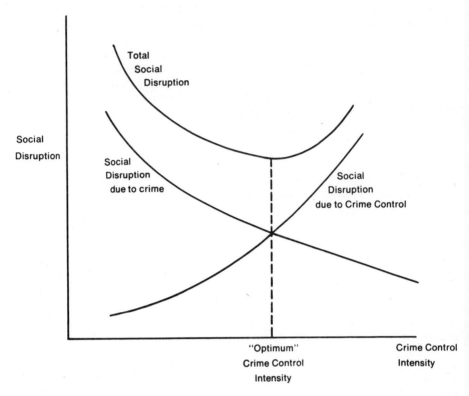

FIGURE 2 –

SOCIAL DISRUPTION AS A FUNCTION OF CRIME CONTROL INTENSITY

resulting from crime. Thus, if we plot social disruption as a function of the intensity of crime control, we might expect a plot such as that shown in Figure 2.

There are two components to social disruption. One is the social costs resulting from crimes. This is presumably a monotonically decreasing function of crime-control intensity. This results from the direct costs of being a victim of crime, the cost of protecting oneself against victimization, and the general fear of victimization. The other component reflects the total social costs resulting from crime *control*, which is presumably a monotonically *increasing* function of crime control intensity. This includes the cost of operating the criminal justice system, welfare costs for offenders and their families, invasion of privacy, and the costs of erroneous arrests or convictions.

The upper curve of Figure 2, the sume of the two components, thus reflects the total social cost associated with crime and its control. Since this may well have a minimum point, we might view that to be the "optimum" level of crime control intensity.

Having thus identified this higher measure of "social disruption," its complexity and its many unquantifiable features preclude operating with it analytically at this time. Nevertheless, considerable value derives from considering these issues, for they pervade many later considerations, such as those relating to technological approaches to improving the effectiveness of crime control, perhaps at the expense of privacy or due process considerations.

This forces us again to focus on crimes as the measure of effectiveness. Even here, however, it is extremely difficult to find relationships between actions taken by the criminal justice system and their effect on crimes. This issue requires effort, but at this point drives the examination to a still lower level.

3. THE CRIMINAL JUSTICE SYSTEM

Focusing on the criminal justice system, we find there are three principal means by which it controls crime: incarceration, correction, and deterrence.

Incarceration involves the physical restraint of identified, arrested, and convicted offenders by placing them under supervision in a prison or jail. During this time, they are physically precluded from engaging in criminal activity against the larger society. It would be desirable to know the crime-reducing consequence of this isolation, aside from the deterrent effect of its threat or any corrective treatment applied during incarceration. This depends on how much crime these people would commit if they were let free. The percentage of crimes leading to incarceration is sufficiently small (on the order of 5%) and the duration of detention is sufficiently short (about 1.5 years in prison and about .4 years in jail), that these same offenders even if released into society, might raise the crime rate only by an additional 5-10 percent. This, of course, assumes that the incarcerated offenders commit crimes at a rate of 1-2 times that of the general crime-committing population. It also ignores whatever difference there may be in the seriousness of the crimes committed by the imprisoned population compared to the broader crime-committing population. These factors need further exploration, but even allowing reasonable margin for their range, it does not appear that incarceration represents the major means by which the CJS controls crime.

The second means by which the CJS tries to control crime is through *correction* of identified offenders, by trying to teach them proper social values, by providing job training, and by various forms of personal and social counseling. This approach may well have future promise, particularly with an increasing technology of education and "behavior control". At present, however, the correction process is still relatively ineffective: about 75-90 percent of arrested individuals find themselves rearrested at some subsequent time, and about one-third of those released from prison will return to prison within five years.

The third principal mode by which the VJS controls crime is through *deterrence*. Evaluation of the effect of deterrence is far more difficult than even incarceration or correction. The difficulty here is in measuring the "non-crimes" that were deterred, based on the concept that there is a reservoir of potential crimes, and the deterrent threat keeps them from appearing. Despite this difficulty in evaluating its effect (or perhaps because of it), deterrence is most commonly regarded as the prime means by which the criminal justice system is able to control crime. The deterrence concept implies a rational weighing of risks against benefits, so that if the perceived risk of apprehension and conviction exceeds the benefit to be gained from committing the crime, then presumably an individual will be "deterred" from committing the crime.

The deterrence concept is based on a *perceived* risk. It is well known that different individuals may well perceive the same situation differently, and may well apply different utility weights to different components of the risk. It is important to know how these perceptions and utilities vary. For instance, what is the relative weight applied to the probability of apprehension compared to the probability of conviction given apprehension? How does the presence of police patrol, or a change in the maximum sentence, or a change in judicial sentencing policies, or a favorable public relations program affect these perceptions and, through them, deterrence? These are issues to be explored in a major research program on deterrence, a program on which only fragmentary beginnings have been made.

Lacking meaningful results from such a program, in order to move on, we can do little better than to accept the conventional wisdom that increasing the probability of apprehension of an individual (all else remaining equal) will result in greater deterrence. We know that this would not be true, say, for a masochist for whom greater risk may well have the opposite effect, or for certain crimes of passion for which the utility in committing the crime is sufficiently high that almost any risk would be acceptable. We also know, from some preliminary studies by Goodman [5], that prison populations are probably less deterrable than non-prison populations, (and this evidence is supported by deterrence having failed at least once in the past), and that there are sharp differences even within the prison population. Nevertheless, acknowledging these limits, we next search for means of increasing the probability of apprehension*.

4.   THE APPREHENSION SYSTEM

Apprehension is something that *can* be measured, since it represents a set of events where "success" was achieved. Apprehension success was measured by sampling calls for police assistance, the crime reports for the subset of these calls that led to crimes, and the arrest reports for the subset of crimes that led to an arrest [6]. With such a sample (taken in two police districts in Los Angeles for one month) one can search for the characteristics of the crime and of the police response that give rise to arrest. At this stage, these are only correlations that must be posed as hypotheses for further exploration in a more carefully controlled way.

In examining the data, it was found that one important feature affecting apprehension is the naming of the suspect in the crime report. "Named-suspect" cases occur when either the victim knows the suspect and identifies him or the suspect is apprehended at the scene of the crime.

These cases, of course, are easy to solve. As shown in Figure 3, the "clearance rate" or

---

* It is not the *true* probability of apprehension that is relevant here. Rather it is the *perceived* probability of apprehension which one wants to increase. This might well be done by means which have little to do with changing the true probability (e.g., by an effective public relations campaign). Furthermore, means of improving the true probability of apprehension that are not perceived (e.g., an unannounced improvement in crime laboratory techniques) will not affect deterrence, at least until the effects are noted.

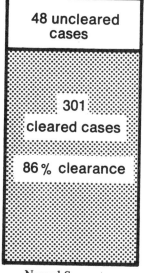

48 uncleared cases	1375 uncleared cases
301 cleared cases	
86% clearance	12% clearance 181 cleared cases
Named Suspects	Unnamed Suspects

FIGURE 3 – CLEARANCE OF CRIMES WITH NAMED AND UNNAMED SUSPECTS IN A SAMPLE OF 1905 CRIME REPORTS

police solution rate of these cases is acceptably high. For the remainder, or "unnamed-suspect cases", the clearance rate is only about 12 percent, and that is probably an over-estimate because of failure to name the suspect in crime reports of cases that were probably "named-suspect" cases.

Clearly, it is desirable to increase the percentage of named-suspect cases, principally by increasing the probability of apprehension at the scene. One means of accomplishing this is by reducing the time it takes the police to respond to a report of a crime in progress*. Examination of alternative approaches first requires the definition of an "apprehension system '. In this system, following detection of the crime by the victim, a witness, or an alarm, the following sequence of events occurs:

1. Communication of the information about the crime to the police, typically by telephone to "complaint clerks" at police headquarters.

2. Decision-making by the police command-and-control system to select an appropriate police response, typically involving the selection of the closest available and appropriate (i.e., having an appropriate number of officers) car.

3. Dispatch of the assigned car, or an alternative one if the assigned one proves to be unavailable.

---

* Another approach would involve improving the probability that the patrol force detects crimes in progress. A search model was formulated to estimate the current detection probabilities, assuming uniform distributions of search effort and crime occurrences. Using data from Los Angeles, and assuming that a street robbery is exposed to detection for two minutes, the expected number of detection opportunities for a street robbery was found to be 0.27 per day, or about two percent of the street robberies. For the average patrol officer, this is an average time between detections of 14 years.

4.   Travel to the scene by the assigned car.

5.   Search for the suspect, first in the immediate vicinity of the crime scene, then in the general vicinity after obtaining identifying information from the person reporting the crime, and finally through detective follow-up.

Each of these steps takes time, and could be reduced. The alternatives examined were the following:

1.   Reducing the delay in calling the police by installing public call boxes more widely in the street or by permitting the public to use existing private police call boxes.

2.   Reducing the telephone queueing delay in calling the police by assigning additional "complaint clerks" to the police communications center.

3.   Increasing the speed with which a police command-and-control system center processes an incoming call* and dispatches a car by using a computerized command-and-control system, in which the complaint clerk puts the information into the computer, and a digital dispatch message is sent to the selected car by teleprinter.

4.   Enabling more accurate selection of the car closest to the scene of the crime by providing more precise information on police car position with automatic car locator equipment.

5.   Reducing patrol-car travel time by reducing the area covered per car through the introduction of additional patrol cars.

5.   COST-EFFECTIVENESS COMPARISON

These alternative approaches can be compared through cost-effectiveness analysis, in which the measure of effectiveness is delay saved per dollar allocated. Since the results depend on the particular conditions in a particular city, specific parameter values must be specified. These values are shown in Table 1. The important variables are the city size, the arrival rate of calls for police assistance, the service rate of the dispatching operation, the service time for a call, the number of complaint clerks, the number of patrol cars on duty, the number of telephones distributed through the city, and the travel speed for the patrol cars. Table 1 shows typical values for a city of about 100 square miles with a population of about 500,000 comparable to Atlanta or Indianapolis.

The results of the detailed calculations are shown in Table 2 for the five types of basic units identified above. The table shows the number of such units currently assigned (considering the possibility of two or three complaint clerks), and the current delay time associated with the current assignment of units.

---

*   In the Los Angeles study it was found that 20—50 percent of the response time was due to delay within the communications center.

TABLE 1 CITY PARAMETERS

Item	Details
Geography...	The City is a 10-by 10-mile square.
Rate of call receipt.............................	40 calls per hour or approximately 350,000 calls per year are handled by the police telephone complaint clerks.
Rate of police mobile unit dispatch.......	30 one-man mobile units are dispatched per hour.
Total mobile patrol force......................	40 one-man patrol cars.
Speed of mobile force...........................	25 m.p.h.
Public telephone distribution...............	1,000 distributed uniformly throughout city.
Call service time..................................	30 minutes average.
Number of call complaint clerks...........	2 or 3.

The fifth column of the table indicates the seconds of delay that could be saved by adding one of the indicated units. Thus, computerizing the command-and-control operations would reduce the processing time from 120 seconds to 30 seconds per call, and adding a forty-first patrol car would save an agerage of 4 seconds in travel time by reducing the average beat sizes.

The sixth column indicates the annual rate of use for each type of unit. Here, all 350,000 calls go through the complaint clerks, but only 264,000 involve the dispatch of a car. The annual cost of an additional unit reflects the amortized investment and operating cost. The cost per additional patrol car is $50,000 per year, reflecting the need for five shifts of $10,000-per-year men to maintain the additional beat continuously. Complaint clerks are paid at somewhat lower rates.

The final column reflects the utility of each of the alternatives, and is given by:

$$U_j = N_j \, D_j / C_j$$

where:

N_j = Annual use of unit j in calls per year

D_j = Average seconds of delay saved per call with an addition of one unit j

C_j = Annual cost of unit j

U_j = Average seconds of delay per year saved per dollar

TABLE 2 – COST-EFFECTIVENESS COMPARISON OF DELAY-REDUCTION ALTERNATIVE

Elements of delay	Basic unit Added	Number of units Currently Allocated	Delay time (seconds)	Seconds of delay saved per call per additional unit	Frequency of use (calls/year)	Cost per yr. of additional unit	Seconds of delay saved per dollar allocated
Public access..............	Public callbox.........	1,000	96	0.0475	10,000	$ 50	9.5
Telephone queue..........	Complaint clerks....	2 } 3	7.2 .042	7.158 .042	350,400 350,400	35,000 35,000	71.7 .42
Command and control..	Computer system...	0	120	90	264,000	200,000	119
Car position................	Car locator............	0	20	18	264,000	100,000	47.5
Patrol mobility............	Patrol car.............	40	216	3	264,000	50,000	21.1

From Table 2, we note that for the case represented here, the most useful investment would be in an automated command-and-control center. The second most attractive alternative would be the addition of one complaint clerk if there are only two currently in service, although if three were already assigned, additional complaint clerks would be of little benefit. Thus, were this a satisfactory analysis for a particular city, the city could then proceed to a more detailed design of the command-and-control system, perhaps repeating the analysis with alternative configurations of the command-and-control system.

In fact, however, the analysis is far from adequate, and is only illustrative at this point. Specific data must be collected for a particular city. Averaged variables need to be treated in more detail. Diurnal and seasonal variations in demand and service capacity should be incorporated into the model. Geographical distributions of crimes and allocations within the city must be considered.

More accurate estimates of the potential time savings through computerization must be obtained before making a design or development commitment. At least two increasingly detailed iterations of this model would be required, perhaps dropping some of the alternatives at each stage and representing the remaining ones with greater precision.

Furthermore, there are side benefits and costs associated with each of the alternatives which could not be taken into account in this or any other cost-effectiveness comparison. These include the creation of a central data base made possible by the computer, or the other services that can be performed by an extra man when he is not answering a call. These considerations certainly must enter the allocation decision.

And, finally, there is the long chain of logic that led to the use of response time as the measure of effectiveness in the cost-effectiveness comparison. The decision-maker must be satisfied with the chain (or provide a better substitute), and the research community must begin to address the operationally important research questions that have been raised.

6.   SUMMARY

The process reported in this paper tried to develop a rational basis for investing police resources. In the largest view, we began with a desire to reduce the total social cost or disruption associated with crime and its control. Then we focused on crime, on the criminal justice system, and on deterrence as its means for controlling crime. We assumed that deterrence is related to the threat of apprehension and, by an analysis of field data, concluded that police response time is related to apprehension probability. Finally, through a cost-effectiveness comparison of alternative approaches to reducing response time, we found that automated command-and-control systems were most efficient for one case.

In following this process we uncovered, and necessarily left for later, a number of important questions. These include such questions as how one can evaluate the social costs of crime control, the trade-offs among different types of crimes, means for assessing what specific actions deter what groups of people from committing what kinds of crimes, what perceptions most affect deterrence, further validation of relationships between response time and the probability of apprehension, and further development and replication in other cities of the cost-effectiveness analysis. Where a city does have an increment of resources to commit, this approach represents a means whereby it can structure its problem and use cost-effectiveness analysis to help in making that decision. The open questions are explicitly addressed. For the researcher, the approach formulates clearly the critical questions which must be addressed in order to rationalize the operation of the criminal justice system.

7.   ACKNOWLEDGEMENTS

Many contributions and suggestions to the work reported here were made by Ronald Christensen, Herbert Isaacs, Sue Johnson, and Richard Larson.

REFERENCES

1.   Blumstein, A. et al, (1967); *Task Force Report: Science and Technology*; President's Commission on Law Enforcement and Administration of Justice; Government Printing Office; Washington, D.C.

2.   Sellin, Thorsten and Marvin Wolfgang, (1964); *The Measurement of Delinquency*; John Wiley and Sons, New York, N.Y.

3.   U.S. Federal Bureau of Investigation; *Uniform Crime Reports*, (annual); Government Printing Office, Washington, D.C.

4.   Christensen, R. in Chapter 5 of *Task Force Report: Science and Technology* op. cit., p. 56.

5.   Goodman, Leonard, et al, (1966); A Study of Value of Crime Prevention Measures as Perceived by Criminal Offenders; unpublished paper; Bureau of Social Science Research; Washington, D.C.

6.   Isaacs, Herbert H.; "A Study of Communications, Crimes, and Arrests in a Metropolitan Police Department"; Appendix B to *Task Force Report: Science and Technology, op. cit.*, pp. 88-106.

A PROPOSE DES OBJECTIFS ET DES CRITERES DE CHOIX PUBLICS

F. Perret

INTRODUCTION

Traditionnellement, tous les économistes qui ont travaillé sur la question de la détermination de critères de choix publics ont pris comme point de départ et fondement de leur démarche les préférences individuelles. Celles-ci étant supposées exprimables sous la forme d'un préordre complet, le probléme global (tel par exemple qu'il a été abordé par Arrow* est le suivant: peut-on agréger les préordres complets individuels en un préordre complet global?

Bien que le résultat obtenue par Arrow fut négatif, de nombreux auteurs dans un souci pratique ont cherché à utiliser des fonctions d'utilité individuelles et une fonction d'utilité collective. Ils en ont déduit moyennant quelques hypothèses complèmentaires un critère de choix collectif baptisé le plus souvent Critère du Surplus ou de l'Avantage collectif†. Celui-ci dans son principe, est censé exprimer de façon synthétique l'ensemble de ce qu'il faut prendre en compte lors de la préparation de choix publics.

Il va se soi en réalité que cette méthode de choix est insuffisante, ne serait-ce que parce que les fonctions d'utilité sous leur forme "normale"** rendent très mal compte de l'ensemble de ce qui intéresse les gens et les pouvoirs publics. On va donc tenter, ici de définir une nouvelle approche, laquelle n'est en fait qu'une tentative de justification théorique d'une préoccupation très pratique.

L'objet de notre démarche est d'aboutir (si c'est possible) à *proposer* l'utilisation effective de tel ou tel critère de choix pour l'évaluation et la sélection des décisions publiques.

On admettra que ces critères doivent pouvoir être utilisés par la puissance publique; ils doivent donc être cohérents avec ses objectifs. Il ne s'agit donc pas d'être le moins de monde normatif et de dire ce que devraient être les critères de choix gouvernementaux mais de chercher ce qu'ils pourraient être.

On admettra encore comme principe (à charge de précisions ultérieures) que les objectifs gouvernementaux ont quelque rapport avec les préférences individuelles; aussi ce papier commence-t-il par quelques remarques à ce sujet.

1. PRELIMINAIRES SUR LES PREFERENCES INDIVIDUELLES

Traditionellement, le choix individuel est supposé fondé sur une préférence: si je choisis A au lieu de B, cela signifie que je préfère A à B. Le second élément du

---

* Voir Arrow : Social choice and individual values.
† Voir en particulier Lesourne : le calcul économique.
** Fonctions ne dépendant que des quantités consommées.

raisonnement est aussi important que la premier: si on me donne ce que je préfère, je m'en trouve mieux.

On préfère partir ici des hypothèses suivantes:
— La préférence est une opinion de l'individu. Cette opinion est telle que si une personne préfère A à B, alors elle choisira A plutôt que B. L'implication inverse *n'est pas* en général supposée vraie.
— Quant à l'idée de "mieux", clef des théories Economiques du Bien-Etre on la liera à celle de préférence en supposant équivalentes les deux formules:
— L'individu préfère A a B.
— L'individu *pense* qu'il se trouvera mieux en A qu'en B.

La terme "pense" a été souligné pour traduire le fait que son imagination et son jugement peuvent se trouver en défaut, c'est-à-dire infirmés par la suite et par lui-même*.

Sans entrer dans le détail d'un exposé sur les choix et préférences individuels qui est hors de notre propos, indiquons simplement—ce qui est nécessaire pour la suite de l'exposé—que cette structure d'hypothèses correspond à l'idée selon laquelle les sujets d'intérêts de la plupart des gens sont nombreux et variés et correspondent à un certain nombre d'objectifs distincts et supposés irréductibles les uns aux autres. On admet ainsi qu'il y a des situations où on finit toujours par choisir une solution parce qu'il faut bien choisir mais ou on ne peut dire qu'on préfère ce qu'on a choisi. Un choix ne correspond à une préférence que lorsqu'aucun des objectifs poursuivis n'est maltraité par le choix.

On donne ainsi aux préférences individuelles une structure d'ordre partiel et non plus d'ordre complet.

Admettons encore sans insister que les facteurs limitatifs de l'accomplissement des objectifs individuels (les contraintes) sont aussi multiples et divers que les objectifs. Ces contraintes expriment que l'obtention de quoi que ce soit réclame du temps et de l'argent, ces deux éléments étant les denrées rares fondamentales que l'individu a à gérer.

Ces contraintes et ces objectifs posent à l'individu un problème formellement identique au problème classique de l'optimum de Pareto: un certain nombre de fonctions objectif sont à maximiser qui sont non comparables entre elles.

Remarquons ici pour les besoins de la suite de l'exposé le résultat suivant: de même que dans le cas classique de l'optimum de Pareto, le point finalement choisi sur la frontière du possible aurait également été obtenu si on avait pris dès le départ une fonction objectif unique, somme pondérée des différents objectifs de l'individu, à condition de choisir une pondération adéquate. Cette pseudo-fonction objectif unique sera évoquée par la suite sous le nom de fonction unitaire.

Du point de vue qui nous occupe, cette façon de présenter les préférences et choix

---

* Cette façon de présenter les choses aboutit à reconnaître que l'individu peut se tromper, mais peut également être trompé par un conditionnement social biaisé.

individuels possède un certain nombre d'avantages. Elle est tout d'abord plus large que la vue traditionnelle exprimée par les fonctions d'utilité: en principe tout ce qui peut concerner l'individu y est pris en compte. Elle insiste ensuite sur la prudence qu'il faut conserver en utilisant la notion de préférence dont la signification est fondamentale du point de vue Economie du Bien-Etre. (Les distinctions faites ici n'ont d'ailleurs d'importance et d'intérêt que de ce point de vue). Elle permet enfin de mettre en valeur les possibilités d'instabilité dans ces préférences, ce qui incite également à la prudence lorsqu'on juge de la valeur globale de ces méthodes. Nous n'avons malheureusement pas la place de développer ici ce dernier point, malgré son importance.

2.   LES BASES DU COMPORTMENT GOUVERNEMENTAL

Changeons à présent de point de vue, et intéressons nous spécifiquement aux problèmes de gouvernement.

2.1   La Contribution de DOWNS

Dans son ouvrage "An economic theory of Democracy", Anthony DOWNS développe une thèse qui rend compte de la façon dont fonctionne le système politique à deux partis, un des deux partis étant au pouvoir et l'autre constituant l'opposition. Selon DOWNS la motivation essentielle des hommes politiques est la recherche du pouvoir; le principe majoritaire donnant le pouvoir au parti ayant recueilli le plus de voix, l'hypothèse fondamentale de schéma consiste à dire que tout se passe comme si les programmes de chaque parti étaient établis de façon à maximiser le nombre de voix. Les électeurs de leur côté choisissent le parti le plus propre à se comporter comme ils le souhaitent; ils établissent leur jugement non seulement sur le programme annoncé par chaque parti mais également sur la façon dont le dit parti s'est comporté dans le passé lorsqu'il était au pouvoir (ceci de façon à tenir compte de la "sincérité" du parti).

Bien que sommaire dans ses considérations de principe, cette théorie permet néanmoins d'éclairer sous un jour unificateur un certain nombre de phénomènes politiques réels. Quelques variantes intéressantes pourraient d'ailleurs être étudiées qui, sans remettre en cause le principe de la démarche, permettraient d'intégrer quelques supplémentaires.

2.2   La Constitution des Objectifs Gouvernementaux: 1° Partie

L'approche qui va à présent être dessinée se situe en aval de celle de DOWNS. Quoique fondées sur des outils conceptuels différents, les deux ont, sinon des points réellement communs, du moins des aspects très proches qui permettent à l'une de préciser l'autre.

Notre objectif est en effet de chercher comment on pourrait définir des critères de choix publics. Le mérite de DOWNS est d'analyser un mécanisme expliquant les liens qui peuvent exister à l'intérieur d'un cadre institutionnel donné entre les préférences individuelles et les choix gouvernementaux. On va ici supposer a priori l'existence de ce lien et essayer de l'expliciter formellement sous un angle différent mais complémentaire de celui de DOWNS.

On a cherché plus haut à mettre en valeur le fait que les préoccupations et les objectifs individuels sont nombreux et divers. On considèrera alors un principe que tout ce qui intéresse un membre de la communauté intéresse les pouvoirs publics: l'ensemble des objectifs gouvernementaux n'est autre selon cette hypothèse que la réunion des ensembles d'objectifs individuels. Cette affirmation, pour satisfaisante qu'elle soit logiquement n'en est pas moins insuffisante pratiquement car il est bien clair que ces différents objectifs ainsi juxtaposés forment un ensemble dépendant, contradictoire et en outre d'une lourdeur de nature à le rendre inutilisable pour l'evaluation effective des décisions possibles; il se trouve que cet ensemble peut être considérablement allégé sans perte de généralité.

L'individu doit dans ses choix courants opérer un arbitrage entre ses différents objectifs cela est au moins aussi vrai au niveau de la puissance publique. On peut alors analyser le problème en suivant deux voies quelque peu différentes; la première consiste à prendre en compte les préférences individuelles par l'intermédiaire des fonctions unitaires et à traiter ces différentes fonctions unitaires comme on a traité les différents objectifs individuels: le problème se ramène alors plus ou moins au choix d'une pondération des fonctions unitaires individuelles. Cette approche présente toutefois des difficultés insurmontables dont la plus importante est incontestablement la quasi impossibilité à laquelle on se heurterait si on voulait effectivement déterminer les fonctions unitaires individuelles. Il existe toutefois, partant du même principe, un moyen de transformer formellement notre problème* qui amènera à envisager une façon plus directe et plus pratique de le traiter qui constituera la seconde approche.

On considère que l'état du monde peut être entièrement décrit par la valeur prise par un certain nombre N de paramètres x_1, x_2,..., x_N. Ces différents paramètres ne sont pas indépendants les uns des autres; un certain nombre de relations existent entre certains d'entre eux qui résultant de l'existence de lois physiques ou psychologiques; supposant celles-ci en nombre fini, on les écrira sous la forme générale.

$$f_i (x_1, x_2, \ldots, x_N) = 0 \quad i = 1,2, \ldots, n.$$

Outre ces lois exprimant des liaisons strictes, il existe un certain nombre de contraintes entre ces variables provenant de limitations physiques ou psychologiques; supposant celles-ci au nombre de m, on les écrira sous la forme générale.

$$g_j (x_1, x_2, \ldots, x_N) \leqslant 0 \quad j = 1, 2, \ldots, m.$$

Les différents objectifs de l'individu k s'expriment en fonction des valeurs prises par les paramètres de définition du monde: si celui-ci a K_k objectifs, chacun de ceux-ci peut être considéré comme revenant à souhaiter que les valeurs prises par des fonctions $f_1^k(x_1,...,x_N) \ 1 = 1,...,K_k$ soient maximales. Ces valeurs étant à présent admises comme de nouveaux paramètres complémentaires de définition de l'état du monde, on peut alors considérer que celui-ci sera dorénavant caractérisé par un certain nombre $N + N'$ de paramètres, N' étant le nombre d'éléments de la réunion des ensembles d'objectifs individuels. Les objectifs de l'individu k s'expriment alors par la recherche d'une valeur maximale pour les variables $x_{k_1},\ldots,x_{k_{K_k}}$

L'individu k accordant une pondération implicite $\lambda^k_1,..., \lambda^k_{K_k}$ ses différents objectifs et admettant que la marge de manoeuvre du pouvoir politique se ramène au

---

* Qui est, rappelons-le de nous interroger sur la possibilité de déterminer des critères de choix publics qui soient effectivement utilisables.

choix d'une pondération implicite μ_1 ... μ_h (h nombre d'individus) aux préférences des différents nombres de la communauté, tout se passe comme si la puissance publique cherchait à maximiser la fonction unitaire collective*.

$$W = \sum_{k=1}^{h} \mu_k \sum_{i=1}^{K} \lambda_i \, x_{k_i}$$

Nous avons eu l'occasion de souligner plus haut que les différents objectifs des différents individus étaient dépendants et contradictoires. Il import donc de simplifier le problème (la fonction W) en conséquence.

Dans son état actuel, le problème de choix s'écrit

$$\text{Max } W = \sum_k \mu_k \sum_i \lambda_i \, x_{k_i}$$

sous les contraintes

$$f_1. \, (x_1 \, \ldots \, x_{N+N'}) = 0$$
$$\vdots$$
$$f_{n+N'} \, (x_1 \, \ldots \, x_{N+N'}) = 0$$

$$g_1. (x_1 \, \ldots \, x_{N+N'}) \leqslant 0$$
$$\vdots$$
$$g_m \, (x_1 \, \ldots \, x_{N+N'}) \leqslant 0$$

La prize en compte des relations f comme définissant implicitement certaines variables en fonction des autres permet de réduire le nombre des variables en cause à un nombre sensiblement moindre de variables indépendantes au regard de ces relations.

Posant alors $N'' = N n$ et supposant que ce sont les variables x_1, x_2 ,,, $x_{N''}$ qui sont *choisies* come variables indçependantes on peut réécrire le problème

$$\text{Max } W = \phi \, (x_1, x_2, \ldots, x_{N''})$$

$$G_1 \, (x_1, \ldots, x_{N''}) \leqslant 0$$
$$\vdots$$
$$G_m \, (x_1, \ldots, x_{N''}) \leqslant 0$$

Ce très simple artifice formel est un premier pas vers la simplification du problème posé: on n'a pas besoin de considérer séparément tous les éléments de la réunion des ensembles d'objectifs individuels; il suffit de considérer *un* ensemble de variables indépendantes.

2.3 La Constitution des Objectifs Gouvernementaux: 2° Partie

Ces préliminaires nous permettent à présent de décrire une vue plus opératoire des choses en limitant l'arbitraire.

Dans ces activités quotidiennes, lorsqu'il définit par exemple une politique des transports ou une politique de l'énergie, le Gouvernement ne prend pas en compte les préférences individuelles en les considérant d'abord séparément, et puis en les agrégeant suivant le processus formel qui vient d'être décrit. On peut considérer au

---

* Notons en passant que notre problème serait résolu si on arrivait d'une manière ou d'une autre à déterminer la nature des x_{k_i}, et les valeurs des λ_i et des μ_k

contraire qu'il repère *directement* un certain nombre de ces variables indépendantes dont il a eté question ci-dessus, que ce sont elles qu'il considère pratiquement lorsqu'il prend ses décisions, et que ces variables ont quelques liens avec les préférences individuelles.

Plus précisément, le processus formel décrit au paragraphe précdent n'est jamais explicité (en supposant qu'il ait un fondement réel). Tout semble se passer comme si les pouvoirs publics prenaient directement en considération la valeur des variables* x_1, x_2, .. $x_{N''}$ comme représentant les objectifs finaux entre lesquels il opère ses arbitrages: un peu plus de croissance, un peu plus d'inflation, etc. . . .

La recherche des coefficients μ_k, correspondant à la pondération implicite des préférences des différents individus qui sous tend ces arbitrages gouvernementaux, devient dans ces conditions un travail quasi impossible. L'utilité pratique en est de plus assez douteuse du fait que l'aide et les conseils de l'économiste risquent fort d'être sans portée s'il n'utilise pas le même langage—celui des objectifs partiels poursuivis—que celui du pouvoir politique qu'il est appelé à servir.

Le problème reprend alors une forme classique: la connaissance des frontières symbolisées par les contraintes G. (x_1 ... $x_{N''}$) $\leqslant$ 0 et l'observation de l'activité gouvernementale devraient nous permettre, si on adopte une optique de préférence révélée, sinon de déterminer la fonction $\phi(x_1$ ... $x_{N''})$, du moins de "cerner" son gradient, cette connaissance permettant à son tour une systématisation de la préparation des décisions, une meilleure cohérence et donc une plus grande efficacité des choix.

La première partie du raisonnement consistait à transformer formellement le problème des choix gouvernementaux en partant des préférences et des choix individuels et en les pondérant d'une façon adéquate. On a dit que dans la pratique courante le processus n'est pas aussi raffiné (ce serait sans doute extrêmement difficile) et le Gouvernement considère directement un certain nombre d'objectifs "à atteindre" et arbitre entre ceux-ci. Supposant que l'on connaisse parfaitement toutes les préférences individuelles, il n'est pas a priori évident qu'il existe une pondération individuelle qui aboutisse à la voie suivie par le Gouvernement; il paraît donc fort possible que le formalisme de la première approche soit, en ce sens, creux. Il est néanmoins, par contre évident que les options gouvernementales ne devraient pas se trouver fort éloignées de ce qui correspondrait aux options individuelles: le contrôle démocratique est en principe là pour éviter de telles errances. Reprenant le cadre conceptuel de DOWNS, on devrait pouvoir affirmer que le Gouvernement est contraint, sous peine d'éviction, de censure populaire, d'exprimer "assez largement" les préférences individuelles. Si en effet le Gouvernement se comportait "trop mal" dans un domaine important et si on savait comment se comporter "mieux", l'opposition ou les oppositions devraient ne pas manquer d'en profiter pour assurer en utilisant ce point la chute du Gouvernement.

Il n'y a de valeur que par rapport à des objectifs et inversement la définition des objectifs permet d'établir la valeur à attribuer à chaque chose: la définition des objectifs gouvernementaux et les arbitrages opérés entre ceux-ci permettent en principe de définir directement une valeur marginale des différents éléments qui concourent à l'achèvement de ces objectifs.

---

* Ou tout autre jeu de variables indépendantes.

Une fois analysé le comportement observé des pouvoirs publics, on peut définir une "valeur gouvernementale" pour chaque chose, laquelle sera utilisable pour effectuer les calculs économiques: on constatera ainsi que le Gouvernement attache par exemple une valeur faible au téléphone marginal (ou a l'agrément de celui qui le possède). Qu'il attache au contraire une grande valeur à l'équipement électrique et une valeur de plus en plus grande à l'éducation et à la recherche.

L'économiste sera là pour aider à atteindre une plus grande cohérence, pour mettre en valeur la signification et les conséquences de tel ou tel choix, mais certainement pas pour exprimer approbation ou réprobation au nom de je ne sais quelle éthique révélée dont il aurait le privilège.

3.   CONSEQUENCES PRATIQUES

3.1   Le Surplus Corrigé

Les éléments de l'état du monde sur lesquels protent les objectifs individuels (et donc gouvernementaux d'après nos hypothèses) peuvent grossièrement être divisés en deux grandes catégories. Seront rangés dans la première tous ceux d'une nature telle que les préférences individuelles correspondantes puissant être révélées par les mécanismes économiques normaux, c'est-à-dire essentiellement le marché; la seconde catégorie regroupera le reste.

On admettra alors que les préférences de première catégorie des individus sont convenablement représentées par des fonctions d'utilité de type classique ne dépendant que des quantités consommées. On admettra encore (l'hypothèse contraire serait contradictoire avec ce qui a été dit précédemment de la constitution des objectifs gouvernementaux) que parmi les objectifs qu'il retient le pouvoir politique introduit la maximisation de ces fonctions d'utilité individuelles. En d'autres termes ceci signifie que le Surplus (qu'on pourrait d'ailleurs à la rigueur remplacer par une fonction d'utilité collective normale) figurera *parmi* les indicateurs utiles auxquels le pouvoir politique se réfère au moment de prendre une décision.

Les autres objectifs individuels, exprimés par certains individus eux-mêmes, par différents groupements et par les partis politiques son assimilés et pris en compte directement par le Gouvernement qui les regroupe et les synthétise à sa guise suivant un certain processus, celui précisément que nous avons voulu décrire ci-dessus. A ces objectifs correspondent d'autres indicateurs destinés eux aussi à la préparation des décisions et qui pourraient venir se juxtaposer à celui fourni par le critère du Surplus.

Ces différents objectifs sont a priori quelconque: ils peuvent concerner la distribution des richesses, le taux d'inflation, le déficit de la balance des paiements, la culture et l'éducation des citoyens ou le dépeuplement de la basse Bretagne: tout ce qui peut être considéré comme ayant une influence sur le comportement gouvernemental.

Autrement dit et pratiquement, au terme provenant de l'utilisation du critère du Surplus viendront s'ajouter une foule de bonifications et de pénalités provenant de modifications favorables ou défavorables de l'état du monde du point de vue d'autres objectifs. L'esquisse de base constituée par le Surplus pourra être ainsi plus ou moins altérée, parfois même complètement bouleversée: ce n'est pas parce que le terme de Surplus est cité en premier qu'il est toujours effectivement premier: nombreuses sont les préoccupations gouvernementales non directement relatées à des consommation.

Le critère du Surplus reprend donc ici un rôle plus modeste: un parmi les autres. Il n'en conserve pas moins un rôle particulier du fait de la qualité qu'il possède de résumer et de synthétiser tout un pan, malgré tout assez important dans bien des cas, des conséquences d'une décision. Il porte en outre sur le seul type d'objectifs dont une exploration satisfaisante est déjà réalisée.

3.2   La "Révélation" des Préférences Gouvernementales

Il serait souhaitable, dans la mesure où on veut arriver à obtenir une véritable cohérence des choix gouvernementaux, de parvenir à l'utilisation d'un étalon de valeur unique. Selon les principes classiques, il est indispensable de suivre la démarche des "préférences révélées" pour évaluer les taux de substitution marginaux entre les différents objectifs et atteindre ainsi le but fixé.

Beaucoup de gens se penchent ou se sont penchés sur ce problème: définir quelles sont les préférences gouvernementales. La plupart d'entre eux ont abandonné la tâche soit parce qu'ils ont jugé le travail impossible soit (ce qui revient au même) parce qu'ils ont jugé que les résultats qu'il était possible de trouver étaient instables et non significatifs.

Il est a priori bien évident qu'il est inutile d'aller trouver tel ou tel ministre pour lui demander s'il préférerait tant de beurre ou tant de canons. La résponse qu'il donnerait (s'il en donne une) s'apparenterait fortement aux réponses que ferait n'importe qui lorsqu'on lui demande "que feriez-vous si . . .? " Il est bien connu que les réponses ainsi obtenues ne sont absolutment pas représentatives de ce que feraient effectivement les gens dans telle out telle circonstance.

Il est d'ailleurs clair que les pouvoirs publics ne sont pas représentables sous la forme d'une entité une homogène et cohérente. Les décisions possibles sont d'abord imaginées par les uns, reprises par d'autres, modifiées et altérées jusqu'à aller pourrir dans un obscur tiroir ou au contraire jusqu'à ce qu'un des leaders du système la reprenne à son compte et la fasse adopter. Où se trouvent alors les préférences sur ce sentier tortueux et aléatoire?

Le seconde méthode théoriquement possible pour déterminer les "préférences" gouvernementales est d'utiliser proprement les principes de la "préférence révélée", c'est-à-dire d'observer les choix effectivement faits par le Gouvernement, la situation actuelle et son évolution, de déterminer les caractéristiques du domaine du possible et de déterminer quelle est ou quelles sont les fonctions objectifs cohérentes avec les situations observées. Les difficultés d'application de cette méthode sont, elles encore, multiples: elles tiennent d'une part à l'absence d'une définition nette de l'ensemble des objectifs, d'autre part à la difficulté de détermination du domaine du possible (cette détermination modifiant d'ailleurs ce qu'on pourrait appeler des "contraintes" d'ignorance, lesquelles jouent en fait un rôle important), au caractère évolutif et changeant des opinions et préférences.

Enfin, pour couronner le tout, en supposant qu'on ait réussi à surmonter toutes ces difficultés, il est fort possibles qu'on n'aboutisse qu'à une indétermination partielle du résultat du fait que la situation observée a toutes chances de se situer dans un coin du domaine du possible (ou au moins un coin "relatif").

3.3 Remarque Finale

Il semble à l'expérience que ce problème de révélation soit dans bien des cas beaucoup plus théorique que pratique.

D'une part il peut arriver qu'on puisse obtenir par des voies plus directes des ordres de grandeur raisonnables de ce qu'on pourrait prendre comme valeur pour certains éléments: on peut citer par example les problèmes de sécurité et de lutte contre les accidents, et le problème correspondant d'évaluation de ce que la collectivité est disposée à payér pour égargner des vies. Les résultats qu'on peut obtenir par le biais d'analyse spécifique de certaines décisions ou réactions seront certainement très imprécis mais ils permettront néanmoins de diminuer considérablement l'acuité du problème.

On se trouve en outre actuellement dans une situation telle que le plus urgent dans bien des secteurs n'est pas de chercher à obtenir de telles évaluations, mais bien plutôt de ne chercher qu'à faire preuve de bon sens pour déceler des incohérences et des aberrations grossières.

Est-donc à dire que la démarche et les considérations qui précèdent sont sans intérêt? On peut penser que leur intérêt est moins de préciser une méthode pratique à suivre que d'éclairer la signification et l'orientation de ce qu'on peut faire: il faut y voir en particulier une tentative de réhabilitation théorique de la prise en compte explicite d'objectifs multiples.

COST BENEFIT ANALYSIS IN EVALUATING ALTERNATIVE PLANNING POLICIES FOR GREATER LONDON

A. D. J. Flowerdew

"Andy Cobham: Do I have to know about economics before I'm permitted to build my cities?"

Arnold Wesker. *Their Very Own and Golden City*

1.   DISCLAIMER

This paper is based on work carried out by the Cost Benefit Studies Section, Survey and Research Group, Planning Department, Greater London Council, which I was in charge of from February, 1966 to December, 1968. It does not necessarily reflect the policy of the Greater London Council in any way.

2.   INTRODUCTION

The Greater London Council was set up in 1963 as part of a major re-organisation of local government in London. It covers an area of 620 square miles, with a population of nearly 8 million, and is more than five times the size of the former London County Council with more than double the population. At the same time 32 new London Boroughs were established, with populations of about a quarter of a million each, covering the whole area apart from the square mile of the City of London. Local authority functions and powers are split between the G.L.C. and the London Boroughs. In particular, the planning function is divided, with the G.L.C. carryingout a strategic role and the Boroughs being responsible for detailed planning in their areas.

The major task of G.L.C. planning is the preparation and maintenance of the Greater London Development Plan, due to be submitted to the Minister of Housing and Local Government sometime around the date of presentation of this paper. This Plan will consist of a series of policy statements on subjects like population, housing, employment, transportation, open space and shopping. These policy statements will be supplemented by maps, and by research material presented simultaneously, product of a research group about 50 strong, possibly the largest planning research team in the world.

Research in planning, as in other fields, has several aims. It has to specify the data which must be collected for analysis, it must carry out the analysis of data to define more precisely the planning problems to be solved; it must forecast the likely effects of alternative planning policies, including the 'do-nothing' alternative, and it must evaluate these effects, so as to guide decision-makers on which policies should be adopted. It is with the last of these activities that I am concerned here.

3.   STRATEGY

The use of the word strategy is intended to imply that the policies for each major subject should be consistent with each other. It would be foolish, for instance, to adopt a policy of encouraging economic growth while at the same time lowering housing densities, maintaining the Green Belt and discouraging commuting. There would then be no labour to produce the economic growth. This seems obvious, but there is an understandable tendency, for planners, politicians and private citizens alike, to suggest that through their ingenuity in devising plans, the interests of every section of the community can simultaneously be advanced. If policies are considered separately, this self-deception can be maintained, but when they are taken together, in the light of the constraints placed by availability of capital, labour and land, it is clear that planning is a question of compromise, or of allocating scarce resources, not of panaceas. Three examples for illustration: much housing in Inner London is crowded or unfit; housing considerations suggest re-housing at lower densities, and taking more land, but the same areas are often desperately short of parks and play areas. Traffic management schemes (usually re-routing traffic round one-way systems) have succeeded in maintaining Central London traffic overall journey speeds, despite a large growth in the volume of traffic*; but the use of formerly quiet residential streets by fast and heavy traffic has increased environmental costs. Satisfying housing demand efficiently implies more investment in public housing and low price accommodation in poor areas, and in owner-occupied property in the better-off places, yet this policy is likely to increase social problems associated with one-class communities, the effects of which are realised in extreme form in parts of the United States. These examples could be multiplied.

The major strategic issue for London is that of centralization versus decentralization. In over-simplified terms, is it better to encourage the centralization of activity in London, or to shed as much as possible of the activity to new or expanded towns, counter-magnets, or new cities in other parts of the country. For some time now, both central and local government have been pursuing a policy of decentralization influenced by the Barlow Report (1940), the Abercrombie plan and the views of most of the planning profession. Whether for this or for other reasons, the population of the G.L.C. area has been falling slowly since the early 1950's, and is expected to fall quite dramatically in the next decade.

Now that decentralization policies are beginning to bite, should public authorities continue to encourage them or should they hold back and remove some of the existing constraints and incentives? (The constraints and incentives include: Office Development Permits, Industrial Development Certificates, regional subsidies such as capital allowances, SET rebates, etc.—central government; land use zoning and plot ratio restrictions and new and expanded towns schemes—local authority.) It is almost impossible to quantify how far the projected population decrease is caused by planning measures, and how far it is a natural process: moreover to get a complete picture it would be necessary to consider how much is invested by Government in London relative to the rest of the country. So to obtain the basis for a judgement it is necessary to examine in detail the likely costs and benefits of the alternative strategies.

The main costs and benefits to be considered are:

(i)   productivity. Output per man in manufacturing industry is higher, job for job, in

---

* J.M. Thomson (1968) however puts this down to better driving and better cars.

Greater London than in the rest of the country—in particular the rest of S.E. Region. Not much can be deduced from these figures (which date from 1958; 1963 Census of Productivity data are not available at the time of writing). But on a detailed analysis the most plausible hypothesis seems to be that the productivity differences reflect external economies of scale. In so far as these result from specialisation, close geographical ties between firms and their customers, suppliers and competitors or the volume and range of services available, one might expect such a productivity difference to exist also in the service sector where direct productivity measurement is not possible. If the productivity differences are real, one could expect losses in output from decentralizing economic activity. The problem of measuring this loss with any degree of precision remains.

(ii)   housing and infrastructure. Costs here depend very much on the pace of decentralization. It seems unlikely that many areas of London would have vacant property, beyond the usual float of vacancies required by the market. What is most likely is that decentralization would reduce the need for new building and bring down occupancy rates. There is an obvious benefit here, which may be partly offset by the construction of a greater number of new dwellings. Much of the social infrastructure however is likely to cost more on decentralization—at least that which is associated with urban uses, and with the possible exception of roads (see below). If open space provision is also regarded as infrastructure, on the grounds that it is a community need, decentralization would bring benefits. Measurement of these factors is clearly quite complicated: perhaps a rough guide could be obtained by comparing new or expanded town costs to the extra costs of renovating or re-building an equivalent number of houses in the conurbation, including land costs where new land has to be taken for modern density standards, and with some allowance for increasing open space provision.

(iii)   congestion and travel. Congestion costs in London are well known to be heavy, both on road and rail, and journeys to work are often formidably long. Such factors can be costed, but there are some quite difficult problems to consider. Since expensive and extensive transport investments are on the way, against what system should one measure congestion costs? And what assumptions are to be made about future pricing policy and other controls, on road and rail, parking and taxes? In principle one should no doubt compare optimum pricing and investment policies for the centralization and decentralization cases (if the implied assumption of rational behaviour on the authorities' part is sustainable) but such a study would need to be of an order of magnitude more sophisticated than the £1 million, 5 year London Transportation Study. This study, advanced for its time, nevertheless failed to take into account the price demand relationship, failed to produce a social rate of return calculation for the G.L.C's proposed roads programme as such and failed to produce a meaningful comparison of the relative merits of investment in road and rail improvements.

While one can look for short cuts on some of these points, a clear indication of the right strategy must wait for the next batch of information and research. Crude numerical studies carried out at the G.L.C. suggested that the answer was not obvious. In this situation a compromise strategy for London seems right at the present time—not to resist the trend for people and firms to move out, but to be more selective in operating the incentives for them to do so.

This section has dealt with strategy at some length, in the hope of dispelling the rather widespread belief that the solution to London's problems is obvious, and planning should therefore be concerned with means of getting there, rather than with considering what the overall objective should be.

4.   POLICIES/PROJECTS

More was achieved (and far more research effort was used) in carrying out cost benefit studies into particular policies or projects. Four case studies will be described here. Two were in fact carried out in support of policy research, two intended to help in development projects, but in effect all four can be regarded as case-studies. The case studies are disguised in this account to avoid identification, and simplified to avoid the paper becoming too long: I hope nevertheless to put over some of the flavour of the work. They deal respectively with Central London redevelopment, a suburban town centre proposal, residential density, and a proposed new civic centre.

4.1   Central London Redevelopment

Central London—broadly the area surrounded by the mainline termini—contains within it many areas which do not resemble or function as effective parts of the centre of a large conurbation. Commercial inertia, coupled with the additional friction on changing land use which planning policies impose, have left areas which attract the attention of architects, planners and entrepreneurs as potential sites for ambitious redevelopment. This study concerned one such district: the Committee was to be advised on the most suitable land use zonings for the district, part of a Comprehensive Development Area. For various reasons a number of unconventional possibilities were eliminated and the alternatives were boiled down to three:

  A.   retention of commercial and some office uses
  B.   replacement of these by residential
and   C.   a mixture of A and B.

Capital costs of acquisition and clearance and resulting land values had been estimated in the normal way, showing a very large loss of Scheme B over Scheme A, which was not much reduced by the compromise proposal. But this was unlikely to satisfy the Committee as clinching the matter, especially since it had requested particular attention to be paid to the problem of traffic congestion. It was suggested that Scheme A should be debited with the cost of road works to cater for the traffic generated by commercial uses, but in the dense mesh of Central London a road scheme could hardly be judged within the limited area of this one district. Anyway there were other factors to consider. There was thought to be a case for increasing the residential population of the centre to cut down on commuting problems. A cost-benefit study was called for.

The major factors to be incorporated in the study, apart from those in the financial appraisal, were taken to be the effects on road congestion of removing the traffic generated by commercial land-uses; the change in commuting expected by increasing household potential in the centre; and environmental changes. In assessing these factors, two complicated problems of principle arose. The first is that one needs to make assumptions that alternative locations for residents in Scheme A and for firms in B (unless assumed to go out of business): the second that we are recommending land-use zonings, not actual buildings, so that costings, traffic generations, etc., can only be taken as average values. Because of this second problem we baulked at assessing the environmental changes: it seemed wrong to suppose that new commercial development would ipso facto be better or worse than new housing. The first problem was treated by assuming that the change from commerce to residential would not be compensated by an equivalent change in the reverse direction elsewhere in Central London, and that if housing is not provided here it would have to be increased at the fringe of the conurbation.

4.2   Congestion Costs

If one form of development is likely to generate more traffic than another on an already overcrowded network of roads, this traffic will impose extra external costs on the environment. These external costs will arise because the traffic generated by the development will tend to reduce the speed and hence the journey times of the traffic already on the network. The consequent reduction in speed cannot of course be precisely calculated, but estimates of the average reduction in speed have been produced by the Road Research Laboratory in the work for the Smeed Report on Road Pricing (1964). The formula used in that report relates the marginal social cost of congestion for an additional vehicle mile of traffic on the network to current vehicle speeds, the desired speeds of vehicles and to the social costs of additional time spent in travelling, which is composed of evaluation of an individual's time together with that portion of operating costs which varies with operating time. The desired speed which is assumed corresponds to the speed at which traffic would flow along the network in the absence of other vehicles. The equation takes the form

$$M = b \, (d-v)/v^2 \, ,$$

where M is the marginal social cost of an additional vehicle mile, b is a constant derived from the mix of traffic on the roads, the marginal operating costs, and time values, d is the desired speed and v the actual speed on the network.

To apply this formula to traffic generations it was necessary to derive an estimate of the most likely number of additional generations by type of vehicle, time of day and distance travelled. Since we were dealing with Central London redevelopment it seemed reasonable to suppose that all trips were radiating out from the centre. This was a useful assumption since it meant we did not have to take into account the direction of travel. There is a reasonably good relationship between distance from the centre of London and vehicles' average speeds. We assumed that desired speeds would also be likely to increase as distance from Central London increased since the density of the road network itself becomes less, the obstructions fewer, and one would not expect free flow in Central London in any case to reach the levels that it does on suburban roads. The formula can now be applied to produce a marginal social cost derived from the number of additional traffic generations which can in turn be related to the amount of floor space provided. Figure 1 overleaf illustrates the process.

Estimating the social cost of congestion on public transport posed rather different problems. We were fairly easily able to calculate the expected effect on the length of journey to work. Clearly providing more homes in the central area and fewer jobs is likely to reduce the average length of travel, and our best estimate was that this was approximately two train loads of commuters per day. It is less easy, without detailed

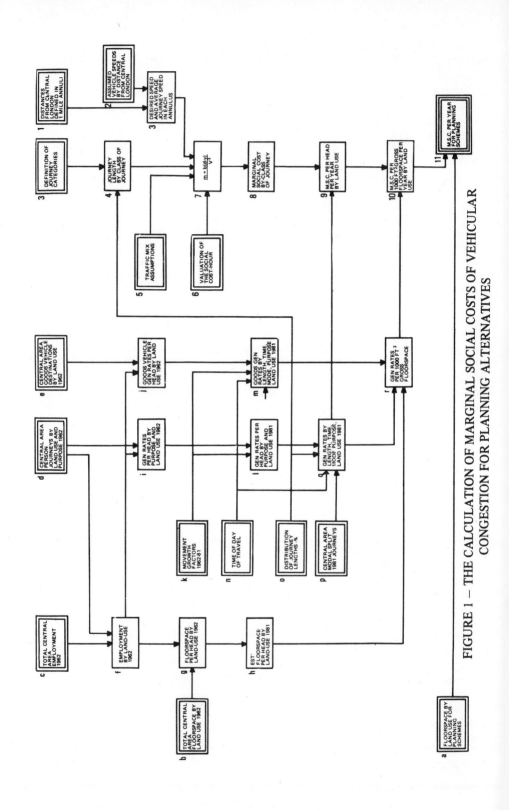

FIGURE 1 – THE CALCULATION OF MARGINAL SOCIAL COSTS OF VEHICULAR CONGESTION FOR PLANNING ALTERNATIVES

knowledge of British Rail and London Transport operating costs, and what the policy is for providing extra services once congestion in overcrowding terms has reached a certain level, to evaluate the social cost involved, even if one could get a reasonably good measure of the social cost of discomfort from overcrowding.

At this stage, therefore we examined the figures which we had already obtained. Inclusion of the congestion costs effects had reduced the differential between Scheme B and Scheme A by something like a third, indicating that road congestion was certainly a significant factor in location policy but it did not seem in this case to be sufficiently large to outweigh the financial losses involved. It was our judgement that the public congestion cost was not likely to be greater than that on the roads. We therefore concluded that Scheme B–and the same applied to Scheme C–were not really improvements on Scheme A. It is however worth noting that the same calculations, applied to particular sites in the area, did not necessarily show the same results. There were instances where a particular proposed commercial development, while showing a purely financial profit, produced a social loss when congestion costs were taken into account. This indicates that it may be of some value to go through these calculations in considering whether or not to adopt such schemes.

The implications for land use policy as a whole in Central London are less clear. The analysis briefly described above can really not be taken to apply to anything other than marginal alterations in the existing land use pattern. In so far as it indicates that road congestion alone is not an argument for reducing the amount of land allocated to employment generating uses, it may be taken as one justification for continuing this kind of activity and possibly expanding it within the central area, a policy which in some ways conflicts with the objectives, for example, of the Location of Offices Bureau. It would however be rash to make any such sweeping conclusions on the basis of a purely marginal study, which in itself has not covered by any means all the important factors.

5. TOWN CENTRES

Most of London's shopping centres are located at junctions of main roads and along stretches of busy arterial routes in and out of London. In the inner areas the buildings themselves are often fifty and more years old. The growth of traffic since the war, in particular the growth of car based shopping, had led to great interest by the local authorities in preparing renewal schemes. At the same time private developers, finding that the scope for office building was limited by controls, have tended to turn to shopping redevelopments as the next best likely source of a high return on capital.

As a result there are getting on for a hundred schemes for redevelopment of shopping centres within Greater London alone. Many of these schemes include both development of roads and shops, and the more ambitious ones often incorporate a public transport interchange and a number of new civic buildings. Many of them are envisaged as a partnership between public and private development, public development being responsible for roads, very often some housing and civic buildings as well. The Ministry of Housing and Local Government will prepare a priority list of schemes to which they are prepared to allocate resources from a central pool.

The criteria for priorities in these town centre redevelopment schemes–and there must be priorities for the total expenditure involved would come to thousands of millions of pounds—must take into account two factors. Firstly, the individual viability of these schemes interpreted not in a narrow commercial sense—will the shops pay the developers?—but in a social sense—do the total benefits for this scheme provide an adequate social return on the costs involved? Secondly, whether the resulting balance of provision is desirable, for it may be that two redevelopment schemes close together could each in isolation provide an adequate return, but the combination of them results in an over provision of shopping. Hence planning must take into account the overall pattern of new centres provided in addition to the merits and demerits of each individual case. The study to be described here in outline was concerned solely with the evaluation of individual schemes. It was undertaken in order to establish whether it would be possible to institute a system for evaluating each town centre proposal, in the same way that the Ministry of Transport assesses road proposals, and allocates money on the basis of the results. The centre studied in the pilot was typical of many redevelopment schemes. The existing centre lay at the intersection of two major roads, and it was proposed to redevelop within a ring road so that most of the new shopping development would be in a pedestrian precinct.

It proved possible to establish a rate of return for this particular scheme although a number of difficulties were encountered, some of which really need to be overcome before it could be claimed that the method is really sound. One of the most difficult of these was in evaluating the benefits from improved shopping facilities. The only data available were on increased rents paid by shopkeepers to the developers which had to be forecast, of course, to produce a commercial rate of return. This return does not however take into account any additional benefits for the shopkeepers which may be created nor benefits to the shoppers themselves. The only benefits credited to the shoppers themselves were savings in accident costs, because vehicle/pedestrian conflict in the centre would be virtually eliminated. In fact no non-financial costs and benefits were assessed, except for traffic. The analysis of traffic was based on an assignment technique, developed especially to deal with small networks. Incidentally, this showed the ring road to be a rather poor solution to the traffic problem, since the road was of too low capacity to handle the peak flows of vehicles, and traffic distances were increased on this network against the previous one. (The scheme was later revised with a much more satisfactory road network.)

A rate of return was however calculated, and it was about 5%. Taking into account unquantified factors, which on the whole seemed to be against the scheme, with the exception of consumer surplus for shoppers, it was concluded that the scheme was perhaps a doubtful starter. A more detailed description of the study is given in Saalmans (1967).

6.   DENSITY

Among the most pressing redevelopment problems are the large areas in Inner London of mainly 19th century housing where a high building density and high occupancy rates combine to produce severe overcrowding. Some few of these areas—Earl's Court, Hampstead, etc.—have been largely taken over by groups of single people or childless families for whom high density living can be attractive, and who can afford rents which will maintain the property in good condition. But much is in really bad condition and at or approaching slum level. Redevelopment is clearly desirable, and in at least some cases money should not be lacking—two of the richest London Boroughs, Westminster and Kensington and Chelsea contain large chunks of such property in

Paddington and North Kensington—but the problem of overspill or what to do with the surplus population if redevelopment is confined to approved residential densities, is tricky.

In any case, if density standards are to be taken seriously, a critical examination is necessary. We decided to take as a case study a small area, currently inhabited at 250 persons per acre, and compare the effects of redevelopment at densities equivalent to 250, 140 and 75 persons per acre, assuming the overspill population could be housed on the fringe of the conurbation. Again this was a marginal study; it was recognised that if low densities turned out preferable for large areas of Inner London, further comparisons would have to be made with housing beyond the Green Belt.

The most easily quantified factors, land and construction costs, journeys to work and congestion costs, turned out to be fairly evenly balanced, the extra costs involved in high density construction being nearly equal to the cost of acquiring more land on the fringes. Two more intangible factors appear capable of a decisive influence on the study.

The first is the cost of compelling some proportion of people to move from where they live, involving some disruption of communities, family ties, and so on. Measures of these costs are not yet established: it is possible that some limits could be set by considering what extra rents unwilling movers would have to pay to move back, or unwilling stayers would need to pay to move out. Social surveys could establish what proportion would accept a move. From these data a crude measure could be obtained. The social cost involved depends on how it is decided who should stay; if matters can be arranged so that those who are least resistant to moving do so, the cost can be minimized.

The second intangible factor relates to the benefits obtained from housing of various types. High densities do not necessarily mean high flats of course, but the higher the density the less easy it is to match the provision of dwelling types to the preferred choices of the families. So benefits from reducing densities can be expected by enabling people to occupy more preferred types of housing.

Two approaches are possible here. One is to infer relative preferences from rent levels in the private housing market. The main objection to this procedure is that private and public housing markets in London cater on the whole for very different classes of people, not so much with regard to income level, as to family structure and geographic mobility. The second approach is via a survey in which people are asked, first to rank their choice of housing types, and second to estimate the differential rent which would induce them to shift to a less preferred type, or allow them to go to a more preferred type. There are obvious difficulties in this approach, but it is hoped that it can be tried.

7. CIVIC CENTRE

When the London Boroughs were set up many of them were amalgamations of existing authorities: consequently their municipal and civic facilities are spread over a number of locations. There is an argument for centralizing these, and we carried out a study on one such proposal. Three alternative sites for the new centre were to be compared, and it was also proposed to incorporate some new facilities.

The list of costs and benefits considered were as follows:

     (i)   Construction, demolition and clearance.
     (ii)   Land costs and replacement of public open space.
     (iii)   Effect of concentration on costs and services.
     (iv)   Journey to work costs.
     (v)   Accessibility of residents to existing facilities.
     (vi)   Benefits from new facilities.
     (vii) Running and maintenance costs.
     (viii) Imponderables (aesthetic: civic pride).

The first two items in the above list were obtained: there was some uncertainty with regard to one site, located in the middle of a proposed large open space, there being some support for the view that use of the open space would be enhanced by the civic centre. On balance it seemed best however to include the replacement cost of open space, because of the counter argument that breaking up a continuous green area could have a greater social cost than using the whole of a small area. (By analogy taking 10 acres out of Hampstead Heath could not necessarily be compensated for by an equivalent acreage not adjoining the Heath.)

Sketchy studies were carried out on (iii), (iv) and (v), enough to indicate the rough orders of magnitude and demonstrate that they were relatively small. Taking a generous view the capitalized value of benefits would be around quarter of a million pounds, compared with construction costs of several millions.

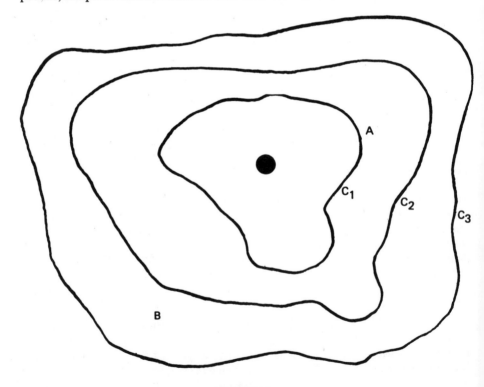

FIGURE 2

Benefits from new facilities were estimated by a Hotelling type analysis, using data from an existing recreation centre (Swiss Cottage) and an existing Central Library. The method used analyses the costs paid to use such facilities, including travel costs and time valuation, and produces an implied demand curve. It is illustrated in Figure 2.

The central blob represents some attraction such as a swimming pool, fishing pond, library etc. The squiggly lines are equi-cost contours dividing up the map into regions where the cost of travel to the blob is the same. Thus it costs C_1 to travel from point A and between C_2 and C_3 to travel from point B. The population inside C_1 is p_1, and the number visiting the blob from this region is n_1; similarly the population between C_1 and C_2 is p_2, and so on. Normally one would have:

$$\frac{n_1}{p_1} \geqslant \frac{n_2}{p_2} \geqslant \frac{n_3}{p_3} \ldots$$

It is assumed that the population is homogeneous within each ring with regard to their desire to visit the blob (an assumption that would not be satisfied if they had chosen where to live because of **proximity** to it). But if this is so, then of the people living inside C_1, at least a proportion n_2/p_2 must be receiving some surplus benefit, since this proportion of people travel from outside the ring. If we assume a linear demand curve then their benefit will be

$$p_1 \left\{ \frac{n_3}{p_3}\left(\frac{C_2 + C_3 - C_1}{2}\right) + \left(\frac{n_2}{p_2} - \frac{n_3}{p_3}\right)\left(\frac{C_2 - C_1}{2}\right) \right\}$$

Similarly we can calculate a surplus for those inside C_2. Even without assuming a linear demand curve, we can estimate upper and lower bounds for the total surplus. Details need not be described here.

There are considerable problems in applying this method to real data, not least the existence of competing facilities in the neighbourhood (to account fully for these one needs to use a gravity model formulation). But the figures produced—about £85,000 per year for the recreation centre and £25,000 for the library—seemed plausible. The method of course does not take into account health and education benefits except in so far as these are appreciated and valued by consumers.

The last two items were not estimated. The short fall between capitalized benefits and costs was around £5 million and it seemed unlikely that they could possibly make up the difference. Item (vii) is likely to increase the cost side, especially for new facilities.

Analysis of the separate elements of the proposal showed that the Recreation Centre was the best bet, though in no case were benefits more than 80% of the costs.

ACKNOWLEDGEMENTS

The work described in this note is to be credited to members of the Cost Benefit Studies Section rather than to me. The people concerned are Carol Barnett, Robin Carruthers, Richard Carter, Donald Hoodless, Frank Little, Peter Saalmans, Bob Stannard and Ray Thomas. To each of them grateful thanks, and also to Donald Cross and Ian Carruthers, Head and Deptuy Head of Survey and Research Group and to many other colleagues too numerous to mention.

REFERENCES

Road Policy, the Economic and Technical Possibilities (Smeed Report) H.M.S.O., 1964.

Royal Commission on the Distribution of the Industrial Population (Barlow Report) Cmd., 6153, H.M.S.O., 1940.

Saalmans, P.D. (1967) Evaluation of Town Centre Redevelopment Schemes, *Proceedings of P.T.R.C. Seminar on Urban Renewal Cost Benefit*, 25-31.

Thomson, J. M. (1968), 'The value of traffic management', *J. Transport Economics and Policy*, 2, Nos. 1, 2 and 3.

CHOIX EN PRESENCE DE CRITERES MULTIPLES : UN ESSAI D'APPLICATION AUX TECHNIQUES DE PREPARATION DES DECISIONS POUR L'AMENAGEMENT DU TERRITOIRE

Claude Bozon
Alain Maugard

1. INTRODUCTION

L'utilisation de plus en plus fréquente, dans les entreprises privées et dans les administrations, de certains outils d'analyse, comme les graphes de pertinence, l'analyse coût-efficacité, l'analyse de systèmes, l'analyse multicritères, ainsi que l'instauration de nouvelles procédures, comme le P.P.B.S. aux Etats-Unis (Planning-Programming-Budgeting-System) ou la R.C.B. en France (Rationalisation des Choix Budgétaires), et les procédures de programmation de la recherche, invitent à repenser en termes nouveaux la préparation des décisions pour l'aménagement du territoire.

Il faut donc examiner comment de telles méthodes et de telles procédures pourraient être utilement appliquées à la préparation des décisions d'un organizme responsable de la fonction d'aménagement du territoire :

En décrivant de façon succincte un schéma de conception globale, l'attention se portera sur tous les niveaux de l'analyse, où se posent des problèmes de choix en présence de critères multiples, et sur toutes les étapes de la procédure, où l'analyse multicritère est susceptible d'apporter des résultats opérationnels.

Le point de vue des critères multiples sera ici privilégié, car il paraît un outil d'analyse particulièrement adapté à l'aménagement du territoire. En ce domaine, en effet, se posent des problèmes de *cohérence intersectorielle* à tous les niveaux géographiques (région, département, communes); il en est ainsi, lorsqu'il s'agit de choisir un parti d'aménagement qui intéresse plusieurs secteurs (agriculture, équipment, santé, éducation, ...), défenseurs chacun de leurs points de vue at de leurs préoccupations sectorielles.

En outre, *la pluralité des niveaux géographiques de décision* oblige à considérer que des intérêts de caractère national, régional, départemental, local, poussent, respectivement, les décideurs.

Enfin, l'interdépendance des moyens envisageables implique une cohérence fonctionnelle de l'aménagement du territoire. Ainsi, le choix d'une solution d'aménagement dépend, à la fois, des secteurs économiques qu'elle recouvre, des décideurs qu'elle concerne et des autres partis déjà pris, ou des solutions qui lui sont éventuellement complémentaires.

La mise en place d'une technique de préparation des décisions en matière d'aménagement du territoire conduit à envisager les étapes suivantes :
                   description morphologique des concepts et des moyens,

- modélisation,
- définition des systèmes de préférence,
- mise au point des procédures.

Pour la clarté de l'analyse, ces quatre étapes seront successivement envisagées.

Les deux premières étapes montreront, comment on peut décrire la politique d'aménagement du territoire, en termes de choix en présence de critères multiples.

Les deux dernières étapes montreront, comment les arbitrages politiques, qu'exige l'aménagement du territoire, peuvent s'aider utilement des techniques d'analyse multicritère et d'agrégation de préordres.

2. LA POLITIQUE D'AMENAGEMENT DU TERRITOIRE PEUT ETRE DECRITE ET MODELISEE EN TERMS DE "CHOIX EN PRESENCE DE CRITERES MULTIPLES"

2.1 Description Morphologique des Concepts

Au premier stade de l'analyse, le projet est de mettre en place le langage qui sera utilisé, et de générer le vocabulaire qui sera employé; il s'agit d'une phase purement descriptive.

(i) les concepts de finalités–le plan des finalités:

–La finalité est l'expression d'une orientation ou d'une volonté politique.

–Tous ces concepts abstraits, qui ne préjugent pas des moyens qui seront utilisés pour les satisfaire, appartiennent à un même *plan*, dit *plan des finalités*, ou *domaine du souhaitable*.

–Pour les distinguer, nous utiliserons un repérage dans un ensemble produit $F = F_1 \times F_2 \times \dots \times F_n$ ou F_1, F_2 .... F_n sont chacun des ensembles de description indépendant des autres; ils seront abusivement appelés *descripteurs indépendants*.

Pour être fine et opérationnelle la description morphologique doit faire apparaître le plus de descripteurs indépendants possibles. A titre d'exemples, des descripteurs indépendant pourraient être:

F_1 – Emploi, culture, santé, éducation, etc.,

F_2 – Catégories, socio-économiques,

F_3 – Découpage spatial: national, régional, départemental, communal,

F_4 – Etc.

–Pour chaque concept, ainsi repéré dans l'espace des descripteurs indépendants, il faut envisager les étapes suivantes, dans le passage du qualitatif ou quantitatif:

mission: une mission est l'énoncé général d'une finalité.

but: c'est une mission, à laquelle est jointe une échelle quantitative de réalisation.

objectif: c'est un but, auquel on a précisé un point dans l'échelle quantitative.

Voice deux exemples:

1er exemple:

MISSION = améliorer les possibilités d'emploi dans l'Ouest de la France.

BUT = améliorer les possibilités d'emploi dans l'Ouest de la France en utilisant comme échelle le pourcentage des emplois à créer en France, dans les 5 ans à venir.

OBJECTIF = améliorer les possibilités d'emploi dans l'Ouest de la France par l'implantation dans ces régions de 35 à 40% des emplois nouveaux à créer en France, dans les 5 ans à venir.

2ème exemple:
MISSION = Freiner le développement de la population dans la région parisienne.
BUT = Freiner le développement de la population dans la région parisienne, en utilisant comme échelle la population de cette région.
OBJECTIF = 14 millions d'habitants dans la région parisienne en 1985.

La génération des finalités, missions, buts et objectifs peut être entreprise. concurremment d'ailleurs, de plusieurs manières:
—par l'analyse systématique des textes d'orientation politique,
—par des comparaisons internationales,
—par des techniques de table ronde, d'entretiens, d'enquêtes (du type Delphi, par questionnaires itératifs, par exemple),
—par la recherche, lorsque cela est possible, de descripteurs indépendants.

(ii)   Les centres de décision: le concept de module de décision

Comme il a été dit plus haut, les problèmes d'aménagement du territoire se caractérisent par la multitude des centres de décisions. La première question à se poser est de savoir quels sont les niveaux de choix.
Le terme de niveau de choix suppose qu'il y ait possibilité de décision; c'est-à-dire qu'à chaque niveau doit correspondre une possibilité de décision et un système de finalités; pour distinguer ces niveaux il est possible de faire deux coupes:

—*la coupe horizontale* concerne des décideurs, non subordonnés les uns aux autres, mais non indépendants, car leurs decisions relatives interfèrent et influent les unes sur les autres. En terms de théorie des ensembles, les décisions des uns ne sont pas des sous ensembles des décisions des autres, mais elles ont presque toujours des parties communes.
On peut citer au niveau le plus élevé:
le Gouvernement et les Ministères
les organisations syndicales et professionnelles
les entreprises
les organisations régionales et locales
etc.

—*la coupe verticale* concerne, pour chacune des têtes de chapitre définies ci-dessus, la succession des niveaux ce choix, où chaque décision peut être considérée comme une application d'une décision précédente.
Pour le Ministère de l'équipement et du logement, ce sont par exemple:
les directions de l'administration centrale
les services régionaux de l'équipement
les directions départementales de l'équipement.

L'analyse doit porter sur les centres de décisions ayant une influence significative de *droit* ou de *fait*. Ces centres de décision seront appelés *modules de décision*, ou "décideurs".

Une fois effectués leur dénombrement et leur regroupement par catégories, l'attention. doit se porter sur les *intentions* des décideurs, par grandes catégories, et sur leurs *moyens d'action*.

L'analyse *des intentions et des comportements* yise à mettre en évidence les critères, (ou points de vue), implicites ou explicites, qui président aux choix des différents décideurs. Notamment, on se proposera de recenser les points de vue, qui ont vraiment influé sur des décisions réellement prises, au cours des dernières années :

Critères psychologiques,
Critères sociologiques,
Critères d'efficacité et de coûts
Particularismes locaux.

L'analyse des *moyens d'action* vise à caractériser un décideur par le type des moyens d'action qu'il utilise, c'est-à-dire par *ses méthodes générales d'action*. Parmi celles-ci, par exemple, on peut engisager :

Formation–Information
Règlementation
Financement
Avis et conseil
Activité de constructeur ou de maître d'oeuvre
Conception
Etc.

(iii)   Le concept de moyens–Eléments de programmes ou projets–Programmes

Alors que les finalités, appartenaient au domaine du souhaitable, les moyens appartiennent au domaine du réalisable.

Deux notions seront distinguées : l'élément de programme (ou projet) et le programme. A titre de comparaison, la première notion correspondrait, dans notre langage, à des syllabes ou à des lettres, la seconde à des mots.

a)   Les Eléments de programmes (ou projets)

Un élément de programme est caractérisé par un quantum d'action, par son échelle géographique et par sa finalité opérationnelle ; c'est lui qui assure le lien entre la programmation et la gestion.

A titre d'example, sont éléments de programmes :
une subvention aux investissements des entreprises de telle catégorie.
la création d'une zone industrielle de —— hectares, dans telle agglomération.
une recherche sur les micro-climats artificiels.
la modification des conventions collectives sur le régime des vacances annuelles.
la construction d'un canal à grand gabarit sur telle liaison.

La génération de ces éléments de programmes peut être entreprise–concurremment d'ailleurs–de plusieurs manières :
par un recensement systématique des décisions et des actes d'aménagement du territoire effectués en France,
par des somparaisons internationales,
par des techniques de table ronde, d'entretiens, d'enquêtes (type Delphi, par exemple),
par la méthode de l'analyse morphologique.

A titre d'exemple, une analyse morphologique pourrait comprendre les descripteurs suivants:

un niveau fonctionnel: subvention, interdiction, règlementation, démonstration, formation, recherche, construction, etc.

les groupes-cibles, selon des caractéristiques sociales et économiques,

un niveau par secteur d'activité, selon une nomenclature à définir,

d'autres niveaux, particuliers à certains points: par exemple, pour les subventions aux industries, le choix entre zones industrielles, reconversion, installations nouvelles, déconcentration, etc.

L'ensemble de ces méthodes conduirait à une génération très large et presque systématique des éléments de programme ainsi définis.

b) *La notion de programme*

La notion de programme provient de ce que l'efficience d'un projet est largement tributaire de la réaction d'agents économiques indépendants (c'est-à-dire dont les décisions ne sont pas programmées simultanément à celles du décideur). Si nous considérons, par exemple, le décideur Etat, hormis le cas assez rare d'une action directe (implantation d'un service administratif dans tell région, . . .) l'efficacité de ses décisions apparaît comme une variable aléatoire. Cette remarque conduit à distinguer les éléments de programme, qui ont un effet par eux-mêmes, dès qu'ils atteignent un certain seuil, et ceux qui n'ont d'effet que s'ils sont accompagnés d'autres éléments de programme cohérents. Ce sont ces notions, qui permettent de définir les programmes.

En effet, un élément de programme peut avoir par lui-même un effet, à condition qu'il atteigne un certain seuil; ainsi, une subvention aux investissements n'aura d'effet, que si elle compense au moins les désavantages subis par l'investisseur. Un tel projet, du moment qu'il atteint la taille critique, représente déjà, à lui seul, un programme.

Par contre, certains projets n'ont d'effet que s'ils font partie d'un ensemble cohérent de plusieurs projets: c'est cet ensemble, qui constitue un programme. Par exemple, l'action sur l'aménagement du territoire de la construction d'un canal à grand gabarit n'atteindra son plein effet, que si elle est accompagnée d'une politique de zone industrielle et d'une politique de la main-d'oeuvre (formation professionelle, . . .)

Ainsi, les choix en matière d'aménagement du territoire ne sont pas des choix entre projets, mais des choix entre programmes et des choix portant sur la taille de certains programmes au-dessus d'un certain seuil d'efficience.

A l'issue de cette analyse, on peut espérer définir un programme par son objet. Il faut, toutefois, s'interroger sur les types de décisions qu'il conviendra de prendre, pour que le programme remplisse effectivement sa mission. On distinguera les décisions à effet direct, semi-direct ou indirect. En outre, il serait souhaitable d'analyser si les décisions sont d'ettet immédiat (court terme) ou plus lointain (moyen terme et long terme).

Pour conclure sur cette première étape, le vocabulaire qui sera utilisé vient d'être mis en place et correspond à l'articulation suivante:

à la notion de finalité est liée celle d'orientation politique,
à la notion de décideur est liée celle de méthode d'action et de critères de jugement,
à la notion de moyens est liée celle d'ensemble cohérent d'actions ou programmes.

2.2   Modélisation et Structuration de l'Analyses

A ce stade de l'analyse, on dispose donc d'une simple description des concepts de l'aménagement du territoire, qui ne pourra être convenablement utilisée qu'après structuration et modélisation, c'est-à-dire passage du descriptif au normatif.

En ce domaine, deux approches successives entrent en jeu:
d'une part, l'analyse modulaire des centres de décision ou l'établissement d'une structure de décision,
d'autre part, la construction de graphes de pertinence pour ces décideurs.

(i)   *Structure de décision—analyse modulaire*

L'analyse modulaire se propose de faire une simulation des mécanismes de décision; elle est déjà utilisée dans l'analyse des grands systèmes. En terme d'analyse de système, elle consiste en une analyse de la structure d'organisation actuelle: il s'agit de dresser un graphe des flux de décisions, des flux d'information, des flux des moyens d'actions, qu'échangent les différents modules de décision.

Les problèmes posés par cette analyse du système "organisation actuelle" ne seront pas développés plus avant, car ils ressortent de techniques particulières de la décision qui, à elles seules, exigeraient un exposé particulier.

Pour la suite de l'exposé, nous retiendrons que l'analyse modulaire permet d'induire une structure dans l'organisation de la décision, ou *"structure de décision"*, qui permet, pour l'ensemble des décideurs, de procéder à une répartition systématique des tâches et de construire un cadre d'actions.

(ii)   *Construction de graphes de pertinence pour les décideurs*

A ce stade de l'analyse, chaque décideur connaît son environnement, par *la structure de décision*; il lui reste à structurer, à organiser le domaine du souhaitables (plan des finalités) et celui du réalisable (plan des moyens).

Pour effectuer ce travail de structuration, les représentations en graphes sont d'un grand secours.

Au niveau des moyens, c'est-à-dire des éléments de programmes et des programmes, la structuration en graphe se fait relativement facilement par le mécanisme de l'inclusion: les éléments de programme s'emboîtent entre eux pour former des programmes; ces derniers s'emboîtent à leur tour entre eux pour former de "grands" programmes; sauf cas spéciaux, on aboutit à un graphe particulier: un *arbre*, (l'arbre étant caractérisé par la présence de niveaux et l'absence de boucles).

Au niveau des finalités, les difficultés sont plus nombreuses: il s'agit d'établir une *structure logique* entre les concepts, qui fasse apparaître les préoccupations politiques du décideur. Or, à mesure que l'on recherche les liaisons effectives entre concepts ou liaisons *pertinentes*, on est souvent amené à engendrer de nouveaux éléments. Par ailleurs, il semble que la nature du graphe que l'on obtient dépende fortement de la façon d'aborder le problème. Il y aurait alors autant de *structures logiques* que de *problématiques*; cependant il paraît possible d'indiquer, pour toutes les problématiques, quelques règles et considérations générales:

a)   Tout au long d'un graphe logique*, il faut prendre soin de garder un même opérateur de construction, par exemple:

  que faut-il faire pour . . .
  est nuisible à . . .
  est utile à . . .
  est contradictoire avec . . .

b)   Une structure logique n'a pas de sens, si elle ne présente pas suffisamment d'alternatives; c'est-à-dire, si tous les éléments issues par leur origine d'une même élément supérieur sont reliés entre eux à leur niveau par l'opérateur *et* et non pas l'opérateur *ou* ou l'opérateur *et ou*; en d'autres termes il faut qu'à tous les niveaux du graphe logique il y ait suffisamment de liaisons par *ou* ou par *et ou*.

c)   La définition même du graphe logique interdit de faire apparaître des des éléments qui ne répondent pas à la question de l'opérateur; ainsi les contraintes extérieures et les éléments extérieurs contradictoires avec les éléments internes du graphe ne peuvent pas être pris en considération.
Les éléments qui entrent dans la composition du graphe sont si possible relevés de façon exhaustive. Dans les domaines techniques, cette exigence est relativement facile à remplir. Par contre, dans le domaine social, il est impossible de descendre en dessous d'un certain niveau, vues la complexité et la diversité des actions possibles aux niveaux les plus bas.

L'utilisation du *graphe logique* peut être envisagée de la façon suivante:

Le graphe logique révèle non seulement les éléments appartenant au domaine d'analyse du décideur, mais aussi les "interfaces", c'est-à-dire les cases, qui sont à la frontière de deux domaines différents.

Compte tenu des interfaces ainsi mises en évidence, et de son cadre d'action (mis en évidence par la structure de décision), chaque décideur peut chercher à déterminer sa *structure pour action*; l'opérateur de son graphe est "que puis-je faire pour "? "

Souvent, il aura à plaquer cet opérateur au bas de la structure logique. Parfois, cet opérateur peut être utilisé sur des éléments intermédiaires du graphe logique. En somme, le décideur introduit un mode d'appréciation dans la structure logique pour en faire, compte tenu des interfaces et de la structure de décision, une *structure pour action*. A ce niveau, on doit aussi rechercher le maximum d'alternatives dans les actions proposées. Par ailleurs, la structure pour action doit évidemment intégrer les résultats de la structure des moyens.

---

* Il faut noter que le graphe met en évidence à la fois des liaisons *d'inclusion* des éléments inférieurs dans le éléments supérieurs, mais aussi des relations de *définition* de l'élément supérieur par les éléments in-férieurs.

A la fin de ces deux premières étapes (description, structuration et modélisation), il faut s'interroger sur les avantages que l'on peut attendre d'une telle démarche:

Le premier résultat est d'avoir élargi considérablement le champ de choix ou, plus précisément, le champ de conscience de choix. On a généré, de façon quasi systématique, les éléments de programmes et les programmes, étendant ainsi la connaissance du domaine du réalisable. On a élargi de même et structuré, de façon systématique, le champ du souhaitable et ceci pour chacun des modules de décisions.

Le deuxième résultat est d'avoir posé le problème de la politique d'aménagement du territoire en termes de choix en présence de critères multiples.

Poser le problème en terme *de choix*, c'est introduire la volonté délibérée, dans les graphes logiques et les structures pour action, d'obtenir le maximum d'alternatives.

La mise en évidence des critères multiples s'opère à deux moments; d'une part, lorsque l'analyse modulaire fait apparaître les différents centres de décisions, caractérisés par leurs motivations ou critères propres de jugement; d'autre part, lorsque la structure logique du plan des finalités fait apparaître des missions, buts, objectifs, qui seront poursuivis par les décideurs politiques.

3. **ESSAI DE RESOLUTION DE CE PROBLEME DE CHOIX PAR LES TECHNIQUES D'ANALYSE MULTICRITERES ET D'AGREGATIONS DE PREORDRES**

Les deux dernières étapes de l'analyse concernent l'évaluation ou le choix des systèmes de préférence et la mise au point des procédures. Elles vont permettre de montrer l'apport, que l'on peut attendre des techniques d'agrégation de préordres dans les problèmes de *sélection* d'alternatives.

3.1 Le Choix des Systèmes de Préférence ou Evaluation

Dans le champ de choix, ainsi élargi et structuré, il s'agit de choisir les décisions ou les politiques à mettre en oeuvre. De nombreuses techniques sont applicables.

On pourrait, par exemple, dans les graphes logiques, être tenté d'appliquer des valeurs, au moins marginales, aux progrès réalisables vers les finalités; dans le graphe des moyens, faire des estimations des probabilités d'efficacité et de coûts des différentes actions envisagées; on pourrait alors calculer l'utilité probable de toute action élémentaire et dresser des bilans actualisés portant sur de vastes ensembles de décisions et sur des politiques.

Cette approche théorique du problème paraît hautement irréaliste; il faut donc envisager une solution moins ambitieuse, mais plus opérationnelle.

Il est en effet extrêmement difficile, sinon impossible, d'attribuer des valeurs valculées a priori aux progrès vers les finalités situées à la partie supérieure du graphe logique; les décideurs politiques ne pourraient pas accepter cet ensemble de valeurs, qui dissimulerait les arbitrages possibles aux niveaux les plus élevés. Par exemple, la construction d'une échelle unique de valeurs, en matière d'avantages apportés par les différentes politiques routières, aurait pour effet de dissimuler à l'attention politique les problèmes extrêmement importants de l'arbitrage entre les gains de sécurité et notamment de vies humaines avec des augmentations de temps de parcours et de coûts de circulation; de tels arbitrages ne doivent pas être proposés une fois pour toutes aux décideurs politiques, puis-qu'ils évoluent dans le temps en fonction des réactions de l'opinion publique et des relations décideurs-opinion publique.

Par contre, dans le graphe des moyens on peut rechercher des rationalités partielles par l'utilisation des techniques classiques de calcul économique, dont l'analyse coût-efficacité (au sens strict du terme).

L'apport de l'analyse multicritères est de mettre à jour les choix implicites et explicites qui sont opérés: pour ce faire les structures de graphe doivent être hiérarchisées à tous les niveaux.

(i)   Les critères de jugement à chaque niveau du graphe doivent être explicités

On peut alors faire une distinction entre critères internes et critères externes. Les critères internes sont des critères inhérents aux problèmes propres du module de décision. Les critères externes sont souvent des critères généraux de jugement, qui doivent être introduits par souci de cohérence, afin d'être assuré que tous les modules de décision prennent en considération certaines contraintes générales de l'aménagement du territoire.

Les éléments qui entrent en compétition dans le jugement seront classés, tout d'abord, selon chacun des critères. A chaque critère est associé une échelle de quantification: classer un élément revient alors à le repérer dans cette échelle; il faut noter que la finesse de l'échelle dépend exclusivement du degré de finesse que l'on peut atteindre dans le jugement, sans risquer de commettre des erreurs significatives.

(ii)   La pondération des critères doit être explicitée

Tout jugement agrège implicitement les préordres: soit qu'il donne un poids constant à chaque critère, soit qu'il en privilégie certains de façon dictatoriale, soit qu'il donne un poids variable aux différents critères, ainsi qu'il apparaît dans les tableaux ci-après.

Pour chaque tableau les cases de la matrice indiquent la note globale d'un élément qui est obtenu selon les 1er et second critères des notes correspondant à ses coordonnées.

a)   somme pondérée des critères

1er critère / 2ème critère	0	1	2	3
0	0	1	2	3
1	1	2	3	4
2	2	3	4	5

b)   critères dictatoriaux

Dans le cas présent le 1er critère est dictatorial par rapport au second.

1er critère / 2ème critère	0	1	2	3
0	0	3	6	9
1	1	4	7	10
2	2	5	8	11

N.B. L'ordre lexicographique est un exemple d'agrégation de préordres avec des critères dictatoriaux.

c)   poids variable des différents critères

1er critère / 2ème critère	0	1	2	3
0	0	1	3	5
1	1	2	5	8
2	2	4	8	13

Quoiqu'il en soit, on peut songer, parfois, à aider un décideur, ou l'ensemble d'experts faisant office de décideurs, en lui présentant une liste de critères regroupés par grandes catégories; lesquelles, éventuellement, seraient à leur tour regroupées en super-catégories: il pourrait, ainsi, dans un premier temps, donner un ordre d'importance aux super-catégories, puis aux catégories à l'intérieur de chaque super-catégorie, puis enfin aux critères à l'intérieur de chaque catégorie. L'ensemble de ses jugements serait rendu cohérent, par l'introduction *d'un héritage* que chaque élément recevrait de l'élément supérieur et transmettrait à l'élément inférieur, selon le schéma suivant:

grande catégorie   catégorie   critères

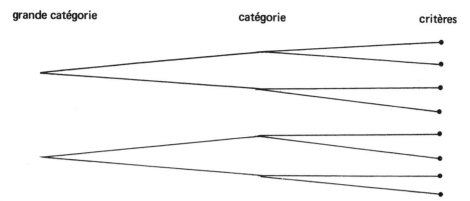

(iii) La hiérarchie de chaque niveau se propage, par héritage, aux niveaux inférieurs, le long des lignes interniveaux du graphe: en clair des éléments inférieurs, issus d'un élément supérieur bien classé, auront, toutes choses égales par ailleurs, un classement définitif meilleur, que s'ils étaient issus d'un élément supérieur mal classé. Cette méthode de notation des graphes permet ainsi de classer des éléments hétérogènes, au niveau inférieur, qui, directement, n'auraient pas été comparables.

Cette analyse multicritères devrait être particulièrement adaptée:
—d'une part, au classement des éléments du bas du graphe logique,
—d'autre part, au classement des variantes de programme en ensemble d'actions cohérentes, qui satisfont à un même objectif.

On a pu, ainsi. concretement, aborder le problème suivant: étant donné l'état actuel de la liaison Paris-Lyon, les travaux en cours et les objectifs de la politique du gouvernement, quelles mesures peuvent être prises d'ici 1971 et quelles orientations apparaissent souhaitables au cours du VIème Plan, dans le domaine du transport de voyageurs entre Paris et Lyon.

3.2 Mise au Point des Procédures

Les outils d'analyse et dévaluation, qui viennent d'être décrits, sont à utiliser selon des procédures, qui doivent maintenant attirer toute notre attention. En effet, l'application brutale de ces outils par le centre de décision chargé au niveau national de la fonction aménagement du territoire risquerait d'amener celui-ci à un traitement centralisé des problèmes correspondants, ce qui serait, en soi, une grave contradiction. Il convient donc d'adapter le schéma, qui vient d'être décrit (description, modélisation, évaluation) à des procédures, qui en permettront une bonne utilisation.

L'aménagement du territoire, considéré comme la mission d'assurer une cohérence fonctionnelle aux différents niveaux géographiques entre les différents secteurs, doit s'exercer de manière très souple et procéder par une programmation d'objectifs (ou, peut-être, une programmation fonctionnelle) et non pas par une programmation de moyens. Ainsi, en prenant une filière verticale (national, régional, départemental, local), on agira de telle sorte que le niveau géographique inférieur ait le maximum de liberté, compatible avec le besoin de cohérence. A chaque niveau, les décisions seront telles, qu'elles ne feront que guider ou encadrer celles des niveaux inférieurs, en leur donnant la possibilité d'exister. En somme, il est essentiel de veiller à ce que les niveaux supérieurs ne prennent pas de décision relevant de niveaux plus bas et qu'elles assurent leur propre rôle, qui est de créer des possibilités de décisions pour les niveaux inférieurs.

Pour ce faire, on peut penser à une procédure du type suivant:

(i)   Un organisme d'Etat, au niveau national, chargé de l'aménagement du territoire, élabore et communique:

aux responsables des politiques sectorielles et horizontales, les différents objectifs d'aménagement du territoire qui les concernent.

aux différents niveaux de décentralisation géographique, et en particulier aux régions, les critères de cohérence à respecter.

(ii)   Chaque ministère, pour la (ou les) politique(s) sectorielle(s) ou horizontale(s), dont il est responsable, élaborerait, par une procédure déconcentrée, sa politique, en tenant compte des objectifs d'aménagement du territoire qui lui ont été communiqués et de ses propres objectifs, ainsi que dè leurs consquences sur l'aménagement du territoire.

Ainsi, pour le secteur des Transports, où les travaux sont le plus avancés, deux graphes ont été étudiés. Le premier graphe répond au souci de replacer les problèmes de transports dans le cadre de l'aménagement du territoire; ce travail, effectué à partir de textes officiels, articule les buts d'aménagement du territoire en deux catégories:

favoriser la création de pôles de développement

assurer des liaisons entre pôles de développement

Le second graphe indique comment le décideur transport intègre les objectifs d'aménagement du territoire, ainsi qu'il apparaît dans la finalité: entrainer ou accompagner le développement économique des régions défavorisées.

(iii)   Au niveau régional enfin, un organisme assurerait la mise au point des programmes par amalgame des programmes des ministères sectoriels (ou horizontaux) traduits au niveau de la région, compte tenu des critères de cohérence communiqué par l'organisme central d'aménagement du territoire.

Il faut noter que ces critères de cohérence pourraient être tout ou partie de certains graphes logiques du décideur aménagement du territoire, qui se trouveraient ainsi injectés au niveau régional comme critères; ce sont généralement des critères externes, déjà structurés en catégories de critères et en grandes catégories, comme il a déjà été indiqué dans le paragraphe sur l'évaluation: à ces critères externes s'ajouteraient, évidemment, des critères locaux ou internes, liés aux particularités régionales.

Il semble que la combinaison de ces critères, de natures fondamentallement différentes, ne pourrait pas s'effectuer selon un système de pondération fixe. En effet, deux axiomes de combinaison paraissent raisonnables:

1er axiome:

un programme régional considéré comme prioritaire au regard de critères externes ne peut être fortement déclassé en raison de critères internes.

2ème axiome:
un programme régional non considéré comme prioritaire au regard de critères externes, peut être fortement reclassé en raison de critères internes.

Les deux axiomes induisent le tableau suivant:

critères internes \ critères externes	0	1	3
0	0	1	3
1	1	2	5
2	2	4	8
3	3	8	13

Pour chaque critère la note 0 est la meilleure. 1, 2, 3, etc, sont respectivement moins bonnes.

Le tableau peut se lire de la façon suivant: un élément noté 3 selon les critères externes et noté 2 selon les critères internes sera noté 8 de façon globale; ainsi les cases de la matrice fournissent la règle d'agrégation des préordres.

(iv)   Au niveau départemental et local, on peut envisager un schéma analogue à celui qui vient d'être décrit pour le niveau régional.

Les programmes ainsi élaborés aux niveaux inférieurs seraient communiqués à l'organisme central d'aménagement du territoire, qui devrait s'assurer de leur cohérence au niveau national: problèmes interrégionaux, problèmes d'équipements d'intérêt national, problèmes internationaux. Pour pouvoir assurer cette mission, il paraît nécessaire que l'organisme central construise lui-même un graphe logique et un graphe pour action, détaillé et très élaboré, d'aménagement du territoire.

Pour que la préparation des décisions en matière d'aménagement du territoire se réalise, effectivement, selon la procédure qui vient d'être précisée, il conviendra de fournir aux différents centres de décision les informations en nombre et en qualité suffisantes, afin d'éviter qu'ils ne prennent des décisions fondées sur des points de vue partiels. Par ailleurs, l'organisme central, qui a délégué une part importante de ses pouvoirs de décision, devra s'assurer, en contre partie, de la bonne utilisation qui en est faite, par la mise en place d'un contrôle de gestion. A cet effet, il pourra utilement se servir d'un graphe très élaboré des finalités et des moyens.

4.   CONCLUSIONS

L'exposé, qui précède, présente un caractère apparemment très abstrait. Toutefois, les études déjà réalisées par le Service des Affaires Economiques et Internationale du

Ministère de l'Equipement et du Logement, laissent entrevoir, à relativement bref délai, des possibilités intéressantes d'applications concrètes de l'analyse multicritères aux grands problèmes que pose l'aménagement du territoire.

Ces études ont été particulièrement développées dans le secteur des transports et les quelques exemples cités au cours de l'exposé,—élaboration des graphes de la politique des transports, analyse de la liaison Paris-Lyon,—donnent une première idée des applications qui pourront être faites de ces nouvelles techniques, dès la préparation du VIeme Plan (1971-1975) et en liaison avec le développement en France des procédures de "rationalisation des choix budgétaires" (R.C.B.).

SECTION 3

DEFENCE and R & D

Chairman :   **G. R. Lindsey**
Director General, Defence Operational Research
Establishment, Canada

Speakers :   M. C. Heuston
Cost—Effectiveness Branch, SHAPE Technical Centre,
Netherlands

H.M. Dathe
Operations Research Gruppe der IABG, Germany

R.L.R. Nicholson
Mintech/UKAEA Programmes Analysis Unit U.K.

COST-BENEFIT ANALYSIS AT THE SHAPE TECHNICAL CENTRE

M. C. Heuston

1. INTRODUCTION

This briefing presents a review of Cost-Benefit Analysis at the SHAPE Technical Centre, which is located in The Hague. The sub-title should, perhaps, be "The Problems of Developing a Capability for Cost-Benefit Analysis," because this type of analysis, as a formal discipline, is rather new at the Centre. There are no studies, nor have there been any, which can properly be labelled as cost-benefit studies. As a consequence, STC is not in a position to describe specific applications nor even offer new concepts or sophisticated mathematical formulae. STC has, however, been involved in the initial development of a capability to do this type of analysis—a capability which has been specifically requested by SHAPE. It is the problems connected with this early development effort which can be discussed here and which may be of some help to other European organisations.

The problems arising out of the STC's development programme on this analytical technique are at this time of a very practical nature and are focussed on two important aspects. The first aspect concerns the nature of the NATO environment for cost-benefit and/or cost-effectiveness analysis. Cost-benefit analysis and cost-effectiveness analysis will be used here interchangeably. We have been asked such questions as, "What is the need for this kind of analysis? What kind of SHAPE plans lend themselves to this type of an analytical approach? How often might there by SHAPE requests for studies? Who would use the results?" Finally, "Is there an immediate requirement for application to some particular system trade-off or force mix problem?"

The second aspect concerns the nature of the effort required to solve a very critical problem which is the key to the success of the development of a cost-benefit capability at STC; that is the data base. All organisations in the same profession, both commercial and military, have faced this same critical problem. From personal experience, there are many organisations which fail to take it seriously and to recognize the magnitude of the effort required to solve it. In NATO, SHAPE and STC there are several conditions which make the data problem even more difficult to solve and requiring a much larger effort than normaly might be necessary at any Ministry of Defence (MOD) or organisations within a particular country. STC does not have final answers to any of these questions and problems. It is doubtful that there are conclusive solutions. However, this paper can offer some personal comments based on current operations which may be helpful to the cost-benefit profession in Europe. These personal comments do not presume to reflect future plans of any part of SHAPE or STC.

2. ORGANISATION OF CONTENTS

The content of this briefing is organised into the following major topics:—
General Background

3.   GENERAL BACKGROUND

Several years ago the NATO Ministers emphasized the need for planning future military forces to achieve greater effectiveness for the money available. The constraints on economic resources were being felt to an increasing extent by all members of the Alliance. Official direction was given by the member countries through their ministers to consider the cost and effectiveness implications of future force plans.

The Military Committee of NATO, in turn, also emphasized the importance of carefully considering the costs of proposed programmed force structures.

There are many possibilities for improving the NATO military forces. Not all of these improvements can be achieved by the participating countries simultaneously. Improvements could consist, to name a few, of more troops, better training of troops, more weapons per unit, better quality weapons, and greater quantities of stocks. Many of these improvements are very costly, and some do not improve effectiveness as much as others. The military budgets of the NATO countries cannot absorb all conceivable improvements irrespective of their usefulness of overall NATO defence.

SHAPE organised, recently, an effort to deal with the evaluation of the effectiveness and cost implications of their proposed forces. They also directed the SHAPE Technical Centre to organise a small staff to develop the analytical tools and to perform the necessary evaluation studies. Both the SHAPE effort and the STC effort have taken many months to get up to full scale operation.

4.   THE STC ROLE

STC, known originally as the SHAPE Air Defence Technical Centre, was organised in 1955 to assist SHAPE in many technical and scientific aspects of air defence. The scope of SADTC was expanded in 1963 to embrace both air and land warfare. The organisation has been financed by NATO since 1960.

Currently, there are three Research Divisions: Operations Research, Systems Research, Communications, and a Command and Control Group. There are 106 Scientists from most of the NATO countries divided, about equally, among the three Divisions and the Groups.

STC, as a whole, supports SHAPE with a broad range of research, including some laboratory work, primarily on land-based air defence radars. The Operations Research Division is currently performing several effectiveness studies of individual weapon systems and methods of air base survivability. Also, some war gaming of land, air and sea forces is being handled by a part of this Division.

Last year STC organised a Cost-Effectiveness and Cost Analysis Group. STC proposed to SHAPE two major tasks in its Work Programme to be devoted to Cost-Effectiveness Analysis and to the supporting function of Cost Analysis. Both of these were to be the responsibility of this new Group within the Operations Research Division. The effectiveness analysis, from a weapon system and battle force point of view, had long been an important subject of research for the Operations Research Division. However, cost analysis had never been developed into a formal discipline. Neither had cost-effectiveness analysis, as a discipline, received major attention.

The initial staff consisted of only a few Scientists and has by now added several more. This team has the responsibility for the initiation and development of the cost-effectiveness discipline at STC, and for the conduct of studies in this area, including cost analysis as they are required to support SHAPE planning. Most of the effort, to date, has been spent on the preparation of analytical tools, primarily on the data requirements of cost analysis, of the overall cost-effectiveness work. More will be described about these aspects later.

5.   THE PLANNING ENVIRONMENT

5.1   General

SHAPE has the responsibility of making proposals for the best ACE forces under its command. These proposals are made in a formal way periodically and usually cover a five year period of time. They usually deal with the total forces of all NATO countries in terms of individual units, such as infantry battalions, fighter bomber strike squadrons and destroyers. This activity represents a part of SHAPE's planning cycle.

To arrive at these proposals, consideration is given by SHAPE to a great many aspects of the current and future environment. Consideration is given at least to the present and possible future threats to NATO, the ACE forces in being, and the technological, economic and other resource limitations of the NATO nations. Consideration is also given to the political factors and to whatever guidance has been issued by the NATO Ministers.

5.2   Cost-Effectiveness Aspects of SHAPE Planning

In general terms, Cost-Effectiveness Analysis, as it has evolved during the last ten years or so, usually offers a very wide range of application to mamangement planning. It is usually described in public literature as an aid to decision-making. It has found uses for commercial, as well as government and military planning problems. The kinds of applications range from assisting in the decision process concerning overall Department of Defence force plans and individual weapon system selections, to studies by contractors proposing new hardware. Cost-effectiveness applications have found their way even into very short-range planning for the manufacture of hardware components.

For typical military decision-making, a commonly used classification of decisions includes the following*:—

(i)   Operations Decisions (Strategy and Tactics)
(ii)   Procurement or Force Composition Decision
(iii)   Research and Development Decision.

The purpose of the cost-effectiveness analysis is not to make these decisions which

---

* C.S. Hitch and R.N. McKean, *"The Economics of Defence in the Nuclear Age,"* Harvard University Press, Cambridge, 1961 p.131.

usually arise out of the military planning process, but to assist the judgement of the planner by laying before him, in a systematic fashion, the important implications of various alternative course of action.

The cost-effectiveness implications of alternatives are usually evaluated as the major part of a particular study. The evaluation is performed (to oversimplify) through the mechanics of estimating the appropriate total effectiveness measurements and total system costs of the alternatives which are proposed to meet the assumed future threat; and the effectiveness and costs are then related via appropriate model techniques and selection criteria. This process is common to most types of cost-effectiveness studies, which are usually classified as follows*:—

> System Configuration Studies
> System Comparison Studies
> Force Structure Studies

From a personal point of view, after an examination of the current environment, SHAPE planning offers rather limited possibilities for the application of cost-effectiveness analysis. SHAPE does not have responsibilities in all of the areas of decision problems listed earlier. In the first place, their planning problems appear to be more concerned with making proper recommendations to the Nations than with actual decisions. In the second place, their direct management of the forces is restricted to war time operation.

More specifically, for example, SHAPE has little, if any R & D planning. It appears that the SHAPE staff does not make decisions in this area in the same sense as an MOD does, and makes few substantial recommendations to the Nations for long range research and development of future combat weapon systems. Neither are they involved with continuous procurement problems of major combat systems in the same sense as an MOD would be. They do have important procurement problems for some supporting hardware. However, it would seem that their major planning decisions are involved in their force composition recommendations.

In general, their primary concern is with current operations and with the planning, in a limited sense, of future peacetime operations and wartime deployments.

Thus, the biggest opportunities for the application of cost-effectiveness analysis by SHAPE is largely restricted to one class of problem—i.e., Force Composition Recommendations. These recommendations are concerned with the total force, mixes of force, improvements to various units of the force, and broad operational procedures, including training. The type of cost-effectiveness analyses most useful for this are force structure studies with some support from system comparison studies. Rarely will system configuration studies be of interest. This is quite a different environment for cost-effectiveness studies than can be found in the typical MODs.

It must be strongly emphasized, however, that even within this limited area of opportunity, the need for cost-effectiveness analysis is very serious and very great. It can make a very valuable contribution to improving the usefulness and the creditability fo the SHAPE recommendations to the Nations.

---

* Washington Operations Council, *"Cost-Effectiveness Analysis,"* edited by T.A. Goldman, Praeger Publishers, New York, 1967, p.15.

6. PROBLEMS OF DEVELOPING ACE CAPABILITY

6.1 Elements of the Capability

The basic elements of cost-effectiveness analysis or cost-benefit analysis have been described in many ways and can be found in many books and documents. The elements differ depending upon the background of the author (i.e., mathematician, social scientist), as well as the specific applications to which the author has addressed himself.

The broad categories of elements usually mentioned, include the following*:–
    The Objective (or Objectives)
    The Alternatives
    The Costs
    A Model
    A Criterion

For the cost and model elements, there is one common aspect. This concerns the mechanics of the analysis–i.e., the tools, computational procedures, estimating methods, models, and evaluation techniques common the kinds of application arising out of the planning problems.

The estimating methods are an important part of the mechanics of the analysis. They usually include: (a) estimating methods pertinent to preparation of the effectiveness measurements, and (b) estimating methods pertinent to the cost measurements. Both of these are not without important problems associated with concepts and definitions. However, both are very sensitive to one fundamental problem.

6.2 Data Base

This one fundamental problem represents the key to the success of any cost-benefit or cost-effectiveness analysis. It concerns the *data base*. Without sufficient data of the right kind, the estimates of effectiveness and costs used as inputs to the analysis are meaningless. In the case of STC the evaluation of alternative SHAPE plans and the ranking of the alternatives, which are the output of a cost-effectiveness study, are credible only if the input data are credible. This credibility does not require 100% accuracy. It does require a level of detail and reliability consistent with the uses to which the answers will be put, the inherent differences between the alternatives under consideration, and the amount of time or budget available to do the study.

There are many individuals who give lip service recognition to the importance of the data base, but not many who are willing to take action to prepare an adequate library of data. It takes work of a simple statistical clerical nature. It requires digging into sometimes sensitive and proprietary areas. It requires the expenditure of unusually large sums of money to collect and store the data, and it requires, often, the upsetting of long traditionally entrenched ways of data reporting. These factors, and others, often make the effort to prepare an adequate data base unattractive to management, to senior professional individuals who may be involved in collecting, and above all to those agencies from which the data must come. These agencies rarely see the benefit to

---

* ibid, p.4.

themselves for releasing the data and often, what is worse, they see the loss of power through the disclosure and dissemination of information which otherwise is known only to a privileged few. The effort to overcome these difficulties is great and not many organisations doing cost-effectiveness analysis are willing to allocate their limited manpower and budgets to the preparation of adequate data base.

Since the NATO Ministers and the Military Committee and SHAPE have emphasized the need for cost-effectiveness analysis, as applied to Proposed Forces, and since STC has embarked upon the formal tasks of cost-effectiveness and cost analysis, the preparation of this data base has been of the utmost importance. There are several conditions which distinguish the problems of data collection by STC from other efforts, either in Europe or in the North American Continent. The nature of this effort and some of the problems and conditions which present unusual challenges will be presented next.

6.3   STC Data Requirements

The requirements for data for military cost-effectiveness studies, in general, depend upon the nature of the studies. The requirements depend upon such aspects of the studies as the kind of systems and military forces considered in the studies; the time scale—i.e., the calendar on fiscal years covered—the need for accuracy.

In general terms, the kinds of data required pertain to the military forces (e.g. land, air and sea) and units which comprise those forces (e.g. battalions, squadrons and ships) within the Allied Command Europe. Both units currently in the military inventory committed to NATO of each country, as well as planned units (i.e. new weapon systems) are of interest.

More specifically, the data are of two kinds. First, they consist of estimates of (1) the effectiveness of the ACE units and forces, and (2) the cost of these units and forces. Second, the data also consist of the physical and operational characteristics of military units and the major combat hardware included in the unit, such as the 155 mm self-propelled artillery pieces in Artillery Battalions, or F-104 aircraft within Fighter Bomber Strike Squadrons.

Both the estimates of effectiveness and of costs are usually made in gross terms. The costs which STC is interested in are not of accounting accuracy. The degree of accuracy achievable and desirable for cost-effectiveness studies varies with the use of the study results, the nature of the study, and many other factors. For SHAPE and STC, much less accuracy can be tolerated than usually required by MODs.

The general scope of the data requirements at STC is very broad and icnlusive. There is need for data on every type of military combat unit in ACE—i.e., every type of land force combat unit, such as Infantry Battalions, Brigades and Divisions; air force units, such as Fighter Bomber Stroke Squadron Bases; and sea force units, such as Destroyers. There is need for data on current hardware, such as the F-104, as well as possible future hardware, such as a new fighter aircraft. There is need for estimates of effectiveness and costs which have already been prepared as well as the supporting information such as numbers of troops, quantities of supplies, etc.

The STC requirement for data is not uniform in terms of the amount of detail for all forces, all systems and all countries. Some weapon systems are not as critical as others. Those systems to which the final overall estimates of effectiveness and costs are most sensitive, require the most attention to accuracy and, therefore, the greatest amount of detailed data.

6.4 The Collection Problem

Virtually no cost data were available within STC last year, at the beginning of the STC costing studies. As a consequence, STC not only had to define which data were required, but also find out the sources of these data and to experiment with ways of collecting them. If the data were not available either because they could not be released, or did not, in fact, exist, STC had to learn how to search for related data which could be used to project the necessary estimates. STC also had to learn to collect data on related systems which could be used in analogies in order to estimate costs for the military weapon system of primary interest in the force structure. This learning process and the data collection effort is by no means complete.

In general, the sources of information, in terms of agencies accessible to STC, are as follows:–
— NATO Headquarters
— SHAPE and its Subordinate Headquarters
— The MODs.
Most of the cost data which has been collected has come from one primary source, the MODs. The data have come directly from the MOD, or, indirectly, through the International Staff of NATO, and through SHAPE.

The data collection problem is time-consuming and expensive. It cannot be done by sitting in one's office waiting for the appropriate material to be automatically dropped on the desk. The data must, literally, be searched for, using a vigorous and persistent policy, much like a detective tracking down clues. Often the best, most valuable, pieces of data are obtained through personal contacts with individuals who have a piece of information which normally cannot be found in official documents.

One of the unique aspects of all the data collection problems which face STC stems from the nature of the NATO Alliance. There are eleven countries with significant military forces which must be contacted for data. In general, each country has a different management reporting system for the government and for the military establishment. The countries have different traditions and different attitudes towards the traditional ways of defining and recording the cost of procuring and operating military units, for example. The sources of data in NATO, as represented by the MODs, are separated geographically, and communication by STC to them is difficult, not only by differences in language, but also the mechanical means of communication, such as telephone and mail. All these aspects, and others, make the data problem for STC difficult, time-consuming, costly and frustrating.

Another unique aspect of the problem which may be worth considering, since it may also influence the actions of commercial companies doing military contract work on NATO systems: there is no centralized NATO agency for the collection of peacetime management type of information, such as procurement and operating cost of NATO military equipment. The International Staff at NATO comes closest to it with some of their statistical reports on costs. However, these reports do not provide the unit detail data in a form suitable for cost-effectiveness studies. SHAPE comes close to it with some of its reports on effectiveness. However, these reports do not reflect the kinds of battle effectiveness measurements needed for many kinds of cost-effectiveness studies. This means that data must be collected from numerous sources, each of which may use somewhat different definitions of the information recorded.

7.   SUMMARY AND CONCLUSIONS

This briefing has presented some observations concerning STC's effort to develop a cost-effectiveness analysis capability. Only two important aspects of their effort have been discuseed—i.e., (a) the environment and possible need for this type of analysis within the SHAPE planning cycle, and (b) the data requirements. In the case of the latter, the STC experience spent on the cost side has been discussed.

In summarizing, the opportunities for the application of cost-effectiveness studies by STC for SHAPE appears, at this time, to be limited—more limited than those which may be open to individual countries. SHAPE planning does not require the results of cost-effectiveness studies for the prupose of making decisions in the same sense as normally done in each country. There appears to be little requirement for:—

    (i)   Military R & D decision planning, and

    (ii)   military production planning.

SHAPE planning does deal with operations and with the options for procurement in current NATO weapon system and forces. These options are severely limited by the inflexibility of the national budgets and other political difficulties. The cost-effectiveness approach can make valuable contributions in helping SHAPE to make reasonable recommendations about improvements in each force in the light of overall ACE effectiveness and budgets.

The key to the development of a capability to perform cost-effectiveness analysis within this limited environment lies in the establishment of an adequate data base. This still means a large requirement for data for all military forces, land, air and sea, and for all countries. But the nature of the data required is more aggregative than needed by individual countries, and more detailed than normally presented by these countries.

The preparation of the data base at STC is handicapped by the very nature of the NATO Alliance. Conditions and policies of the Alliance tend towards the separation fo the member countries and make it difficult to collect common data sufficient to optimize the effectiveness of the forces of the Alliance for the total budget of the Alliance. Eleven separate sources of data, eleven different definitions of csots and effectiveness, are examples of a few difficulties facing STC. The collection of data suitable for NATO cost-effectiveness studies is a costly and time-consuming effort, even it if deals with a relatively high order of aggregation.

In concluding, there are two pay-offs of this effort which should be mentioned. One deals with the direct pay-off of cost-effectiveness studies with good data inputs to the SHAPE planning cycle and to the improvement of the recommendation of better overall forces, more effective and less costly. The second pay-off deals with the development of common definitions, cost estimating techniques, and effectiveness analysis techniques at STC which may stimulate the improvement of even better methods of analysis in the individual countries.

OPTIMUM ALLOCATION OF RESOURCES TO R & D PROJECTS

H.M. Dathe

1. INTRODUCTION

Research and development in the scientific and technological field are characterized by increasing numbers of possible realisations and by growing costs per single activity. Today, a rational allocation of finance and capacity resources in this area is more important than ever before. In this paper, the problems involved in this task are discussed and a procedure which may be of help in solving them is proposed.

A frequent difficulty in R & D decisions is the fact that the alternatives under consideration cannot be compared by the same measure of effectiveness. The only objective which candidate projects of a national space program, e.g., have in common is their intended contribution to scientific and technological progress. More general, in this type of task we have to determine that distribution of expandable resources which maximuzes the estimated total benefit of the R & D program.

It must be emphasized that the field of basic research should not be touched by this type of cost-benefit investigations. Work in this area has to cover a spectrum as broad as possible to facilitate the definition of future R & D projects, notwithstanding whether an immediate benefit of these activities can be established or not.

However, as soon as programs of a certain magnitude for applied research and development are defined, studies on optimum allocation are necessary. If they take into account possible errors in the cost and benefit estimates, they are suited to provide a useful guide for the decisionmaker. This is the objective of the general procedure proposed here. A comparison with some other concepts of R & D planning was given recently [4].

2. TYPE OF COST-BENEFIT MODEL

In developing a method for the allocation of R & D funds we have to start with the establishment of a model for the cost-benefit relationship of a single project. This model has to be

- general to cover the needs of a large range of applications,
- realistic to provide a frame-work for the use of available input data,
- practicable with respect to an optimization technique and to the consideration of uncertainties.

An example for the payoff of research programs as function of cost is presented in Fig. 1 (Branch, 1), where the miss distance reduction for a missile guidance system is plotted. The diagram shows the well-known "diminishing marginal return" characteristics. In Fig. 2 (Branch, 2) for another research project the cost-benefit relationship, starting at zero, is given.

While the dimension of the cost variable are currency units, the definition of the benefit measure is much more difficult. Only in special cases as with the guidance

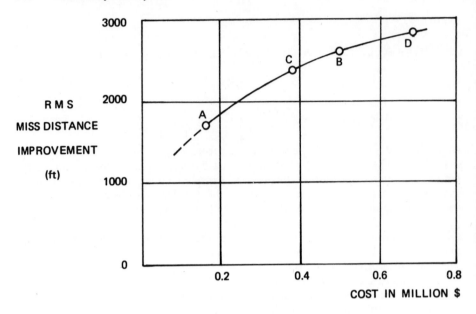

FIG. 1   ERROR REDUCTION PROGRAMS FOR A MISSILE
GUIDANCE SYSTEM

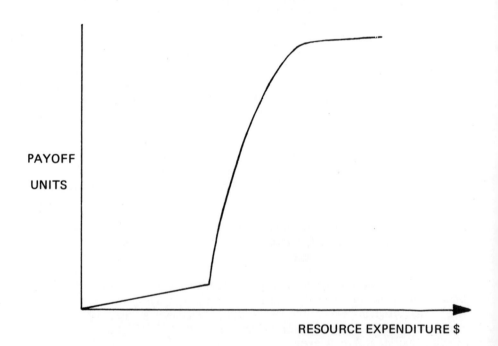

FIG. 2   PAYOFF vs. EXPENDITURES FOR A RESEARCH
PROJECT

system an objective measure—e.g. miss distance reduction in feet—can be used. Frequently, the only possibility are subjective evaluations of benefit scores.

A standardized form of the cost-benefit curve for a R & D project is based on experience and statistical data [3] and is exhibited in Fig. 3. For small expenditures the benefit value is growing slowly, afterwards quicker, until the increase reaches its maximum. For higher cost values, benefit growth is decreasing and the curve approaches the upper boundary. Beyond saturation point S, no additional benefit is gained how large the increment in expenditures may be. In extension of the case described by Fig. 1. every point of the curve is a hypothetical termination of a R & D activity.

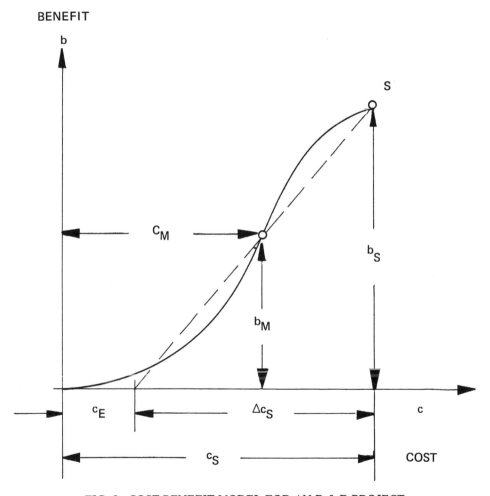

FIG. 3   COST-BENEFIT MODEL FOR AN R & D PROJECT

As a "skeleton" of the S-shaped characteristics, the dotted line in Fig. 3 can be used. It served to Define the following basic parameters of a project:

— entry cost, c_E

— saturation cost, c_S

— saturation benefit ratio, b_S/b_{S_O}, in relation to a reference project,

the estimation of which is relatively easy. However, because of the sensitivity of the optimum allocation to the local gradient of the cost-benefit curve, these basic informations have to be transformed to the S-shaped curve.

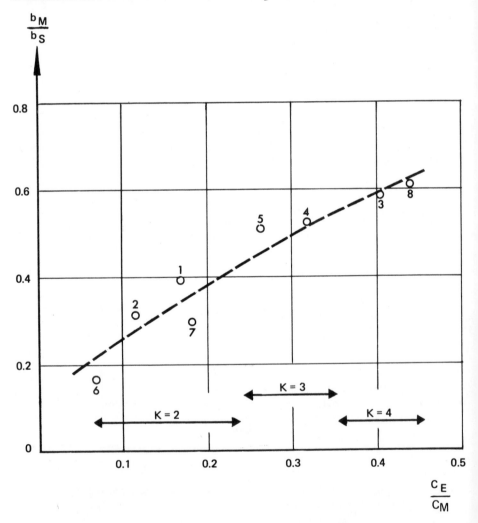

FIG. 4   PARAMETERS OF THE TWO COST - BENEFIT MODELS

For this final model, the use of the following functional relationship between benefit b and cost c of project number i is appropriate:

$$b_i = L_i \; c_i \; K_i \left(\frac{M_i}{N_i + c_i} - 1 \right)$$ (1)

The limit of validity of this equation is the saturation point (index S):

$$c_i \leqslant c_{S_i} \; ; \qquad \frac{db_i}{dc_i} \bigg|_{c_{S_i}} = 0$$ (2)

K_i, L_i, M_i and N_i of Eq.(1) are constants, for the integer values of exponent K_i certain ranges are defined in Fig. 4.

As will be shown, this model fulfills most of the requirements which were stated above for the cost-benefit relationship.

3. PREPARATION OF INPUT DATA

Only three basic parameters were defined as necessary for the linearized model. Two of them, c_E and c_S, must be determined by cost analysis. The estimation of the benefit measure, b_S/b_{S_0}, is facilitated by the fact that only relative values have to be assessed for alternative projects.

The transformation procedure from the linearized to the S-shaped model is derived and explained in Appendix A. Useful for this transformation are empirical values as plotted in Figs.4 and 5. P of Fig. 5 denotes the gradient of the linearized model and Q stands for the gradient of the S-shaped curve at the crossing point of both models. Q is approximately equal to the maximum benefit increase.

If more accurate data on the cost-benefit relationship are available as demonstrated in Fig. 2, they should be used. In the major number of examples where this is not the case, the transformation to the S-shaped model, Eq.(1) forms a reasonable basis for further study.

When considering uncertainties in the input data, it is assumed that the characteristics of the cost-benefit ratio remain valid and that one of the following two conditions applies:

   (a)   Constant cost values but possible benefit decrease (Fig. 6).
        If the correction factor ψ_i is defined by

$$b_i = \psi_i \cdot b_{i_0} \; ; \quad \psi_i \leqslant 1$$

we have

$$\frac{b_i}{c_i} = \psi_i \left(\frac{b_i}{c_i} \right)_0 \quad \text{for } c_i = \text{const.}$$

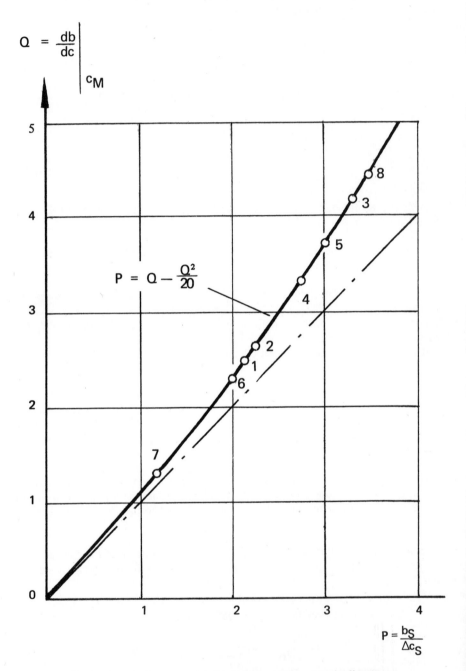

$$Q = \frac{db}{dc}\bigg|_{c_M}$$

$$P = Q - \frac{Q^2}{20}$$

$$P = \frac{b_S}{\Delta c_S}$$

FIG. 5   GRADIENT VALUES OF THE TWO COST-BENEFIT
MODELS

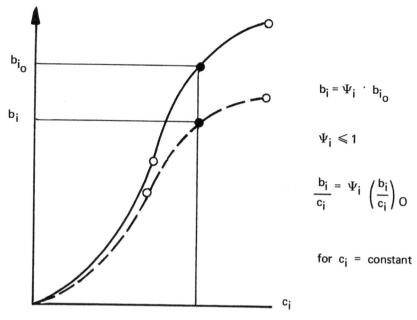

FIG. 6   BENEFIT UNCERTAINTY FOR CONSTANT COST

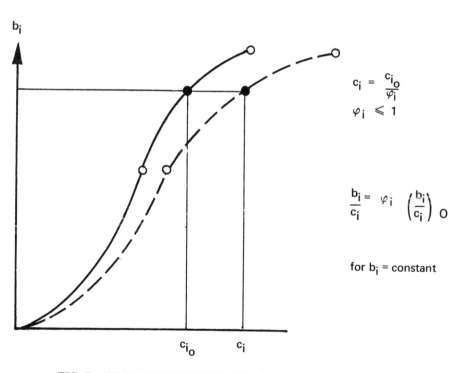

FIG. 7   COST UNCERTAINTY FOR CONSTANT BENEFIT

(b)   Constant benefit values but possible increase of cost (Fig. 7).
If the correction factor φ_i is defined by

$$c_i = \frac{c_{i_0}}{\varphi_i} ; \quad \varphi_i \leqslant 1$$

we have

$$\frac{b_i}{c_i} = \varphi_i \left(\frac{b_i}{c_i} \right)_0 \quad \text{for } b_i = \text{const.}$$

In both cases, the original cost-benefit curve does not present mean values of a distribution of estimates but is considered as a theortetical (optimistic) assumption which may experience some degree of deterioration in practice.

The decision between the two conditions (a) and (b) depends on the choice of R & D policy and on the kind of input estimate. If the question is what amount of research work may be finished with a given budget level we have a problem of type (a). Then, the factor ψ_i may be interpreted as a project probability of success. On the other hand, if the achievement of a certain development objective is a prerequisite, all uncertainties are cost risks as in case (b). R & D work which pays attention to the established state-of-art is frequently of that type.

Combinations of type (a) and (b) are not considered here. It should be mentioned that during the early phases of a project the effects of both types have only small differences.

Numerical values for ψ_i or φ_i should be estimated as input data in addition to the expected project parameters. They have to be reconfirmed at an early project review term. The consquences of these uncertainties are discussed in Sections 4.3 and 5.

As an example, the cost-benefit curves of 8 R & D proposals are plotted in Fig. 8. Among these projects, some have a relatively slow start before they grow to remarkably high benefit/cost values, others produce an early return but are inferior afterwards. This set of characteristic curves—expressed by the coefficients of Eq.(1) with exponent K=2, 3 or 4—is believed to be suitable to illustrate the following steps of the allocation procedure.

4.   OPTIMIZATION PROCESS

4.1   Determination of Promising Projects

The problem of optimum allocation of resources may be formulated as follows:
A number i=1, ..., n of R & D projects is considered, the cost-benefit relationship of which is given by the same basic law, Eq.(1). The projects are characterized by different coefficients K_i, L_i, M_i and N_i. The objective of the optimization is to maximize the total benefit B of all projects n:

$$B = \sum_{i=1}^{n} b_i = \text{max} \tag{3}$$

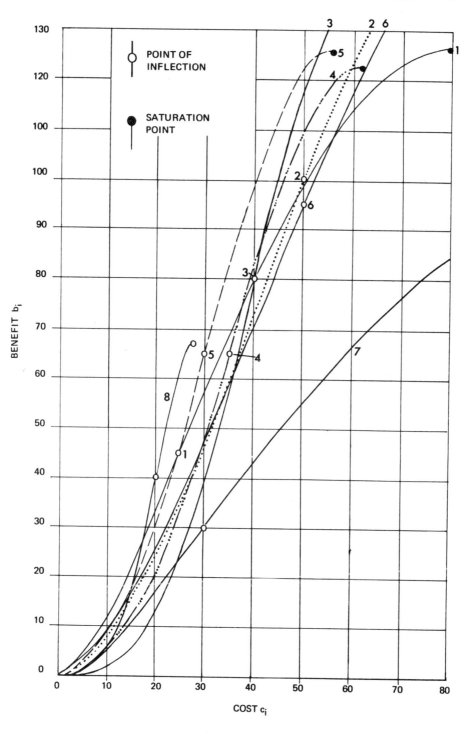

FIG. 8   COST-BENEFIT CURVES OF EIGHT R & D PROJECTS

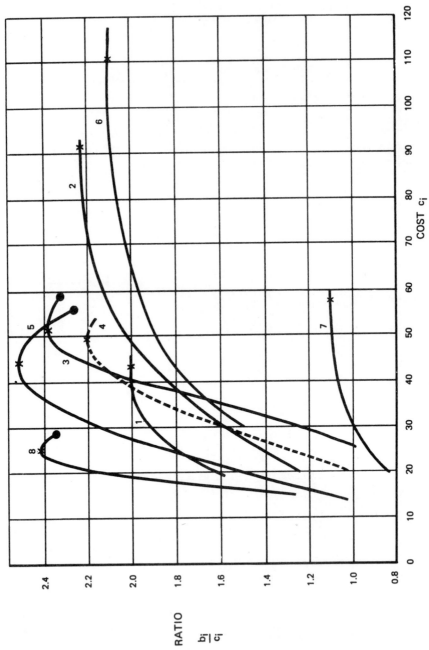

FIG. 9 BENEFIT/COST RATIO OF EIGHT PROJECTS

for a given level of total cost

$$C = \sum_{i=1}^{n} c_i \qquad c_i \geqslant 0 \tag{4}$$

It is assumed that no interdependence exists between the benefit values of the n projects.

The condition that some of the projects in favour of others may get no support at all ($c_i = 0$) prevents the direct application of an optimization technique. However, to select the promising projects from the alternatives under question can be done in a simple and illustrative manner: If the cost/benefit ratios of the single projects are plotted over single cost, Fig. 9, those candidates which are superior to others in a certain interval are easily identified. In our example, these are the projects No. 3, 5 and 8. The 7 possible combinations of peak values $(b_i/c_i)_{max}$ of one or more of these 3 candidates are first approximations to the optimum allocational mix [3].

The exact determination of optimum combinations of these selected projects for any level of budget is described in the following Section. While this applies to the nominal values, the variance of the estimates is considered in Section 4.3.

4.2 OPTIMUM MIX

The optimization task is again the same as described by Eqs.(3) and (4) with the exception, that only m projects ($m \leqslant n$) are considered which all have to be taken into account. Now, after suspension of the condition $c_i = 0$, the Lagrange multiplier method [5] is applicable.

A payoff-function may be defined as follows

$$\Phi\,(c_i) = \sum_{i=1}^{m} b_i - \lambda \left(\sum_{i=1}^{m} c_i - C \right) \tag{5}$$

It is a problem with only one degree of freedom, therefore, one multiplier is sufficient. After insertion of Eq.(1) we have:

$$\Phi(c_i) = \sum_{i=1}^{m} L_i \cdot C_i^{K_i} \left(\frac{M_i}{N_i + c_i} - 1 \right) - \lambda \left(\sum_{i=1}^{m} c_i - C \right) \tag{6}$$

The conditions for maximum benefit are obtained by partial differentiation of this function:

$$\frac{\delta \Phi}{\delta c_i} = L_i \left[\left(\frac{M_i}{N_i + c_i} - 1 \right) K_i \cdot c_i^{K_i - 1} - \frac{M_i \, c_i^{K_i}}{(N_i + c_i)^2} \right] - \lambda = 0 \tag{7}$$

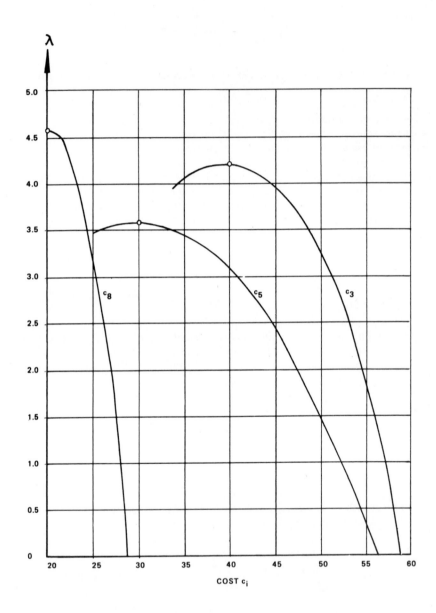

FIG. 10   LAGRANGE MULTIPLIER FOR THE PROJECTS NO. 3, 5 AND 8

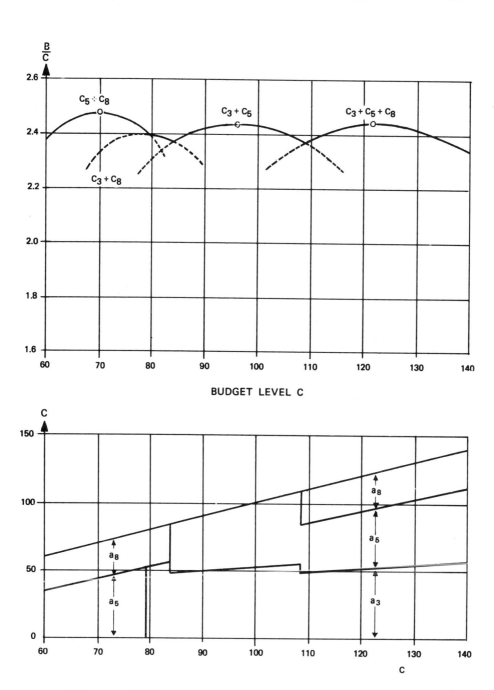

FIG. 11   OPTIMUM MIX AS FUNCTION OF BUDGET LEVEL

These are m equations for the unknown variables c_i ($i=1,2,...,m$) which all are tied together by the same factor λ. It is now easy to compute λ for the m projects as function of c_i and to draw a chart for the values between $\lambda=0$ and λ max, Fig. 10. In the example under consideration, every horizontal cut for λ=const. gives the optimum distribution of expenditures c_i for one of the four combinations $c_3 + c_5, c_3 + c_8, c_5 + c_8$, and $c_3 + c_9$. By restricting the range of admitted λ values it is assured that the c_i do not become negative.

The result of the optimization is presented in Fig. 11, where the benefit ratio B/C is plotted versus the budget level C. Each mix of projects is only within a certain cost interval superior to its alternatives. In the lower part of the chart the optimum distribution of the total budget to the projects is shown.

As far as this example for the allocation of R & D funds is considered to be typical, the following general conclusions can be drawn:

-   A concentration on a small number of projects is necessary to achieve the level of optimum benefit.
-   The optimum composition of the mix of projects is a function of budget level. If in spite of large changes in budget level the type of mix is maintained, substantial benefit losses are the consequence.
-   Over the whole range of budget under consideration, the benefit ratio is of a more or less constant magnitude. There is no evidence from this example that increased expenditures lead to higher efficiency.

4.3 Variance of Estimates

The allocation procedure developed so far is based on undistributed estimated values for cost and benefit. Now, in this Section the uncertainties of these data are taken under consideration. We first assume that the abscissa values of the S-shaped curve, the expenditures, are constant while the benefit figures remain below of the estimations (case (a) of Section 3).

The factors of uncertainty in this case are designated ψ_i, i.e., if the main projects under study have the numbers 3 and 5, the probabilities of success with respect to benefit level are ψ_3 and ψ_5. It is difficult to make a prediction about the magnitude of these probabilities. What reasonably can be done after the R & D budget is defined is to study the consequences of different values i for the optimum allocation using the relations of Section 3(a) and the Lagrange multiplier method explained in Section 4.2. The results of such an analysis for C=90 and 105 in our example are plotted in Figs. 12 and 13.

In these charts, ψ_3 and ψ_5 are used as coordinates so that a survey on the allocation c_5 and the benefit ratio B/C over the range ψ_i=0.4 .... 1.0 is obtained. B/C is decreasing with both ψ_3 and ψ_4. The optimum value of c_5 is remaining nearly constant as long as the ratio ψ_3/ψ_5 is maintained, but it is decreasing when ψ_5 become inferior relative to ψ_3.

In Fig. 13 for a budget level of C=105, a constant value of $\psi_8 = 0.8$ is assumed. For a

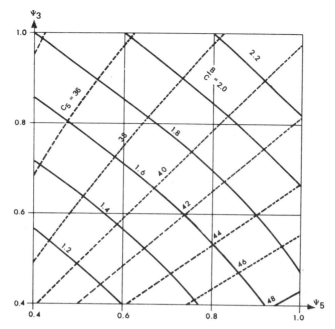

FIG. 12   OPTIMUM MIX OF PROJECTS 3 AND 5 FOR A BUDGET LEVEL OF C = 90

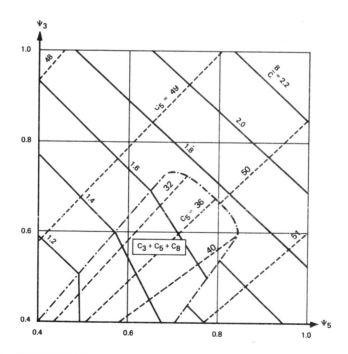

FIG. 13   OPTIMUM MIX OF PROJECTS 3 AND 5 OR 3, 5 AND 8 FOR A
BUDGET LEVEL OF C = 105   ($\Psi_8 = 0.8$)

range of both ψ_3-and ψ_5 figures, the optimum mix $c_3 + c_5$ is replaced by $c_3 + c_5 + c_8$ to avoid remarkable benefit losses. These charts help to define cases in which it is sufficient to have a rough estimate on both ψ_3 and ψ_5, and others, in which these values are relatively sensitive.

Case (b) of Section 3 is characterized by cost uncertainties, while the benefit level of the project output is kept constant. As one example of that kind, single project cost increases 0 and 10% (i.e. $\varphi_i = 1,0 \dots 0,9$) are being considered in Fig. 14 for a large range of total cost levels. With growing uncertainty, the optimum for every mix is getting a possible shift towards a higher budget. For each combination except of $c_3 + c_8$ a dominance interval can be defined. However, if the uncertainty range surmounds 10%, the allocational decision may become difficult. Charts as Fig. 14 could also help to select relatively stable points on the budget scale and would provide a safeguard against unforseen risks.

5.   REVIEW OF PROJECT IMPLEMENTATION

While this paper is dealing with the allocation of R & D funds, the analysis of single project activities, their time phasing and evaluation are excluded from study. The decision made at the beginning of a R & D program has to rely on the information available at that date. On the other hand, the amount of information on possibilities and limitations of certain R & D fields is increasing after the projects have started. In some cases this may lead to remarkable changes in the prospects of running R & D work and to the evidence that a still larger loss in total benefit ratio has to be prevented. Therefore, project reviews are a necessity in order to achieve an adequate allocation of resources.

As an example, the results of such a review subject to the following assumption will be presented:

a)   Project uncertainties are considered as defined in Section 3(b), i.e., cost is increasing to achieve the benefit as specified.

b)   The date of review is the "1/3 term", i.e., one third of the funds for each project is spent.

c)   The percentage of deviation from the cost-benefit curve will approximately continue during the following phases of the project.

d)   The budget $C = 120$ is distributed to the activities $c_3 + c_5 + c_8$. While the cost of Project No. 3 remains unchanged, No. 5 and 8 exhibit increases between 0 and 40%.

The effect of single project cost transgression on the total benefit cost ratio is shown in Fig. 15, above. The dotted line marked "$c_{8R} = 9$" is valid for the case that Project No. 8 is not continued after the 1/3 term and that the initial expenditure of 9 units for No. 8 is lost. This measure brings an improvement if Project 8 has an increased cost of 25 to 40% or more. The lower chart of Fig. 15 demonstrates that the optimum allocation of c_5 is relatively insensitive to cost transgressions Δc_5.

Unpredicted cost increases in R & D should be the exception, not the rule. But if they occur, early measures must be taken to keep the benefit/cost decrease at the minimum. Re-allocations of funds which do not improve the overall B/C ratio have to be avoided in any case.

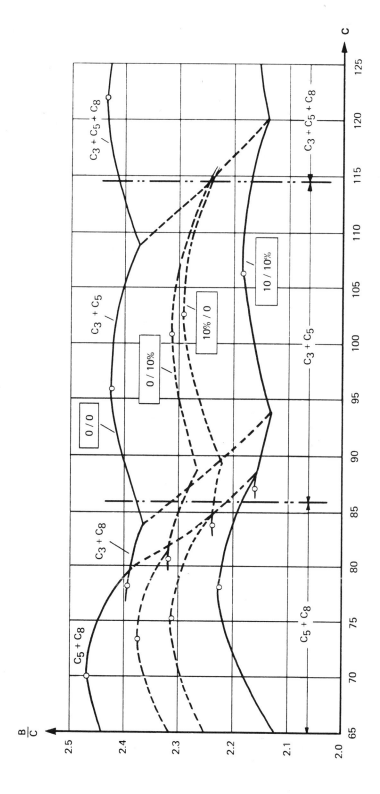

FIG. 14   CHANGE OF OPTIMA AS CONSEQUENCE OF COST INCREASES

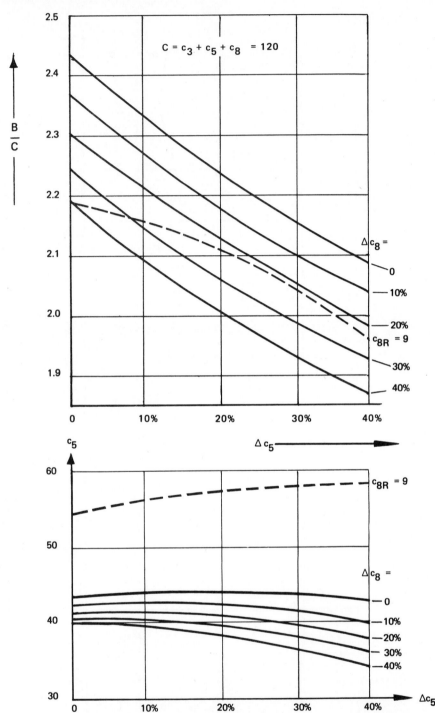

FIG. 15   REVIEW OF R & D PROGRESS (1/3 TERM): MINIMIZATION OF
B/C - DECREASE

6.   CONCLUSIONS

Those familiar with the practice of R & D planning might emphasize with D.G. Jones [6], that a suitable management of project implementation frequently is more important than an utmost care in project selection. But equally true is the statement, that without a well-grounded allocation of funds to large R & D projects the danger exists that valuable resources would be wasted.

The steps of the allocation procedure explained in this paper may be summarized as follows:

1.   Selection of appropriate cost-benefit model
2.   Definition of benefit measure
3.   Transformation of input data into model characteristics
4.   Determination of candidate projects
5.   Optimum allocation of resources
6.   Estimation of uncertainties, sensitivity analysis
7.   Definition of R & D program
8.   Review of project implementation
9.   Eventual re-allocation of funds.

Such a formal method may serve a dual purpose: it is not only an aid in preparing R & D decisions in accordance with all relevant informations at hand, it also can be a guide for provision, control and improvement of these essential input informations.

7.   REFERENCES

1.   G.A. Branch, I. Peschon: "Allocation of Research Funds". Paper presented at Joint ORSA/TIMS National Meeting, San Francisco, May 1968.

2.   G.A. Branch: "Example of a Resource-Allocation Technique". *SRI Report*, 1968.

3.   H.M. Dathe: "Die Planungsforschung als Hilfsmittel für Entwicklungsentscheidungen". *Jahrbuch 1967 der Wissenschaftlichen Gesellschaft fur Luft- und Raumfaht,* Verlag Friedr. Vieweg & Sohn, Braunschwieg 1968.

4.   H.M. Dathe: "Die Optimierung von Mittelzuweisungen fur Forschungsund Entwicklungsvorhaben". *Unternehmensforschung,* Band 13, Heft 1 (1969)

5.   H. Everett: "Generalized Lagrange multiplier method for solving problems of optimum allocation of resources". *Operations Research,* 11 (1963), oo. 399-417

6.   D.G. Jones: "Research and Development Profitability Considerations in a Large Company". *Operations Research Quarterly,* Vol. 18, No. 3 (1967)

APPENDIX A: Transformation from the linearized to the S-shaped cost-benefit model

As explained in Section 2, the following basic parameters of the linearized model, Fig. 3, are given:

$$c_E = \text{entry cost,}$$

$$c_S = \text{saturation cost,}$$

$$b_S = \text{saturation benefit.}$$

With the gradient of the linearized model

$$P = \frac{b_S}{\Delta c_S} = \frac{b_S}{c_S - c_E}$$

the maximum gradient of the S–shaped curve

$$Q = \frac{db}{dc}\bigg|_{c_M}$$

can be taken from empirical data in Fig. 5. With this value of Q and by means of the chart b_M / b_S over c_E / c_M, Fig. 4, the c_M and b_M data may be estimated.

Let us now look at Eq. (1) for the S-shaped model. If we omit index i for simplification, we have

$$b = L \, c^K \left(\frac{M}{N + c} - 1 \right)$$

The value of exponent K can be read from the empirical curve, Fig. 4, according to the magnitude of c_E/c_M. The three unknown coefficients L, M and N have to be determined from the following three equations for c_S, b_S and c_M (and for Q).

For the maximum gradient of the S–shaped curve this equation is valid:

$$Q = \frac{db}{dc}\bigg|_{c_M} = L \left[\left(\frac{M}{N + c_M} - 1 \right) K \, c_M^{K-1} - \frac{M \, c_M^K}{(N + c_M)^2} \right] \tag{A1}$$

From the fact that the gradient vanishes at the saturation point we get:

$$\frac{db}{dc}\bigg|_{c_S} = 0 = \frac{M}{N + c_S} - 1 - \frac{M c_S}{K(N+c_S)^2} \tag{A2}$$

and for the saturation benefit b_S :

$$b_S = L \; c_S^{\;K} \left(\frac{M}{N + c_S} \right) - 1 \tag{A3}$$

If we eliminate L from equation (A1) and (A3):

$$\frac{M}{Q} \left[\frac{K \; c_M^{K-1}}{N + C_M} = \frac{c_M^{\;K}}{(N + C_M)^2} \right] - \frac{K}{Q} \; c^{K-1} = \frac{M}{M} \frac{c_S^{\;K}}{b_S} \frac{c_S^{\;K}}{N+C_S} = \frac{c_S^{\;K}}{b_S}$$

or

$$M \left[\frac{1}{Q} \; \frac{K \; c_M^{K-1}}{N + C_M} \quad \frac{c_M^{\;K}}{Q \, (\, N+C_M)^2} \; - \; \frac{c_S^{\;K}}{b_S \, (N+C_S)} \right] = \frac{K}{Q} \; c_M^{K-1} \; - \; \frac{c_S^{\;K}}{b_S} \tag{A4}$$

Eq. (A2) may be written as:

$$M = \frac{(N + C_S)^2}{N + \dfrac{K-1}{K} \; C_S} \tag{A5}$$

Both Eqs. (A4) and (A5) contain M = f(N) explicitly. It is convenient to plot Eqs. (A4) and (A5) into an appropriate chart and to determine the values of both M and N at the intersection of the two curves. The last step is to calculate the remaining unknown variable, L, from Eq. (A3).

THE PRACTICAL APPLICATION OF COST-BENEFIT ANALYSIS TO R & D INVESTMENT DECISIONS

R.L.R. Nicholson

1. INTRODUCTION

Research and Development are, in many countries, major activities for both Governments and Industries when measured in terms of cost; table 1 shows both types of spend for a number of industrial countries. The pursuit of R & D by industrial companies at their own expense can be regarded as a particular form of investment subject to analysis which, while it may prove difficult in some respects, has at least clear ground rules. The costs are those to the company and the benefits are likewise. The wider implications of any resulting innovation are of interest to the company only insofar as they affect its markets and prestige and hence its profits with or without growth.

As distinct from financial Investment Analysis as applied by companies, Cost-Benefit

Table I - EXPENDITURE ON R & D BY SOME INDUSTRIAL COUNTRIES (1963/64)

	Gross National Expenditure on Research and Development (Million U.S. Dollars)	Percentage of Gross National Product at Market Price	Government Funds as Percentage of Total	Proportion of all Research Funded by Government *except* Space and Defence Research
United States of America	21,035.0	3.3	63.8	28.7
United Kingdom	2,159.9	2.3	56.6	37.9
Germany	1,436.3	1.4	40.4	36.8
France	1,299.1	1.6	63.3	48.7
Japan	892.0	1.4	27.8	27.8
Canada	425.1	1.1	54.5	45.8
Netherlands	330.4	1.9	40.0	38.0

Source: A Study of Resources devoted to R & D in O.E.C.D. Member Countries in 1963/64, O.E.C.D., Paris, 1967

Analysis as usually described and understood* appears to be a tool applicable to the selection of many R & D programmes funded by governments; for much R & D leads to innovation which clearly has both long term and wide effects, obscure though these may be.

Yet there is but little published case study material [2] [3] and reviewers of cost-benefit analysis seem agreed that progress in application to R & D has been slow. [4] [5] among them the uncertainty of estimates of costs, the complex nature, multiplicity and diffusion of the benefits [1], the lack of knowledge of the future, and so on. Perhaps, too, attempts made to relate benefits directly to the scientific outcome of basic research have been premature. These factors, together with the difficulties in the macroeconomic correlation of levels of R & D expenditure with economic growth [6], may lead us to suspect that progress is slow because the goal is impossible. But "R & D" is a tag describing a wide spectrum of activity within which there is much objective-oriented Government sponsored R & D where the relationship of the work to the objectives can be seen with sufficient clarity to merit attempts at analysis.

This paper presents comments on the problems of analysis as seen by an organisation concerned with advising on the selection of R & D programmes in such areas. We will exclude the heavy investment in research, mostly basic in nature, as part of the education system; the criteria for such expenditure are bound up with total objectives of the educational system. We will exclude other basic research which may have impacts on society remote in time and place from the location of the work and for which the choice of funding will normally be on other criteria than the microeconomics of cost-benefit analysis.

It is also proposed to exclude defence research. The objectives are not readily expressed in economic terms so that it is usual to set them as operational requirements. Appraisal then uses the techniques of cost-effectiveness.

2.   GOVERNMENT FINANCED APPLIED R & D

There remain a number of areas where Governments fund applied research, either in industrial companies, in universities or in government laboratories. For example:

    (i)   where the public sector are major consumers and some stimulus or control is considered necessary on R & D time scales, e.g. development of cheap nuclear power, desalinated water, educational techniques;

    (ii)   where the end-objectives are primarily welfare or amenity, e.g. fire protection, air and water pollution;

    (iii) where government has a central co-ordinating role, e.g. specification of standards, road and other transport research, safety;

---

*   As, for example, by Prest and Turvey [1], as "a practical way of assessing the desirability of projects where it is important to take a long view (in the sense of looking at repercussions in the further, as well as the nearer future) and a wide view (in the sense of allowing for side effects of many kinds on many persons, industries, regions, etc.) i.e. it implies the enumeration and evaluation of all the relevant costs and benefits."

(iv) where innovation could affect a wide sector of industry in the short or long term but where there is currently insufficient incentive, interest or resources to do the work in any one sector or company, e.g. marine or underwater technology, support to research associations;

(v) where work in the field of defence, or of other categories (i)-(iv) above has led to an aggregation of scientific capability and facilities which can rapidly be deployed for different social and industrial objectives and where such deployment offers advantages in cost, timing and effectiveness over other means to reach the objectives, e.g. work on desalination of water in U.S. and U.K., use of engine testing facilities, pursuit of "spin-off";

(vi) through indirect support of privately financed R & D, e.g. via tax concessions on capital write-off (this class of support perhaps is less likely to be mission oriented than the others above).

Clearly such work leads to a wide spread of benefits and beneficiaries; but much of it is such that the vital links between the R & D and the attainment of benefits can be established. Such links are necessary if cost-benefit analysis is to be of use in decisions on the choice of programmes. Macroeconomic approaches such as the use of Input-Output Matrices to find residual or technical coefficients do not yet constitute an adequate basis for R & D project selection.

3. PROBLEMS IN R & D PROGRAMME ANALYSIS

There are many problems in applying cost-benefit analysis to R & D projects or programmes which are doubtless common to other applications; but there are some features of R & D which pose problems of analysis different in the degree of their severity from those encountered in other evaluations. In this section I will outline some of these and suggest how they may often be tackled.

3.1 Uncertainty

The first major uncertainty arises because we do not know whether the objectives will be achieved by the proposed programme of research and development. This is not just a question of the reliability of estimates of cost or of time to completion (though these themselves are uncertain features). Our existing knowledge of the laws of science, our experience of similar situations and of past achievements—all these may be used to set down objectives for applied research which are believed to some degree to be attainable. Such objectives will be expressed in operational terms but will be subject to implicit or explicit economic constraints. The uncertainty here is whether this "constrained" objective can be attained regardless of input of research resources. However brilliant our research teams, we do not yet know whether reverse osmosis can be applied to make fresh water from the sea at costs under, say, $1 per 1,000 gallons; or whether processes can be found to make textiles permanently non-flammable at a cost of less than 3d. per pound.

Clearly we need to qualify the outcome of analysis to take account of such uncertainties and this is normally done by estimates of "probabilities". In this case we have to apply subjective estimates made by those best qualified by knowledge and experience, i.e. by the experts in the field. Since the estimates are subjective, we attempt to improve them by widening the number of experts consulted to obtain a consensus of judgments [7]. In practice one tries to get subjective views on the distribution of probabilities, their limits and the shape of the distributive curve.

It may be possible to improve the estimates by a breakdown of the R & D process since we are seldom dealing with a single stage development. For example, research aimed at finding materials suitable for engine components which have to operate at high temperature may be concentrated on metal alloys, coated metals, ceramics or composites. We have to estimate the likelihood that any material will:

    (i)   resist the corrosion of gases at high temperature, and

    (ii)   exhibit the necessary physical properties, and

    (iii) be formable without losing its properties.

It may be easier for the expert to set the bracket of his estimates by considering each sub-objective separately.

It may be that the R & D programme will achieve partial attainment of the objective. It is unlikely that the effect of this on the benefit analysis can be calculated in a simple proportional manner. The market and benefits for, say, a desalination process will be sensitive to the costs of the product water and there is high elasticity of demand; the penetration of new materials into markets will be sensitive to the properties of the materials (i.e. their utility) as well as their price. The effects of partial attainment of objectives call for a separate analysis.

Uncertainties in timing and cost, as mentioned above, are factors of concern. It is not intended to discuss here the methods of R & D cost estimating and programme planning. The sensitivity of the analysis to variations in the cost of R & D can usually be shown. The effects of variation in timing are more complex. Apart from corrections in discounted cash values, the interactions of the R & D with the benefits must be examined for changes in the markets, the effect of competing technologies, and so on. There is, of course, some trade-off possible between timing and cost, i.e. to ensure a higher likelihood of attaining the objectives by a given date through increasing the input of research resources; but such trade-off is often limited by the needs of the objectives which call for establishing the life of the product, e.g. the fatigue properties of aircraft or engine components, the behaviour of nuclear fuel under reactor conditions, performance under stress and thermal cycling conditions, the life of surface finishes in various environments, etc. While engineers and scientists give great attention to techniques for "accelerating" tests and to the optimal planning of test procedures, there are often cases where a sequence of lengthy tests is unavoidable because of the interplay of technological properties within systems. The costs of testing—involving expensive facilities such as wind tunnels, engine test beds, furnaces, rigs, materials testing reactors, laboratories for chemical or biological assay—often form a large proportion of the cost of R & D projects and the programme analyst must pay attention to such features to identify the scale or potential variations in cost and timing.

Uncertainties in assessing the levels and values of benefits are perhaps common to many cost-benefit analyses. But R & D has one particular additional aspect in that attainment of the scientific or technological objectives may not be followed by exploitation—the problem of "coupling" or "diffusion". There is an array of obstacles which can prevent the attainment of benefits from R & D which is, in the scientists' or engineers' eyes, successful. While policies for technology transfer [8] and steps to improve the ·mechanisms of coupling [9] have been outlined and while practices are improving in this matter, there is no panacea for all the potential failures in transfer.

This problem is particularly acute for government funded research*. It has become necessary and customary to qualify benefits by some factor to allow for such uncertainty; as I hope to show later the process of cost-benefit analysis can hopefully shed some light on the potential obstacles to particular innovations.

Since the prime objective of the analysis is to aid decision between options, quantified judgments on these uncertainties have to be expressed in the form of subjective probability distributions to be combined with the values of costs and benefits. It is not proposed to dicuss here the methods of combining subjective probability distributions which are dealt with in the literature [7].

Decision theory can then be applied based on "expected values". Most of the methods suggested in the literature and used in practice for ranking projects take account of uncertainty by using "probability" factors such as:

P_t -   probability of technical success

P_c -   probability of commercial success.

How these are combined to give ranking numbers is discussed in section 4 but here it may be noted that many recognise that these factors are not probabilities in the statistical sense but rather are factors indicating confidence levels in the estimates of benefits.

As discussed in the next section, R & D projects have several stages. The early stage may in fact be aimed at reducing uncertainty in estimates of the outcome and the problem arises as to whether cost-benefit analysis can be used to set levels of effort for all such work including other means of reducing uncertainty such as market surveys, design studies, etc.

4.   CONDITIONAL NATURE OF THE BENEFITS

In most cases the realisation of benefits from R & D programmes is conditional

---

* A good, though perhaps extreme, example is the research that has been carried out by or for a number of governments on the disinfestation, sterilisation and pasteurisation of food. Some marginal benefits can be foreseen but the pay-off has to be qualified by the likelihood of public acceptance of irradiated food—or of what authorities and manufacturers believe to be the acceptability to consumers. Irradiation still has emotive connotations and the likelihood of successful application is low; the use is largely confined to military supply where consumer attitudes may be said to be constrained.

on other investments. The pattern of events is usually conceived as "Research-Development-Investment-Production-Sales-Consumer-Satisfaction". This is, of course, over-simplified and misleading if used as a universal guide. The end product of R & D is knowledge and the confidence that brings and sometimes this can be exploited without further investment. A company may do research to find new uses for an existing product for which it has or expects to have spare production capacity; the end product of computer research may be a new software code; public funded research may lead to changes in building regulations reducing investment rather than increasing it; and so on. But often the costs of R & D represent only a small fraction of the total resources needed for exploitation, a point stressed in a number of publications [10], and general figures for the ratio of research:development:capital investment figures of 5:15:80 have been quoted [11] though these must be treated with caution since there is much variation between industries.

It needs to be clear in cost-benefit analysis whether we are estimating the return on the whole spectrum of exploitation or just the R & D sector. In fact we are usually concerned with the decision on the R & D alone, or even on some part of it; the other commitments are made later.

In the literature, and in practice, values for decision or ranking purposes are of two types, for example:

(i)   Project number = $\dfrac{P_t \times P_c \times (p - c) \times V \times L}{\text{total costs}}$

where
$$
\begin{aligned}
P_t &= \text{"probability" of technical success}\\
P_c &= \text{"probability" of commercial success}\\
p &= \text{price}\\
c &= \text{cost}\\
V &= \text{annual sales volume}\\
L &= \text{life of product}
\end{aligned}
$$

(ii)   Project number = $\dfrac{P_t \times P_c \times \dfrac{I_1}{1+r} \times \dfrac{I_2}{(1+r)^2} + \dfrac{I_n}{(1+r)^n}}{\text{total discounted R \& D costs}}$

where r = discounted rate
I_n = net income in year n

i.e. these methods use benefit-cost ratios for ranking purposes.

Such methods can be misleading since projects can be terminated before being taken to the exploitation stage either because of lack of technical success or because of a fresh evaluation of the needs or market. Revised formulae are needed of the type:

Expectance of Total Benefit/Expectance of Total Cost

$$
\frac{P_R\, P_D\, P_M\, \overline{(I(r) - C(r))}}{\overline{R(r)} + P_R\, \overline{D(r)} + P_R\, P_D\, \overline{M(r)} + P_R\, P_D\, P_M\, \overline{F(r)}}
$$

where P_R, P_D, P_M are the probabilities of success at the research, development and marketing stages respectively.

$\overline{I(r)}$ — expected income discounted.

$\overline{C(r)}$ — expected production or operating costs discounted.

$\overline{R(r)}$, $\overline{D(r)}$, $\overline{M(r)}$ discounted costs of research, development and marketing respectively.

$\overline{F(r)}$ — discounted value of investment necessary after marketing success has been achieved.

In practice a frequent course is to estimate the net benefits on the basis that the necessary investments subsequent to the R & D stage will be adequately rewarded in the prices of the product or services which are sold by those exploiting the R & D. The return on capital, plus a profit margin, is included in the techno-economic estimates of products and services, these estimates being an essential constituent of any evaluation. It may be noted that two outstanding hindsight cost-benefit studies of R & D by Griliches [2] and Grossfield and Heath [3] both make assumptions that the capital invested has been adequately rewarded and compare net benefits with R & D costs. This procedure is probably satisfactory provided a check is made that the amount of later investment is not so large as to disturb the general pattern of capital investment and thus require some divergence of opportunity cost from the market value or form some constraint on the exploitation.

If comparing projects, we need, of course, to ensure that all the analyses are done on a similar basis. To the objection that quite small inconsistencies in what costs to include will have a larger effect on the ratio of net benefit to R & D costs than on the return on the whole project, it may be remarked that the spread of net benefit to R & D cost ratios is often high and we are not usually faced with small differences.

5.   R & D AS AN OPTION TO OTHER MEANS

The analyst of R & D programmes must first pay attention to the objectives; he may be breaking into a loop of the evaluation process since frequently there is feedback from the analysis to the objectives; he must also examine whether there are other means towards the objective which appear a priori to offer a cheaper route. In some cases this will be obvious at the start and the alternative means will effectively set the target economic constraints mentioned in paragraph 3.1. The development of nuclear power is a clear example, the targets being set by the expectations of the cheapest alternative method of power generation at the time at which the proposed development can be exploited. The use of technological forecasting techniques may help the analyst here. Another example is provided by desalination; a public body sponsoring research in this field will set its targets by the prospective costs of schemes for long distance pipelines, or other means of transporting fresh water to the areas of need.

Sometimes the R & D will interact with other courses. The fire bill to a community will be composed inter alia of the costs of losses by fire, of preventive measures, and of services to save life and reduce damage. These may be reduced by the development of less flammable materials, better detection systems, more efficient extinguishers, etc. The same may be attained by having more fire brigades, more inspectors or better publicity on the dangers of fire. We may find that the levels and distribution of fire brigades, the numbers of inspectors, or the amount spent on advertising are the subject to forces which tend to optimise them (i.e. such that marginal additional benefits are less than marginal additional costs and marginal reductions in cost are exceeded by the increased losses) to an extent not true of R & D. But the latter will interact with the other costs and cause a change in optimum level.

Consider the optimum for installation of detector systems as represented in Figure 1. The optimum levels of installation of current detectors are, say, C_1 —such detectors being a mixture of rapid, costly instruments and slower, cheaper devices. Development of a rapid, cheap detector moves the optimum to C_2. There is a benefit because the total costs will be lower but the reduction cannot be gauged from simply considering the change in cost per detector.

Comparison of R & D with other projects must, of course, allow for the differing levels of uncertainty. The decision maker's action will be affected by his attitude towards risk. We cannot assume that if P_R x B_R = £Xm = P_C x B_C (where B_R, B_C net benefits from a research and conventional project respectively) that both projects are equally

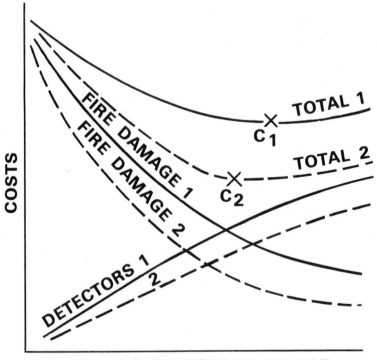

FIG. 1 – ILLUSTRATION OF INTERACTION OF R & D ON
OPTIMUM INSTALLATION OF FIRE DETECTORS

desirable if, say, $P_R = 0.5$ and $P_C = 0.95$. We may correct for this by looking for a higher "expected value" return from the R & D than from more certain projects.

6.   R & D AS AN OPTION TO OTHER R & D

The objectives of our programme may be met through other programmes of research. That a project to develop a composite material for a set of uses or markets must be considered in the light of prospective advances in metal alloys or ceramics is obvious. The use of satellites to relay educational television must take account of future developments in land lines and microwave links. What is not always so clear is that the objectives may be invalidated by other advances. A new biological process for extracing metals from low grade ore will affect our views on how much to spend on instruments to analyse the sea-bed. Ideally we would like to consider together all R & D programmes aimed at the same objective but this is seldom possible; we are forced back to treat the alternatives as a factor of uncertainty and attempt to improve judgment by technological forecasting in the relevant fields.

While the combined consideration of R & D options is seldom possible, it is occasionally so. A government agency may be responsible for a number of nuclear power development projects aimed at the same end; or in the case of desalination research it may see a number of alternative and competing processes. Figure 2 shows a

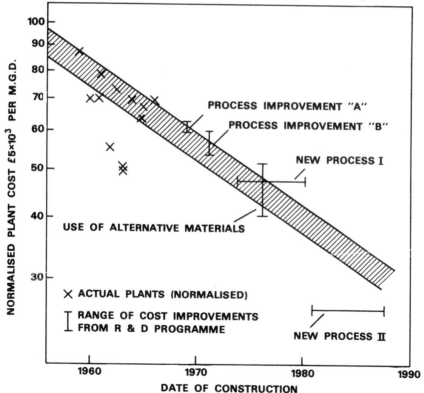

FIG. 2   ANTICIPATED CAPITAL COSTS DESALINATION PLANTS
COSTS NORMALISED TO 2 M.G.D. UNITS WITH P.R. 8:1

technological forecast in which "normalised" capital costs of desalination plants are used as a parameter of technological performance—and indeed of economic performance, for the costs of water and the benefits are related to the capital costs. The figure shows that we have five R & D programmes from which to choose. The number of options is much larger since we may select one or more processes or process improvements. In this case systematic analysis of the different combinations must be carried out assessing the marginal gains from working on additional processes; the cost-benefit analyses must take account of the time scales, the shape of the demand vs. time curve, the life of each improvement before it is overtaken by other advances, etc. Next, the analyst must ask whether the public body needs to fund the R & D itself. There are few fields in which any one organisation is uniquely engaged. Will the knowledge from someone else's R & D be available? And equally important, when will that be? The problems are often those of timing or of compatibility of objectives. But in any event a check must be made of the marginal benefits of one's own sponsorship. Two cautions are needed here. First, one must not assume that the prospective supplier of knowledge is certain of success with the target timescales and economic constraints. Secondly, one cannot purchase R & D knowledge off the shelf like a kilo of apples. The customer has to be sophisticated and the costs of relying on others include that of maintaining a small but "technologically-viable" home-based team. This factor has been an important one in the funding of certain research programmes by the governments of medium to small sized countries.

7.   MECHANICS FOR REALISING THE BENEFIT

The diverse nature of R & D is matched by correspondingly diverse mechanisms by which it is exploited to individual or general gain. While reference has been made to the fact that some cases require no supporting investment, in many the first step in exploitation requires the manufacture of new products or provision of new services by one or more companies, for example materials, machine tools, instruments, chemicals, process plant, electronic components and so on. Since probably at least one-half of the customers of "high technology" products are other companies we find a chain of production-production links before the benefits, if any, reach the consumer. This applies to much public-funded as well as privately financed R & D. This can be illuminated a bit further by attempting a broad classification of the benefits that can arise.

8.   TYPES OF BENEFITS FROM R & D

The R & D, whether performed by the producer or elsewhere, is followed by investment of resources into the manufacture and sale of new products; or the sale of new or extended services; or the sale of existing products or services but arrived at by new or changed processes. Of course some of the investment may be transferred to others by means of contracts for input resources (materials, components or services) but it is usually possible to identify one or more parallel companies who effectively control the success of the exploitation by their investment and performance. The returns to these companies may be by way of:—

(i)   increased profits through new or expanded markets for new products.

(ii)   protection of existing levels of profit. New processes or products will arise affecting present levels. The investment will be considered on a marginal basis, i.e. on the marginal differences between investing and not investing.

(iii) increased market penetration through quality or service improvements.

(iv) lower input costs—the return being either by way of lower costs themselves, through increased slaes reflected by lower prices (depending on the price elasticity of demand), or through greater output per unit cost.

These benefits are obvious and do not need illustration. The point to the cost-benefit analyst and to the government agency concerned with the successful exploitation of public funded R & D is to check that the market forces or imperfections are likely to be such as to allow a producer surplus enough to encourage the initial stage of exploitation. For example, the price paid to the producer should reflect the buyer's judgment of the benefits that he will gain from the purchase but modified in the light of the risk that he considers he is taking by using a new product or service. The demonstrable benefits must be such as to more than balance any uncertainty or risk that pertains to the buyer and to give a return to the producer at least commensurate with his own risk.

9. CONSUMER SURPLUS

For many R & D projects we can, from our knowledge of the structure of industry, forecast that other companies, together with public sector organisations, will buy new products or services because the latter give them marginal benefits. Such will take the same forms as applied to the primary exploiter, viz: increased profits, protection of profits, lower input costs, improved quality or service leading to larger or more secure markets. There may be one or more such companies or organisations in the vertical chain. In practical cases, we need, in the decision-taking stage, to project the possible chains of use since this will often show a spread of applications and markets and what we may call the intermediate consumers/producers surplus to such companies frequently appear to be many times larger than those to the primary exploiter even after allowance is made for the primary exploiter to recoup a share of such benefits by his pricing policy.

For example, consider a new material for an engine component. The primary exploiter makes the material for sale to engine manufacturers. The price will be set by the price-demand schedule but it will not more than partially reflect the advantages to the various engine manufacturers since these will differ between them depending on on their market situations. Differential pricing to the various manufacturers is unlikely significantly to increase this reflection of advantage (particularly if the material passes via a sub-contractor for components). The engine manufacturers are unlikely to gain significantly through lower input costs and, indeed, the material cost of components may have little effect on the overall cost of the engine. The advantage is more likely to be in the increased market penetration achieved through offering improvements in operational performance. In a competitive situation the manufacturer may recoup only a fraction of the value to his customers of such improvements in performance. The latter may be calculable in terms of reduced operating costs, e.g. longer periods between maintenance, lower fuel consumption, since we often know the relationships between technological parameters and operating economics.

One approach then is to project the course by which our objectives will be met; to follow the chain of exploitation, to identify and estimate the markets or demand using the best forecasting techniques at hand. This is a time-consuming but essential part of the analysis. Our aim is to identify the "surplus"; the split between the various producers in the chain is only of concern to ensure that there is no apparent disincentive to exploit; such disincentive may be avoided if the parties bargain together or even merge [5].

Another approach which may be available to us is to compare the costs of providing the final product or service to consumers (not the prices) with the cheapest alternative expected at the future time. Comparison of nuclear generating costs with those from other sources is one example. Water costs from desalination is another. In some cases parametric costing formulae have been historically derived which may be projected to the future. The use of composite materials may lead to weight savings in aircraft, high speed marine craft and other vehicles. The extent to which substitution leads to weight saving may be a complex matter since there are many design interactions, but once these are estimated the worth to operators may be derived from relationships between money and weight for the different types of craft although we do not know how the advantage will be exploited in any particular instance, e.g. by increased passenger capacity, or lower fuel costs.

In other cases we can calculate the savings in resource costs to public authorities. Research in which is called Industrial Aerodynamics contributed to the design of a suspension bridge for the Severn estuary which could be compared with a slightly earlier similar design (for the Firth of Forth) made before the research was available. A cost saving of about £1m was deduced.

Another instance is the use of hydrological research and radio-isotope tracers to establish the movement of silt in estuaries. Dredged silt is dumped in areas out ot sea from some of which it shows a homing instinct. Choice of areas where it is content to stay put saves the port authorities considerable dredging costs and the historical costs have in one instance been calculated. (Projection of savings to other ports is hazardous but it may be possible to show that the range of saving is many times any necessary marginal additional research cost.)

A further example of resource saving lies in fire research aimed at revising standards for buildings and materials such that the costs of protection against fire spread and damage can be reduced while retaining the same standards of safety and protection. The approach in planning is one of cost-effectiveness; subsequent action, e g. legislation, leads to benefits.

These approaches assume that resources released have opportunity cost at their current or projected market values. They overlook the transfer payments or sectional dis-benefits (e.g. to the dredging companies; incidentally it would be difficult to persuade the research scientists that defeating nature's perversity was of no benefit even if the opportunity cost of dredgers was zero). Sometimes a problem may arise as to whether the labour rates in a particular industry are the right reflection of opportunity cost since the labour "saved" may not be employed in the same industry.

10.   OTHER ECONOMIC OBJECTIVES

Prudence dictates that the benefits and costs ascribed to R & D should be those which can be clearly seen and clearly linked with the programme. However, it may be that some wider effect can be identified with equal clarity, for example where technological innovation will lead to changes in the balance of regional employment, thus increasing or decreasing social costs. Alternatively there may be some impact on a nation's foreign exchange situation through an increase or decrease in imports or exports. These effects can be separately identified to the decision-maker; their weight will depend on policy at the time.

11. WELFARE AND AMENITY BENEFITS

Not surprisingly R & D leads to benefits in the economically less tangible areas—a few of these "benefits" will doubtless be regarded by some as cleaning up the mess of other technology. Some examples are given to prove the point, which will not be laboured here. The problems of how they are handled are common to other applications of cost-benefit analysis:

Factors	*Examples of Research Leading to Improvements*
Reduced loss of life	Fire research, aviation
Improved health	Air pollution
Reduced injury and risk of injury	Fire research
Quality improvements (above that covered by market factors)	Fish processing and handling
More leisure time	High speed transport
Amenity—visual	Use of isotopes and hydrology to trace underground water flow—may lead to less need for reservoirs
—noise	Rotary engines
—olfactory	Waste disposal processes
—other	Numerically controlled machine tools (working conditions)
	Use of aerodynamics research to help town planning
Prestige	By-product of research having other major objectives, e.g., high speed vehicles, space
Entertainment	Ditto

Some of these have directly measurable economic effects—costs of hospital treatment, loss of working hours, reduced costs of attaining given safety standards, laundering costs through dirty air, and so on—and such benefits can be included along with those described in section 9. But others may have to receive notional treatment, or be left as a stated residual. Where such benefits are main objectives of the R & D, then some defined target of performance, e.g. reduction in loss of life, or acceptable noise level can be specified and the evaluation becomes one of cost-effectiveness rather than cost-benefit analysis. The problem does become difficult if one is trying to compare programmes or optimise a portfolio containing work leading to both tangible and intangible benefits. Within a single programme it is best to split the objectives and apportion the costs by objectives as best one can.

12.   LEVELS OF CRITERIA

To select from a number of R & D programmes by using cost-benefit analyses we need to be sure the latter are carried out on a consistent basis. The choice can be obscured by the fact that much R & D is exploited through an industrial chain. It would not be sensible to assume that all benefits from publicly-funded R & D are reflected in the returns to the companies who are the primary exploiters, i.e. are at the first stage in the chain.

Also the question arises from government agencies as to whether the first members in the chain should not make some return (by cash payment, royalties, etc.) towards the cost of government investment in R & D, whether this is done in the firms concerned, or in a government laboratory; particularly this is so where some innovation or specific capability has arisen in government work and where timely exploitation requires a continuation of government-industry collaborative work. A decision to spend government money could thus be based on the prospects of return to the laboratory or the sponsoring organisation. An analogy here is the case of contract R & D institutes where the payment is the sole criterion. In practice the willingness of a firm or firms to contribute, in return of course for certain advantages, measures more than a financial return. It confirms judgment that the R & D involved is likely to lead to benefits; and it establishes the first vital link towards exploitation and partially removed the bugbear that R & D will fail to be exploited to the country's advantage through lack of communication.

A different level of benefit is implied when the investment is regarded as being in aid of a particular industry or sector of the economy. The measures of return relate to the ' performance" of the sector concerned, i.e. improved productivity, and perhaps contribution to foreign exchange balance. These benefits are "assumed" on a sub-optimal basis for we would need to relate the performance of the industry to other sectors of the economy to know if the net effect was beneficial, e.g. by means of econometric models.

Thirdly, we may assess the R & D on the grounds of benefit to the community as a whole, taking account as best we can of the spectrum of exploiters and users, and other residual social benefits. This is in fact the proper basis inferred by "cost-benefit analysis".

The analyst must make the basis clear to the decision-maker and avoid false optimisation of a selection of research products through using various levels of criteria.

It may be observed that changing the basis on which costs and benefits are estimated may change not only the level of R & D investment but in some cases the objectives and technological direction of the R & D programmes themselves.

13. OPPORTUNITY COST OF RESEARCH RESOURCES

Analysis of individual investments in R & D programmes should, it may be argued, use the opportunity costs of research resources. Such resources have, of course, a market value but since this value varies but little across a range of R & D activities (including a number of large fields such as defence, the universities, and basic research, where market mechanisms do not operate) the value is unlikely to reflect opportunity cost in terms of profit earning. In practice, however, too little is yet known of the opportunity cost of the various types of research resource to vary from the market value with any confidence. It may be possible to do so within a particular laboratory if all of the projects can be measured in benefit terms; and if the application of cost-benefit nalaysis to publicly-funded R & D is extended, we will get more light on the subject.

14. CONCLUSION

As in other applications of cost-benefit analysis, pre-decision studies on R & D programmes may require the use of systems analysis and modelling as well as various forecasting techniques. Little has been said of these. We have concentrated on a few aspects of applying analysis to R & D situations. While there are obvious limitations such studies can, it is believed, help not only in the decision-making process but also in the planning of R & D programmes.

In putting together the picture of benefits likely to arise from R & D careful attention has to be paid to the incentives or disincentives that such benefits imply. The general economic and social benefits do not appear as a cash return to the investors up the chain of exploitation.

Mention has been made of the uncertain nature of research. In deciding to invest in Government R & D, we have to take account not only of the scientific uncertainties but of the chances of successful exploitation. Mapping the pattern of benefits can thus assist in assessing not only the level of gain but also the probability of attaining it. It has also an important role in defining the objectives of the programmes, of influencing their orientation and structure, and of identifying opportunities for increasing their effectiveness.

ACKNOWLEDGMENTS

I have drawn upon the work of my colleagues in the Programmes Analysis Unit to illustrate points in this paper; they, and members of the Economics and Statistics Division of the Ministty of Technology, have also made constructive comments. I wish to acknowledge both forms of help.

REFERENCES

1.   Prest, A.R., and Turvey, R. (1965) 'Cost Benefit Analysis: A survey' *Economic J.*, vol. 75, pp. 683-735

2. Griliches, Z. (1958) 'Research costs and social returns: Hybrid corn and related innovations' *J. Political Economy*, vol. 66, pp. 419-431

3. Grossfield, K., and Heath, J.B. (1966) 'The benefit and cost of Government support for research and development', *Economic J.*, vol. 76, pp. 537-549

4. Foster, C.D., (1968) 'Cost-benefit analysis in research', in *Decision making in national science policy*. A. de Reuck, M. Goldsmith, J. Knight, eds. Churchill, London

5. Peters, G.H. (1968) *Cost-benefit analysis and public expenditure*, Eaton Paper 8, 2nd edition, Institute of Economic Affairs, London

6. Williams, B.R. (1965) 'Economics in unwonted places', *Economic J.*, vol. 75, pp. 20-30

7. Winkler, R L., (1968) 'The consensus of subjective probability distributions', *Management Science*, vol. 15, pp. B61-B75

8. Brooks, H., (1967) *'National science policy and technology transfer'* NSF Report 67-5, National Science Foundation, Washington, D.C.

9. Davidson, H., (1968) *The transfer process from science to technology*, Institute on the Worth of Planning and Control Processes in R & D Management, American University, Washington, D.C.

10. Central Advisory Council for Science and Technology (1968) *Technological innovation in Britain*, H.M. Stationery Office, London.

11. U S. Department of Commerce (1967) *Technological innovation: Its environment and management U.S. Government Printing Office, Washington, D.C., PB-174103*

SECTION 4

NATURAL RESOURCES

Chairman: **P. de Wolff**
          Instituut voor Actuariaat en Econometrie,
          Amsterdam, Netherlands

Speakers :   P. F. Gross
          Associate Professor of Administration and Director,
          Computer Centre, University of Saskatchewen, Canada

          L. J. Locht
          Institute for Land and Water Management Research,
          Netherlands

          D. J. Clough
          Chairman, Department of Management Sciences,
          University of Waterloo, and President, Systems
          Engineering Associates Ltd., Canada

A SYTEMS APPROACH TO PUBLIC POLICY- MAKING IN FORESTRY — A CASE STUDY

P.F. Gross

1. INTRODUCTION

1.1. Management Science and Forest Management Decision Making

The use of the techniques of scientific management (or Operations Research) for decision making in the area of Natural Resources would appear to be growing steadily.

In the Forest Management sector, some of the first applications of Linear Programming were reported by Bethel and Harrell [1957] in Plywood Production/Distribution, and the number of applications has increased since 1960 when a Forest Management Control Conference was held at Purdue University. Early papers by Machol [1960] and Courtu and Ellertson [1960] related to farm economics. Other papers by Jones [1960] related to the use of linear programming in minimising transportation costs for a pulpwood agency supplying pulpmills from a number of sources. Later papers by Curtis [1962] and Loucks [1964] use more complex models of different forest processes.

The use of simulation techniques in Forest Management has been reported by Balderson and Hoggatt [1962] in modelling complex marketing processes for the U.S. Pacific Coast plywood industry. Later work by Newnham and Smith [1964], Gould and O'Regan [1965] and Walton [1965] indicates that simulation is an accepted technique in forest management processes.

With this historic development, it is not surprising that applications of scientific management to more basic processes such as the replacement of equipment for sawmills, or to the relative profitability of timber management as a whole, are now being more frequently reported, although Broido et al [1965] comment that " . . . the decision making processes with respect to 'conservation of wildland resources' have not been as elaborately developed as those found in most industrial, agricultural and many governmental activities . . ."

In the determination of the profitability of sawmill operations, some of the most significant work has been done by the Southern Forest Experiment Station, New Orleans, Louisiana, and is reported by Row et al [1965]. In this report, a method is suggested of optimizing profits, given four factors:
—amount, quality and cost of timber
—possible sawing patterns and their yields
—machine time available on the mill equipment
—sales requirements
The methodology used consisted of time studies of sawing activities in a single sawmill with two bandsaws, a sashang, a vertical line resaw and a horizontal resaw, the mill having a capacity of 200,000 board feet per 8 hour day. Regression analysis was then

used to determine lumber and by-product yields as a function of sawing patterns and log diameters. Linear programming was used finally to determine the most profitable sawing patterns. Similar studies have been reported by Jackson and Smith [1961] and by Smith and Harrell [1961].

Methods of estimating the cost of sawing lumber from logs of any size have been suggested by Anderson [1964], admittedly for small sawmills and for pine lumber.

This summary of the application of management science to forest management problems would seem to indicate a variety of attacks on different problem areas. The application of the traditional methods of profitability accounting in forest maturity analysis by Bentley et al [1965] indicates that the problems of handling the time element in such an analysis are the same problems faced by other workers attempting to rank likely investments in other areas of the private sector.

1.2   Systems Analysis and PPBS in Public Policymaking

By way of contrast, the use of the tools of systems analysis and the development of a model of public policymaking within the area of Natural Resources is, as yet, still in the embryonic stages.

Leaving aside the important pioneering steps by Eckstein, Maass and associates at Harvard University in the application of benefit-cost analysis to water resource systems [refer Eckstein, 1958 and McKean, 1959], and some tentative steps taken by Mack and Myers [1965] in evaluating public investment in outdoor recreation facilities, the forest sector has come forth with few pioneering attempts to incorporate the tools of systems analysis within the public policymaking processes. Perhaps the exceptions to this general statement are the attempts by the Forest Service, U.S. Department of Agriculture, to apply the Program-Planning-Budgeting System (PPBS) to Forest Resource Management. McKean [1959, pp247-278] described the first exploratory attempts to develop a performance budget for the Forest Service, while a slightly modified PPB approach to the same problem is described by Hinrichs and Taylor [1969]. In essence, these approaches, as with most analyses using the PPB approach and subsequent cost-effectiveness comparisons, attempt to rationalise existing budgeting processes with a view to enabling a more rational comparison to be made of different strategies of managing, protecting and researching forest resources.

To date, the literature has not revealed any attempts to extend the comparatively narrow aspects of systematic analysis inherent in the PPB approach to the much wider problem of public policymaking in the forest sector. In recent years, there has been a plethora of literature on the overall decision making process in the public sector with particular emphasis on:

first, reemphasising the role of the polity within the public policymaking processes by including some facility within the decision-making model for recognising the phenomena that Dror calls "political feasibility" [Dror, 1968 and Dror, 1969a]

second, examining the relationship between the analytical and political approaches to public spending in particular [Schultze, 1968]

third recognising the role of comprehensive planning within a public policymaking system [Dror, 1967].

Despite the fact that many of the variables and their interrelationships within the public policymaking process are unknown, and despite the fact that much of the literature is too erudite to be of use to the practitioner, the volume of new literature on public policymaking is indicative of the general concern of many public administrators and academicians to develop a more systematic model of the public policymaking processes. Such a model would extend far beyond somewhat dated models which stress the existence of a "power elite" or a pluralist society in the decision processes. Some of Yehezkel Dror's work provides a first approach to rationalising the attempts by a policy analyst to show that the crux of public policymaking is the interrelationship between interest groups, the executive and legislature, at any of the three levels of government.

As the next section of this paper indicates, the extension of a small pilot study of the efficiency of forest sawmilling processes to a systems analysis of the public policymaking processes was a natural consequence of recognising the dangers of sub-optimisation in the decision making process in the forest sector.

2.   BACKGROUND TO THIS STUDY

2.1   Overview

The study was unique for a number of reasons, and therefore the results may not have universal implications. Firstly, this was a joint study by a public sector forest agency and private sector sawmill owners into the efficiency of the sawmilling process. The expressed purpose of the study, which came through discussions between the forest management advisory branch in the state agency controlling use of forests and the sawmill owners, was to find methods of making efficient use of the rapidly dwindling hardwood resources in the State, where it was estimated that the forests would be depleted by the year 2000. Secondly, the nature of the *modus operandi* of public agency and private sawmills who process the timber, is such that each sawmill operates on an annual quota system, with quotas determined solely by the agency on the basis of estimated modal efficiency of sawmills in a region, as described further on.

There were more basic reasons for the motivation of both parties in a joint study, and these reasons are briefly discussed here.

(i)   Sawmill Aspirations

On the one hand, the sawmill owners were anxious to determine, through a joint study, whether their particular milling processes were efficient by comparison with other mills in the study and with other sawmills at large. Generally, it could be said that sawmilling in this State is not efficient, in that there is general agreement that (a) there are too many sawmills milling hardwood timber, and (b) there are too many *small* sawmills i.e. those cutting under 200,000 super feet of timber annually, say. Since sawmilling involves a process whereby raw material is converted into finished goods, other by-products and waste, requiring combinations of different mechanical devices, there is no doubt that, *ceteris paribus*, one large sawmill of capacity A super feet is far more efficient, in its use of natural resources and its production processes, than ten smaller mills of capacity 0.1A super feet. Of particular concern to the sawmill owners is the choice of the headsaw, which is the saw that first breaks a log down into smaller sections called flitches, which are further broken down by other processes [Figure 1 is a schematic of the overall milling process]. Traditional methods of deciding when to invest in headsaws (and indeed in other saws to a certain extent) usually involve rather simple decision rules such as—replace the saw when it falls to pieces—*or* replace the headsaw when a competitor replaces his and appears to be more efficient that he was previously! Such decision rules do not require the keeping of accounting records, and there is no need to calculate rather elaborate optimum replacement period formula or evaluate cost-benefit considerations. However, a large number of sawmills are moving from *ad hoc* decision making to the use of the new techniques of investment analysis, and it was this transition that led a few of the larger sawmill owners to agree to a joint study of the whole production process in their mills, wiht a view to seeking better indicators of the effectiveness of existing milling techniques and equipment.

(ii)   Public Sector Forest Management Aspirations

On the other hand, the public agency viewed these studies of sawmill production efficiency as being a means of verifying (or otherwise) some rather *ad hoc* decision making criteria used in the exercising of its powers as regulator of the usage of forest resources in the State. Firstly, all sawmills in the State are privately owned, with timber being supplied to the mills from a number of State forests, on an annual quota basis. (This situation should be contrasted with U.S. environment, where nearly three-quarters of the commercial forest area or 367 million acres was in private ownership on January 1st, 1963, but public lands, with slightly more than a quarter of the acreage, contained nearly half the growing stock (Hinrichs et al. 1969 at pp.261)). This quota is determined by a rather cursory assessment of the modal efficiency (measured usually on a percentage recovery basis) of sawmills in a region, and the application of quotas for each mill is then made on the basis that a particular sawmill should be capable of efficiently milling X super feet of log input in the coming year. As can be seen, this decision-making rationale penalises the efficient sawmills (which are usually the larger automated sawmills) and relates to only one measure of efficiency (percentage recovery) which does not consider log input quality in any cause-effect relationship. To this date, it has not been possible to quantify a relationship between percentage recovery and log quality, mainly because of lack of a meaningful measure of the latter, particularly in hardwoods, which are generally of (increasingly) poorer quality that softwoods in this region of Australia. Secondly, the decision as to whether to restrict quotas (i.e. to close mills down in effect) in any year is a political decision ultimately, and while it was obvious to agency management that the modal efficiency of sawmilling could be improved by shutting down the large number of small inefficient sawmills, this might normally be construed as a restraint on free enterprise. In fact, it would be so if it were not for the fact that the rate of extinction of available hardwood resources is so rapid as to soon require fairly regular production efficiency studies by agency personnel. However, a proxy variable for efficiency was available in the form of efficiency of headsaw operation in each sawmill, although it was recognised that the study of one production unit might not be a true measure of overall mill efficiency, Since this study was viewed as a forerunner of many other studies increasing in complexity, it was decided, however, to proceed with the headsaw evaluation and with studies of other equipment concurrently.

So at this point, the study resolved itself into a public agency determination of private

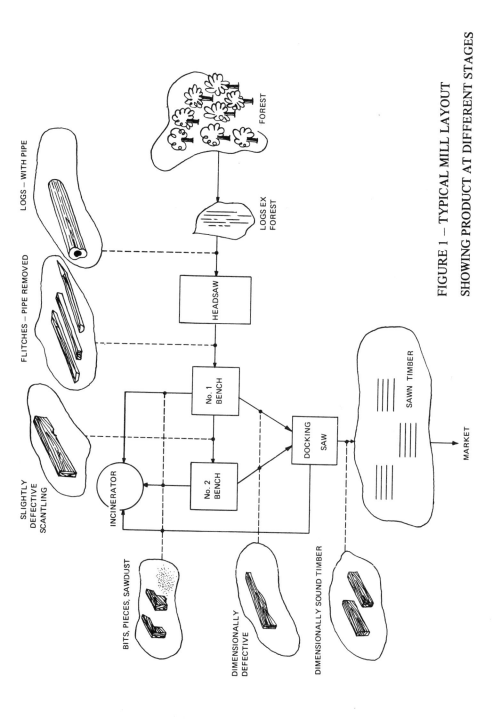

FIGURE 1 – TYPICAL MILL LAYOUT
SHOWING PRODUCT AT DIFFERENT STAGES

sector sawmill efficiency, with a view to first, using techniques of investment analysis and production control to enable both public and private sectors to evaluate some measure of sawmill efficiency, second, extending the analysis of a small sample of mills to an overall cost-effectiveness analysis of different methods of public sector regulation of usage of forest resources by *all* sawmills in the State. As will be indicated, the cost-effectiveness analysis discussed in this paper involved an extension of the basic method of the traditional C–E analysis to a model of public policymaking proposed as a result of the initial pilot study of headsaw operation, which was itself a form of cost-effectiveness analysis (used in a literal sense here, even at the risk of offending those purists who content that cost-effectiveness analysis is strictly a phenomenon of the public sector) using a mathematical model of the equipment replacement situation.

2.2   The Public and Private Interests in Forest Management Efficiency

Basically one can recognise at least four distinct stages between the planting of the seedling and the marketing and usage of a finished timber product. In simple layman's terms, these four stages are the *afforestation-deforestation* stages (where timber is grown and then cut down for milling or other uses, such as in household fireplaces), the *milling* stage (where the log is converted into some marketable product (such as scantlings and structural timber for construction, or wood pulp for paper) and finally the *marketing* stage (where the finished product is sold for commercial or other usage).

In each of these three stages, a number of factors complicate decision-making for private sector management and public policymaking in the public sector, and in an endeavour to indicate how some of the decision criteria might cut across private/public boundaries (as was revealed in this rather unique situation studied), Table 1 summarises some of the pertinent problem areas. A brief explanation is in order to explain, *inter alia*, what Table 1 does *not* attempt to illustrate.

Firstly, Table 1 does not depict a model of *all* the relevant parameters and variables in the public policymaking process in the forest environment under study. It is illustrative rather than exhaustive. At best, Table 1 attempts to illustrate some of the important players, their roles in the decision making process at different stages of forest resource usage and the decision making tools (if existent) that are in use at this stage. Obviously, scientific management techniques, *per se*, are applicable in a comparatively narrow area of decision making. Equally obvious is the fact that by examining the overall process through looking at the components (or *sub-systems*, as represented by the separate processes in Stages I through IV) of that process and the interactions of those subsystems within the whole process (or *system*) depicted in Table 1, we are in fact implementing a systems analysis of the overall process. This exposition of a fact that will be obvious to the systems practitioner, but perhaps obscure to the reader confused by the tendency in the literature to equate systems analysis to specific techniques of Operations Research or Management Science (or to O.R. or Management Science alone), is an attempt to obviate confusion in the use of systems jargon [see Quade, 1966].

Secondly, no attempt has been made to superimpose a scheme for determining the political feasibility of any one decision made in the overall process. Obviously some decisions relate mainly to constraints on agency budgets, such as a decision to increase the numbers of staff in a forest products research group. Thus the format of Table 1 could be expanded into a more extensive *program and financial plan* so as to satisfy

TABLE 1 - ACTORS, INPUTS, INTERACTIONS AND DECISION TOOLS IN OVERALL FOREST RESOURCE USAGE[1]

Stage	Average Duration	Program Elements[2]	Main Actors[3]	Inputs into Policymaking	Impact of Interactions	Decision Tools
I. Afforestation	50–100 years	1. Forest Development - planting - seeding	Agency		Weak	Precedent
		2. Forest Protection and Use	Agency/Public	1. Budget Constraints	Weak	Precedent
		3. Fire Fighting	Agency/Public	2. Resource Constraints	On Demand	Precedent with no scientific mgt. approach
		4. Forest Research		3. Market demands		
		- range surveys and data collection	Agency	4. Public Opinion	NA	Computer data base
		- range management	Agency	5. Interest Group	NA	Precedent
		- product investigations	Agency	6. Pressure	NA	Precedent
		- resource investigations (incl. quota determination)	Agency/Mill Owners/ Polity	7. Rules of Game	Strong	Statistical
		- long range market demand/supply studies	Agency/Mill Owners/ Polity	8. Technology	Weak	Statistical
		- mill production studies	Agency/Mill Owners	9. Political Leverage	Weak[4]	LP, Simulation, Production Planning and Control
		- mill licence granting	Agency/Mill Owners/ Polity		Strong	Ad hoc
II. Deforestation	1–3 months	5. Road Clearing, Construction and Maintenance	Agency		NA	Precedent
		6. Logging	Agency		NA	Precedent
		7. Haulout	Agency		NA	Precedent
		8. Inspection	Agency		NA	Precedent
III. Sawmilling	1–2 months	9. Sawmilling	Mill Owner		NA	Precedent
		10. Treatment/Storage of Finished Product	Mill Owner		NA	Precedent
		11. Transportation of Finished Product	Mill Owner		NA	Precedent
IV. Marketing	variable	12. Short range (6–12 months) market demand studies	Mill Owner		NA	Ad hoc
		13. Transportation Subsidy Studies	Mill Owner/Agency/ Polity/Interest Groups		Weak	Ad hoc
		14. Transportation Studies	Agency/Polity/ Interest Groups		Weak	Ad hoc

Note
1. Terminology follows Dror (1969, p.8–12) NA means not applicable or very relevant.
2. "Program" is *not* used in the strict PPBS sense here, except perhaps for Stage I. The list of elements is illustrative, not exhaustive.
3. Capacities of each actor should be obvious, although affected by historical precedents, personal relations etc. as noted by Dror (1969, p.8–9)
4. This study was a general exception to the rule, as the study involved four different mills on a comparative basis.

the six major goals of a PPB system [as outlined by Schultze [1968, p19-23], bridging the gap between the *program budget* and the *appropriation structure*. Perhaps it might be possible to use an extension of Dorr's "political feasibility" estimation methods to develop the *special issues studies*, even though we are a long way from recommending the trip-facet Delphi method suggested by Dror for prediction of political feasibility (Dror, 1969a pp12-190]. Alternatively, the traditional cost-benefit or cost-effectiveness analyses are seen as being more relevant in the special studies in the forest sector.

Thirdly, and most relevant in this paper, the comparatively micro nature of the sawmill production efficiency studies that were a basis for commencing this study can be seen in Table 1 within the overall framework of the global process of forest growth and usage. Any analysis of the process that considers sawmills in isolation is in danger of sub-optimising overall decision making processes.

To put this latter point in better focus, Section 3 outlines the nature and results of the initial study undertaken of the micro process of sawmilling, and Sections 4 and 5 extend the results observed in this micro analysis of sawmill operation to the comparatively macro analysis of the interacting phases of the whole process.

3.   THE ANALYSIS OF SAWMILL OPERATIONS

3.1   Introduction

Since this initial study of sawmill operation was carried out in sawmills owned by the private sector, but where the quota of timber used by each mill is allocated by a Forestry Commission (for which this study was undertaken), the very fine distinction that exists between some traditional methods of investment appraisal in the private sector, and cost-effectiveness analysis in the public sector, was tested to its extreme. Essentially, the description that follows is of a cost-effectiveness analysis in the public sector, was tested to its extreme. Essentially, the description that follows is of a cost-effectiveness analysis in the *private* sector, where the results, as they reflected mill efficiency, were of some importance to the agency in the *public* sector.

It is assumed that the reader is familiar with the traditional methods of investment appraisal (such as payback period, DCF or Internal Rate of Return and Present Worth concepts) used in the business sector [Dean, 1954 and Vassilatou-Thanopoulos, 1965]. It is also assumed that the problems of using these techniques, particularly those that attempt to recognise that one dollar in the hand now is worth more than one dollar received a year hence, are understood by the reader. (The particular problems of determining the social discount rate in benefit-cost analysis in the public sector have been referred to by Peston [1968], Weisbrod [1965] and Due [1968]).

In this initial study, an evaluation was made of a mathematical model of the equipment replacement siutation; specifically, the Least Cost Model as proposed by Fetter and Goodman [1957] (or the equivalent Least Average Annual Cost Model as has been used by Eilon et al [1968] in vehicle replacement). The one attractive feature of the model is the convenient form of output that can be produced—such as a series of graphs showing replacement cycles for different values of the basic parameters (discount rate, operating cost growth rate, etc.). The sawmill owner with little formal education can, with little training, be taught to read off values from a graph, whereas the outputting of a single benefit-cost ratio as an output does little in the way of allowing the sawmill owner to estimate the effects of "what if" situations. This practical difficulty of using a single index (such as a benefit-cost ratio) to represent a multitude of assumptions is often neglected in formal discussions in academic circles, but is not overlooked in discussions by hard-headed practitioners.

3.2   The Least Cost Model

In mathematical terminology, this model postulates that the cost C of a single cycle of replacement (T) is given by the formula:

$$C = B - S(T)e^{-it} + \int_0^T E(t)e^{-it}\, dt \dots\dots\dots\dots\dots (1)$$

where B = prime cost of equipment at time zero in the equipment acquisition cycle.

S(T) = salvage value at the time of replacement T. Thus the salvage value is a function of time.

e^{-it} = discounting factor to allow for the different time values of money.

E(t) = operating cost at any time t in the replacement cycle T. Thus, the operating cost would normally increase with time.

$$\int_0^T E(t)e^{-it}dt = \text{cumulative sum of all operating costs in the cycle T.}$$

Since a single cycle of replacement does not recognise that the sawmill operation is a continuing process, we can extend the simple model represented by equation (1) to cover an infinite number of replacement cycles, in which case it can be shown (Fetter and Goodman [1957]) that:

$$C = \left[B - S(T)e^{-it} + \int_0^T E(t)e^{-it}dt \right]\left[\frac{1}{1 - e^{-it}} \right] \dots\dots (2)$$

The model represented by equation (2) suggests that, in comparing two pieces of equipment, the equipment with the lesser value of C should be selected. The optimum value of C can be determined by methods of differential calculus, or using the graphs given in the Fetter and Goodman [1957] paper if certain common assumptions are made. The optimum replacement cycle T for each machine can also be determined.

In this study, both C and T were determined for each type of headsaw, assuming:
—that the salvage value $S(t) = Be^{-kt}$, i.e., the normally accepted negative exponential salvage value model.
—that the operating cost E(t) = E + Gt where E = operating and maintenance cost at time zero, assuming that some minimum maintenance is required on the equipment before it comes into operation.

G = cost increase gradient per unit time.

As Fetter and Goodman have shown, the Least Cost Model is particularly sensitive to variations in G, i and S(T), a situation that does not lead to complete satisfaction with the usage of this model.

Another factor that is relevant in considering this model in a replacement situation is that the model does not consider revenues or returns from the investment. It is possible to set up a Profit Maximisation model to overcome this situation, such that the profit P of an infinite series of replacement cycles is given by:

$$P = \left[\int_0^T [R(t) - E(t)] e^{-it} dt + S(T) e^{-it} - B \right] \left[\frac{1}{1-e^{-it}} \right] \qquad \ldots (3)$$

where R(t) = revenue earned at time t.

It can be shown that under conditions of constant revenue and by redefinition of E(t), the Profit Maximisation model can be resolved into the Least Cost Model. In the sawmills studied, the conditions of constant revenue are potentially present, since a state quota system acts as a constraint on widely varying returns. However, it is possible to cut different marketable patterns of timber from a given log, thus changing the revenue earning pattern. Hence the constant revenue assumption may not be present.

In view of the desire to compare the results of using the mathematical model with the results suggested by a benefit-cost ratio, it seems likely that the Profit Maximisation model is the more appropriate model to use in this study. The output of the Profit Maximisation model is the present value of the profit of a certain optimum replacement cycle T.

3.3   Parameters Required by Replacement Models

The estimation of E(t) and R(t) is difficult even if sawmill owners divulge costs, and even the, the accounting records may not be easily searched. Production rates, operating efficiency and variability of log input makes estimates even more difficult. The traditional problems of determining discount rate and duration of earnings for the model pale by significance.

Section 3.4 details the extent of measurement required to achieve a single result having some aura of legitimacy.

3.4   The Study Technique

The study technique consisted of protracted time and output studies by a study team of 6-8 members for one week in each of four sawmills, one using a Framesaw and the other three using Canadian saws. The characteristics of each mill are contained in Table 2.

The time study included the headsaws and benchsaws as did the volume recovery and efficiency studies. Queue sizes at each unit and variations from intended dimensions of flitches were also measured, since any comparison of the headsaws must take into account the amount of network necessary through faulty sawing at the headsaw. As the appended tables indicate, considerably more information was extracted than would be necessary for a comparison of headsaws only, so as to allow simulation models of sawmill operation to be developed at a later stage.

Characteristic	MILL 1	MILL 2	MILL 3	MILL 4
1. Type of headsaw	Frame	Canadian	Canadian	Canadian (Gibson Carriage)
(i) Number of operators	1-2	2	2	2
(ii) Methods of loading log to deck	Gantry Crowbar	Winch	Livechain	Winch
(iii) Av. speed of feed	7-24 inches/min.	86 inches/min.	219 inches/min.	138 inches/min.
(iv) Equipment for turning and/or unloading	Overhead winch	Pneumatic dogs and Cant & Hook	Hydraulic flippers	Hydraulic dogs, pneumatic Flippers
2. Follow-up Benches				
(i) No. of No. 1 Benches	2	1	1	1
(ii) No. of operators	5-6	3	3	3
(iii) No. of No. 2 Benches	-	1	1	1
(iv) No. of Operators	-	3	3	3
(v) No. of docking saws	2	2	2	2
(vi) No. of operators	2	2	2	2
3. Type of Transport				
Headsaw to No. 1 Bench	Transfer Chain & Skids	Powered Chain and motorized rollers	Powered Rollers and skids	Powered Rollers and powered skids
No. 1 Bench to Docking Saw	Skids	Skids	Skids	Skids
4. Type of product being cut	Scantlings Boards Structural Timbers	Scantlings Boards	Scantlings Boards	Scantlings Boards

TABLE 2 - SUMMARY OF MILL CHARACTERISTICS

FRAMESAW	CANADIAN SAW
1. Winch log onto tracks, position for cutting and attach chains.	1. Winch log to carriage.
	2. Set log in desired position and dog.
2. Saw logs.	3. Move log to saw and align.
3. Remove chains.	4. Saw log.
4. Unload sawn logs to convery or skids for transport to No. 1 Bench.	5. Unload sawn flitch.
	6. Return carriage to initial position
	7. Turn log down onto sawn face and align for next cut.
	8. Repeat operations 3-7.
	9. Repeat operations 3-5.
	10. Unload sawn slab and heart.

TABLE 3 – MODE OF LOADING/SAWING ON HEADSAWS

Table 3 summarises the pattern of operation in loading and sawing logs at headsaws.

Table 4 summarises for each mill the times of various phases of the loading/sawing operation (including handling, manipulation, sawing and unloading times) plus input log characteristics. The unload time of the Canadian saw has been included in the "time to manipulate" classification, since this time is negligible compared to the equivalent time for the Framesaw.

Table 5 summarises the input log defects and various log measurements (length, top diameter (UB) and mid girth (UB) made prior to log breakdown.

Table 6 attempts to give some idea of the log quality, which has some relationship to the percentage recovery from the log. The concept of a "log quality index" has been suggested by Page [1962], but was not applied here because of the comparatively high percentage defect in the hardwood timber submitted for milling. The table also summarises some of the output variables measured in the study.

Table 7 is the matrix of correlation coefficients between the various factors outlined in Table 4, while Tables 8A—E summarise the effects of regressing the various operation times on length, top diameter, mid girth and NHV. The significance of these tables is discussed further on.

In an endeavour to test the effect of flitching to dimension on the headsaw on the percentage recovery and the production rate per man at subsequent benchsaw operations, measurements were made of the various mean times of operation at the No.1 benches for all four mills. Table 9 summarises the results of this aspect of the study.

TABLE 4 – SUMMARY OF RELEVANT FACTORS IN THIS STUDY

FACTOR	MILL 1				MILL 2				MILL 3				MILL 4			
	MIN	MEAN	MAX	S.D.	MIN	MEAN	MAX	S.D.	MIN	MEAN	MAX	S.D.	MIN	MEAN	MAX	S.D.
A. Length log (ft)	8.0	15.5	24.0	3.9	8.0	15.0	21.0	3.7	9.5	14.9	19.7	2.3	8.0	15.5	24.0	3.6
B. Top diameter ub (in)	10.0	23.7	47.0	8.6	16.0	26.0	39.0	5.6	14.0	25.4	39.0	7.5	14.0	27.9	44.0	9.8
C. Midgirth ub (in)	41.0	76.6	134.0	26.3	52.0	84.0	122.0	16.5	46.0	82.5	126.0	24.9	42.0	90.2	159.0	31.1
D. Volume log (NH)	14.0	373.5	1287.0	268.8	102.0	482.0	1230.0	248.5	119.0	416.0	920.0	231.5	103.0	557.1	1653.0	397.9
E. Time to load (secs)	18	124	842	204	43	276	789	217	19	55	200	46	21	102	310	23
F. Time to manipulate (secs)	114	822	2569	742	79	471	1179	309	7	242	570	166	27	403	1585	363
G. Time to saw (secs)	425	815*	1941	361	21	126*	387	113	10	49	127	36	14	82	260	73
H. Time to unload (secs)	105	673	3046	780	2	53	218	71	–	–	–	–	–	–	–	–
I. Delays (secs)	–	–	–	–	0	60	866	137	0	107	1050	280	0	291	4857	1050
J. Total time (secs)	987	2420	5951	1409	196	987	1902	636	54	454	1449	378	103	877	5290	1140
K. No. logs measured	–	75	–	–	–	–	32	–	–	–	40	–	–	–	42	–
L. No. logs timed	–	16	–	–	–	–	12	–	–	–	20	–	–	–	20	–

Note * In *Mills 2-4*, the method of disposal of defect is in the form of boxed heart directly from the output side of the Headsaw to the incinerator. In *Mill 1*, boxed heart was carried to the No. 1 Benches with the other flitches.

Species	Mill 1 Number	Mill 1 Percent	Mill 2 Number	Mill 2 Percent	Mill 3 Number	Mill 3 Percent	Mill 4 Number	Mill 4 Percent
Blackbutt	–	–	9	17.3	2	4.8	19	45.2
Sydney Blue Gum	8	10.4	–	–	16	38.0	8	19.0
Red Mahogany	2	2.6	–	–	–	–	4	9.6
Tallowwood	41	53.3	43	82.7	21	50.0	11	26.2
White Mahogany	2	2.6	–	..	–	–	–	–
Brushbox	12	15.6	–	–	3	7.2	–	–
Ironbark	5	6.5	–	–	–	–	–	–
Grey Gum	4	5.2	–	–	–	–	–	–
Flooded Gum	3	3.9	–	–	–	–	–	–
TOTAL	77	100.0	52	100.0	42	100.0	42	100.0

TABLE 5 – SUMMARY OF LOG SPECIES PROCESSED AT EACH MILL

Variable	Mill 1	Mill 2	Mill 3	Mill 4
1(a) *Variation from intended flitch dimension. ($\frac{1}{32}$")	$4 \begin{matrix} +12 \\ -4 \end{matrix}$	$18 \begin{matrix} +22 \\ -18 \end{matrix}$	–	–
(b) No. of flitches measured	87	42		
2(a) Average % recovery on GHV	76.1	44.6	45.6	34.6
(b) Average % recovery on NHV	88.8	49.5	58.6	42.5
(c) No. of logs measured	29	31	20	27

*Indicates (a) top and bottom saw misalignment for Canadian Headsaw.
(b) average deviation from intended dimension (including oversize allowance) at 2'0" intervals along flitch for Frame Saw.

TABLE 6 – SUMMARY OF OUTPUT VARIATIONS BETWEEN MILLS

FACTOR/MILL	A LOG LENGTH	B TOP DIAM	C MID GIRTH	D N.H.V.	E TIME LOAD	F TIME MANIPULATE	G TIME CUT	H TIME UNLOAD	I TOTAL TIME
B 1	0.391	1.000							
B 2	-0.336								
B 3	0.069								
B 4	0.182								
C 1	0.349	0.731	1.000						
C 2	-0.283	0.974							
C 3	0.096	0.984							
C 4	0.257	0.961							
D 1	0.750	0.625	0.673	1.000					
D 2	0.277	0.709	0.803						
D 3	0.369	0.885	0.920						
D 4	0.533	0.844	0.924						
E 1	-0.084	-0.082	0.110	-0.035	1.000				
E 2	-0.204	0.685	0.768	0.670					
E 3	-0.295	-0.190	-0.167	-0.191					
E 4	0.310	0.711	0.802	0.816					
F 1	-0.083	-0.422	-0.339	-0.081	-0.073	1.000			
F 2	0.230	0.742	0.720	0.760	0.541				
F 3	0.123	0.149	0.182	0.271	0.098				
F 4	0.266	0.801	0.888	0.907	0.867				
G 1	0.699	0.495	0.690	0.903	0.012	-0.145	1.000		
G 2	0.229	0.708	0.687	0.789	0.496	0.837			
G 3	0.221	-0.085	-0.055	0.061	0.059	0.869			
G 4	0.229	0.801	0.870	0.865	0.847	0.951			
H 1	0.600	0.162	0.317	0.626	-0.125	0.224	0.770	1.000	
H 2	0.192	0.517	0.453	0.489	0.398	0.828	0.585		
H 3	–	–	–	–	–	–	–		
H 4	–	–	–	–	–	–	–		
I 1	0.480	-0.002	0.212	0.559	0.041	0.593	0.643	0.887	1.000
I 2	0.163	0.762	0.739	0.735	0.580	0.988	0.799	0.824	
I 3	0.212	0.327	0.360	0.486	0.166	0.652	0.537	–	
I 4	-0.085	0.430	0.428	0.331	0.188	0.427	0.377	–	

TABLE 7 – CORRELATION COEFFICIENTS

Independent Variable	MILL 1 Partial Regress Coeff. (Std. error)	MILL 1 Variability acct. for	MILL 2 PRC (SE)	MILL 2 VAF	MILL 3 PRC (SE)	MILL 3 VAF	MILL 4 PRC (SE)	MILL 4 VAF
A. Length	−2.011 (22.216)		−1.272 (32.455)		−9.221 (7.573)		−2.363 (5.650)	
B. Top diameter	−8.228 (11.541)		−36.717 (35.346)		−5.351 (8.396)		−4.806 (4.661)	
C. Mid girth	4.742 (5.584)	7.8%	20.465 (19.284)	66.8%	0.624 (3.071)	15.3%	2.252 (2.346)	71.0%
D. NHV	−0.059 (0.416)		−0.078 (0.829)		0.075 (0.165)		0.078 (0.092)	
Constant	−30.889		−51.925		24.190		0.246	
B. Top diameter	−8.254 (11.050)		−37.403 (28.720)		−6.331 (8.482)		−5.111 (4.484)	
C. Mid girth	4.886 (5.127)	7.7%	21.034 (11.884)	66.8%	2.089 (2.868)	7.0%	2.781 (1.925)	70.6%
D. NHV	−0.087 (0.273)		−0.107 (0.329)		−0.069 (0.117)		0.047 (0.055)	
Constant	−60.109		−55.551		7.648		−5.007	
C. Mid girth	2.826 (4.248)	3.4%	6.146 (3.372)	59.8%	0.101 (1.047)	3.7%	0.841 (0.910)	68.3%
D. NHV	−0.140 (0.258)		0.123 (0.289)		−0.045 (0.110)		0.073 (0.051)	
Constant	−83.547		−40.647		6.643		−3.662	
D. NHV	−0.025 (0.187)	0.1%	0.545 (0.191)	44.9%	−0.035 (0.042)	3.7%	0.116 (0.019)	66.7%
Constant	128.264		−5.745		7.021		1.061	

TABLE 8A - SUMMARY OF REGRESSION ANALYSIS OF LOAD TIME ON VARIOUS FACTORS

Independent Variable	MILL 1 Partial Regress Coeff. (Std. error)	MILL 1 Variability Acct. for	MILL 2 PRC (SE)	MILL 2 VAF	MILL 3 PRC (SE)	MILL 3 VAF	MILL 4 PRC (SE)	MILL 4 VAF
A. Log Length	-42.462 (68.662)		39.676 (29.008)		-12.431 (26.721)		-45.648 (16.763)	
B. Top diameter	-43.967 (35.669)	28.2%	48.406 (31.592)	82.3%	-10.329 (29.624)	12.4%	-12.303 (13.829)	90.1%
C. Mid girth	-12.944 (17.258)		-6.463 (17.236)		-0.928 (10.838)		1.106 (6.691)	
D N.H.V.	1.532 (1.285)		0.020 (0.741)		0.573 (0.583)		0.926 (0.274)	
Constant	3250.640		-108.950		51.368		60.710	
B. Top diameter	-44.510 (34.728)		69.823 (28.893)		-11.649 (28.757)		-18.196 (16.166)	
C. Mid girth	-9.908 (16.113)	25.7%	-24.200 (11.956)	77.5%	1.048 (9.724)	11.2%	11.316 (6.942)	85.2%
D. N.H.V.	0.952 (0.856)		0.938 (0.331)		0.378 (0.396)		0.337 (0.199)	
Constant	2633.823		4.162		29.068		-40.789	
C. Mid girth	-21.019 (13.914)		3.591 (4.053)		-2.611 (3.508)		4.412 (3.276)	
D. N.H.V.	0.663 (0.846)	15.5%	0.509 (0.347)	61.1%	0.424 (0.370)	10.3%	0.429 (0.183)	84.0%
Constant	2507.437		-23.660		27.220		-35.859	
D. N.H.V.	-0.198 (0.654)	0.6%	0.755 (0.204)	57.7%	0.171 (0.143)	7.3%	0.657 (0.072)	82.3%
Constant	932.057		-3.268		17.422		-11.296	

TABLE 8B - SUMMARY OF REGRESSION ANALYSIS OF MANIPULATION TIME ON VARIOUS FACTORS

Independent Variable	MILL 1 Partial Regress. Coeff. (Std. error)	MILL 1 Variability acct. for	MILL 2 PRC (SE)	MILL 2 VAF	MILL 3 PRC (SE)	MILL 3 VAF	MILL 4 PRAC (SE)	MILL 4 VAF
A. Log Length	-10.381 (15.025)		- 2.796 (9.928)		1.009 (5.938)		-8.168 (4.473)	
B. Top diameter	-12.493 (7.805)		30.111 (10.813)		-2.728 (6.583)		-1.156 (3.690)	
C. Mid girth	6.875 (3.776)	86.4%	-12.008 (5.899)	84.2%	0.039 (2.408)	9.5%	0.261 (1.858)	82.5%
D. N.H.V.	0.930 (0.281)		0.482 (0.254)		0.074 (0.130)		0.156 (0.073)	
Constant	-147.694		9.438		6.774		8.946	
B. Top diameter	-12.361 (7.631)		28.602 (8.834)		-2.621 (6.351)		-2.210 (3.902)	
C. Mid girth	6.133 (3.541)		-10.758 (3.655)		-0.122 (2.147)		2.087 (1.675)	
D. N.H.V.	1.072 (0.188)	85.9%	0.417 (0.101)	84.0%	0.090 (0.087)	9.3%	0.050 (0.048)	78.7%
Constant	3.105		1.468		8.584		-9.214	
C. Mid girth	3.047 (3.165)		0.626 (1.432)		-0.945 (0.775)		1.249 (0.769)	
D. N.H.V.	0.992 (0.193)	82.8%	0.242 (0.123)	63.1%	0.100 (0.082)	8.4%	0.061 (0.043)	78.2%
Constant	-31.993		-9.929		8.167		-8.616	
D. N.H.V.	1.116 (0.142)	81.5%	0.285 (0.070)	62.3%	0.008 (0.032)	0.4%	0.126 (0.017)	74.9%
Constant	196.414		-6.374		4.623		-1.663	

TABLE 8C - SUMMARY OF REGRESSION ANALYSIS OF CUT TIME ON VARIOUS FACTORS

Independent Variable	MILL 1 Partial Regress Coeff. (Std. error)	MILL 1 Variability acct. for	MILL 2 PRC (SE)	MILL 2 VAF	MILL 3 PRC (SE)	MILL 3 VAF	MILL 4 PRC (SE)	MILL 4 VAF
A. Log Length	52.102 (66.489)		2.557 (10.742)					
B. Top diameter	-42.847 (35.540)		19.451 (11.699)					
C. Mid girth	5.219 (16.712)	50.7%	-6.700 (6.383)	53.3%	NA		NA	
D. N.H.V.	1.730 (1.245)		0.149 (0.275)					
Constant	-282.477		-3.613					
B. Top diameter	-42.181 (33.970)		20.831 (9.543)					
C. Mid girth	1.493 (15.761)	47.9%	-7.844 (3.949)	52.9%	NA		NA	
D. N.H.V.	2.441 (0.838)		0.208 (0.109)					
Constant	474.364		3.677					
C. Mid girth	-9.036 (13.560)	41.2%	0.448 (1.286)	24.9%	NA		NA	
D. N.H.V	2.167 (0.825)		0.080 (0.110)					
Constant	354.592		-4.624					
D. N.H.V.	1.797 (0.598)	39.2%	0.111 (0.063)	23.9%	NA		NA	
Constant	-322.673		-2.081					

TABLE 8D – SUMMARY OF REGRESSION ANALYSIS OF UNLOAD TIME ON VARIOUS FACTORS

Independent Variable	MILL 1 Partial Regress Coeff. (Std. error)	MILL 1 Variability Acct. for	MILL 2 PRC (SE)	MILL 2 VAF	MILL 3 PRC (SE)	MILL 3 VAF	MILL 4 PRC (SE)	MILL 4 VAF
A. Log Length	17.087 (110.560)		86.870 (67.044)		-39.054 (56.193)		-76.349 (151.996)	
B. Top diameter	-107.711 (57.434)		90.582 (73.016)		-8.502 (62.297)		8.627 (125.391)	
C. Mid girth	4.245 (27.788)	51.7%	-5.511 (39.386)	79.2%	-10.210 (22.791)	30.9%	18.267 (63.119)	22.4%
D. N.H.V.	4.136 (2.069)		-0.321 (1.713)		2.060 (1.226)		-0.042 (2.485)	
Constant	2778.139		-251.016		116.631		1.855	
B. Top diameter	-107.493 (55.032)		137.473 (66.053)		-12.650 (61.001)		-1.230 (120.918)	
C. Mid girth	3.023 (25.534)	51.6%	-44.347 (27.332)	74.2%	-4.003 (20.626)	28.6%	35.343 (51.924)	21.1%
D. N.H.V.	4.367 (1.357)		1.689 (0.757)		1.448 (0.840)		-1.028 (1.490)	
Constant	3026.351		-3.357		46.574		-167.909	
C. Mid Girth	-23.810 (23.740)		10.371 (8.745)		-7.977 (7.414)		34.877 (23.591)	
D. N.H.V.	3.677 (1.444)	36.2%	0.845 (0.748)	60.2%	1.498 (0.782)	28.4%	-1.022 (1.317)	21.1%
Constant	2721.125		58.135		44.567		-167.575	
D. N.H.V.	2.693 (1.068)	31.2%	1.557 (0.455)	54.0%	0.724 (0.307)	23.6%	0.776 (0.521)	11.0%
Constant	936.498		0.759		14.637		26.585	

TABLE 8E - SUMMARY OF REGRESSION ANALYSIS OF TOTAL TIME ON VARIOUS FACTORS

| TIME | MILL 1 | | MILL 2 | MILL 3 | | MILL 4 | |
(Secs)	No. 1A	No. 1B	No. 1	No. 1	No. 2	No. 1	No. 2
1. Av. time pickup/flitch	77	28	15	30	25	23	25
2. Av. cutting time/flitch	165	102	60	72	91	127	94
3. Av. refeed time/flitch	253	180	86	176	132	200	158
4. Av. delay time/flitch	39	181	3	12	21	245	197
5. Av. total time/flitch	534	491	164	290	269	595	474
6. No. of flitches timed	41	50	36	22	35	22	28

TABLE 9 – COMPARISON OF AVERAGE TIMES OF OPERATIONS ON FOLLOW-UP BENCH(ES)

RELEVANT FACTOR	MILL 1	MILL 2	MILL 3	MILL 4
1. Ave. Recovery - from *Tables C and E* showing ave. NHV and % recovery on NHV (s.ft.)	0.888 x 373.5 = 332	0.495 x 482 = 249	0.586 x 416 = 246	0.425 x 557 = 237
2. Mean Total Time/log-from *Table C* - (secs)	2420	987	454	877
3. Ave. Volume of Output/hr. = $\frac{(1)}{(2)}$ - (s.ft/hr.)	493	912	1950	967
4. Ave. Volume of Output/8 hr. day-(s.ft/day) (rounded off)	4000	7300	15600	7800
5. Ave. Volume of output/240 day year (s.ft/year)	1,000,000	1,750,000	3,750,000	1,870,000
6. Actual quotas for each mill (s.ft/year)	1,050,000	2,200,000	4,500,000	1,720,000
7. Budgeted return $R(t)$ at MH and quota volume.	10500 x 5.55 x 0.8 = 46600	22000 x 5.55 x 0.5 = 61600	45000 x 5.55 x 0.5 = 124900	17200 x 5.55 x 0.5 = 48000

Note: (a) The first five factors are tabulated to indicate that the actual output volume observed during the period of investigation was in fact in accordance with the expected volume if the mill was to process its quota. A comparison of the actual sawn volumes observed (5) with the quota input volumes (6) indicates that the mills could easily meet their quota working at the observed rate of processing. (b) The calculation of $R(t)$ in (7) is given by $R(t) = $ (Quota Volume) x (Manufacturing Margin/100 sawn) x (Recovery percent) where the recovery percent is reckoned as 0.8 for Mill, and 0.5 for the other mills. Mill 1 is cutting a large proportion of heavy structural timbers, hence the high recovery

TABLE 10 - COMPARISON OF REVENUES R(t) FOR MILL OPERATION

	Mill 1	Mill 2	Mill 3	Mill 4
1. Least Cost Model				
(a) Range of replacement cycle (years)	2 – 14 +	1 – 14 +	0 – 6	1 – 8
(b) Least Cost ($)	11950–12380	16240–17760	15050–16710	19200–22160
2. Profit Maximization Model				
Range of Replacement cycle	14 +	14 +	14 +	14 +

TABLE 11 - LEAST COST AND PROFIT MAXIMIZATION MODEL RESULTS
(using three values of K and i = 0.10)

Table 10 summarises the calculations of the budgeted revenues R(t) when each mill operates at the manufacturing margin and at a certain level of quota. The purpose of some of the timings made during the study might be apparent now, since the presence of observers in any mill could have caused Hawthorne effects. The comparison of items (5) and (6) in Table 10 indicates that the mills were all working fairly close to normal speed during the time and work studies, thus giving some strength to the hypothesis that no Hawthorne effect of a negative or positive nature occurred during the study period.

Table 11 summarises the optimum replacement cycles (T) and the equivalent minimum costs (C) of these cycles of replacement for each mahcine.

The table also uses the revenue calculations from Table 10 and other observed data to calculate the optimum replacement cycle (T) and the equivalent profit (P) of using this replacement cycle, from the Profit Maximisation model. It will be seen that the replacement cycle varies somewhat from the replacement cycles given by the Least Cost Model (Items 6 and 7).

4. DISCUSSION OF RESULTS OF INITIAL STUDY

It would seem that at least four factors could affect the comparison of the headsaws:
—the *real* effect of log quality on percentage recovery.
—the *possible* effects of the quota system as in inhibitor of mill production efficiency.
—the effect of variety in log input size and volume.
—the effect of sawing accuracy on total mill operation.

(1) Research in forest management has not established any real indication of the true relationship between log quality and percentage recovery. In this study, a subjective assessment of log input to the mills suggested that log input to Mill 1 might have been of slightly higher quality than inputs to the other mills. It is considered that any measurement of revenues or costs must take the variable nature of the "log quality index" that could be applied to all mills, such as to modify the output volume measurements (and therefore the revenues).

(2)   On the other hand, the effects of the quota system are very real, and are reflected in the operations of Mills 2-4, where the Canadian headsaws are not being used to capacity. Furthermore, the observations of the queues at benches revealed that, even with the Canadian saw operating at under its rated speed, the bench-saws would not be able to cope with an increased output from the headsaw, requiring either replacement or duplication of existing benchsaws. The problem of sawmill management is to balance the cost of delays caused by an inadequate supply of flitches from the headsaw against the cost of idleness of the headsaw, plus the cost of providing intermediate flitch storage when the headsaw operates at full speed.

For this reason, the quota system can have an effect on the Canadian saw as an investment, since it inhibits its speed of operation more than it does for the Framesaw (Table 4 highlights the speed of differences).

(3)   The regression analysis summarised in Tables 7 and 8 would seem to indicate that NHV and mid girth of input logs have some effect on output and suggests that, within the range of operations observed, the optimum total time per unit output is obtained from the log with the largest volume or girth, a situation that has been noted by other workers [D.S.I.R.,1963] in softwood milling. Thus, Mill 1 with the small average NHV should be at a disadvantage with Mills 2-4.

(4)   There is no doubt (Table 6) that the Framesaw has a superior ability to flitch to dimension, and the percentage recovery is also superior. These two aspects constitute secondary benefits (in the public sector cost-effectiveness sense) that must be taken into account in any analysis. The question is—secondary benefits to whom? In this study, part of the benefit of better quality logs reverts to the private sector managing the sawmills, while part of the benefits of higher percent recoveries accrues to the public, since public forests are used to better advantage. The mechanism for imputing the cost of a social benefit in this situation is rather complex, but not completely insoluble. Given the non-existence of a proven relationship between log quality and volumetric output, these benefits cannot yet be quantified, and it would seem that the timber industry has much research to complete before the practical problems of using this form of cost-effectiveness analysis in forest management can be overcome.

It will be noted that there is no apparent evidence that flitching to dimension leads to a reduced size of flitch at the No. 1 bench. At Mill 1, where there was no transfer chain for the last 20 feet of travel from headsaw to No. 1 benches, this was a real disadvantage, since Table 4 indicates that 15% of the total time of processing a flitch was "pickup time". With suitable conveyor design, the hypothesis that flitching to dimension is a secondary benefit that leads to reduced handling at later processes might have been proved.

(5)   A summary of the foregoing is that the headsaw evaluation can *not* be considered in isolation, without involving a consideration of a number of factors that relate to secondary benefits. In fact, the consideration of the sawmill as a production line might lead to a more realistic assessment of investments in *any* piece of equipment in the mill. This particular finding is explored further in Section 5.

(6)   A brief comment is also made as to the effect of uncertainty in the measured parameters. In this pilot study, the action taken to assess the impact of varying parameters such as log size, log quality, frequency of bench breakdown etc. was to

present the results as a *range* of results rather than as single values. This aspect is discussed further in Section 5.

5.   EXTENSION OF PILOT STUDY RESULTS

Two aspects of the results seem obvious.

First, while the measure of mill efficiency used in the pilot study (viz. least cost or profit maximisation replacement time *plus* secondary benefit to private and public sectors) may not be an *optimum* measure, it is a more *relevant* measure than methods currently used, albeit a *static* model since the parameters observed in the study, as well as the process itself, have stochastic elements. [Ralph Turvey's pertinent comments at the start of this Symposium on methods of overcoming uncertainty in the process parameters, emphasise the dangers of using static cost-effectiveness models, and are germane here.] However, if the public agency was to use continuing mill studies of this type for assessing mills for quotas, a large study team would be kept busy all year, and thus the costs of mill studies would exceed the cost of thepresent *ad hoc* assessment system. It must be worthwhile considering the role of a simulation model of mill operation for the whole State, where the oeprating characteristics observed in the pilot study would be observed in every sawmill in the State, perhaps using a regional study as a first evaluating effort.

Figure 2 outlines the model flow chart in a very broad block diagram that would normally be understood by a reader with some background in O.R. methodology. At this stage, it is considered that the output of such a model of the sawmilling operations in the State (i.e. Stage III for all mills in the State, in terms of Table 1) might be, given variable mill quotas, sizes of equipment configurations—resource usage measures (in terms of percent recovery and accuracy of finished product, for example, for all mills) —saw mill utilisation measures, perhaps in terms of the standard measures used in waiting line or queuing theory (viz. percentage utilisation of each bench, queue lengths, total mill utilisation etc.) —overall State *supply* patterns, given variable demand, variable numbers of mills or policy decisions to close down certain mills or restrict quotas.

Thus the agency has the power to determine possible implications of "what-iff" situations, and this ability to predict operating results may inspire policy makers at agency and political levels to have more faith in their decisions to close down X mills or to refuse extensions of quotas to certain mills that refuse to improve their efficiency of milling scarce timber resources.

Second, while this simulation model may add strength to decisions as to sawmilling processes, there is still no comprehensive decision strategy to improve and link decision making in *all* stages depicted in Table 1. Since in any reputable system analysis one cannot isolate a part (or sub-system) of problem by neglecting its interactions with other parts (or sub-systems), it would seem that the boundaries of the pilot study must be pushed even wider to ascertain which sub-system interdependencies are important (Quade [1966] is worth studying on this topic should the reader wish to have clearly defined the role of systems analysis techniques in a PPB system).

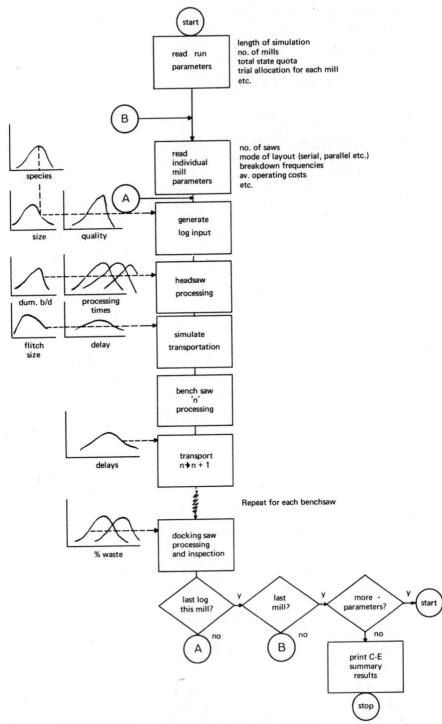

FIGURE 2 : SAWMILL SIMULATION MODEL

Figure 3 is a schematic showing the interfacing between the four stages in the forest growth and usage cycle. In proposing this schematic of a so-called comprehensive planning and decision process, one is always conscious of at least three of the fallacies of comprehensive planning alluded to by Dror [1967]. These three fallacies are: the fallacy of "maximisation of comprehensiveness" (where a planner can optimise a decision model out of existence through complicated comprehensive planning), the fallacy of "free input" (where the costs of manpower and other resources used in building the model go out of sight as comprehensiveness increases), and the fallacy of "plans as output" (where reality as to comprehensive plan *output* is ignored).

Figure 3 illustrates a number of features that may not be immediately obvious. Firstly, an attempt has been made to set up the basis for an overall systems analysis of all stages of the process, depicted in its implest form. Essentially, the series of interconnected boxes in Figure 3 are sub-system models in an overall simulation model. The forest growth-usage model of Gould and O Regan [1965] and/or of Walton [1965] (sometimes referred to as the Harvard Forest Simulator) is essentially the Stage I–II operation. With a simulator of this type, it is possible to simulate growth processes, and to incorporate the effects of bushfires, floods and other variables on the growth processes and stripping processes, and to incorporate the effects of bushfires, floods and other variables on the growth processes. The deforestation subsystem model incorporates the ability to vary parameters such as different patterns of stripping different stands of timber. Obviously, it would be possible to incorporate a mechanism to observe different cost-effectiveness ratios for different variations of all relevant parameters. Since the real-time growth patterns are 50–100 years, the computer-based simulation model is a powerful tool in policymaking that allows compressions of the time span of policy decisions on "what-if" situations such as whether to grow new stands, where to locate them likely outputs given these inputs and different stripping patterns etc....

The output from the Stage II model is not strictly input to the milling model because of the regeneration time of 50–100 years. No policy maker is going to try to predict whether timber will be in use in 50 years, let alone what the specific demand will be. Strictly the interface between the Stage II–III models might therefore be a *data bank* on existing stands, which then is used as input to the Stage III model.

Secondly, the simulation model in Phase III is obviously the model depicted in Figure 2. Given perhaps a computer-based data bank on forest inventory as its input, the model simulates the effects of variable numbers of mills, equipment usage, labor force availability, log input quantity and quality and mill efficiency to produce an output that is useable in cost-effectiveness analyses of the effects of variations in input quota, mill sizes and equipment configurations.

Finally, this output of finished volumes of sawn and other products becomes input, with product demand statistics, into a transportation simulator and a market simulator similar to the Balderson and Hoggett [1963] or Jones [1960] models. The output of the model is various market strategies, given certain transportation modes and market locations. The effects of variations in distribution patterns, transportation methods and curing patterns would be built into such a model.

Without emphasising the fact much further, the role of the data bank as the input for Stages III–IV is important, and in many areas of the world, data on forest stands are

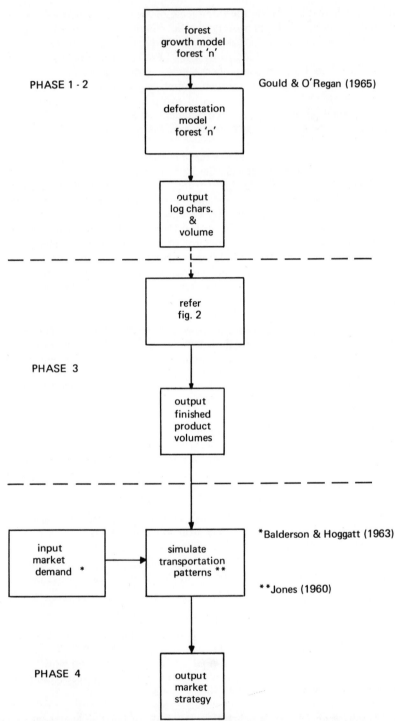

FIGURE 3 : A FOREST GROWTH-USAGE MODEL

being acquired from sample plots and whole stands for computer storage and subsequent retrieval. The high cost of this method of data storage should be considered in the light of its importance to the model proposed, and to the value of the model as a component, along with political and other components, of the overall public policymaking process.

6. CONCLUSIONS

As does Blumstein's paper given in this Symposium, this paper presented a case study of the power of systems analysis in moving from a complicated policymaking environment to a study of subsystems making up the whole system. The role of systems analysis in moving from a complicated policymaking environment to a study of subsystems making up the whole system. The role of systems analysis as a means of viewing the relationships of various stages in the forest growth-use-regeneration-marketing cycles has been proposed.

The role of *specific* techniques of systems analysis, such as cost-effectiveness analysis and simulation, has been emphasised within the framework of a model that attempts to distinguish *operating* planning (Stages III–IV) from policymaking and long range planning (Stages I–II). Any one technique is seen as complementary to and not necessarily replacing other techniques used for analysis.

At this stage, this paper does not suggest a definite mechanism for handling the political factors related to public policy, but the recent work of Dror, Quade, Schultze and others gives some indication of how the political and budgetary processes might interact. The necessity of moving from a narrow PPB–systems analysis syndrome to a broader analysis of public policymaking, as reflected in this paper, has been noted by Dror in a recent analysis [Dror, 1969b].

Finally, the unique relationship of the parties involved in the pilot study discussed herein and the existence of an accessible computer-based data bank is seen at this stage as a prerequisite to further development of parts of the total model suggested. It is emphasised, in conclusion, that while this model of forest growth and utilisation may provide a convenient theoretical framework for policy analysis, such refinement of the various subsystem elements and linkages is required before one could claim that a discrete policy issue could be fully analysed meaningfully at this stage.

7. ACKNOWLEDGEMENTS

The typing expertise and patience of Miss Shirley Wenger (Secretary, Faculty of Administration, University of Saskatchewan, Regina) and Barbara A. Gross has been much appreciated in the preparation of the paper, as have been the comments of academic and government colleagues on three continents. The residual errors still remaining are, of course, mine.

BIBLIOGRAPHY

1. Anderson, W.C. [1954] *Pine Sawmilling Costs by Log Size*: Station Paper No. 43, Southeastern Forest Experimental Station, Asheville, North Carolina–June 1954.

2. Balderson, F.E. and Hoggatt, A.C. [1962] *Simulation of Market Processes*: Institute of Business and Economic Research, University of California, Berkeley, California IBER Special Publications No.1.

3. Bentley, W.R. and Teeguarden [1965] "Forest Maturity Analysis"—*Forest Science* 11, 1: 76-87.

4. Bethel, J. and Harrell, C. [1957] "The Application of Linear Programming to Plywood Production and Distribution"—*Forest Products Journal* 7, 7(July): 221-227.

5. Broido, A., McConnen, R.J. and O'Regan, W.G. [1965] "Some Operations Research Applications in the Conservation of Wildland Resources" - *Man. Science* 11, 9, Series A (July) 802-813.

6. Courtu, A.J. and Ellertson, B.W. [1960] "Application of Linear Programming Procedures to Farm Forestry Problems" —: *Proceedings of Forest Management Control Conference,* Department of Forestry and Conservation, Purdue University, (Indiana). pp.177-190.

7. Curtis, F.H. [1962] "Linear Programming in the Management of a Forest Property"—*J.For.* 60, 9: 611-616.

8. Dean, J. [1954] "Measuring the Productivity of Capital"—*Harvard Business Review.* Jan/Feb: 120-130.

9. Dror, Y. [1967] —Comprehensive Planning: Common Fallacies Versus Preferred Features—*In* Van Schlagen F. 9ed.) *Essays in Honour of Professor Jac. P. Thijsse.* The Hague, Mouton Co., pp.85-99.

10. Dror, Y. [1968] *Public Policymaking Reexamined*: San Francisco, Chandler Publishing Company.

11. Dror, Y. [1969a] *The Prediction of Political Feasibility*—Rand Corporation Publication P-4044, (April 1969). 19pp....

12. Dror, y. [1969b] *Systems Analysis for Development Decisions: Applicability, Feasibility, Effectiveness and Efficiency*—Rand Corporation Publication P-4159 (August 1969), 27pp....

13. D.S.I.R. [1963] *Sawmill Study—Work Cycle Times on a Rackbench*: D.S.I.R. Special Report No.17, H.M.S.O., London.

14. Due, J.F., [1968] *Government Finance: Economics of the Public Sector*: Irwin, Homewood (Illinois).

15. Eckstein, O. [1958] *Water Resource Development: The Economics of Project Evaluation*: Harvard University Press, Cambridge.

16. Eilon S., King J. and Hutchinson, D. [1966] "A Study in Equipment Replacement"—*Oper. Res. Quart.* 17: 59-71.

17. Fetter, R.B. and Goodman, T.P. [1957] "An Equipment Investment Analog"—*Ops.Res.* 5, 657-669.

18. Hinrichs, H. and Taylor, G.M. [1969] *Program Budgeting and Benefit-Cost Analysis—Cases, Text and Readings*: Goodyear Publishing Co., California. pp258-270.

19. Hunt,G. [1956] "Sequential Arrays of Waiting Lines" *Ops.Res.* (Dec.) 674-683.

20. Gould, E.M. and O'Regan, W.G. [1965] "Simulation—A Step Towards Better Forest Planning": *Harvard Forest Papers No.13*: 86pp....

21. Jackson, N.D. and Smith, G.W. [1961] "Linear Programming in Lumber Production"—*Forest Products Journal* (June) 272-274.

22. Jones, T.A. [1968] "Linear Programming Applied to a Wood Supply Problem"— in: *Proceedings of Forest Management Control Conference, Department of Forestry and Conservation, Purdue University (Indiana)*: 191-207.

23. Loucks, D.P. [1964] "The Development of the Optimal Program for Sustained Yield Measurement"—*J.For.* 62, 7: 485-499.

24. Machol, R.E. [1960] "A Demonstration of Linear Programming"—in: *Proceedings of Forest Management Control Conference, Department of Forestry and Conservation, Purdue University (Indiana)*: 168-176.

25. Mack, R. and Myers, S. "Outdoor Recreation" in: Dorfman, R. [1965] *Measuring Benefits of Government Investments*: Brookings Institution, Washington, D.C. pp. 71-116.

26. McKean, R. [1959] *Efficiency in Government Through Systems Analysis*: Wiley, New York.

27. Newnham, R.M. and Smith, J.H. [1964] "Development and Testing of Stand Models for Douglas Fir and Lodgepole Pine"—*For.Chron.*40:4.

28. Page, M.W. [1962] *Studies of Equipment and Practices Employed in the Sawmilling of Jarrah (First Report)*: C.S.I.R.O. Project U.9., Experiment U.9/21, Laboratory Report No.85.

29. Peston, M.H. [1968] "Reflections on Public Authority Investment" in Prest, A.R. [1968]: *Public Sector Economics*: Manchester Univ. Press, Manchester, pp.133-137.

30. Quade, E. [1966] *Systems Analysis Technique for Planning-Programming-Budgeting*, Rand Report P-3322, March, 31 pp.

31. Row, C., Fasick, C. and Guttenberg, S. [1965]: *Improving Sawmill Profits through Operations Research*: U.S. Forest Service Research Paper SO 20, 26pp. illus.

32. Schultze, C. [1968] *The Politics and Economics of Public Spending*, Washington, Brookings Institution.

33. Smith and Harrell, C. [1961] "Linear Programming in Log Production", *Forest Products Journal* (January), 8-11.

34. Vassilatou-Thanopoulos, E. [1965] *Financial Analysis Techniques for Equipment Replacement Decisions*, New York, National Association of Accountants, Research Monograph No.1, (Mayl), 67pp.

35. Walton, G. [1965] *A Study to Develop a Computer Program for Forest Management Simulation*, unpublished thesis submitted for degree of Master of Forest Sciences, Harvard University, June.

36. Weisbrod, B. [1965] Preventing High School Dropouts, *In* Dorfman, R. (ed.) [1965], *op.cit.* , p.117-171

EVALUATION OF RURAL RECONSTRUCTION PROJECTS WITH THE AID OF A MODEL OF REGIONAL ECONOMIC GROWTH

L.J. Locht

1. INTRODUCTION

At the Institute for Land and Water Management Research in Wageningen (ICW) a method of economic evaluation of rural reconstruction projects is in preparation for the Netherlands Government Service for Land and Water Use. The main lines of this method will be treated below, some comments on differences with current thought will be added. The author is well aware of a lack of scholarly thoroughness on many issues involved.

The rural reconstruction projects concerned cover an earmarked region and consist of a proposal for coherent investments in land, water and buildings, to pull agriculture and recreation. Claims on the land and water resources for main roads and waterways, extension of towns and nature conservancies enter the projects as data, though open to negotiations on design and other details. There are many of these projects in the Netherlands. The investment amounts to some $10.000 per agricultural worker in such a project region.

The method of selection now is use was published ten years ago. A description in English is given in Land Reclamation and Improvement [1960]. However useful that method is, there were critics from the onset. Preparations for a new technique started some eight years ago. At that time the author published the essence of his proposal [Locht 1962]. Now many partial studies have been completed, but the method as a whole is only applicated in retrospective calculations.

2. FRAMEWORK OF THE CALCULATION FOR AGRICULTURE

First and foremost the calculation with regard to agriculture will be treated and that with the aid of the inserted scheme. In the head of this diagram the disciplines and the board concerned are given, in the frames the involved magnitudes. If the magnitudes enter as data-exogenes—the frames are square, if they are consequences-endogenes—the frames are circular. Some of the exogenes are the instruments of the agency concerned. The relations between the magnitudes are indicated with arrows. The frames and arrows are plotted in the matching discipline or board column.

After arguing on one or two features of this scheme under 2.1 and 2.2, the steps in the calculation will be treated one by one under 3, 4, 5 and 6 citing some examples of the researches performed. This will be done proceeding from the right to the left of the diagram. This sequence is preferred because it permits to elaborate on the problem posed to each research step before treating its solution.

2.1 Stepwise working procedure

A feature of the procedure is its stepwise character, e.g. reallotment → scale of lots, in the first step; change of scale of lots → shift in the vector of claims on labour, in the

completed or in execution (771,470 ha)
applied for (1289,600 ha)

0 10 20 30 40 50 km

Figure 1   Map of the areas involved in rural reconstruction in The Netherlands
(1–1–1968)

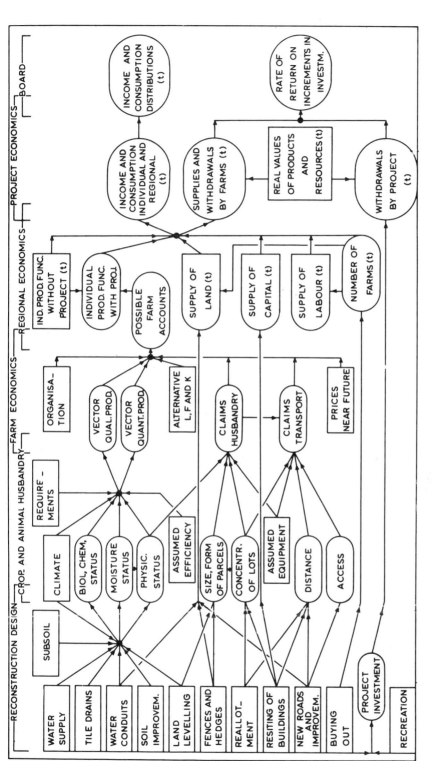

Figure 2   Diagram of the calculation procedure

second step; changes of vector → shift in the production function, in the third; etcetera. Another sequence is: water supply → groundwater table → moisture status → crop yield as a shift of the production functions. Thus the procedure of solving the model to the exogene **variables is** refuted and with that an uninterrupted computer program as well, at least for some time to come. The stepwise procedure is advocated because:

—the system is so large that otherwise at best only very large computers would meet its requirements; those who propose a closed computation—e.g. Hufschmidt [1966]—seem to be tempted to omit important aspects,

—each researcher solves his own problems with his own techniques, be it optimalization, simulation or estimation. He checks as an expert the results in magnitudes of his own discipline.

—research in each segment is autonomous as usual. The project economist only handles a modest step of his own. His role as the spider in his web seems to have no chance in this case.

As a consequence the scheme is also a scheme for the distribution of tasks over the researchers. In first instance the separate research steps are run simultaneously: each step is not built on the results of its preliminary steps, but uses possible levels of its input variables. The results of a step are functions, graphs or tables. E.g. the farm economist starts with a range of possible vectors of claims and finishes with farm accounts. Of course there are instances where a research group handles more than one step. In that case the computations may run ininterrupted over this range.

2.2   Model of economic growth

A growth pattern is not an integral part of current benefit-cost approach and that because of the assumed competitive model. At best it appears as an amendment, or as an informational side line for economically underdeveloped nations; e.g. Marglin's contribution to the well-known Harvard Water Program [1962]. Where Marglin treats the selection of investment for India [1967] he does not introduce a growth model either. He seems to take the time streams of benefits and costs as data.

A full drawn justification of the use of a growth model would need a survey of the tests of the here rejected competitive model and this goes beyond the scope of this essay. An early and fundamental rejection is Gunnar Myrdals display of *cumulative causation* [1957]. As is well-known the growth's path is neglected by assuming a competitive model because in the competitive model optimalization of income leads automatically to optimalization of growth of income; this by means of changing prices, mobility of the resources labour and capital and the mobility of the demand for these resources. In the course of the prelimianry studies for the model it was found—as others have found before—that:

—income differentials of farmers are not much good at reallocating labour; granting claims for subsidies interferes,

—on many farms investments depend on savings and imitation. A reasonable productivity is only a constraint,

—marginal products of labour in agriculture are often far below current wages. In several instances those of land were higher than current rents. In this production function study only accounts of 'middle of the road' cases were used. The accounts were very detailed and accurate. The Netherlands Agricultural Economic Research Institute made the data available.

It is the author's opinion that in many regions where projects have to provide a stimulus, the competitive model does not hold at all; neither in this country nor in the U.S.A. Where it holds for the case with the project, it does not hold for the case of reference; and that by definition, because the raison d'etre of the project is that pulling is necessary.

There is nothing new in the rejection of the competitive model [for instance Eckstein, 1961; Bos, 1961; OECD, 1967]. The familiar conclusion is declining the benefit-cost approach or limiting its scope: not much would be gained by representing the involved long term consequences in an individual project appraisal. The author takes, with Bos, the stand that there are no grounds for using quite different benefits for relatively small programs on one side and all embracing investment planning on the other.

If the adaptations of the competitive model occur, they will be taken account of in the here used model of growth, just as far as they occur, and with the appropriate time

Table 1. Cobb-Douglas function applied to accounts of Dutch farms, averaged over three years; compared with application of Rasmussen to accounts of British and Irish farms (marginal productivities are calculated at arithmetic means of variables) ($R \geqslant 0.96$ in all cases)

	Netherlands* 1961/62-1963/64		Great Britain 1954/55-1957/58	Ireland 1955/56-1957/58
	coefficients	marg. prod.	marg. prod.	marg. prod.
DAIRY FARMS				
rent	0.118(0.025)	1.5	2.6	1.3
labour	0.097(0.040)	0.28	0.6	0.3
capital	0.194(0.043)	0.18	0.16	0.34
purchases	0.583(0.024)	0.96	1.0	1.4
ARABLE FARMS				
rent	0.256(0.032)	1.65	2.1	1.2
labour	0.175(0.046)	0.4	0.8	0.8
capital	0.082(0.036)	0.10	0.20	0.15
purchases	0.436(0.053)	0.61	1.05	1.4
MIXED FARMS				
rent	0.058(0.020)	1.1	1.2	0.9
labour	0.083(0.035)	0.3	1.0	0.5
capital	0.103(0.030)	0.15	0.19	0.25
purchases	0.691(0.020)	1.06	1.0	1.5

* For dairy farms with < 1.9 labour units; arable farms with evaluated wages at < fl. 19,000; mixed farms with < 1.7 labour units. Number of farms is 216, 118 and 233 respectively.

lag: perfect mobility is a special case and merits a place only in a more general model.

3. SUPPLY TO BOARD

According to the given scheme the board is provided with:

a.   not just one project design for the region concerned, but a few proposals (I, II, etc.) with their technical content. These proposals are supposed to be the best ones (technical efficiency) at their investment levels. These are only proposals which would lead to an $^r\Delta J$ —as defined below—between about 8% to 3%; the internal rate of return over total investment being larger,

b.   the internal rate of return over the stream of the differences between I, II, etc. in output and resources over a period of 50 years $^r\Delta J$. Next an undiscounted total of the claims on resources in the construction period for each of the proposals (J_I, J_{II} , etc.) and the differences between these proposals in sequence (ΔJ).These together are a proxy of a demand curve for investment funds (as in fig. 3 below),

c.   estimates of value-added on the farm firms (businesses) in the course of time (Y_{bt}) and its regional total ($Y_{B,t}$); as also the equivalents in consumption (C_{bt} and C_{Bt}). This is the income redistribution effect and the consumption redistribution effect,

d.   an impression on the probability of the results. This is not studies systematically yet.

In some models for benefit-cost analyses and project-design, all effects are reduced to a stylish single measuring rod in money, utility or willingness to pay. To reduce the outputs b, c, d to one output it is necessary to use the consumption redistribution preference of the board and its preference with regard to risk distributions. By playing a choice-game with the board their general preferences may be measurable indeed. However, the members of that committee are not willing to play it. Besides they feel that the weight to be given to an impetus for a certain region and the 'possibility' to accept a more risky proposal, is a matter of statemanship to be decided upon at the last possible date. This is one reason for not integrating uncertainty of the results in the computations, however important that aspect is.

In current procedure the quotient of average benefits over the years and the whole of the funds procured by this particular government agency (J_g) is used. This requires that benefits are defined net of depreciation and interest over investments of the agricultural businesses (J_b) and those of other agencies. The proposed criterium—$r_{\Delta J}$—is different in that:

—all investments are treated on an equal footing. Because returns on J_b are usually larger than depreciation and interest, the old rate was always higher the more private investments were involved,

—account is taken of the timing of costs and returns. The arguments are that the calculators can make a better estimate of that timing than the board and that the proposals differ in this respect. The criterion is sensitive in particular for changes in the length of the construction period and the length of the 'adaptation' period,

—attention is focussed on the rate of return on increments in the resources used ('marginal' test). The rate for the whole of the funds used in current procedure is misleading. There was a comprehensive project in which filling of ditches gave a high rate of return, the rate of return for the project as a whole was sufficient. This project—B_3—however did not meet the 'marginal' test (see fig. 3).

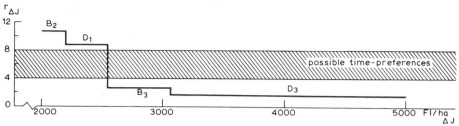

Figure 3   Testing of proposals by the project economist, using returns over increments in investment level as criterion; an application to the proposals of Van Duin et al (1963)

Resistance to the marginal test is often argued with the fact that in other fields in general only one comprehensive proposal is prepared for calculation. However that does not improve the meaning of the mean rate. 'The crying need is to increase the frequency with which increments to projects are analysed' [McKean, 1958]. Spijk [1969] pleads for designing 'alternative' plans in town and country planning in general. This is already done in Switzerland for all the projects for which a public vote is required.

An attempt will be made below to illuminate the decision procedure of the board and the use of the interal rate of return instead of the present value with a fixed discount rate.

The agency operates on a given budget, and in revision of that budget only general conditions and political forces are working. However, it is not a genuine case for capital rationing. It has to be assumed that, if spending its budget would imply that the marginal revenue falls below the minimum rate of time preference, the agency will not exhaust its budget and refuse the marginal-project. If on the other hand the budget constraint would imply that increments to projects with worthwhile revenues have to be cut off, the board will store projects. The board would have conclusive arguments—be it on general grounds—to claim a higher budget for the year, or years, to come. The internal rate of return is sufficient for these decisions. Henderson [1965] arguments that these limits for the *marginal* rate are about 3% and about 8% respectively, are accepted here.

Present values in which discount rates of 3% and 8% have been used, would meet this requirement as well. It is, however, less convenient because the demand curve has to be presented in benefit cost ratios; there will be two curves and for different projects they will start or end at different ratios.

The discussion on time preference does not only show that there are no conclusive arguments for a special rate in between 8% and 3%, but seems to point out as well that there is no unique time preference; consumers time preference varying with the rates of growth of income of the group involved [Feldstein, 1965], producers time preference with the marginal productivity of capital. This, however, does not provide an argument to use a low time preference for stimulation of declining areas in our calculation procedure, because the benefits and costs are the supplies and withdrawals of goods and services to and from the rest of the economy. These may be assumed to distribute throughout that economy and the marginal time preference for the community as a whole is then relevant. As soon as this marginal rate (long term) would be known, it could be used in this case. As will be seen in Section 4 that rate is, however, not yet available.

It is necessary to leave arbitrary decisions to the board if the calculation is sensitive for that decision. It is the internal rate of return which makes this possible.

As mentioned the board is provided with time series of consumption distributions (C_{bt}). Some project plans will be refuted by the board because some—up to now not defined—target will not be reached within a certain period. These will often be the project plans of a small scale. The target may be a grow rate of 4% of the mean income, being the target for the economy as a whole.

After the scheme will have been used for some years it may be tried to derive from the actual decisions of the board a curve for weights on redistribution. This curve is supposed to be sloping downward with the level of C (or Y) attained and with the length of period. In this last case the different time preferences are relevant indeed.

4.   TASK OF THE PROJECT ECONOMIST

According to the given scheme the project economist has to compute the internal rate of return over differences between successive proposals and to select a few proposals for transmitting to the board. He received data on the development in the region and the effort involved in the project for a number of comprehensive proposals for investment as they are chosen by the designers. He introduces the value component.

The project economist fills in—in principle—a simple table for each of the proposals (table 2).

Table 2. Net supplies or withdrawals from other sectors by the farms concerned

Kind	Time in years				
	1	2	...	...	50
Output (O, p_O)	.	.			
Labour (L, p_L)	.	.			
Accumulated Savings (S)	.	.			
Land (F, p_F)	.	.			
Non factor input (I, p_I)	.	.			
$\triangle$ national income (Y. p_Y)	Σ	Σ	$\overline{\cdot}..$	...	Σ

The components of this table are drawn from the well-known equations $(O-I) p_i = Y. p_Y$ and $Y. p_Y = (L + \dot{S} + F) p_i$, where p are the prices. The addition to national income Y_R may be computed with $\Delta O_r - \Delta I_r$ providing for the addition to Y_R in the sector-region r, and $\Delta L_{R-r} + \Delta S_{R-r} + \Delta F_{R-r}$ providing for the addition to Y_R in the other sector-regions of the country. The table does not therefore refer to the resources used on the farms, but to their supplies and withdrawals to and from other sectors. The differences are that in the last case:
—resources which are pushed out of agriculture but stay unemployed are not included (this refers especially to labour and land);
—resources which are procured by way of the project are not included either (this refers to savings and land). It is for this reason that the magnitude savings is used instead of capital; the deliveries of capital goods to the farms are not meant. The

withdrawal of savings is equal to the value of the deliveries of capital less the farmers own savings.

The quantity component of each cell is supplied by the regional analysis, and is multiplied by the value component, of which the project economist has to derive an estimate. He assumes that the resources distribute throughout the national economy and therefore makes use of national data. For The Netherlands a medium range national plan is already available [Centraal Planbureau, 1966]. This provides the value component for some years which, however, cover at most only the period of construction. The building of models for long range planning receives much attention nowadays in Europe [e.g. E.E.C., 1960]. As soon as these plans are turned out these models may be used to derive the production value of L and S in the course of time. The latter would be the time preference in production. For the time being crude estimates from trend extrapolations are used for values O, I and L. For S inserting of a value is avoided, it is incorporated in the internal rate of return.

An analogous table is produced for the net supplies and withdrawals by the governmental agencies concerned. Its content is mainly the funds for investment and the costs for maintenance of the project proper. The quantities are supplied by the project designers, the prices may be shadow prices but are mostly actual prices in the near future in our case. It is essential that maintenance, reinvestment or liquidation, providing the foreseen operation over a uniform and long period—here 50 years— are included.

The streams of benefits and costs in 'cash flows' are added for each proposal. Then the differences between successive proposals are figured out. For the proposals as such and for the differences, the internal rate of return is computed with the well-known formula. The mere entering of re-investments into the computations causes negative cash flows. The experience is that the multiplicity of solutions is not of practical significance in the iterative procedure of the electronic computer. This could be expected [Wright, 1964].

The results are passed on to the designer:
—the proposals which do not meet the 3% requirement, as refuted
—those which are followed by other proposals with higher 'marginal' rates, as inefficient
—those with a marginal rate amply above 8%, for testing a possible intensification of the effort
—those with marginal rates between 8% and 3%, for more details.

Most of the procedure is of course also valid in retrospective calculations. The author performed a calculation for the region Waarland which was retrospective over 10 years and prospective over 40 years. Most the data were drawn from accounts of the individual farms. The reference development was deduced from data on farms in a nearby region. The internal rate of return over the whole investment showed up to be about 8% [Locht, 1968]. This was a case where good results were evident: small holdings were involved, the fields could only be reached by boat, cabbage (which has a negative income elasticity in this country) was cultivated in particular. Important aspects of the reconstructions were reclamation of land (20%) and water discharge, which led the way to the cultivation of tulips and the like.

It is experienced that differences in supplies of L, S and F between proposals are often small. A typical case of a good project is therefore one that attains a good—real—value of O, which would deteriorate without the project. These projects attain a fundamental change in production, mostly to horticulture, ornamental nurseries, meat production.

Aside from economic growth and income redistribution, also for agriculture other objectives are sometimes stipulated. This results for example in benefits from a fine scenery and in particular from leisure. For the time being these are not considered. At the Institute, Spijk [1969] developed a point system of benefits. It may be used to compile these effects and transfer them in an income equivalent.

5.   TASK OF THE REGIONAL ECONOMIST

This is an attempt to reduce the complicated process of economic growth in agriculture to a simple model 'Ce qui est simple est toujours faux, mais ce qui ne l'est pas est inutilisable', Valery). This model consists of:
—a production function on the micro-level. The Cobb-Douglas model is used in the form

$$\log (O.p_O)_{bt} = t \log (1 + \Sigma + \pi) + \lambda \log L_{bt} + \mu \log K_{bt} + \gamma \log F_{bt} + \lambda \log (I.p_I)_{bt} \qquad (1)$$

where O, L, F and I are output, labour, land and nonfactor inputs as before, K is capital, b represents the farm firm (business) and ϵ its efficiency, π the rate of growth of the price level of O. Also used is

$$\log (O_{bt}.p_O - I_{bt}.p_I) = \log (Y_{bt}.p_Y) = t \log (1 + \Sigma + \pi), \text{ etc.} \qquad (1a)$$

—a function specifying the probabilities that a business will be liquidated (2).
In general form this relation is:

$$P = f (A, Y_b, m, d, r, s, t) \qquad (2)$$

where A is the age of the farmer, m the coefficient of professional mobility of the farmers in the region, being a probability for the individual farmer, d the mortality rate, r the retreat rate, s the shift rate. P is defined for periods of 5 years. Applying P to the holdings in existence at t-5 provides the number of businesses (B_t),
—functions for the development in the course of time for each of the inputs.

The regional economist analyzes the region concerned by means of the parameters of the model as they have been without the project. Continuing with these same parameters provides an estimate of the development without the project. (In retrospective calculations, derived parameters for another region are used to check the parameter extrapolations. The results cannot be checked: experience is that in The Netherlands there are always differences between regions in that respect). Next, he inserts a new production function as derived from data of the farm economist for a case with the project and inserts also the buying-out of farms as realized in the project, this is supplied to him by the designer. Continuing with the growth model in this form provides an estimate of the development with the project.

The computations produce the workers which will be pushed out of agriculture in the course of time and their age at the moment this will happen. As also the amounts of savings and investments. These are used to estimate the supplies and withdrawals of S from the rest of the economy.

Below some more remarks on the model are made, the application is not treated here. Some experience is acquired in calculations which were partly retrospective and partly prospective. This concerns Waarland, the region mentioned above in the northwest of The Netherlands and a region in the southeast (Broekhuizen). In both regions the cropping pattern is tending to horticulture. Although many difficulties did arise, they were not refuting the model as such. Data are assembled for a dairy and fruit region in the central part of this country (Tielerwaard-West). This seems to be a more difficult case to handle.

The relative simplicity follows among other things from assuming that:
−a continuous production function on the farm level with aggregated inputs does suffice,
−the effect of the project on the rest of the economy fades away; it cannot turn back to agriculture,
−the multiplier may be omitted for the time being. Van Der Lely [1965] did research to construct an input-output table,
−prices are automomous with regard to this context (the prices are inserted in the farm economists step).

Data for the input-output relation (1) are drawn from two sources: accounts of actual farms in the region before reconstruction provided by accountants and computed

Table 3. Cobb-Douglas function applied to 31 farms in the region Broekhuizen for two periods in parallel planes ($\epsilon + \pi = 1{,}8\%$). Means over three years are used to subdue the effect of weather (R = 0.985)

	Coefficients	Mean values infl.		Marginal productivities	
		1956/58	1963/65	1956/58	1963/65
Labour	0.200 (0.043)	8 185	11 400	0.50	0.60
Tenants wealth	0.137 (0.081)	13 910	21 840	0.20	0.22
Buildings	0.011 (0.021)	11 430	21 610	0.02	0.02
Land*	0.005 (0.049)	56 740	52 340	0.02	0.03
'Imports'	0.718 (0.052)	11 890	21 650	1.25	1.14

* The value for land used here is the market price it would have after 'maximum' improvement

accounts for several production systems, provided by a farm economist as will be treated under 6. Both are still laborious tasks. It is supposed that access to the actual accounts will be simplified becuase many of the accountants involved have opted for uniform and mechanical data processing.

The results with actual accounts for mixed farms in Broekhuizen are given in table 3. For the procedure may be referred to Rasmussen [1962].

As could be expected from the small number of farms included the range of possible coefficients is rather wide; this is a drawback especially in the case of tenants wealth. Besides the function is only valid within the range of the input combination that happens to be in existence. For these reasons the same procedure is applied to computed accounts for the same situation (without the project).

From the computed accounts a function is derived valid for the situation with the project. The direct effect of the project is foremost the difference in the production function: a once and for all shift in the efficiency level and in the coefficients for the resources.

Five main problems still have to be discussed: the Cobb-Douglas model as such, its application on the microlevel, the aggregation of the inputs and the use of any continuous function and the shift in efficiency and price level.

The logical implications of the Cobb-Douglas function and the method of identification used, do meet some objections. At the Institute a conceptionally more promising function is elaborated [Visser, 1968].

For analogous problems the regional production function is sometimes used: data are aggregated over the firms and the parameters are derived from the resulting time-series. In the case treated here, however, it is important to know each farmers position (his residual in the cross-section analysis).

The basic data—whether actual or computed—are in elementary variables: tools, implements, etc. To confront demand and supply in the model, these elementary variables have to be transformed into the units of supply: capital, labour and land with a few subcategories. Up to now, this is done by simple addition of the values of the elementary variables. A conceptionally better approach is to run a programming model for the farm, with the resources as such as constraints.

In fact the data by themselves provide already on input-output relation; computation of the Cobb-Douglas function provides only for the averaging over the original data interpolation, and a method for extrapolation in time. Neither of the first two is by itself necessary with computed accounts. In some research on spacial equilibrium of production is is therefore preferred to use directly the computed accounts—after aggregation; Fahri and Vercueil [1967] for instance have their program select the best 'systeme de production'. That method was proposed for our case by the computer centre RAET at Arnhem. The efficiency of that method depends on the existence, the width and the possibility of perception of the gaps between the production systems. The systems—and with that the gaps—are what indeed is studied with linear programming. In spite of that many positions in between are possible: for instance by using an old implement, sharing one with a neighbour. Next: the gaps may be

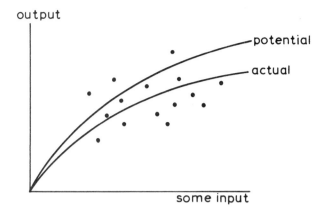

Figure 4   Schematical presentation of the derived function from actual accounts
and that from computed accounts ('potential') in parallel planes
computations. The difference between these curves is the overrating of
efficiency implied in the procedure with computed accounts

perceivable for some 10 years in the future which covers, at most, the construction
and adaptation period. Fahri can bypass this problem because he only looks ahead to
1970, in the case here interpolation is preferred be it within broadly farm-types.
Change of farm-type is only envisaged as accomplished by the project in the
construction and adaptation periods.

The results with linear programming imply a certain level of efficiency. This stems
from the standards used and from the optimalisation the program performs. An
estimate of the overrating of efficiency is derived from solving the Cobb-Douglas
function with actual data and computed data in parallel planes (both without the
project). The thus deduced factor of overrating has to be applied to the computed data
for the cases with the project. Fig. 4 may illuminate this matter.

The deduction of a quantitive relation for the probabilities that a business will be
liquidated, has taken a large part of the time of the author's group at the Institute in
the period of the preliminary studies. A statistical procedure was formulated for
deriving the components of change—death, retreat, professional mobility and
shifts—from available data [Locht and Ploeger, 1968]. These data are the registration
numbers of the farms in the region, broken down according to the age classes of 5
years of the farmers. Series of these data, with 5 years of time in between, are
compared. From these basic data, exits and entries are deduced for every age class
separately (fig. 5). To these derived data on exits for instance, a function is fitted with

	age in years	
time	20 - 25	25 - 30
1955	•―――――	•
1960	•―――――	⟶•
1965	•	⟶•

Figure 5   Schematical presentation of the deduction of data exits and entries for a
number of age classes

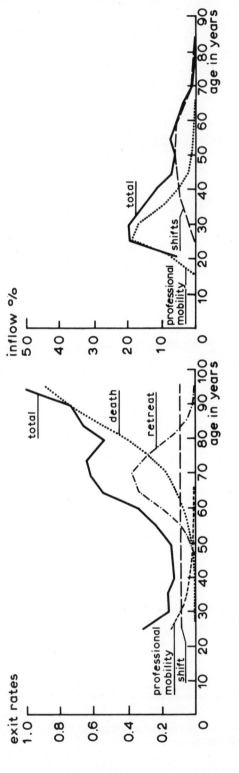

Figure 6   Exit rates (decrease in number of farmers divided by present number of farmers) and inflow (in % of total inflow) of farmers in relation to age (mean of interval, midst of period). Means of 15 agricultural areas with, in total, 6229 holdings larger than 2 ha

consists of death (using a predetermined rate), retreats (using a normal distribution with predetermined σ and deducing the parameters), professional mobility (using a log normal distribution) and shifts (using a constant rate for all age classes). Fig. 6 gives some results.

The parameters derived from this analysis are correlated with other characteristics of the region, especially with growth of income.

The labour on the farms is foremost that of the farmer himself (L_1). The outcome is therefore identical to that above. Labour of members of his family (L_2) is calculated with a trendwise changing rate (L_2/L_1). With foreign labour (L_3) the farmer is assumed to equate marginal output and wages as in the competitive model. The derived formula implies that the impetus of the project to growth of income per capita, is to some extent offset by a difference in decrease of the number of workers.

The development of capital, is the star turn in deduction of the growth rate and its content of cumulative causation. The stand taken here is that in many cases the amount of private investment depends on previous savings and that the investment opportunities do operate only in the selection of the kind of capital goods to be acquired and as a constraint which is actual only in a few cases. The main argument is that in agriculture in The Netherlands research and even knowledge of techniques, is far ahead of application. Might ever there be accumulated savings and no opportunities on a large scale, research and development would pounce upon this. This refers to the supply of opportunities. The demand for opportunities is small because:
—the use of outside accumulated savings is limited by the farmers own savings; the rate between these variables varying with age and sociological factors,
—the amount of the farmers own accumulated savings is small because in the regions where the agency wants to push agriculture, income on many farms is rather low. Besides that, savings are drained some every thirty years.

The argument on this point has to be cut short. A simple graph (fig. 7) is added as an illustration.

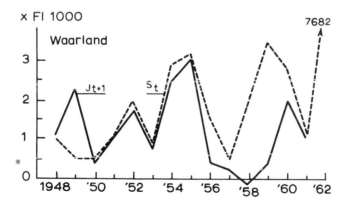

Figure 7   Course of net savings (S_t) and net investments in the following year (J_{t+1}) of farmers in Waarland

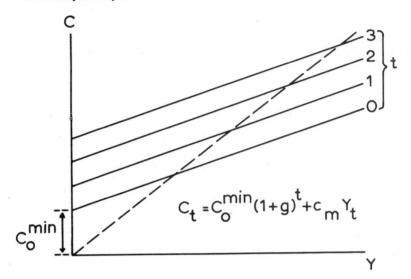

Figure 8   The applied consumption function. With this function it is assumed that minimum consumption (C^{min}) shifts every year with the rate (g); C_t depends on C^{min}, the marginal rate of consumption (c_m) and income (Y). It will be clear that the mean rate of consumption will only be constant over the years at a growth rate of Y equal to g. For the region Broekhuizen C^{min} is Fl. 3059 (prices 1962), the shift g is 1.5% and c_m, 0.43 (R=0.74, n=372): the equilibrium growth rate of income being also 1.5%. In the years of a small increase in income, the mean rate was between 70 and 75%; in the years of more rapid growth, between 63 and 66%

Using this model the effect of the project is very sensitive for the savings quote. In both regions studied this quote showed up to be very high (net savings over 20% of net income before tax).

In our model the savings function shifts every year and the marginal rate is larger than the mean. As long as the marginal rate and the shift are fixed there is only one rate of income growth for which the mean savings rate is constant (see fig. 8). A typical case of a good project is one that operates in a region where without the project the growth rate on many farms is below the equilibrium level and which starts an income growth above the equilibrium level, (it has to be remembered that the project economist inserts the real values for the products. If these real values are much below the actual prices—a heavy subsidy—a good project from the regional point of view may have still a low $r_{\Delta J}$ and be a bad project from the national point of view.

This essay does not deal with the regional growth model in full. It may therefore suffice to state about the other variables:
—that the available land on the farms depend among other things on the continuation of the other farms as in (2). The problem how to distribute the land over the remaining farms is not yet solved in a satisfactory way.
—the estimate of the efficiency of the farm is the mean efficiency and the residual in the cross-section test of (1). The yearly shift of the mean efficiency is derived from

computation with (1), fitting parallel planes to two series of data (each being an arithmetic mean over three years). Whether this development has to studied embodied, disembodied, etc., receives much attention in economics nowadays. The proposed model of growth can follow suit.

—the number of farms in the region B_t follows them (2) and the compilations O, I, L, K and F over the farms bear no problem.

6.   TASKS OF THE OTHER RESEARCH GROUPS

Research in the first three steps of the calculation procedure will only be discussed briefly. Farm economics, crop and animal husbandry and rural reconstruction design are involved.

The problem posed in the scheme to the farm economist is as mentioned to supply computed accounts. At the Institute, Meyerman [1966] and Righolt [1967] derived potentialities for income on farms under the different conditions stemming from proposals for specific projects. They used the technique of linear programming and made their computations for different land input (parametric), a few levels of labour input and a few different equipments. They used vectors for 'normal' claims on labour and capital goods in each season for each crop and vectors of claims when land and water resources would be of the different quality that the proposals for the project assume. Next they used standards for yields per hectare, for fertilizers to be applied, etc. They in fact integrated in some way all the variables for the first three steps in the calculation procedure. They used the actual prices of the past.

For the use of their results in the given scheme some minor adaptations are necessary:
—the number and selection of the programs to run has been set at 27 for each of the possible projects: three levels each for labour, capital and land. The large number of programs is thought to be warranted because the investment involved is considerable;
—in the computations for the cases with the project, prices of the near future have to be used. The prices to be used are not the values used in 4.1, but the actual prices (inclusive of grants). These are provided by a national supply and demand analysis [Agricultural Economics Research Institute, The Hague, 1967];
—instead of only an income level, an account has to be deduced; stipulating the outputs and the inputs. This bears no problems;

The computations with linear programming are indicated in fig. 2 with a dot under the heading farm economics.

The research on crop and animal husbandry has to supply vectors of claims and standards for yields. The Institute for Rationalisation of Agriculture (I.L.R.) at Wageningen published lists of such claims [Postma and Van Elderen, 1963, a revised edition is in press]. At the Institute research is performed based on land-wide inquiries. Some differentiation after size of lots, distance to farm buildings is already incorporated. More differentiation in claims according to factors which vary with the proposals of the project is object of research at the Institute for Land and Water Management Research, for instance on the effect of turning and side borders, a conspectus of this research is given in Van Den Berg, et al [1968].

The vectors for the output have to be provided, differentiated after moisture status of the soil, chloride content of the water, etc. The field is very wide; for the research performed at the Institute may be referred once more to the conspectus mentioned. Although many relations have already been provided in some form, others are still unknown. In those cases the calculation proceeds from an estimate by an expert. The computations on the plant and animal level are indicated with a dot in the matching column.

Rural reconstruction design covers drainage, reallotment, resiting of farm buildings, buying out, etc. Two kinds of data have to be delivered: data to research in husbandry and the costs of the projects as supply to the project economist.

Some of the data from the first group do need computer programs. Van Gelderen [1966] developed such a program for resiting of farmbuildings → distance and concentration of lots; a Working Party of the ICW [1968] for change in groundwater table → moisture content in areas with a microrelief. Each of the relations plotted in our diagram can already be covered in some way.

Research on the costside is mainly performed by the contractors as the Royal Dutch Heath Company and the sub-contractors. It is only partly available for general use [Heath Company, 1963]. On some aspects, such as investments in drinking water supply, telephone and electricity, cost functions are available [Spijk, 1967].

On most aspects the designer has to assume some execution technique, and to figure out the machine and labour time, next he has to apply a tariff. Because of the lack of cost functions it is impossible to build a program for the selection of design. This is the reason that in the given calculation scheme, the procedure starts with proposals of the designer. As is mentioned in Section 4, some proposals are referred back to the designer for more details or testing the scope for intensification of the effort. In this step the designer has to test his design on details with regard to costs and technical efficiency. Deducing of accounting prices from the model is envisaged.

7.   RECREATION

In the actual projects design hardly any recreational facilities whose benefits accrue to farmers or other groups for which the competitive model is not reasonably valid are incorporated. Therefore the calculation procedure envisaged for recreational facilities, has not the characteristics which take the leading part in this essay; a special regional development is not accounted for. The principle of the calculations made for recreation is that a demand curve is derived for the facility, using distance as a proxy for price. The benefits from opening up a new facility are the differences in travel costs and time, an the increase in the consumers surplus. The conceptionally interesting proposal of Klaassen [1968], to measure the benefits as the effect of recreation on the productivity of those who have recreated seems to be rather difficult to apply.

SUMMARY

An explanation is given of a method of evaluation of rural reconstruction projects as suggested to the Netherlands Governmental Service for Land and Water Use. The main feature of the method is an estimation of development in the long run with and without the project. For the project a few proposals are calculated and they are tested on the benefits of the increments in investment.

The method may seem to be a specimen of perfectionism, the funds involved, however, are large so application may be warranted. After the procedure will have been used for some time, it may show up to be unsensitive for some factors and some short-circuiting may possible by introduced.

REFERENCES

Agricultural Economics Research Institute. 1967. Supply and demand, imports and exports of selected agricultural products in The Netherlands. Forecast for 1970 and 1975. 's-Gravenhage.

Berg, C. Van Den, W.C. Visser, J. Wesseling, J.F. Bierhuizen, G.P. Wind, C. Bijkerk and E.W. Schierbeek. 1968. A decade research in land and water management 1957-1967. *Techn. Bull. ICW* 60.

Duin, R.H.A. Van, Th. J. Linthorst and J.B. Sprik. 1963. Cultuurtechnische verbeteringsplannen voor de Veenkoloniën. Rapport ICW 18.

EEC, 1960. Ramingsmethoden voor de economische ontwikkeling op lange termijn 6. Statistical Office, Brussels.

Farhi, L. et J. Vercueil. 1967. Etudes concertées pour la definition d'un programme agricole: Le modèle de prevision 1970. Article pour Economie Appliquée. *Econ. Appliquée.*

Feldstein, M.S. 1965. The derivation of social time preference rates (unpublished paper quoted by Henderson, 1965).

Gelderen, C. Van. 1966. Bepaling en gebruik van de minimale gemiddelde kavelafstand. *Landbouwk. Tijdschr.* 78.6:230-239. Misc. Repr. ICW 35.

Heath Company, Royal Dutch. 1963. Calculatie Vademecum. Arnhem.

Henderson, P.D. 1965. Notes on public investment criteria in the United Kingdom. *Bull. Oxford Univ. Inst. Econ. Statistics* 27.1:55-89.

Hufschmidt, M.M. and M.B. Fiering. 1966. *Simulation techniques for design of water-resource systems.* Harvard University Press, Cambridge.

Klaassen, L.H. 1968. *Social amenities in area economic growth.* OECD, Paris.

Land Reclamation and Improvement, International Institute for. 1960. A priority scheme for Dutch land consolidation projects. Publ. 6 Wageningen.

Lely, G. Van Der. 1965. Nacalculatie van het effect van cultuurtechnische werken. *Landbouwk. Tijdschr.* 77.22:877-884.

Locht, L.J. 1962. Het effect van cultuurtechnische investeringen in afhankelijkheid van de mobiliteit van arbeid en vermogen. *Cult. Techn. Tijdschr.* 2.4:156-168.

Locht, L.T. 1968. Calculatie van het effect van cultuurtechnische projecten, toegepast op het tuinbouwvaargebied Waarland. *Meded. Dir. Tuinb.* 31.9:358-365. Med. ICW 113.

Locht, D.J. en J. Ploeger. 1967. Een methode voor raming van de toekomstige agrarische beroepsbevolking in het bijzonder het aantal bedrijfshoofden, ten behoeve van een cultuurtechnisch plan. Nota ICW 428.

Marglin, S. A. 1962. Economic factors affecting design. In: *Design of water-resource systems*. Harvard University Press, Cambridge : 159 - 225.

Marglin, S. A. 1967. Public Investment criteria. *Studies in the economic development of India 4*. George Allen, London.

McKean, R. 1958. Efficiency in government through systems analysis with emphasis on water resources development. *Operations Res. Soc. Publ. 3*. John Wiley, New York.

Meijerman, G.C. 1966. Cultuurtechnische factoren en ontwikkelingsmogelijkheden voor veenkoloniale bedrijven. V.L.O. 686. Pudoc, Wageningen.

Myrdal, G. 1957. *Economic theory and under-developed regions* Gerald Duckworth, London.

OECD. 1967, Quantitative models as an aid to development assistance policy. Expert group on the use of analytical techniques, Paris.

OEEC. 1960. Regional Economic Planning. Techniques of analysis for less developed area. *Proceedings Conference on Regional Economic Planning*, Paris.

Planbureau, Centraal. 1966. De Nederlandse economie in 1970. Staatsuitgeverij, 's-Gravenhage.

Postma, G. en E. Van Elderen. 1963. Arbeidsbegroting met behulp van taaktijden. Publ. ILR 70.

Rasmussen, K. 1962. *Production function analyses of British and Irish farm accounts*. Univ. Nottingham.

Righolt, J.W. 1967. Bedrijfseconomische aspecten van de landindeling in het veenweidegebied. *Landbouwk. Tijdschr.* 79.8:262-268. Med. ICW 102.

Spijk, P. 1967. Invloed van de situering van boerderijen op de investeringen in openbare nutsvoorzieningen. *De Ingenieur* 67.7:1-9. Misc. Repr. ICW 41.

Spijk, P. 1967. Gedachten over de wekwijze ten aanzien van landinrichtingsplannen: alternatieven en beoordelingsaspecten. (in press).

Visser, W.C. 1968. Some research techniques for multivariate land improvement problems. In: *A decade research in land and water management 1957-1967*. Techn. Bull. ICW 60.

Working Party of ICW. 1968. Determination of the optimum combination of water management systems in areas with a microrelief. Techn. Bull. ICW 56.

Wright, J.F. 1964. The marginal efficiency of capital. *Oxford Econ. Papers*.

COST-BENEFIT ANALYSIS FOR WATER RESOURCE PLANNING IN ONTARIO

Donald J. Clough

1. INTRODUCTION

The problems of cost-benefit analysis discussed in this paper related specifically to the author's experiences in river system planning in Ontario, [1 to 8] and are circumscribed by four important sets of conditions:

(1) The financing of water resource development projects is shared by federal, provincial and municipal governments, according to the terms of a number of different statutes and conventions, under the administration of a number of government departments which espouse a variety of objectives and policies.

(2) A number of professional associations, private groups and public organizations indirectly enter into the decision-making processes along with the government departments and political representatives. The various agencies all have different sets of objectives, measures of value, and powers to influence and to impose legal constraints.

(3) Existing theories and models for the measurement of economic values are elaborate composites of both static and dynamic models from the fields of engineering, mathematical statistics, operations research and economics, incorporating both discrete and continuous variables, deterministic and random variables, unconstrained and constrained functions of variables, complicated transformations and concepts based on weak and sometimes obscure foundations ("concepts without primitives"). State-of-the-art utility and social welfare theories are not practically useful, and equilibrium economic theories are not valid. State-of-the-art theories and models for benefit-cost analysis are inadequate, but evidently necessary expedients for decision-making.

(4) Communication and agreement among professionals is difficult to achieve. Analysts of different schools or professional training are committed to the use of different theories and models, and they themselves participate in the decision-making processes as pressure groups with their own objectives and measures of value. Engineers, economists, operations researchers, mathematicians, geographers, and others involved in analysis and review, either as consultants or as government staff specialists, hold different points of view about the relevance and validity of each other's methods of analysis. Few individual analysts and few organized groups have broad enough professional competence to integrate and assess the contributions of all the disciplines involved.

This paper deals with some of the problems of benefit-cost analysis that arise out of the four sets of conditions described above. Section 2 gives a brief description of the Ontario setting, emphasizing the role of the local Conservation Authorities in initiating multi-purpose water resource plans for the river systems of Ontario, but suggesting the multi-agency involvement in decision processes. Section 3 focuses on the identification of agencies involved, the objectives of the agencies, the alternative plans by which objectives are achieved, and the sets of primitive variables that enter into the analysis (e.g., the primitive variables of the underlying models of hydro-meteorology, bio-chemistry, mathematical statistics, agriculture, engineering, and so on). Section 4 discusses monetary and non-monetary measures of value and focuses attention on the identification of such measures according to agencies, objectives, and plans for achieving the objectives. Section 5 deals with the formulation of transformation models for mapping the primitive variables into measures of value, and cites problems related to flood control, pollution abatement, and other objectives. Section 6 gives brief conclusions concerning research.

2.   THE ONTARIO SETTING

In Ontario there exist over thirty regional Conservation Authorities which have the authority under statutes of Ontario to construct works such as stream channel improvements and storage dams for such multiple purposes as flood control, water supply, pollution abatement, recreation, erosion control, fish and wildlife conservation, irrigation, drainage control, and other purposes. (Hydro-electric power developments fall within the jurisdiction of the Ontario Hydro Electric Power Commission, and stream navigation, excepting small pleasure boating, falls within the jurisdiction of the federal Deparment of Transport.) Each Conservation Authority has jurisdiction over one or more complete watershed areas or complete river systems and is organized as a quasi-political body with members appointed by all of the municipal governments within that Authority's area of jurisdiction. Financial support for capital works is obtained from federal, provincial and municipal levels of government under a number of different statutes (e.g., the Canada Water Conservation Assistance Act, the Canada Agricultural Rehabilitation and Development Act, the Ontario Conservation Authorities Act).

Although the Conservation Authorities may regulate stream flows and storages, the Ontario Water Resources Commission (O.W.R.C.) holds the legal authority to specify stream water quality standards and standards of waste treatment and water treatment. The O.W.R.C. also has the power to carry out pollution studies and to design and recommend waste treatment works. In many cases the objectives of the O.W.R.C. and the Conservation Authorities are complementary.

The initiative for multi-purpose water conservation works generally comes from a local Conservation Authority. If an Authority wishes to seek financial assistance from the senior levels of government, it will generally engage a firm of consulting engineers to prepare preliminary engineering designs and benefit-cost analyses. It will then submit its proposals and requests in the form of a "financial brief" to the appropriate government departments.

Consulting Professional Engineers are generally employed to carry out the benefit-cost analyses because questions of public safety and structural design criteria usually arise in the analyses. The Association of Professional Engineers of Ontario has legal authority to regulate design practices and professional standards and to licence engineers practising in the province.

One of the problems facing consultants at the present time is the lack of an acceptable set of rules or "guidelines" for the analysis of economic benefits. Existing guides such as the U.S. Government's "Green Book" [9], and various derivatives, are not explicit in the specification of acceptable micro-economic theories and models on which methods of measurement and analysis must be based. Professional economists often try to specify measures of benefits as though they are determined by equilibrium conditions of supply and demand in an unconstrained free market economy, but explicit, valid, and useful micro-models of such a mechanism are not specified. Existing constraints on supply and demand functions—imposed by legal statutes, political goals, health and safety standards, customs, engineering design (and cost) criteria, and not least by certain physical laws of nature—are almost universally ignored or are never specified in terms of underlying theories and models.

3. PRIMITIVE VARIABLES

Let us consider a particular river system and suppose that a number of different agencies are interested in water resource developments in the system. Each agency has a number of different objectives, and at least one of these objectives can be achieved by a number of alternative plans. Table 1 shows the structure of a multi-agency decision table which is designed to display sets of *primitive variables*, classified according to agencies, objectives and alternative plans. These primitive variables consist of *decision variables* and *response variables*, which are later transformed into measures of value.

A *plan* is roughly speaking a linguistic statement of a set of courses of action that can be taken by a number of agencies collectively. Technically, howver, a plan can be viewed simply as a label or name to identify a particular set of explicit values of parameters and variables that we call *decision variables*. For example, suppose that a plan involves the construction and operation of a specified system of dams with fixed locations and fixed operating rules. A linguistic description of the plan would incorporate the specification of a set of physical attributes of the dams, a set of resource requirements, land acquisition, engineering and construction sequence, and a set of operating rules for the system. For mathematical modelling purposes, the plan would consist of the specification of a set of values of parameters and decision variables corresponding to the factors described above (e.g., storage capacities in acre-feet, spillway capacities in cubic feet per second, park areas in acres).

It is important to note that if we want to consider alternative construction sequences or alternative operating rules for the same physical system of dams, for example, we have to consider them as distinctly different *alternative plans*. The values of the decision variables are time-dependent and it is necessary to specify a time interval over which the plan has effects. In conventional terminology such an interval is called a *planning horizon*.

An *agency* is either (a) an individual or an organized group of decision-makers who have some power to influence the choice of one of the feasible alternative plans, or (b) an individual or orgnaization that would be affected by the choice of one of the feasible alternative plans (e.g., by incurring costs or receiving benefits). For example, one might consider the following distinctly different agencies which could have particular interests (e.g., as bracketed) in water resource plans:

1. Federal government departments (transport, works, energy and resources, agriculture.
2. Provincial government departments (energy and resources, lands and forests, treasury, municipal affairs).
3. Conservation Authorities (all water conservation matters).
4. O.W.R.C. (pollution regulation).
5. Association of Professional Engineers (permissible structural design criteria).

TABLE 1 – MULTI AGENCY DECISION TABLE

		PLAN 1	PLAN 2	...	PLAN K
AGENCY 1	Objective 1	S_{111}	S_{112}	...	S_{11K}
	Objective 2	S_{121}	S_{122}	...	S_{12K}
	...	...	...	...	...
	Objective J	S_{1J1}	S_{1J2}	...	S_{1JK}
AGENCY 2	Objective 1	S_{211}	S_{212}	...	S_{21K}
	Objective 2	S_{221}	S_{222}	...	S_{22K}
	...	...	...	...	...
	Objective J	S_{2J1}	S_{2J2}	...	S_{2JK}
...	...	...	...	...	...
	...	...	...	...	...
AGENCY 1	Objective 1	S_{I11}	S_{I12}	...	S_{I1K}
	Objective 2	S_{I21}	S_{I22}	...	S_{I2K}
	...	...	...	...	...
	Objective J	S_{IJ1}	S_{IJ2}	...	S_{IJK}

S_{ijk} denotes a set of variables related to agency A_i, objective O_j and plan P_k, where $i = 1, 2, \ldots, I$ and $j = 1, 2, \ldots, J$ and $k = 1, 2, \ldots, K$.

6. Medical Association (micro-organism control and health criteria).
7. Groups of local companies (flood control, zoning bylaws, taxes).
8. Groups of farmers (flood control, irrigation, drainage, taxes).
9. Groups of city residents (flood control, water supply, pollution, taxes).
10. Groups of tourists (recreational opportunities).
11. Political parties (social-political implications).
12. Chamber of Commerce (regional industrial development).
13. Municipal Board (regulation of bond, debenture and other funding arrangements).
14. The professional consultants (design criteria, methods of analysis, private benefits of subsequent contracts).
15. Other citizens outside the river system (economic welfare and regional disparities).

It is necessary to identify the individual agencies because such a classification facilitates the specification of sets of variables that may be controlled by certain agencies or that may affect certain agencies.

An *objective* of an agency is, roughly speaking, a linguistic statement of a set of outcomes or effects that an agency wants to achieve. By itself, the statement of an objective may be rather loose and ambiguous. Technically, however, an objective is simply a label or a name to identify a particular set of *response variables* that have to be measured. Roughly speaking, such variables measure the extent to which an objective is realized if a particular plan is selected. For example, suppose that the agency is a Conservation Authority and that one of its objectives is "pollution abatement". Saying than an objection is "Pollution abatement" may be regarded simply as the name of a set of primitive variables by which pollution is measured—e.g., stream flows, low flow frequencies, dissolved oxygen concentrations, coliform organism concentrations, chemical salt concentrations, and so on. Such variables relate to natural and man-made physical processes and may be deterministic, random, discrete or continuous.

To summarize in the form of mathematical definitions, the table of primitive variables in Table 1 is subdivided into cells which correspond to particular agencies, objectives, and plans. The agencies A_i are indexed by $i = 1, 2, \ldots, I$. The objectives, O_j, which are repeated entirely for each agency, are indexed by $j = 1, 2, \ldots, J$. The alternative plans P_k are indexed by $k = 1, 2, \ldots, K$. In total there are I x J x K cells in the table. The symbol S_{ijk} in a particular cell denotes a set of primitive variables which are related to the agency A_i, the objective O_j, and the plan P_k.

For completeness in the specification of the sets of primitive variables S_{ijk} we may write:

$$S_{ijk} = \{ Y_{ijk}, X_k \}$$

where Y_{ijk} denotes a set of response variables which measure effects on agency i, relative to objective j, given plan k, and x_k denotes a set of decision variables which describe plan k. We may also write

$$Y_{ijk} = \{ y_{ijkr}; r = 1, 2, \ldots, R_{ijk} \}$$

$$X_k = \{ x_{ks}; s = 1, 2, \ldots, S_k \}$$

Here Y_{ijkr} ($r = 1, 2 \ldots R_{ijk}$) denotes one of R_{ijk} response variables contained in the set Y_{ijk}. And x_{ks} ($s = 1, 2 \ldots, S_k$) denotes one of Sk decision variables contained in the set X_k. In particular applications, one or more of the sets of variables Y_{ijk} may be empty, which simply indicates that the model does not measure the effect of plan k on agency i in relation to objective j.

4.   MEASURES OF VALUE

Table 2 shows the structure of a multi-agency decision table which is designed to display *measures of value* relative to agencies, objectives and alternative plans. The symbol M_{ijk} in a particular cell of the table denotes a measure of value for agency A_i relative to objective O_j, as a result of plan P_k. The measure of value M_{ijk} is some function of the set of primitive variables S_{ijk} shown in Table 1.

Ideally, in economic theory the measures of value would be uniquely defined agency utility functions [10]. They would also be additive utilities on the same scale of measurement, or at least transformable to a common scale, so an *aggregate utility function* or a *welfare function* could be properly defined for each plan (as a function of the primitive variables). Given the present state-of-the-art of economic analysis, however, we can only regard such aggregate utility measures as practically out of reach.

In current practice, values are defined in terms of "costs" and "benefits". The "costs" are measured in terms of monetary values according to existing state-of-the-art theories of managerial economics [12,13] and macro-economics. Such costs are usually expressed as present values of the discounted streams of all future resource costs associated with a plan. (In context, the costs may be expressed as total, average or marginal costs.)

In current practice, the "benefits" of a plan are usually classified as "tangible" and "intangible". (It seems inconsistent that costs are not similarly classified). The so-called tangible benefits are measured in monetary terms. The intangible benefits are usually described linguistically, but no monetary or other quantitative measures of value are defined. In practice the terms "tangible" and "intangible" have become synonyms for "measurable" and "non-measurable", on the assumption that the only relevant measure of value is a monetary measure.

Consider the special case in which all the benefits and costs can be measured on a common monetary scale. In this case a *monetary benefit* is simply the negative of a monetary cost. A cost to one agency may result in a saving in cost (a *benefit*) to another agency. A cost incurred by one agency for a particular kind of resource may result in a saving in cost (a *benefit*) to the same agency for another kind of resource.

For example, a municipal government may incur resource costs to construct a dyke, while private individuals and companies may subsequently realize savings in the costs of flood damages (a benefit). Similarly, a farmers' cooperative organization may incur costs to build a common water distribution and irrigation system supplied from a river storage reservoir, and they may thereby realize savings in costs of individual farm irrigation systems and other factors of production.

It is important to recognize that the classifications of monetary costs and benefits used

TABLE 2 — MULTI AGENCY MEASURES OF VALUE

		PLAN 1	PLAN 2	. . .	PLAN K
AGENCY 1	Objective 1	M_{111}	M_{112}	. . .	M_{11K}
	Objective 2	M_{121}	M_{122}	. . .	M_{12K}
	. . .	. . .	. . .	. . .	.... .
	Objective J	M_{1J1}	M_{1J2}	. . .	M_{1JK}
	TOTALS*	$\Sigma_j M_{1j1}$	$\Sigma_j M_{1j2}$	. . .	$\Sigma_j M_{1jk}$
AGENCY 2	Objective 1	M_{211}	M_{212}	. . .	M_{21K}
	Objective 2	M_{221}	M_{222}	. . .	M_{22K}
	. . .	. . .	. . .	. . .	. . .
	Objective J	M_{2J1}	M_{2J2}	. . .	M_{2JK}
	TOTALS*	$\Sigma_j M_{2j1}$	$\Sigma_j M_{2j2}$	. . .	$\Sigma_j M_{2jk}$
⋮	. . .	. . .	. . .	. . .	. . .
	. . .	. . .	. . .	. . .	. . .
	. . .	. . .	. . .	. . .	. . .
AGENCY I	Objective 1	M_{I11}	M_{I12}	. . .	M_{I1K}
	Objective 2	M_{I21}	M_{I22}	. . .	M_{I2K}
	. . .	. . .	. . .	. . .	. . .
	Objective J	M_{IJ1}	M_{IJ2}	. . .	M_{IJK}
	TOTALS*	$\Sigma_j M_{Ij1}$	$\Sigma_j M_{Ij2}$	. . .	$\Sigma_j M_{IjK}$
	TOTALS*	$\Sigma_{ij} M_{ij1}$	$\Sigma_{ij} M_{ij2}$	. . .	$\Sigma_{ij} M_{ijK}$

* TOTALS ONLY APPLY IF MEASURES ARE ADDITIVE.

M_{ijk} denotes a measure of value for agency A_i relative to objective O_j, as a result of plan P_k, where $i = 1, 2, \ldots, I$, and $j = 1, 2, \ldots, J$, and $k = 1, 2, \ldots, K$.

in current practice are based on *arbitrary accounting conventions*. In practice, the designation of costs and benefits seems to depend chiefly on the identification of the different agencies which bear the costs, and on the arbitrary classification of resources to which the costs correspond.

If all the costs and benefits are measured on a common monetary scale, the difference between monetary benefits and costs is called the *net monetary benefit*. In this case it is possible to define net monetary benefits to each of the agencies, relative to its particular objectives, produced by each of the alternative plans. Since the monetary measures are additive, it is also possible to compute total net monetary benefits for each alternative plan. It is clear, then, that an *exhaustive* tabulation of all the revenues and costs accruing to all the agencies on account of the proposed alternative plans (including the alternative of maintaining the *status quo*), would provide the basis for a complete monetary benefit-cost analysis.

One of the major problems in current practice is that benefits which cannot be measured directly in monetary terms, because an organized market and directly measurable prices for certain resources do not exist, are usually left out of the quantitative analysis. This is usually tantamount to the assignment of zero value to such omitted benefits. Even though the theory is available, mathematical models are rarely employed to generate *imputed* marginal values for omitted beenfits—e.g., as shadow prices generated by the dual formulations in mathematical programming models.[14,15] Multi-agency objectives, which may reflect "social goals", impose real constraints which lead to *constrained* elasticities of demand, *constrained* marginal products, and *constrained* marginal costs (as constrained partial derivatives). The classical theory of unconstrained equilibrium supply and demand is of no practical use in such cases.

5.   TRANSFORMATION MODELS

At the present time there exist no general models for the selection of an "optimal" plan from a very large enumerable set of alternative plans for multi-purpose river resource developments. The major limitation is specifying feasible alternative plans, such as alternative locations and sizes of dams, is the cost of obtaining basic engineering data. Generally speaking, only a small number of specified discrete alternatives can be studied within the constraints of time and cost, and someone has to make *a priori* decisions about the choice of alternatives to be included in a benefit-cost analysis. These prior decisions are usually based on a very limited iterative learning process involving "back-of-the-envelope" calculations at the first iteration, preliminary engineering calculations at the second iteration, and then a final full-scale analysis at the third iteration. In any event, the costs of data and analyses are high and the number of alternatives considered is generally limited by engineering judgment. This is an example of what Herbert A. Simon calls "bounded rationality" in specifying objectives, feasible choices, and adaptive and rational administrative behaviour. [16,17]

Current practice involves the use of a variety of sub-models related to different objectives such as flood control, water conservation and recreation. The measures of value generated by these sub-models are then assumed to be *additive*, and the validity of the assumption is often open to question. Some of the sub-models may contain optimization criteria which essentially achieve sub-optimization of the measures of value (maximizing net benefits or minimizing costs) relative to some subset of a set of primitive variables. Examples of such sub-models for the transformation of primitive variables into measures of value are discussed briefly in the following sections.

5.1   Flood Control Sub-Models

Sub-models related to flood control objectives may incorporate a number of component parts which are based on theories from various disciplines and which raise questions of accuracy, precision, relevance and validity. [18,19] A few of the many components are as follows:

(i)   *Topographic mapping*, based on aerial photography and stereoscopy models. Primitive variables—the relative elevations of contour lines—are subject to significant inaccuracies. Common inaccuracies of plus or minus two feet can lead to huge inaccuracies in estimates of potential flood damages. E.g., will a small inaccuracy mean the difference between overtopping or not overtopping a dyke? [6,8]

(ii)   *Land use surveys*, coded to topographic maps. Primitive variables include, for example, crop classification, crop rotation sequences and frequencies, crop quality grades and yields, factors of agricultural production, and changes in production functions such as irrigation-fertilizer inputs.[2,5] Theories and models include, for example, agricultural production functions based on experimental station data.[2,7]

(iii)   *Meteorological and hydrological studies* Primitive variables include rainfall intensities, durations and frequencies; soil percolation and runoff coefficients; temperature-snowmelt frequencies; stream flow velocities, volumes, elevations, frequencies, storage delays; groundwater storages; and so on. All of such primitive variables are interrelated and are functions of time. A multitude of meteorological and hydrological theories and models are employed piecemeal and may be patched together in a flow simulation model.[20] The relevance and validity of many of the underlying theories are untested.

(iv)   *Floodline mapping*. The primitive variables—flood line plots relative to stream flows—may be subject to very large inaccuracies. The flood lines are based on topographic maps and hydro-meteorological models. In general, the flood lines do not correspond to level countour map elevations because flows are dynamic and involve energy gradients. Inaccuracies arise because a good deal of engineering judgment, in the form of *ad hoc* assumptions, enters the calculation of water surface elevations through flooded areas (e.g., downhill and around street systems of a flooded residential area).

(v)   *Flood damage surveys*. Primitive variables include classifications of properties keyed to floodline maps, potential physical damages to structures and their contents[8] —furniture, equipment, inventories of goods—potential damages to crops at various stages of the planting-growing-harvesting cycle[2], potential traffic and business dislocations and delays; and so on. Theories of engineering, production and managerial economics[12] are combined, and many implicit assumptions are made about individual and corporate behaviour[21] and industrial practices (e.g., decisions on replacement of damaged furniture, equipment, and goods, versus normal cyclical replacement practices). Statistical models underlying sample surveys are sometimes employed to estimate precision, but little is done to estimate measurement accuracy.[18]

(vi) Flood routing simulations. Primitive variables include dam storages and spillway capacities, and the hydro-meteorological variables discussed above. The models simulate the effects of alternative plans on reducing flows, changing flood lines, and reducing damages, employing both deterministic and Monte Carlo simulations[2,22,23].

(vii) Flood damage probability models. The primitive variables are flood flows, corresponding flood damages, and frequencies of occurrence Probability models may involve complex stochastic processes (e.g., non-ergodic processes, non-stationary processes, correlated time series, and sometimes simple independent series). The models may be multi-variate (e.g., joint probability distributions for rainfall, snowmelt, river ice-jamming). Generally speaking, the estimation of parameters and validation of such models requires very large numbers of observations, while historical time-series observations are very small in number. As a result, almost all of the statistical analyses of peak flood frequencies used in standard practice, for example, are based on simplified models which *assume* statistically independent evens and which *assume* mathematical forms of probability distributions which can never be validated.[24] Long extrapolations from short time-series of peak flow observations are common.

(viii) Economic analysis. The primitive variables include prices, interest rates, inflation factors, various indices of economic conditions, and quantities generated as outputs of the underlying models described briefly above. The economic models which are advocated by most economists in the field[24] attempt to measure the present values of future streams of costs and flood control benefits. They incorporate a number of implicit assumptions and mathematical structures, as follows:

(a)   The economic models are static. They are based on static production functions (zero input-output time lags), static demand functions (zero time lags between dependent and independent variables), and the existence of "equilibrium" according to the equilibrium theory. But many of the primitive variables and the underlying models are dynamic. A common standard practice, which is strictly speaking invalid, involves integration of primitive variables over certain time intervals, then the application of static (time-averaged) prices to generate measures of cost and benefit.

(b)   The economic models are deterministic. But many of the underlying primitive variables are random functions and the underlying models are probabilistic (stochastic). A common standard practice, which is invalid, involves the estimation of mean values (expectations) of primitive variables first, then the application of static prices to the mean values (expectations) of primitive variables first, then the application of static prices to the mean values to obtain measures fo cost and benefit. Some fundamental questions of mathematical measurability[25] remain unexplored.

(c)   Variables in the economic models are assumed continuous, so that marginal products, marginal revenues, marginal costs and elasticities can be defined in the usual partial-derivative sense.[26] But some of the primitive variables are discrete-valued (e.g., indivisible parcels of farm land at reservoir sites, indivisible production units), so that the classical notions of marginal analysis are not valid.

(d)   Variables in the economic models are unconstrained. In the classical economic models, the concepts of marginal analysis and simple additivity can be applied. But some primitive variables and some combinations (e.g., sums) of the primitive variables are subject to real physical and institutional constraints.[27] In this case the classical notions of marginal values are invalid and would have to be replaced by concepts of constrained marginal values and constrained elasticities (constrained partial derivatives).

(e)   The economic models are often internally inconsistent. In some cases, for example, constant discount factors based on current interest rates may be specified for the transformation of future costs and benefits into proesent values. At the same time, constant future prices may be specified because of uncertainties in price forecasting. The two assumptions may be mutually inconsistent because current high interest rates generally reflect expectations of price inflation.[8] Interest rates and inflation factors are related, but standard models advocated by some economists do not account for such a relationship.

5.2   Pollution Abatement Sub-Models

Until recently there did not exist any acceptable pollution sub-models for the transformation of primitive variables into measures of value. However, Deininger[29], Loucks, Revelle and Lynn[30], and Clough and Bayer[27.28] have proposed mathematical programming models and Clough has applied a model to river systems in Ontario[7,8].

The Clough-Bayer model,[27.28] which is the most comprehensive to date, incorporates a set of water quality constraints and a non-linear objective function (an incremental cost function to be minimized over a finite time horizon). It is an approximation to reality based on a number of simplifying assumptions. The basic assumption, which is an over-simplification, is that a river system (including its tributary branches) can be treated as a closed micro-economic system. Then external diseconomies of internal pollution control decisions need not be taken into account in the model. This assumption seems plausible in a great many cases.

The model is based on the premise that there exists an agency (the O.W.R.C.) which has the technical competence to specify and codify stream water quality standards as "social goals" and which has the constitutional legal authority to lay down the standards as explicit constraints on some of the primitive variables[31] such as minimum dissolved oxygen concentrations, maximum allowable concentrations of biological oxygen demands, dissolved salts, suspended solids, coliform counts, and so on. The stream water quality constraints *must* be met one way or another.

For example, the imposed water quality constraints (agency objectives, reflecting social goals) may be met by improving the efficiencies of some of the waste treatment plants that discharge into the streams. Alternatively, the constraints may be met by building dams to impound spring runoffs and to augment stream flows and dilute waste effluents during summer low-flow periods. In practice there may be an infinity of feasible alternative combinations of stream flow augmentation and waste treatment plans that will satisfy the water quality constraints. The economic pollution abatement benefit of a storage plan (a set of dams with fixed operating rules and construction sequence) is measured as the difference between the relevant incremental costs[12,13] of optimal selections of waste treatment plant efficiencies with and without the storage plan. (It is assumed that the optimal designs would be implemented.) The economic pollution abatement benefits of a number of discrete alternative storage plans can then be measured and compared in the same way. The imputed marginal values of tightening or relaxing water quality constraints (constrained derivatives of the objective function with respect of the constraints at the optimal values) can also be examined, as suggested by Clough and Bayer[27,28].

"It should be noted that in Canada water quality standards are constitutionally the responsibility of the provincial governments. Water quality standards which are either stated explicitly or imputed by the decisions of a provincial agency such as the Ontario Water Resources Commission are indirect reflections of demands of the provincial body politic and objectives of the provincial government. In this case provincial rather than national demands and objectives dictate the constraints which force the economic variables. This raises some perplexing questions concerning the validity of any of the standard economic theories currently used in the measurement of "national" benefits of multipurpose water conservation projects."[27]

5.3   Other Sub-Models

Most of the problems of transforming primitive variables into measures of value relative to flood control and pollution abatement objectives also apply to recreation,[7,8] irrigation,[5] conservation of flora and fauna, and other objectives. Considering recreational benefits, for example, the Province of Ontario has an extensive system of Provincial Parks (Department of Lands and Forests), Conservation Authority Parks, and parks operated by other agencies (e.g., St. Lawrence Parks Commission, Department of Highways, municipalities). At the present time there are no acceptable models for the transformation of primitive variables such as population distributions, road capacities, park capacities, and "demands" for recreation into measures of value, and arbitrary measures are generally applied.[32] It appears that models restricted to facilities on a closed river system are inappropriate because net economies relative to one recreational facility seem to generate net external diseconomies relative to other facilities at other locations (on other river systems). It seems necessary to develop a mathematical programming model of the entire provincial parks system.

6.   CONCLUSIONS ABOUT RESEARCH

At the present time there seems to be a good deal of advanced academic research activity at various academic institutions, and the need for further research is well documented[33]. A single model to encompass all river system activities seems remote at the present time. Considering the multi-agency aspects of the problem, a goal-programming model[15] with a limited number of integer and continuous variables is worth some research effort.

Actual problem-solving by consultants and most of the current academic research involves the application of state-of-the-art theories, models and techniques of analysis. But what is needed at the present time is fundamental research to extend the state-of-art.

7. ACKNOWLEDGEMENTS

I am grateful to the National Research Council of Canada for its continuing support of my water resource research, and to the Ontario Department of Energy and Resources Management for its assistance in data collection.

REFERENCES

Selected Reports by Donald J. Clough to the Conservation Authorities Branch, Department of Energy and Resources Management, Province of Ontario: References 1 through 8 below.

1. *Plan for Flood Control and Water Conservation*, Metropolitan Toronto and Region Conservation Authority, Woodbridge, Ont., 1959.

2. *Flood Control and Water Conservation Brief, Parkhill Creek Watershed*, Ausable River Conservation Authority, Exeter, Ont., 1959.

3. *Flood Control and Conservation Brief, Moira River Watershed*, Moira River Conservation Authority, Cannifton, Ont., 1959.

4. "Benefit-Cost Analysis of Proposed System of Dams on the Speed and Eramosa Rivers", Appendix E, *Grand Valley Conservation Authority Report on Flood Control and Water Conservation,* Grand Valley Conservation Authority, Galt, Ont., 1965.

5. "Benefit-Cost Analysis, Lower Tillsonburg Dam and Reservoir, Big Otter Creek", Appendix E, *Engineering Report, Big Otter Creek,* Otter Creek Conservation Authority, Tillsonburg, Ont., 1965.

6. *Plan for Flood Control and Water Conservation, Grand River Watershed,* Grand River Conservation Authority, Galt, Ont., 1966.

7. *South Nation River Benefit-Cost Analysis*, South Nation Conservation Authority, Kingston, Ont., 1968.

8. *Alvinston Dam Benefit-Cost Analysis*, Sydenham Valley Conservation Authority, Strathroy, Ont., 1968.

9. Federal Inter-Agency River Basin Committee on Water Resources, *Proposed Practices for Economic Analysis of River Basin Projects*, Washington, D.C., 1950.

10. Fishburn, Peter C., *Decision and Value Theory*, John Wiley and Sons, Inc., New York, 1964.

11. Baumol, William J., *Welfare Economics and the Theory of the State* (2nd ed.), Harvard University Press, Cambridge, 1965.

12. Dean, Joel, *Managerial Economics,* Prentice-Hall, Inc., Englewood Cliffs, N.J., 1952.

13. Clough, Donald J., *Concepts in Management Science,* Prentice-Hall, Inc., Englewood Cliffs, N.J., 1963.

14. Koopmans, T.C., *Activity Analysis of Production and Allocation,* Cowles Commission for Research in Economics, Monograph No. 13, John Wiley and Sons, Inc., New York, 1951.

15. Charnes, A. and W.W. Cooper, *Management Models and Industrial Applications of Linear Programming,* Vol. I, Vol. II, John Wiley and Sons, Inc., New York, 1961.

16. Simon, Herbert A., *Administrative Behaviour* (revised), Macmillan, New York, 1956.

17. Simon, Herbert A., *Models of Man,* John Wiley and Sons, New York, 1957.

18. Clough, Donald J., "Accuracy, Precision, Relevance and Evidence in Operations Research", *CORS Journal,* vol. 4, no. 2, July, 1966, p. 97-109

19. Morgenstern, Oskar, *On The Accuracy of Economic Observations,* 2nd ed., Princeton University Press, Princeton, 1963.

20. Linsley, R.K. Jr., M.A. Kohler, and J.L.P. Paulus, *Applied Hydrology,* McGraw-Hill Book Company, Inc., New York, 1958.

21. Cyert, Richard M., and James G. March, *A Behavioural Theory of the Firm,* Prentice-Hall, Inc., Englewood Cliffs, N.J., 1963.

22. Clough, Donald J., "Measures of Value and Statistical Models in the Economic Analysis of Flood Control and Water Conservation Schemes", *E.I.C. Transactions* vol. 5, no. 1, 1961, p. 33-40.

23. Moran, P.A.P., *Theory of Storage,* Menthuen Monographs, John Wiley and Sons, Inc., New York, 1959.

24. Kneese, Allen V., *The Economics of Regional Water Quality Management,* Baltimore, 1964.

25. Burkill, J.C., *The Lebesque Integral,* Cambridge Tracts in Mathematics and Mathematical Physics, No. 40, Cambridge University Press, Cambridge, U.K., 1965.

26. Allen, R.G.D., *Mathematical Economics,* The Macmillan Company, Ltd., London, 1956.

27. Clough, Donald J., and M.B. Bayer, "Optimal Waste Treatment and Pollution Abatement Benefits on a Closed River System", *CORS Journal,* vol. 6, no. 3, Nov., 1968.

28. Clough, Donald J., and M.B. Bayer, "Optimal Waste Treatment and Pollution Abatement Benefits on a Closed River System", *Proceedings, NATO Conference*

on Applications of Mathematical Programming Techniques, Cambridge, U.K., June, 1968.

29. Deininger, R.W., *Water Quality Management: The Planning of Economically Optimal Pollution Control Systems*, Ph.D. Thesis, Northwestern University, 1965.

30. Loucks, Daniel P., Charles S. Revelle, and Walter R. Lynn, "Linear Programming Models for Water Pollution Control", *Management Science*, vol. 14, no. 4, Dec., 1967.

31. Frankel, Richard Joel, *Water Quality Management: An Engineering-Economic Model for Domestic Waste Disposal*, Ph.D. Thesis, Un. of California at Berkeley, 1965.

32. *Senate Document No. 97, 87th Congress of the U.S.A.*, "Policies, Standards, and Procedures in the Formulation, Evaluation, and Review of Plans for Use and Development of Water and Related Land Resources".
                                   and
     Letter to the President of the U.S.A. from Secretaries of Agriculture, Army, Interior, Health, Education and Welfare, June 4, 1964, transmitting *Supplement No. 1* entitled "Evaluation Standards for Primary Outdoor Recreation Benefits", adopted for use by the Departments concerned.

33. Judy, Richard W., "Economic Problems in Water Resource Management", a research position paper available from The Institute for Policy Analysis, University of Toronto.

34. Clough, Donald J., and Samuel Kotz, "On Extreme-Value Distributions, with A Special Queuing Model Application", *CORS Journal*, vol. 3, no. 2, June, 1965, p. 96-109.

35. Clough, Donald J., "An Extreme-Value Sampling Theory for Estimation of a Global Maximum", *CORS Journal*, vol. 1, no. 2, July, 1969.

SECTION 5

TRANSPORT

Chairman : **R. Cruon**
Centre Interarmées de Recherche Operationelle, France

Speakers :   J.-P. Plas
Chief Engineer, SEMA France

Edith Heurgon
Direction des Etudes Générales de la RATP, France

O. Gulbrandsen
Institute of Transport Economy, Norway

J.B. Heath
Economic Services Division, Board of Trade U.K.

APPLICATION DE LA METHODE CAPRI A LA PROGRAMMATION DES EXTENSIONS DES RESEAUX FERROVIAIRES DE LA REGIE AUTONOME DES TRANSPORTS PARISIENS

Jean-Pierre Plas
Edith Heurgon

1. INTRODUCTION

La Régie Automome des Transports Parisiens (R.A.T.P.) est le service public chargé, non seulement de la gestion des transports publics dan PARIS et sa balieue, c'est-à-dire du réseau de transports en surface (autobus) et du réseau ferré métropolitain (á l'exception des lignes de chemin de fer de banlieue gérées par la SNCF), mais encore, depuis quelques années, de la construction des lignes nouvelles et de l'aménagement des infrastructures spécifiques.

L'aménagement et l'extension des réseaux de transport de la Région parisienne constituent donc une des préoccupations principales de la R.A.T.P.

Les extensions du réseau extra-muros s'organisent actuellement autour du réseau Express Régional constitué de lignes à débit rapide et massif qui, pénétrant ou traversant Paris, doivent assurer la desserte de la banlieue. Les extensions du réseau intra-muros reposent, elles, sur les tronçons du Réseau Express Régional à l'intérieur de Paris, sur des jonctions de ce réseau avec le réseau métropolitain actuel et sur des aménagements ou raccordements des lignes de ce dernier.

Le probléme auquel nous avons limité nos travaux est celui des extensions du réseau intro-muros, en admettant que le réseau extra-muros et sa programmation étaient définis par ailleurs.

Cette limitation qui, à premiére vue, pourrait apparaitre comme arbitraire, correspond bien, en fait, à une réalité: d'une part le réseau régional peut être considéré comme drainant un certain trafic vers ou hors de Paris à partir d'un certain nombre de gares qui constituent les points d'échange entre le réseau intra-muros et le réseau extra-muros; d'autre part les futurs aménagements réalisés intra-muros venant en superposition d'un réseau dèjà extrêmement dense, voir figure 1, ne sauraient modifier sensiblement la carte des points desservis, alors que les lignes régionales s'inscrivent dans un réseau peu dense dont elles modifient considérablement la physionomie: la façon d'arborder ces deux types de problème doit donc être très différente; enfin les investissements urbains sont nettement plus onéreux que les investissement en banlieue et les décisions qui les concernent engagent beaucoup plus l'avenir de la Région Parisienne.

Ce papier sera divisé en quatre paragraphes d'inégale importance décrivant respectivement

–le problème et la procédure générale de résolution,

—le modèle d'affectation de trafic,
—le modèle de programmation,
—les résultats.

2.   LE PROBLEME ET LA PROCEDURE GENERALE DE RESOLUTION

2.1.   Définition de Schémas

Le premier travail consiste à définer les différentes possibilités de tracé des lignes express régionales à l'intérieur de Paris. Pour chaque ligne les possibilités raisonnables de jonction de gare à gare, compte tenue de la densité du réseau existant et des contraintes techniques, sont en nombre très limité. De plus des limitations techniques excluent la coexistence de certain ouvrages: par exemple, si la gare AUBER est construite pour la ligne régionale EST-OUEST, il est pratiquement impossible d'envisager la construction au même endroit d'une gare desservant une ligne régionale NORD-SUD.

De ce fait, chaque ligne régionale étant, à l'intérieur de Paris, représentée par un certain nombre de tronçons joignant deux gares il est possible d'extraire de l'ensemble des tronçons ainsi défini les sous-ensembles de tronçons compatibles entre eux et assurant un écoulement rationnel du trafic: chacun de ces sous-ensemble est appelé un schéma.

Pour fixer un ordre de grandeur, retenons qu'une quinzaine de schémas représente pratiquement l'ensemble des combinaisons de tronçons intéressantes.

C'est désormais à partir de ces schémas que les réflexions vont être conduites dans le but de comparer entre eux les différents schémas.

Pour mener à bien cette comparaison il est nécessaire de procéder à une étude détaillée de chaque schéma de façon à définir pour chacun d'eux les conditions optimales de sa réalisation, c'est-à-dire la date de mise en service de chacun des tronçons qui le composent. En effet une fois cette étude réalisée les avantages attachées à chacun des schémas sont connus et la comparaison des schémas peut s'effectuer sans difficulté. Nous nous attacherons donc à décrire comment est effectuée l'étude des conditions optimales de réalisation d'un schéma.

2.2   Définition des Avantages Attachées à un Schéma

On définit l'avantage attaché, pour une période donnée, à un tronçon comme la somme des avantages relatifs à chaque catégorie d'agent concerné, soit les voyageurs, la R.A.T.F. et la collectivité publique. L'avantage pour l'usager est lié à trois éléments:

—la dépense de transport,
—le temps de transport,
—les conditions de confort.

Pour la R.A.T.P., l'avantage est mesuré par la différence entre recettes et charges d'exploitation.
Puisque l'on mesure l'avantage global, recettes d'exploitation de la R.A.T.P. et dépenses de transport des usagers s'annulent puisque, comme nous le verrons plus loin, quelle que soit la programmation d'un schéma les mêmes trafics seront assurés.

En ce qui concerne le confort il n'existe pas actuellement de méthode permettant d'en calculer une valorisation; mais dans le cadre de cette étude ce problème a pu être éludé en admettant que, quel que soit le schéma de réseau adopté, le confort offert aux voyageurs serait le même.

L'avantage à comparer d'un programme à l'autre ou d'un schéma à l'autre résulte donc essentiellement de trois termes, valeur du temps de transport pour l'usager, charges d'exploitation du réseau et enfin dépense d'investissement. Bien entendu comme ces avantages interviendront à des dates différentes le bilan global est obtenu par actualisation à une date de référence de l'ensemble de ces avantages.

a)   Valorisation du temps

Tous les temps de trajets, calculés comme nous le verrons plus loin sont multipliés par la valeur de l'unité de temps.

Le prix du temps augmentant avec le niveau de vie, il semble admissible, en première analyse, de faire évoluer la valeur du temps comme les revenus réels par personne.

Quant à la valeur initiale retenue elle est fondée sur des enquêtes analysant le comportement des voyageurs de la région parisienne. Réalisées par l'Institut d'Aménagement et d'Urbanisme de la Région Parisienne ces enquêtes reposent sur l'idée que le comportement des voyageurs n'utilisant pas les moyens de transport les moins coûteux s'explique par la valeur qu'ils accordent à l'économie de temps et au surcroît de confort, l'un et l'autre de ces avantages pouvant faire l'objet d'une évaluation.

b)   Coûts d'investissement

Il convient de distinguer les investissements en stations ou gares et les coûts d'investissement des lignes. Ces derniers sont évalués à l'aide de coûts unitaire liés à la nature du tracé. Bien entendu ces investissements ne sont pas nécessairement ponctuels.

c)   Charges d'exploitation

Pour un tronçon donné, les coûts d'exploitation sont calculés proportionnellement au trafic assuré et à la longueur du tronçon.

2.3   Mesure du Trafic

a)   Il est nécessaire de pouvoir associer à tout réseau, défini par un schéma dont tout ou partie des tronçons a été construit, la répartition du trafic à l'intérieur de ce réseau, compte tenue de la demande de transport qui se manifeste.

Cette demande de transport est définie par des matrices de trafic dont l'élément d'indice i, j indique le nombre de voyageurs désirant se rendre de la station i à la station j.

Deux matrices présentent un intérêt particulier:

—la matrice du trafic à l'heure de pointe qui permet l'évalutation des flux de voyageurs sur les diverses lignes du réseau ou dans les couloirs de correspondance.

—la matrice du trafix total journalier qui autorise les calculs des bilans économiques pour les usagers.

b)   Ces matrices de trafic résultent de la mise en oeuvre de modèles d'étude des migrations alternantes, modèles qui permettent de déterminer les trafics Paris-Paris, Paris-Banlieue et Banlieue-Paris.

Ces modèles mis en oeuvre pour divers horizons, 1975, 1985,....., permettent donc de prévoir l'évolution du trafic.

Notons que la prise en compte de ces matrices néglige évidemment l'effet induit par les modifications apportées progressivement au réseau qui simultanément accroissent le trafic et modifient l'affectation ont montré que 40% des voyageurs migrants choisissent leurs déplacements intra-muros abstraction faite de la distance et seulement en fonction des lieux d'emploi.

c)   Reste alors à déterminer la répartition du trafic en fonction du réseau, c'est-à-dire à choisir les itinéraires qu'emprunteront les voyageurs pour se rendre d'une origine i à une destination j.

Nous décrivons plus loin les méthodes et programmes mis au point par la R.A.T.P. pour effectuer cette répartition que, effectuée d'une part pour la situation de référence, c'est-à-dire le réseau actuel, d'autre part pour la situation définie par le schéma étudié, met en évidence les changements d'itinéraires et les gains de temps des usagers sur chaque couple origine-destination.

2.4   Programmation des Extensions du Réseau

La programmation des extensions du réseau peut alors être réalisée: elle consiste à déterminer la date de construction de chacun des tronçons retenu dans le schéma éludié, de façon à rendre maximal l'avantage global que retirera la collectivité de la réalisation de ces investissements.

La difficulté du choix de ce programme, provient de ce que les différents investissements du programme, c'est-à-dire les différents tronçons ne peuvent pas çetre étudiés indépendamment les uns des autres. En effet:

1.   L'avantage lié à la réalisation d'un tronçon dépend de la réalisation d'autres tronçons, dès lors qu'un trajet utilise plusieurs tronçons.

2.   Les décisions de mise en service des divers tronçons doivent être telles que la répartition des coûts d'investissement respecte des enveloppes budgétaires quinquennales déterminées à l'avance.

3.   Il convient de respecter une certaine régularité dans le volume des travaux: en effet les travaux souterrains dans Paris nécessitent un équipement particulier et correspondent à un marché étroit; aussi est-il souhaitable d'assurer une certaine continuité à ces travaux.

En choisissant comme variable de décision la date de réalisation de chacun des tronçons, les contraintes du problème et le calcul des avantages se font à l'aide d'équations ou d'inéquations linéaires. Mais les variables de décision du problème ne sont pas continues puisque les décisions concernant un tronçon donné se prennent par tout our rien. Nous verrons plus loin comment la formulation exacte de ce problème s'apparente étroitement aux problèmes classiques de choix d'investissement; c'est pourquoi la méthode CAPRI mise au point par la SEMA en collaboration avec an certain nombre d'entreprises francaises, dont la R.A.T.P., a été retenue pour résoudre le problème.

3. LE MODELE D'AFFECTATION DE TRAFIC

La Régie Autonome des Transports Parisines a mis au point un ensemble de méthodes et de programmes destinés à évaluer les effets à court terme d'un simple remodelage du réseau ferroviaire urbain. Pareille étude exige en effet toute une série d'operations:

—la détermination systématique, pour tout couple de stations (35,000 couples environ), des chemins de temps généralisés minimaux dans la situation de référence comme dans la situation modifiée.

—la comparaison entre eux de ces temps, le calcul de leur différence si elle n'est pas nulle,

—L'inscription des itinéraires (plusieurs milliers) avant et après modification.

—ces résultats, joints à des matrices de trafic, permettent d'établir un bilan économique pour les usagers ainsi qu'une estimation des bariations de charge, à l'heure de pointe, des lignes et couloirs de correspondance concernés.

Ces procédures ne deviennent opérationnelles que moyennant plusieurs hypothèses:

1. *Affection par tout ou rien*

Le choix d'un ininéraire par les voyageurs est motivé par un certain nombre d'éléments:

a)   la durée du parcours à effectuer en train,
b)   le nombre et la longueur des ruptures de charge,
c)   la charge des trains,
d)   les attentes dans les couloirs de correspondance et sur les quais,
e)   le confort.

Pur le calcul du *temps généralisé* d'un déplacement, nous adoptons une formule linéaire simple tenant compte des facteurs a, b, d.

On convient donc d'affecter tout le trafic entre deux stations (origine et destination) à l'itinéraire de temps généralisé minimal. Cette hypothèse d'affectation est peu gênante lorsqu'il s'agir d'évaluer des bilans annuels de temps généralisé. En effet si les voyageurs se répartissent entre plusiers itinéraires, c'est que leurs temps généralisés respectifs son voisins. Par contre elle est plus restrictive pour le calcul de la charge des lignes.

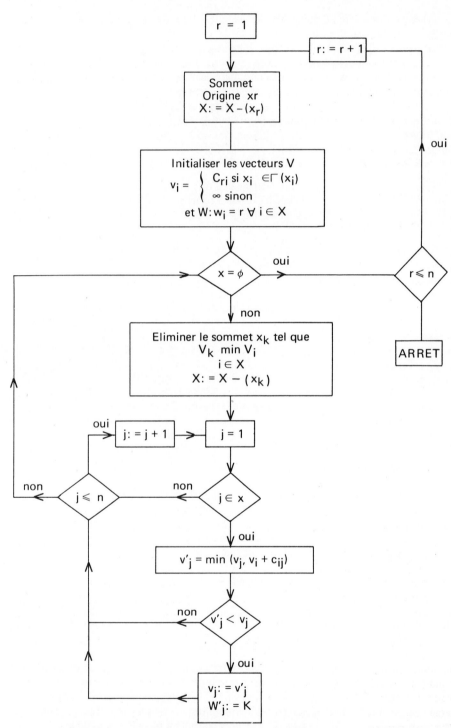

FIGURE 1   ORGANIGRAMME DE L'ALGORITHME DE DANTZIG

2. Le confort, difficile à chiffrer, et la charge des trains ne sont pas pris en compte dans la détermination des itinéraires.

3. L'attente est supposée constante à toute heure et en tout point du réseau. Cette hypothèse revient notamment à régliger les queues dans les couloirs de correspondance et aux portillons automatiques.

4. Le temps généralisé d'une station i à une autre j est considéré l'égal de son symétrique j à i. Cette dernière hypothèse se justifie; nous nous intéressons essentiellement au trafic des migrants qui accomplissent deux voyages quotidiens, le plus souvent, l'expérience le montre, avec le même itinéraire. En outre, elle n'affecte nullement les parcours en train. Pour les ruptures de charge, on est conduit à établir des moyennes sur les temps donnés quai à quai. Cela revient, en somme, à ne pas distinguer les quais. Il en résulte de plus que les flux d'échange dans les stations de correspondance sont calculés, non quai à quai, mais ligne à ligne.

5. On néglige le coût de transport car dans la zone urbaine le tarif est unique.

Le programme *ORANGE** calcule par l'algorithme de Dantzig (voir Figure 1) les plus courts chemins entre tout couple de stations du métropolitain dans la situation de référence, comme dans la situation modifiée.

Le réseau métropolitain peut en effet être figuré par un graphe.

Un seul *sommet* caractérise une station simple. Une *station de correspondance* est définie par:

—un sommet sur chaque ligne
—un sommet Entrée
—an sommet Sortie

On distingue divers types d'arcs:

—des *arcs de parcours* reliant deux stations consécutives: on leur attribue des valeurs désignant les temps interstations moyens (moyenne effectuée sur les temps relatifs aux deux sens du parcours), correspondant à la pointe du soir,

—des *arcs de passage* reliant les différentes lignes d'une même station: on leur affecte des quantités notant les temps généralisés de correspondance. A partir de la brochure FC: *Durée des trajets de quai à quai dans les stations de correspondance du réseau métropolitain,* on calcule un temps physique t_p moyen interligne opérant en général une moyenne sur huit nombres. Pour passer au temps généralisé t_g, on a d'abord essayé la formule préconiseée par l'I.A.U.R.P.:

$$t_g = 2 \, t_p + 1 \text{ mn}$$

Son application a montré que fréquemment les itinéraries calculés différaient des itinéraires observés (après dépouillement de l'enquête cartes blanches). On a testé alors diverse formules faisant intervenir une pénalté plus importante pour la rupture de charge proprement dite. En attendant le résultat de l'étude d'un modèle de

---

* Comparaison de réseaux par l'algorithme de Dantzig.

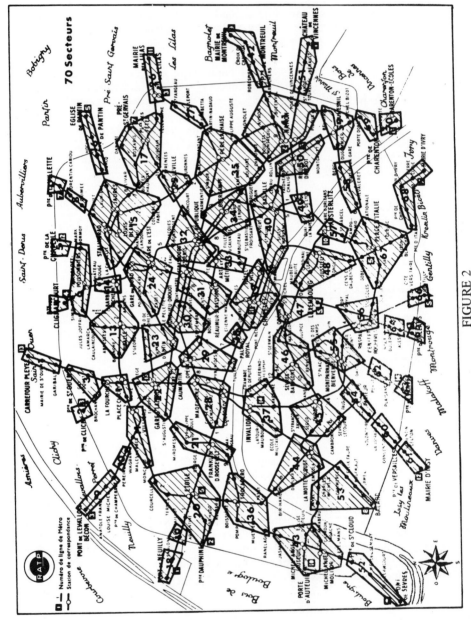

FIGURE 2

comportement des voyageurs à l'égard des possibilités de choix entre plusieurs itinéraires, on a retenu la relation:

$$t_g = 1.4 \; t_p + 4 \; mn$$

qui, tout en conservant la même valeur moyenne du temps généralisé de correspondance que celle de l'I.A.U.R.P. conduit à des choix d'itinéraires plus conformes à la réalité observée.

—*des arcs d'entrée et des arcs de sortie* pourvus de valeurs nulles. Cet argument se justifie car le choix des itinéraires est indépendant des temps d'accès aux quais.

Le nombre de sommets du graphe métropolitain est d'environ 450, celui des arcs de 1 300.

Par des exécutions successives du programme ORANGE, pour chacun des sousgraphes partiels correspondant au fait qu'un tronçon ou un ensemble de tronçons a ou n'a pas été construit, on peut déterminer le trajet qu'emprunteront les voyageurs se rendant de i à j et le temps généralisé correspondent.

L'élément qui dimensionne le modèle CAPRI est le nombre de couples (i. j) concernés par la construction de l'ensemble des tronçons. Si le graphe métropolitain est pris dans sa totalité, ce nombre est fort élevé (entre 2 000 et 15 000). Aussi, avons-nous été contraints à étudier une schématisation plus grossière du réseau.

En regroupant les stations simples autour des stations de correspondance on a ainsi déterminé 80 zones définies à la Figure 2.

LE MODELE DE PROGRAMMATION

4.1   Formulation du Probléme

1.   Nous repérerons les différents tronçons prévus dans les schémas étudiés par l'indice k, variant de 1 à k, et repérons les périodes de temps successives considérées dans l'étude par l'indice t, variant de 1 à T.

Les variables de décision seront alors notées $x_{k,t}$
Ces variables sont bivalentes et ne peuvent prendre que les valeurs O ou l, la valeur l de la variable $x_{k,t}$ correspondant au fait que le tronçon k sera mis en service à la date t.

Ces variables sont soumises à un ensemble de contraintes traduisant le fait qu'un tronçon ne peut être réalisé qu'une fois et ces contraintes s'écrivent

$$\sum_t x_{k,t} \leqslant 1 \quad \forall k$$

2.   Seuls nous intérressent les couples de zones pour lesquels les voyageurs sont susceptibles de recueillir un avantage à la suite de la réalisation du schéma étudié, c'est-à-dire les zones entre lesquelles le trajet le plus court se trouve modifié entre la situation de référence et le réseau enrichi de tous les tronçons nouveaux. Nous repérons ces couples de zone par l'indice ℓ, variant de 1 à L.

Nous désignerons par $N_{\ell,t}$ le nombre de voyageurs désirant effectuer le déplacement ℓ

pendant la période t et $A_{\ell,t}$ l'avantage, recueilli par ces voyageurs, pendant cette période, si les tronçons nécessaires ont été mis en service à la date t.

Pour définir ces tronçons nous utiliserons indifféremment deux notations équivalentes:

——soit un ensemble d'indices k_i (ℓ) dont la signification est que la mise en service de tous les tronçons d'indice

$$k = k_i \quad (\ell)$$

est requise pour améliorer le déplacement ℓ,

–soit l'ensemble des coefficients $B^i_{k,\ell}$ dont la valeur est 0 ou 1, la valeur 1 signifiant que le tronçon d'indice k est utilisé pour améliorer le déplacement ℓ.

3.   Les voyageurs ne pourront obtenir l'avantage $A_{\ell,t}$ que si tous les tronçpns $k_i(\ell)$ ont été mis en service à la date t, c'est-à-dire si

$$\sum_{\tau=1,t} x_{k_i(\ell), \tau} = 1 \qquad \forall i$$

Pour la comodité de l'exposé nous introduirons la variable $y_{\ell,t}$ définie par

$$y_{\ell,t} \leqslant \sum_{\tau=1,t} x_{k_i(\ell),\tau} \qquad \forall i$$

et qui traduit que les voyageurs effectuant le déplacement ℓ obtiennent ou non à la date t l'avantage $A_{\ell,t}$.

L'avantage total recueilli par les voyageurs au cours de la période t peut alors s'écrire

$$\sum_\ell y_{\ell,t} \quad A_{\ell,t}$$

4.   En notant I_k le coût d'investissement lié à la réalisation du tronçon k, le coût des investissemnets s'écrit:

$$\sum_k \sum_t x_{k,t} (I_k \, \alpha_t)$$

dans lequel α_t représente le coefficient d'actualisation.

Notons que cette formule suppose que la dépense d'investissement est entièrement effectuée au cours de la période t. Une formule simple représente le cas où les dépenses d'investissement s'étalent sur plusieurs périodes, mais nous ne la faison pas figurer ici pour ne pas alourdir le texte.

De la même manière, la partie des frais d'exploitation indépendante du trafic est prise en compte dans la formule précédente que nous écrirons plus généralement

$$\sum_k \sum_t x_{k,t} E_{k,t}$$

le term E recouvrant les frais d'investissement, les frais d'exploitation et les coefficient d'actualisation nécessaires.

5.   Le nombre de voyageurs empruntant un tronçon k s'écrit pour la période t.

$$\sum_\ell \beta_{k,\ell} (N_{\ell,t} Y_{\ell,t})$$

et, si les dépense proportionnelles au nombre de voyageurs sont f_k pour le tronçon k. la dépense actualisée correspondante s'écrit

$$\sum_t \alpha_t \sum_k f_k \sum_\ell \beta_{k,\ell} (N_{\ell,t} Y_{\ell,t})$$

6.   Les contraintes financières et les contraintes de régularité s'écrivent de façon évidente

—si ϕ_t est le montant de l'enveloppe budgétaire pour la période t, les contraintes financiéres s'écrivent:

$$\sum_k x_{k,t}\, I_k \leqslant \phi_t \quad \forall\, t$$

—si le montant des dépenses ne doit pas varier de plus de n% d'une période à la suivante, les contraintes de régularité s'ecrivent:

$$(1\text{-}n) \sum_k x_{k,\,t-1}\, I_k \leqslant \sum_k x_{k,t}\, I_k \leqslant (1\text{+}n) \sum_k x_{k,t-1}\, I_k$$

7. En résumé la formulation que nous venons de présenter s'appuie sur deux types en variables:

  1. Les variables de décision $x_{k,t}$ bivalentes, définissant que le tronçon k est mis en service pendant la période t;
  2. les variables de calcul, $y_{\ell,t}$ traduisant que les voyageurs effectuant le déplacement ℓ verront leur trajet amélioré avant la période t.

Les contraintes du probléme sont de quatre types:
  1. Un tronçon ne peut être construit qu'une seule fois, soit:

$$\sum_t x_{k,t} = 1 \quad \forall\, k$$

  2. Un trajet n'est amélioré que si tous les tronçons nécessaires ont été mis en service, soit:

$$y_{\ell,t} \leqslant \sum_{\tau=1,t} x_{k_i\,(\ell),\tau} \quad \forall\, i \quad \forall\, \ell \quad \text{et} \quad \forall\, t$$

  3. Les enveloppes budgétaires doivent être respectées, soit:

$$\sum_k x_{k,t}\, I_k \leqslant \phi_t \quad \forall\, t$$

  4. Les dépenses d'investissement sont régulièrement étalées dans le temps:

$$(1-n)\sum_k x_{k,t\text{-}1}\, I_k \leqslant \sum_k x_{k,t}\, I_k \leqslant (1\text{+}n) \sum_k x_{k,\,t-1}\, I_k$$

Enfin la fonction economique du probléme, prenant en compte les avantages actualisés dont bénéficient les usagers, les dépenses actualisées d'investissement et les charges d'exploitation actualisées, s'écrit:

$$\sum_t \alpha_t \sum_\ell y_{\ell,t}\ A_{\ell,t} - \sum_{k,t} x_{k,t}\ E_{k,t}$$

$$- \sum_t \alpha_t \sum_k f_k\ \Sigma\beta_{k,\ell} \quad (N_{\ell,t}\ y_{\ell,t})$$

4.2   Résolution du Problème de Programmation

Comme le lecteur aura pu s'en rendre compte, dans le problème que nous venons de formuler, contraintes et fonction économique sont des expressions linéaires des variables de décision, problème dont la particularité, et d'ailleurs la complexité, résultant de la présence simultanée de variables continues et de variables discontinues, les variables bivalentes: ce type de problème est connu sous le nom de Programme linéaire en Variables Mixtes.

Différents algorithmes ont été programmes et essayés pour résoudre ce type de problème, algorithmes qui, sur le plan théorique, sont satisfaisants et dont la convergence a été démontrée: par contre il semble que, selon la nature du problème concret qui est proposé, ces algorithmes aient des performances très variables, excellentes pour certains problèmes, très mauvaises pour d'autres.

Nous nous proposons d'utiliser l'algorithme CAPRI spécialement mis au point pour résoudre de tels problèmes de choix d'investissement.

Nous ne décrirons ici que le principe général de cet algorithme, renvoyant le lecteur intéressé en annexe où figurent toutes les justifications mathématiques nécessaires.

Cet algorithme met en oeuvre simultanèment les techniques classiques de résolution de programmes linéaires et une procédure particulière de la classe des procédures "branch and bound" la procédure SEP* (Séparation et Evaluation Progressive).

4.2.1. La procédure S.E.P.

Dans toute sa généralité, cette procédure consiste, étant donné l'ensemble de toutes les solutions possibles dans lequel on recherche la solution optimale:

—à séparer progressivement cet ensemble en sous-ensembles complémentaires de plus en plus "réduits" et de mieux en mieux "précisés";
—à évaluer chacun de ces sous-ensembles de solutions au moyen d'une fonction d'évaluation fournissant:

> une évaluation *par excès* du critère à maximiser c'est-à-dire une valeur supérieure ou égale à la valeur du critère pour la meilleure des solutions contenues dans le sous-ensemble.

> une évaluation *exacte* du critère pour tout sous-ensemble ne contenant qu'une seule solution.

La solution optimale est obtenue lorsque l'on a isolé un sous-ensemble ne comportant plus qu'une solution et que l'évaluation correspondante est plus èlevèe que celle de tous les autres sous-ensembles complèmentaires.

En effet par définition même de la fonction d'évaluation, ces derniers ne peuvent contenir de solutions meilleures que celle qui a été isolée. Bien entendu, la procédure S.E.P. n'est efficace que pour autant que la procdure de séparation et la fonction d'évaluation le soient.

4.2.2. Procédure de séparation retenue

Nous l'exposerons sur un cas très simple où sont confrontès trois projets d'investissement, comportant, le premier deux variantes, 1.1 et 1.2, le second et le troisième trois variantes, respectivement 2.1, 2.2 et 2.3 d'une part, 3.1, 3.2 et 3.3 d'autre part.

La séparation progressive choisie peut être décrite par le graphe ci-dessous qui porte le nom d'arborescence (voir figure 3).

---

* Voir Revue METRA : - volume IV n° 3 1965 "Programmes linéaires en nombres entiers et procédure S.E.P. - volume VI n° 1 1967 "Résolution de programmes linéaires en variables mixtes par la procédure S.E.P.

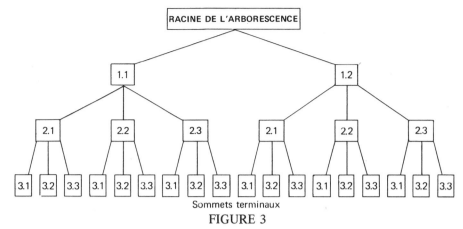

Sommets terminaux
FIGURE 3

La racine de l'arborescence représente l'ensemble des solutions possibles. Les choix progressifs se traduisent par an "arbitrage", d'abord au niveau du premier projet entre ses deux variantes, ce qui conduit à deux sous-ensembles complémentaires, puis successivement au niveau des deux autres projects, ce qui permet, en définitive d'isoler les 18 plans d'investissements possibles, chacun d'eux contenant une variante, et une seule de chaque projet.

Bien entendu au cours de l'exploration de cette arborescence, on ne décrira pas la totalité de des sommets car l'évaluation nous guidera dans l'exploration. Par ailleurs, il est évident que bien d'autres arborescences auraient pu être construites à partir du même exemple en variant l'ordre dans lequel les projets sont "arbitrès". En fait l'arborescence sera construite progressivement en fonction des résultats des évaluations successives.

4.2.3. *La fonction d'évaluation retenue*

A un sommet quelconque de l'arborescence correspondent:

—les projets d'investissement déjà arbitrés, pour lesquels la valeur des variables $x_{k,t}$, est connue, soit nulle, soit égale à l
—les autres projets d'investissements pour lesquels les variables $x_{k,t}$ ne sont pas encore arbitrées.

Le problème correspondant à ce sommet se déduit donc de problème initial en imposant aux variables $x_{k,t}$ correspondant aux projets déjà arbitrés leur valeur réelle, 0 ou 1.

L'évaluation correspondant à ce sommet est obtenue en résolvant le programme linéaire en variables *continues* dérivé du problème réel correspondant à ce commet en rendant contiues sur l'intervalle 0,1 les variables $x_{k,t}$ non arbitrées.

L'ensemble des solutions de ce problème contient en effet l'ensemble des solutions du problème réel correspondant au sommet à évaluer et nécessairement, à l'optimum du problème dérivé correspond une valeur de la fonction économique, valeur retenue comme évaluation, supérieure ou égale à celle qu'elle prendrait à l'optimum due problème réel.

4.*2.4 Le déroulement de la procédure*

1.   L'évaluation

Plaçons nous en un stade quelconque de la procédure, c'est-à-dire en an sommet quelconque de l'arborescence. Au cours de l'évaluation correspondante quatre cas seulement peuvent se présenter:

a)   Le problème modifié n'a pas de solution qui satisfasse aux contraintes donc le problème réel n'en a pas non plus: la branche correspondante de l'arborescence est alors abandonnée, et l'exploration reprend en un autre sommet de l'arborescence.

b)   Le problème modifié a pour solution optimale une solution pour laquelle toutes les variables $x_{k,t}$ valent 0 ou 1, donc cette solution est aussi solution optimale du problème réel: l'étude de la branche correspondante est abandonnée mais on retient la solution trouvée comme solution réalisable, c'est-à-dire qu'il s'agit d'un plan d'investissement possible;
α–Si l'évaluation correspondante est supérieure à toutes les autres évaluations, il s'agit de la solution *optimale* de problème réel et l'exploration est terminée;
β–Sinon l'exploration reprend en un autre sommet de l'arborescence.

c)   Le problème modifié conduit à une évaluation inférieure à la valeur du critère pour au moins une des solutions réalisables déjà construites: l'étude de la branche correspondante est abandonnée.

d)   Le problème modifié a pour solution optimale une solution non réalisable mais sont l'évaluation est meilleure que toutes celles des solutions réalisables déjà obtenues: dans ce cas l'exploration de la branche correspondante devra être poursuivie ultérieurement.

2.   Processus d'arbitrage

Dans les cas a, bβ, c et d où l'exploration n'est pas terminèe, celle-ci reprend en principe au sommet présentant la meilleure évaluation, puisque ce sommet est celui ayant le plus de chances de contenir la solution optimale. Ce principe pourra cependant être transgressé lorsque l'on souhaitera prolonger l'exploration d'une branche même moins bonne qu'une autre en vue de rechercher dans cette branche, une solution réalisable; en effet, comme nous venons de la voir, la connaissance de solutions réalisable permet d'éliminer certaines branches donc d'accélérer le déroulement de la procédure.

Une fois le sommet à arbitrer choisi, l'arbitrage est fait non pas par dichotomie, mais par n-tomie, chaque sommet ayant autant de suivants que le project d'investissement returnu pour l'arbitrage présente de variantes.

3.   Organigramme

En pratique la procédure de résolution se déroule donc conformément à l'organigramme général présenté en figure 4.

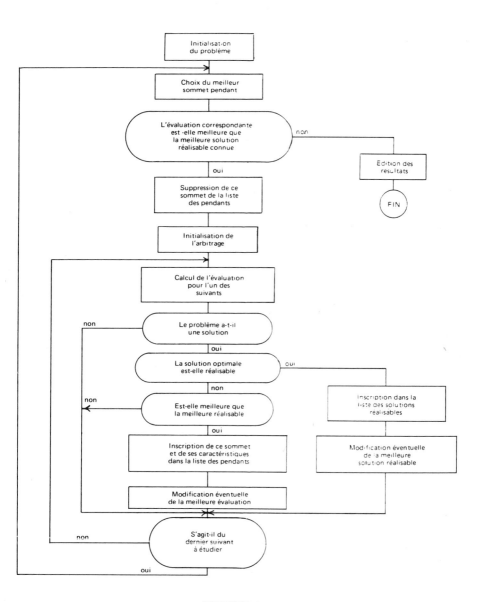

FIGURE 4

5.   RESULTATS

Au moment où nous écrivons ces lignes aucune application complète de cet ensemble de méthodes et de programmes n'a encore été menée à bien.

La raison en vient uniquement du volume considérable d'éléments numeriques que requiert cette étude, chaque type d'élément numérique exigeant à lui seul une analyse extrêment précise et longue.

Certaines de ces analyses sont déjà achevées d'autres sont en cours mai leur achèvment demandera cependant plusieurs mois.

Par contre, les modèles et programmes décrit dans cet article ont tous déjà fonctionné avec succès:

—la RATP a conduit plusieurs études de trafic à l'aide du programme d'affectation

—le programme CAPRI a été utilisé pour résoudre des problèmes d'investissements, relatifs à d'autres entreprises que la RATP, maid de complexité équivalente.

Dès que les éléments numériques nécessaires seront disponibles, les applications pourront donc être conduites rapidement.

ANNEXE: L'ALGORITHME DE PROGRAMMATION LINEAIRE

A.1   Formulation Mathématique

Rappelons tout d'abord la formulation mathématique du problème à résoudre.

Le problème décrit au quatrième chapitra peut être résumé par:

$$(\text{MAX !}) \; Z = \sum_{j \in N} c_j \, X_j$$

sous les contraintes :

$$(1) \qquad \sum_{j \in N} a_{ij} \, X_j = b_i \qquad\qquad \forall \; i \in M'$$

$$(2) \qquad \sum_{j \in N} a_{ij} \, X_j \leq b_i \qquad\qquad \forall \; j \in M - M'$$

$$(3) \qquad X_j \geq 0 \qquad\qquad \forall \; j \in N$$

$$(4) \qquad X_j = 0 \text{ ou } 1 \qquad\qquad \forall \; j \in J < N$$

On notera que les contraintes de type 1 contiennent en particulier les relations d'exclusion des variantes d'un même projet.

L'ensemble J représente l'ensemble des variable bivalentes.

Le problème à résoudre en un sommet quelconque de l'arborescence se déduit du problème initial par définition de deux sous ensembles disjoints J_0 et J_1 appartenant à l'ensemble J et tels que

$$(4') \quad \left| \begin{array}{ll} X_j = 0 & \forall\ j \in J_0 \\[2ex] X_j = 1 & \forall\ j \in J_1 \end{array} \right.$$

La réunion de J_0 et J_1 représente l'ensemble des variables bivalentes arbitrées et le système de contraintes ainsi défini se substitue au système des contraintes de type (4) du problème initial.

Nous noterons ce problème P (J_0, J_1) que nous désignerons sous le nom de problème primal. Nous serons amenés à considérer le problème dual associé qui sera noté P* (J_0, J_1)

A.2 Différentes Voies de Résolution

Trois possibilités ont été envisagées:

—résoudre le problème primal par l'algorithme primal du simplexe;
—résoudre le problème primal par l'algorithme dual du simplexe;
—résoudre le problème primal par l'algorithme primal du simplexe.

a) *Résolution du problème primal par l'algorithme primal du simplexe*

Le problème P (J_0, J_1) peut être présenté de plusieurs façons différentes:

—l'une d'elles consiste à supprimer, par rapport au problème initial P (ϕ, ϕ), le symbole ϕ représentant l'ensemble vide, les variables arbitrées; pour cela, on supprime purement et simplement les colonnes de la matrice correspondant aux variables du sous-ensemble J_0 et l'on transfère au second membre de la matrice, en les changeant de signe, les colonnes correspondant aux variables du sous-ensemble J_1; de cette façon, le problème P (J_0, J_1) contient le même nombre de contraintes que P (ϕ, ϕ) mais le nombre de variables est réduit;

—une autre méthode consiste au contraire à conserver toutes les variables mais à ajouter des contraintes traduisant les arbitrages, soit le système:

$$(4'') \quad \begin{array}{ll} X_j \leq 0 & \forall\ j \in J_0 \\[2ex] -X_j \leq -1 & \forall\ j \in J_1 \end{array}$$

qui se substitue au système (4').

En fait, quelle que soit la méthode employée, on se heurte à la même difficultè: on n'est pas capable d'utiliser l'information obtenue antérieurement dans l'arborescence S.E.P. pour accélérer la résolution de P (J_0, J_1); en particulier, chaque problème devra débuter par la recherche d'une base réalisable (phase 1 de la résolution) généralment assez longue.

b)   Résolution du problème primal par l'alorithme dual du simplexe

Cette méthode a déjà été employée avec succès par certains auteurs. Son intérêt provient en particulier de ce que les calculs sont accélérés par la connaissance pour chaque problème d'une base réalisable.

Par contre, l'algorithme dual du simplexe est moins fréquemment utilisé que l'algorithme primal; partant il est probablement moins performant et n'est pas disponible de façon courante dans les bibliothèque de programmes. Il est donc à craindre que son emploi pratique dans le cadre de CAPRI ne suscite quelque difficultés.

c)   Résolution du problème dual par l'algorithme primal du simplexe

Cette méthode nous a semblé devoir être un bon compromis entre les méthodes précédentes puisqu'elle utilise l'algorithme primal tout en tirant parti des propriétés de dualité. En effet le tableau du simplexe optimal d'un programme linéaire contient toujours implicitement ou explicitement les éléments du programme dual qui lui est associé. Nous allons étudier plus en détail cette méthode dans le paragraphe suivant.

1.3   Résolution du Problème Dual par l'Algorithme Primal

a)   Le problème dual du problème P (J_0, J_1) défini avec les contraintes de type $4''$ s'écrit:

$$(\text{MIN !}) \ w = \sum_{i \in M} u_i \, b_i - \sum_{i \in J_1} u_i$$

avec :

(1*) u_i variable libre $\forall \ i \in M'$

(2*) $u_i \geq 0$ $\forall \ i \in M - M'$

(3*) $\sum_{i \in M} u_i \, a_{ij} + \sum_{i \in J_0} u_i - \sum_{i \in J_1} u_i \geq c_j$ $\forall \ j \in N$

(4*) $u_i \geq 0 \ (\forall i \in J_0)$ et $(\forall i \in J_1)$

En ce qui concerne cette formulation, il y a plusieurs remarques à faire qui nous seront utiles pour la suite.

Remarque 1 (portant sur les variables)

Il y a trois types de variables duales:
—les variables libres u_i $(i \in M')$ qui ne sont pas astreintes à être non négatives et qui correspondent aux égalités du problème primal;
—les variables non négatives u_i $(i \in M - M')$ qui correspondent aux inégalités propres du problème primal;
—les variables non négatives u_i $(i \in J_0$ ou $i \in J_1)$ qui correspondent aux inégalités du problème primal que nous qualifierons de secondaires.

Remarque 2 (portant sur les contraintes)

Le nombre de contraintes du type (3*) ne dépend que du nombre de variables primales quels que soient les ensembles J_0 et J_1. La matrice qui constitue ces contraintes se décompose en deux parties: l'une représente la matrice du problème P* (ϕ, ϕ) et reste fixe, l'autre varie avec les ensembles J_0 et J_1.

Remarque 3 (portant sur la fonction économique)

L'ensemble des coefficients de la fonction économique se décompose également en deux parties dont l'une représente la fonction économique du problème P (ϕ, ϕ) et l'autre varie avec l'ensemble J_1.

Remarque 4 (portant sur l'enchaînement des calculs)

D'après les remarques 2 et 3, nous pouvons alors générer facilement la formulation d'un problème P (J_0, J_1) à partir des éléments du problème P* (ϕ, ϕ) (c'est-à-dire matrice, second membre et fonction économique) et des ensembles J_0 et J_1.

Par ailleurs, chaque base optimale d'un problème dual correspondent à un sommet (J'_0, J'_1) de S.E.P. qui se trouve sur le chemin $(\phi, \phi) \rightarrow (J_0, J_1)$ constitue une base réalisable pour le problème P* (J_0, J_1) ce qui permet d'éviter la phase 1 de l'algorithme primal du simplexe.

Remarque 5

—D'après le théorème de dualité P (J_0, J_1) n'a pas de solution optimale si P* (J_0, J_1) n'a pas de solution réalisable ou bien si la fonction économique de P*(J_0, J_1) n'est pas bornée inférieurement. D'après la remarque 4, le premier des deux cas possibles ne peut se produire que pour le problème P* $(\phi \phi)$. Dans ce cas là, il y aura lieu de vérifier la formulation du problème initial. Par conséquent, l'impossibilité d'un problème d'un problème P (J_0, J_1) avec J_0 U $J, \neq \phi$ sera indiquée par une fonction économique non bornée inférieurement de P*. (J_0, J_1)

—Du théorème de dualité découle également que Z $(J_0, J_1) < w(J_0, J_1)$ pour toute solution duale-réalisable.
Donc, à condition d'avoir déjà trouvé une our plusiers "évaluations exactes", c'est-à-dire correspondant à des solutions réalisables, on peut arrêter le calcul de résolution de P* (J_0, J_1) dès que la valeur courante de la fonction économique devient inférieure à l'une des évaluations exactes.

b)   Sur le plan pratique, on est obligé de présenter le problème P* (J_0, J_1) sous forme standard et de faire disparafre les variables libres si l'on ne dispose pas d'un code de programmation capable de traiter des variables libres. On peut envisager plusieurs façons de le faire.

1)   Remplacer les égalités du primal par deux inégalités:

$$(\forall\ i\ \epsilon\ M')\ \sum_{j \epsilon N} a_{ij} X_j = b_i \quad \leftrightarrow \quad \left| \begin{array}{l} \sum\limits_{j \epsilon N} a_{ij}\ X_j\ \leq\ b_i \\[3mm] \sum\limits_{j \epsilon N} (-a_{ij})X_j\ \leq\ (-b_i) \end{array} \right. \qquad (\forall\ i\ \epsilon\ M')$$

ce qui implique dans le dual de remplacer les variables libres par la différence de deux variables non négatives

2)   Remplacer le système des m' égalités du primal par un système de $(m' + 1)$ inégalités :

$$(\forall \; i \; \epsilon \; M') \; \sum_{j \epsilon N} \; a_{ij}X_j = b_i \quad \leftrightarrow \quad \left| \begin{array}{l} (\forall \; i \; \epsilon \; M') \; \sum_{j \epsilon N} \; a_{ij} \; X_j \leq b_i \\[2mm] \sum_{j \epsilon N} \sum_{i \epsilon M'} \; (\text{-}a_{ij})X_j \leq \sum_{i \epsilon M'} (\text{-}b_i) \end{array} \right.$$

Ce qui entraîne pour le dual de rendre les variables duales toutes non négatives et d'augmenter leur nombre de 1.

3)   Appliquer le procédé précédent au système des relations d'exclusion seulement et transformer les autres égalités en inégalités par une méthode proposée par M. SIMONNARD qui permet à la fois d'éliminer autant de variables contiues qu'il y a d'équations disponibles au départ.

Ceci implique pour le dual à la fois une diminution du nombre de variables et une diminution du nombre de contraintes.

C'est cette dernière méthode qui a été retenue et nous arriverons finalement à une formulation du type suivant:

Primal   P (J_0, J_1) Dual   P* (J_0, J_1)

$(\text{MAX !}) \; Z_1 = \sum_{j \epsilon N_1} \; \gamma_j X_j$ $(\text{MIN !}) w_1 = \sum_{i \epsilon M_1} u_i \beta_i - \sum_{i \epsilon j_1} u_i$

$\sum_{j \epsilon N_1} a_{ij}X_j \leq \beta_i$ $\forall \; i \; \epsilon \; M_1$ $u_i \geq 0$

$X_j \leq -1$ $\forall \; j \; \epsilon \; J_1$ $u_j \geq 0$

$X_j \leq 0$ $\forall \; j \; \epsilon \; J_0$ $u_j \geq 0$

$X_j \leq 0$ $\forall \; j \; \epsilon \; N_1$ $\left\{ \begin{array}{l} v_j + \sum_{i \epsilon M_1} u_i \alpha_{ij} + \sum_{i \epsilon J_0} u_i \sum_{i \epsilon J_1} u_i = \gamma_j \\[2mm] v_j > 0 \end{array} \right.$

COST-BENEFIT ANALYSIS IN TRANSPORTATION

O. Gulbrandsen

1. INTRODUCTION

1.1 The Problem of Resource Allocation

In our communities decisions on allocation of resources for the construction of infrastructure and other fixed real capital are taken continuously. Such decisions are made within important sectors, such as the sectors of transportation, health, education, defence and industry, etc.

The consequences of the decisions are very comprehensive throughout our communities. It is of great importance, therefore, that such allocations are as correct as possible. This fact is further stressed by the following two conditions:

(i) The resource allocations are, in most cases, irreversible, i.e. the fixed real capital may not, or only in part, be converted into the original form of resources.
(ii) The total amount of resources available for allocations is often very limited.

1.1.1 Benefit of Resource Allocations

Some of the resource allocations which are made may subsequently be characterized as not very satisfactory. Other allocations result in fixed real capital which apparently is satisfactory but actually nobody knows whether a different resource allocation would result in a much greater benefit to the community.

An important task to be performed in order to make the decision procedure more reliable is, therefore, as follows:

Task 1:
Elaborate methods for quantitative determination of the total benefit of resource allocations within a system.

The solution of this problem is being complicated by the fact that the benefit of resource allocations to one part of the system as a rule strongly depends on the standard of other parts of the system.

1.1.2. Maximization of the Benefit of Resource Allocation

The fixed real capital resulting from decisions on resource allocations usually has a long "lifetime". When it has been incorporated into a system it will, for a long time, influence what may be considered as optimal allocations to the same part of the system. Thus the benefit of fixed real capital depends both on decisions which will be taken in the future and on decisions regarding other parts of the system to-day. It is, therefore, desirable to make decisions simultaneously both in time and space.

In addition to task 1, the following is important for the reliability of the decision procedure:

> Task II:
> Elaborate methods for simultaneous determination of long term optimal decisions for all parts of a system.

1.1.3 Discussion of the Resource Allocation Problem

To-day, task II has advanced further than task I. The main reason for this is perhaps the theoretical character of task II which demands less collection and processing of data. For many systems, task I is to-day at its very beginning, as only a small portion of benefit wihtin a certain part of the system may be quantified, as well as only a small portion of the indirect benefit of other parts of the system can be determined. Strictly speaking, the optimal allocation of resources may not be made before both task I and task II are fully accomplished. Nevertheless, the results of calculations according to a method deriving from task II will be of great use for the decision-makers, even if only the part of the benefit quantitied so far is taken into account in the optimization process.

The procedure could be as follows:

(i)   A great number of solutions are brought forward and ranked according to the value of the quantifiable part of the benefit for the system. The number of factors which the decision-makers have to estimate is thus reduced.

(ii)   Then the not quantifiable parts of the benefit of the different solutions have to be estimated by the decision-makers. (The quantitatively highest rated solutions will usually not be the best according to the not quantifiable benefits).

(iii) The profit of not quantifiable benefit must be balanced against the loss of the quantifiable part of the benefit, and on this basis the final decisions have to be made.

Task I will, of course, be developed continuously but will probably never find its final solution. There will always be room for appreciations, which implies that the procedure described above in principle always will have to be followed in the future as well.

1.2   Content of the Following Chapters

In the following chapter the resource allocation problems will be described further.

Then follow two chapters in which the principles of optimization methods developed at the Institute of Transport Economy in Norway will be described.

Thereafter, the important problems of the determination of benefit of resource allocations and other input of the optimization calculations will be discussed. Finally, some closing remarks are given.

2.   PRESENTATION OF THE PROBLEM

2.1   The System under Study

The system is defined as a limited part of our communities, in which decisions on allocation of resources may be made relatively independently of other parts of the communities. In the transportation sector, such systems may be:

> a system of roads
> a railway system
> an air transportation system
> a system of ports
> e t c

2.2 Time Periods

For a system as described above, the time period which has to be taken into account in connection with the planning of resource allocations is called the planning period. This time period may be divided into shorter periods called resource allocation periods.

2.3 Resource Budgets

If there exists limitation in the amount of different types of resources which may be allocated to the system, resource budgets must be determined for each of the resource allocation periods. It may be necessary to operate with both upper and lower limits of resource allocations.

As an example of lower limits may be mentioned a system which the decision-makers consider as an employment area where a certain minimum of employment must be maintained. The resource budgets will have to be specified for each resource allocation period.

2.4 System Parts

Furthermore, it must be possible to divide the system into system parts. The system parts are selected in such a way that they constitute operational units, i.e. from an operational point of view the selected system parts should be independent of each other to the greatest possible extent and each system part represent a natural resource allocation object.

2.5 System Part Standard

Moreover, different operational and technical standards must be defined for each system part. When the system changes from one standard to another, allocation of one or more types of resources may be necessary. The need for each type of resource for each possible change of system part standard must be determined.

2.6 The Benefit Function

For the system as a whole, a quantifiable measure of efficiency must be defined, i.e. an objective function or a benefit function of the system. The benefit has to be given as a function of the standard of the various system parts.

2.7 The Objective

The resource allocation problem of our system may be formulated as follows:

Determine which standard each system part shall have in each time period, so that the benefit of the system during the entire planning period is maximized and, at the same time, none of the adopted resource budgets is exceeded.

Task II, as mentioned in chapter 1.1.2, will consist of a calculation method allowing the determination of or the search for these system part standard combinations with acceptable calculation costs.

3.   OPTIMUM RESOURCE ALLOCATIONS IN SYSTEMS CONSISTING OF INTER-DEPENDENT PARTS

3.1   Inter-Dependence Between System Parts

The various parts of a system may be defined as inter-dependent when a change of standard within one part of the system modified the benefit of the standard of another system part to a considerable extent.

As an example of inter-dependence may be mentioned the distribution of traffic on a road net. If the standard of one road is increased, it may influence the traffic flow and structure and thereby the benefit of other parts of the road net.

3.2   Problem Solutions

Calculations which have to be made for the determination of the optimal solution will become quite complicated when the system parts must be considered as inter-dependent. However, it has proved to be possible to solve the problems by applying a kind of guided random search among feasible solutions. According to these principles which, in part, are already known, the method MOCAPRI has been developed at the Institute of Transport Economy in Norway for the solution of such problems. The method is available as a program for electronic computer and includes the Monte Carlo method as part of the search for the best solutions.

The main principles of the method are shown in the flow diagram of figure 1. The figure will be discussed in chapter 3.2.1 but some terms ought to be defined in advance:

The benefit of a standard of a certain system part may, as a rule, be divided into two parts:

(i)   The *independent* benefit is the part of the benefit which is rendered by the standard of one system part, independently of the standard of other system parts

(ii)   The *inter-dependent* benefit is the part of the benefit which is rendered by the standard of one system part, because it exists in combination with the standard of the remaining parts of the system.

In addition, the term *development policy of a system part* has to be defined:

The development policy of one system part is a ranged set of standards foreseen for this system part, one standard for each time period during the entire planning period.

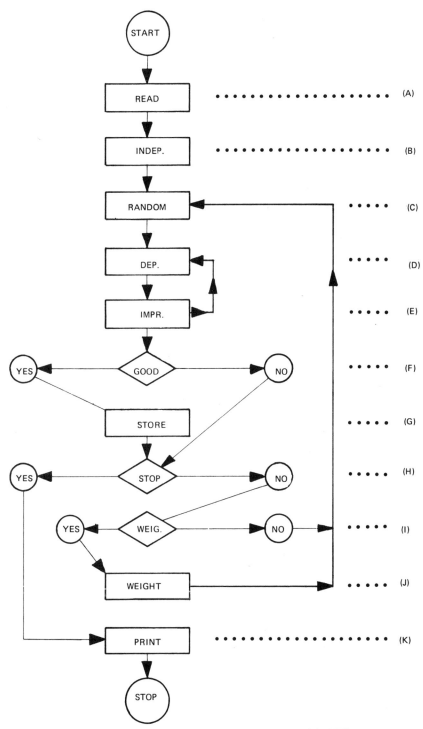

FIGURE 1   FLOW DIAGRAM FOR MOCAPRI

The development policy gives an unambiguous picture of how the standard of one system part may vary throughout the planning period.

In practice, the number of standards defined for each system part is small and the number of resource allocation periods is usually not very great. Consequently, the number of development policies which may be defined is limited. In addition, not all changes of standard of a system part are technically possible or even logically significant. This fact implies that the number of interesting development policies for one system part in most cases is very small and they may, therefore, be listed for each system part. In this way, calculation time is saved by searching among these policies instead of among the standards as originally indicated.

3.2.1. *The Flow Diagram of MOCAPRI*

When the necessary data have been read into the computer (Figure 1(A)), the discounted value of the independent benefit is calculated for each development policy pertaining to each system part (B).

A certain development policy will then be selected at random for each system part by the Monte Carlo technique (C). It is important that this process results in practical and feasible solutions and this is obtained through the performance of the following two steps of control during the handling of each system part:

(i)   A table is set up in which all possible combinations of standards of the various system parts are shown. In connection with the random drawing of a development policy for a certain system part, the table is consulted for each resource allocation period in order to control whether the proposed technical standard is possible in combination with the technical standard in the same time period of the system parts which have already been handled by the random procedure.

(ii)   Controls are also performed in order to ensure that the additional resource consumption resulting from the development policy drawn does not exceed the upper budget limits.

When a complete and feasible solution for the whole system is determined, the total quantifiable part of the benefit is calculated. First, the discounted value of the inter-dependent benefit (D) is calculated for the whole system. The independent benefit (calculated under (B)) is then added for each of the development policies selected.

Then a systematic improvement process (E) of the randomly selected solution is started. This is performed by the following procedure for each part of the system:

(1)   If the lower limit of the resource allocations is not satisfied, all policies with higher resource consumption are pointed out.

(2)   From this group, the policies which are technically and budgetary feasible as compared with the rest of the system parts are selected.

(3)   Each of these feasible policies is then introduced separately into the solution and the inter-dependent and independent benefit of the system is calculated.

(4)   In the case of not satisfied lower budget limits, the best feasible solution, if any, is accepted. If not, it is accepted only if it is better than the original solution.

When this improvement process has been performed for all parts of the system, the combination of development policies may be changed and the process is repeated until no more improvements are possible.

In order to explain the remainder of the flow diagram, we have to imagine that the whole calculation process has been carried on for sometime and that several different "best solutions" resulting from different random start solutions are produced and stored.

Thereafter, it is controlled (F) whether or not the last improved solution is better than the poorest of a set of previously produced improved solutions. If so, the last solution is stored (G) and the poorest of the old solutions is rejected.

The whole process is interrupted (H) and output is given (K) if the probability of obtaining a better solution by a new run is small. If it proves necessary to continue the process, it will be examined (I) whether or not periodical change in the development policy weights shall be made.

If so, each of the development policies appearing in the sets of the stored best solutions is given an extra weight (J). In the subsequent calculations, this will give a higher probability of these policies being selected during the random choice procedure (C). The reason why we are operating with such weights is to increase the converging ability of the process towards the optimal solution. If the increase of such weights is too fast, the probability of arriving at a local optimum is high. In order to counteract this tendency, the weight must be changed very carefully (small changes) at the beginning of the process but as the number of runs increases, the probability of having gone through all important solution areas will be greater, so that the weight may be increased gradually with less risk.

3.2.2 The Calculation Process

A result of the optimization process will then be a set of the best solutions having been found. If desirable, it is possible to print out all the solutions successively as they result from the improvement process. By the relatively simple testing of the optimization program which has been performed so far, the calculation time on the electronic computer was only a few minutes. However, more complicated cases will require one or more hours before the process converges.

4.   OPTIMAL RESOURCE ALLOCATIONS FOR SYSTEMS CONSISTING OF INDEPENDENT PARTS

In some systems, the various parts may be regarded as almost independent of each other. This fact simplifies the problem and gives the possibility of finding an exact global optimum by operations research methods.

In several road investment problems in Norway it has been possible to treat the different parts of a road system as approximately independent. This is the case especially for rural road systems where the various roads of the system form a network only to a small extent but merely being independent roads across the country.

The so-called DYPRI method has been developed at the Institute of Transport Economy for the solution of such resource allocation problems by a combination of the operations research methods Dynamic Programming and Lagrange Multipliers combined with numerical calculations on electronic computer.

4.1   Dynamic Programming

The method of one-dimensional Dynamic Programming may be applied in solving optimization problems which imply that one type of resources has to be allocated to the various parts of the system at a specific moment.

Similarly, problems implying that different types of limited resources simultaneously have to be distributed optimally between the various parts of the system may be solved by multi-dimensional Dynamic Programming. When dealing with such problems it is assumed that the efficiency of allocation of one type of resources to one system part will be influenced by the amount of other types of resources allocated to the same part of the system. The solutions will be found when the limitation of the resource budgets of the different types of resources for allocation is taken into account.

4.2   Time Priority Rating

The multi-dimensional method may be applied in finding the optimal priority rating of the allocation of one type of resources to the various system parts. This is performed in the following way:

(i)   Our long term planning period is, as mentioned above, divided into resource allocation periods.

(ii)   Limitations of the resource budgets for allocation are determined for each resource allocation period.

(iii)   This same type of resources being spread over several resource allocation periods may then be considered as different types of resources, one for each resource allocation period, which may be allocated to the same set of system parts.

The optimal allocation plan for the type of resources in question may then be determined for all resource allocation periods simultaneously by the application of multi-dimensional Dynamic Programming. The influence on the efficiency of the allocation of a certain amount of resources in one time period by the quantities being allocated to the same system part in other time periods, will then be taken into account.

4.3   Four-Dimensional Dynamic Programming Problems

In most cases, it will be sufficient to determine an optimal resource allocation for four time periods. If it is necessary to establish a priority list of resource allocations for a planning period of twenty years, this planning period may, for instance, be divided into four resource allocation periods of five years each. The problem of a system consisting of several hundred system parts may be solved directly on the forthcoming generation of electronic computers. However, on the most usual computers of today, the calculation costs would be reduced if Dynamic Programming was combined with the technique of the Lagrange Multipliers. This will also be the case in the future of still larger systems.

The following functional equation of the four-dimensional priority problem will then be valid:

$$f_N(x_1, x_2) = \max_{\substack{0 \le x_1, N \le x_1 \\ 0 = x_2, N = x_2}} \left\{ \max_{\substack{0 \le x_3, N \le \infty \\ 0 \le x_4, N \le \infty}} [g_N(x_{1,N}, x_{2,N}, x_{3,N}, x_{4,N}) \right.$$

$$\left. - \lambda_3 \cdot x_{3,N} - \lambda_4 \cdot x_{4,N}] + f_{N-1}(x_1 - x_{1,N}, x_2 - x_{2,N}) \right\}$$

where every set of values of the Lagrange Multipliers λ_3 and λ_4 gives a two-dimensional problem, where

$f_N(x_1\ x_2)$	= optimal efficiency of a system containing N system parts and a total resource budget for time period No.1 and 2 of x_1 and x_2 respectively.
$x_{1,N}, x_{2,N}, x_{3,N}, x_{4,N}$	= resource allocation to system part No. N in the time periods 1, 2, 3 and 4 respectively.
$g_N(x_{1,N}, x_{2,N}, x_{3,N}, x_{4,N})$	= efficiency of system part No. N when allocating resource quantities $x_{1,N}, x_{2,N}, x_{3,N}$ and $x_{4,N}$ during the four time periods respectively.

4.3.1 Solution of the Problem

The problem is solved in the following way: First, the inner maximization of a specific set of value of λ_3 and λ_4 is carried out. In this way, a new efficiency function for the first and second time periods is calculated for every system part.

$$q_i(x_{1,i}, x_{2,i}) = \max_{\substack{0 \le x_{3,i} \le \infty \\ 0 \le x_{4,i} \le \infty}} [g_i(x_{1,i}, x_{2,i}, x_{3,i}, x_{4,i}) - \lambda_3 x_{3,i} - \lambda_4 x_{4,i}]$$

for $i = 1, 2, 3, \ldots, N$.

Expression (1) and (2) gives the following functional equation:

$$f_N(x_1, x_2) = \max_{\substack{0 \le x_{1,N} \le x_1 \\ 0 \le x_{2,N} \le x_2}} [q_N(x_{1,N}, x_{2,N}) - f_{N-1}(x_1 - x_{1,N}, x_2 - x_{2,N})].$$

When the two-dimensional problem is solved, i.e. when the optimal amount of resources $x_{1,i}$ and $x_{2,i}$ are found (where i = $_{1,2}$ ....,N) the corresponding quantities $x_{3,i}$ and $x_{4,i}$ are given as a result of the maximization (2). The next step is to calculate:

$$\dot{x}_3 = \Sigma_{i=1}^{i=N} x_{3,i} \qquad \text{and} \qquad \dot{x}_4 = \Sigma_{i=1}^{i=N} x_{4,i}.$$

If there is a deviation between the calculated quantities x_3, x_4 and the original x_3, x_4, a new set of values of λ_3 and λ_4 must be tried out.

The procedure is repeated until the amount of resources allocated in time periods 3 and 4 respectively equal the budget values x_3 and x_4.

The process is usually started by the values $\lambda_3 = \lambda_4 = 0$. If the results of this set give solutions where both x_3 and x_4 are less than x_3 and x_4 respectively, our problem is solved. Otherwise, the calculations have to be continued with other λ-values until the budget restrictions are satisfied. This search procedure may be carried out in a logical and rational way necessitating only a few calculations before the final result is obtained.

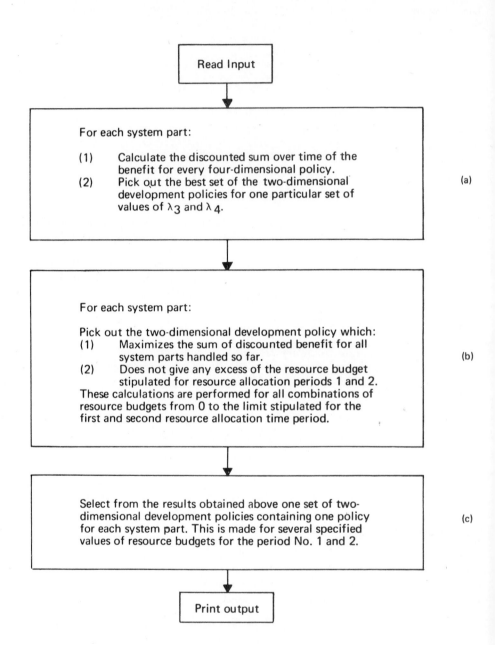

FIG.2   MAIN PROGRAM SECTIONS IN THE FOUR DIMENSIONAL DYNAMIC
PROGRAMMING CALCULATIONS

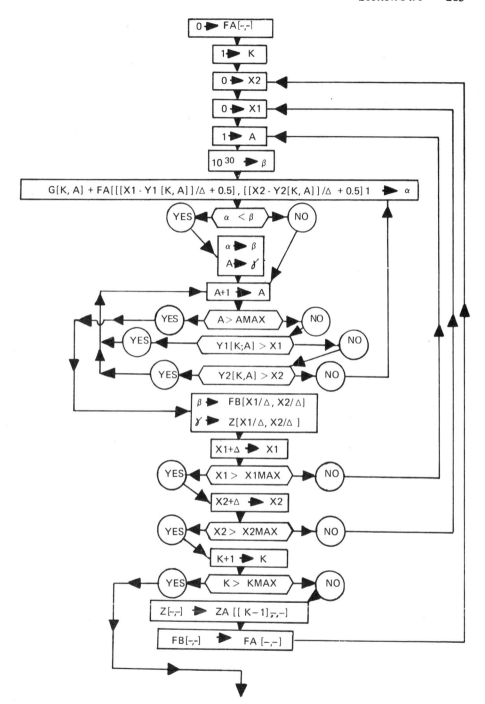

FIG.3   FLOW DIAGRAM FOR TWO DIMENSION DYNAMIC
PROGRAMMING

4.3.2 Flow Diagrams

In the DYPRI method both problems presented by equations (2) and (3) are solved by numerical calculations. Figure 2 shows the main pattern of the optimization calculations.

Section (a) in the figure 2 solves the problem of equation (2) in the traditional way. Sections (b) and (c) solve the problem presented by equation (3). The section (b) is of the most general interest and a detailed flow diagram is given in figure 3.

The following matrices have to be defined:

$$G(K,A)$$
$$Y1\ (K,A)$$
$$Y2\ (K,A)$$
$$Z\ (X1/\Delta, X2/\Delta)$$
$$ZA\ (K, X1/\Delta, X2/\Delta)$$
$$FA\ (X1/\Delta,\ X2/\Delta)$$
$$FB\ (X1/\Delta,\ X2/\Delta)$$

Where	K	=	System part number in chronological order.
	A	=	Two-dimensional development policy number.
	G	=	Sum of the discounted value of the benefit of development policy A for system part K.
	Y1	=	Resource quantity for allocation necessary in the first resource allocation period of development policy A for project K.
	Y2	=	Resource quantity for allocation necessary in the second resource allocation period for development policy A for project K.
	X1	=	Resource budget for the first resource allocation period varying from zero to the budget limit for this period.
	X2	=	Resource budget for the second resource allocation period varying from zero to the budget limit for this period.
	Δ	=	Size of intervals in which resource budgets are investigated.
	Z	=	Code number for the optimal policy of one system part for budget combination X1 and X2.
	ZA	=	The values Z given for each system part K.
	FA	=	The accumulated value of benefit of the optimal policies for the projects handled so far.
	FB	=	FA.

In addition, we have the following properties:

α, β, γ	=	Variables for intermediate data storage
X1 MAX	=	Maximum limit of resource budgets for resource allocation period No. 1
X2MAX	=	Maximum limit of resource budgets for resource allocation period No. 2
K MAX	=	Number of system parts involved
A MAX	=	Number of two-dimensional development policies for one system part.

This diagram follows very closely the corresponding diagram contained in Chapter 1 of the book mentioned under reference (3), but in figure 3 it is extended to two-dimensional problems. The detailed explanation of the flow diagram may, therefore, be found under reference (3).

4.3.3 Calculations Performed

The method was subsequently used for solving long term priority rating problems of road investments in some Norwegian counties, i.e. Sogn and Fjordane, Hordaland and Trøndelag, and calculations are now being processed for the Rogaland county. A run covering 100 projects demands 30 minutes of calculation time on the electronic computer UNIVAC 1107.

5.   INPUT DATA PROBLEMS

It has been found that in addition to the problem of developing a satisfactory method for the calculation of optimal resource allocation, the process of collecting and analyzing necessary input data is most difficult.

Task 1 mentioned under section 1.1.1 concerning determination of the benefit of resource allocations within a system is an important part of this work.

5.1 The Quantifiable Part of the Benefit

The objective function of the system has to express the benefit of various types of resource allocations to each system part by the same unit of measurement. In addition, the fact that the allocation of one type of resources to one system part may result in different types of benefit further complicates the problem. The benefit is often expressed in monetary units for large and complicated systems. However, the benefit could also, for example, be expressed in units such as time, number of workers, number of machines or number of meter or tons of a special commodity within the system, if so is preferred by the decision-makers. The monetary unit of measurement of the benefit may also be expressed in different ways such as, for instance, gross income, total costs or net income of the system. As far as the income is concerned, it has to be mentioned that it is not necessary to take into account the income of one system part deriving from another part of the system in question. This is only a transfer of resources within the same system and does not contribute to the total benefit. Furthermore, if the benefit is expressed in terms of gross income of the system, it is a mistake to include such resource transfers. The income to be taken into account is the income which is brought into the system from the outside, but if the system in question subsequently has to be considered as part of a greater system, then this income will appear as an internal transfer of resources. In view of these considerations, it will often be advantageous to define the benefit as a cost function.

In practice, two conditions will determine the formulation of the objective function:

(i)   Preferences or wishes on the part of the decision-makers

(ii)   Possibilities of quantifying or measuring with necessary accuracy the properties for the system in question.

It is difficult to discuss generally the first of these conditions but the latter may be divided into two aspects as follows:

—   What degree of accuracy is necessary, i.e. how sensitive is the final result (the optimal solution) in relation to errors in input data.

—   What are the costs in time and money of obtaining a certain accuracy of properties measured primarily.

These conditions will be discussed further below.

5.2 Sensitivity Investigations

Some investigation of the sensitivity of the calculation results of optimal priority rating in relation to errors occurring in the input data has already been carried out by the Institute of Transport Economy in Norway. This work has now been restarted. However, a lot of research has to be made in this field in order to obtain satisfactory results, because of the great number of input data and their complicated inter-actions. The following conditions will further complicate the method:

(i)   The possibility of establishing a good scale for measuring the sensitivity and when such a scale has been worked out, how to differentiate between low and high sensitivity .

(ii)   The importance of correct construction of a model or the priority rating method itself. For instance, how realistic is the assumption concerning independence between system parts in the various cases.

(iii) The representativity of the quantifiable parts of the benefit as a measure of the total benefit of resource allocations within the system.

The last two paragraphs have partly been dealt with above. In the following section, therefore, reference will be made only to the first paragraph (i).

The problem to be handled is the same that occurs when measuring temperatures. There are several ways of measuring, none of which may be said to be right or wrong, but only more or less useful in practice.

5.2.1 "Instrument" of Measurement of Sensitivity

First, a starting point has to be established: a specific system with a defined quantitative objective function and an established priority rating method as well as a given set of input data for the priority calculations are chosen. It is assumed that the objective function, the priority rating method and the set of input data are "correct". The results of the priority rating calculations, i.e. the optimal value of the objective function, N_O, and the connected set of the development policies, U_O, may then also be considered as "correct".

Thereafter, an error in one of the input data (for instance, an error in a parameter of the objective function) is then introduced, calculations of the optimal priority rating are carried out and the following two errors may be observed:

(i)   The optimal value of the objective function, N_1, is changed.

(ii) The connected set of development policies, U_1, is also changed.

The introduced error in the input data is of no importance if error (ii) does not appear $(U_1 = U_0)$, because the development policies will be the same if put into effect in real life.

However, the error in the input data may be of importance if error (ii) appears in the result $(U_1 \neq U_0)$. In this case, if the input error is connected with a parameter of the objective function, error (i) in the result will not give a correct picture of the influence of the input error. The correct procedure would be to adopt the false set of development policies U_1 for calculation of the benefit by means of the "correct" objective function. The result of these calculations may be called N_{10}. The difference N_0-N_{10} is then the correct difference in benefit resulting from the realization of the false set of development policies U_1 instead of U_0.

On the basis of the difference N_0-N_{10}, it may be stated that an instrument of measurement of the sensitivity has been constructed which will react according to errors in the calculation results. However, a scale for this instrument has not been established so far.

5.2.2 Sensitivity Scale

It is often difficult to evaluate the importance or the size of the errors occurring in the value of the objective function, because the benefit usually is defined as the sum of discounted benefit over a long time period and for several parts of the system.

The calculated error N_0-N_{10} may be important but very small, however, in comparison with N_0. It is, therefore, necessary to define a more appropriate scale of measurement for this error.

Establishing a scale is to choose two fixed points and to divide the intermediate area.

An idea would be to proceed as follows: Choose the poorest and the best set of development policies as two such points. As a by-product when applying Dynamic Programming calculations for independent system parts, a tabulation of the value of the objective function of all defined development policies of all system parts may be obtained. One set of development policies, U_P, consisting of the poorest development policy for each system part will give the value N_P for the objection function. Another set of development policies, U_B, containing the best development policy for each system part will give the value N_B for the objective function. As far as the inter-dependence of system parts is concerned, it is necessary to perform special maximization and minimization calculations in order to determine the sets of development policies and the corresponding values of the objective function pertaining to the best and the poorest solution respectively. The difference

$$N_B - N_P$$

is the maximum error which might ever be obtained. This value may be divided into 100 and the actual calculated error of the objective function, i.e. $N_0 - N_{10}$, may be measured according to the following percentage scale:

$$\text{Result error} = \frac{(N_0 - N_{10}) \cdot 100}{N_B - N_P}$$

5.2.3 Evaluation of the Error

When one single result of a sensitivity calculation has to be evaluated, the difficulty of distinguishing between unimportant, tolerable and important errors still remains. However, this distinction may probably be fixed if discussed with the decision-makers.

An evaluation of the absolute value of the errors in the result, however, is of no interest if the purpose of the research planning is to divide the research resources for determination of input data in such a way that the errors are minimized.

5.2.4 Practical Experiences

Some sensitivity calculations have been performed according to the principles mentioned above and the following conclusions may be drawn:

Generally speaking, input errors appearing systematically and pointing in the same direction for all system parts (i.e. equal percentage error) give relatively small errors in the result, as compared with input errors which may vary randomly from one system part to another.

Below, some particular results obtained in an investigation of a road system consisting of 25 independent roads, i.e. system parts, are listed. The objective function was defined as the discounted sum of road investment and maintenace costs, operating costs of cars and trucks, passenger time costs, as well as accident costs on the part of persons and material.

If an error in the result of one percent is tolerable, the following errors may be tolerated:

(i)   A change in the discounting rate of interest from 8 to 12 %.

(ii)   A randomly and normally distributed error in the traffic volume with a standard deviation of 15%.

(iii)   A randomly and normally distributed error in the fraction of leisure driving about the average of 50% with a standard deviation of 10%.

(iv)   A systematic 10% too high estimate of investment costs of the system parts. It was difficult to assess a too low estimate as the resulting "optimal solution" would have exceeded the budget limits if put into effect.

(v)   An increase in costs per accident from 16,000 to 24,000.

An error in the result of only 0.1%, i.e. 1/10 of a tolerable error, was caused by:

—   Increase of the price per hour of passenger time in traffic of $0.5.

—   A systematic error in traffic volume of 20%

Special attention should be paid to the investment costs and too low estimates should particularly be avoided. The greatest possible accuracy in traffic forecasts should be aimed at in order to avoid random variations. The dividing of the traffic volume into categories should be especially kept in mind, if the price per hour of these categories is different.

5.3 Observation and Analysis of Data

In the following sections the most common procedure of obtaining the most important input data will be described.

5.3.1 Traffic Volume Forecasts

The purpose of forecasting is to give an estimate of the volume of the different traffice categories for each system part for each resource allocation period. In most cases, the following steps will be taken:

(i)   The traffic volume forecasts are based on observations of traffic and of the conditions that general traffic. In large systems, it is not economically possible to observe all traffic, but samples of present traffic from each system part have to be made. In addition, similar historical data, if existing, have to be collected.

(ii)   Based on these samples, the total traffic volume has to be calculated for each category within each system part.

(iii) From the traffic within each system part, the traffic volume departing from each traffic generating zone and arriving at every traffic attracting zone is estimated.

(iv)   Data describing the course of generation and attraction of traffic have to be observed for the same zones.

(v)   The forecasting model may then be formulated on the basis of the information obtained under (iii) and (iv) and a quantification and evaluation of this model may be made.

(vi)   Forecasts are then worked out for the independent variables of the models.

(vii) The future origin/destination volume table may be calculated from the results obtained under (v) and (vi).

(viii) If the assignment of traffic on system parts is independent of the system part standard, this may be performed by reversing the calculation process (iii), which will produce input for the optimization process. If such independence cannot be assumed, the assignment of traffic to system parts has to be made within the optimization process.

5.3.2 Resource Requirements for Standard Change of System Parts

Alternatives for future possible standards have to be given for each system part. These alternatives must be accompanied by such a detailed technical description that it will be possible to calculate the amount of the different types of resources required when a system part is going to change from one standard to another. It is often necessary to set up cost models according to the following guidelines:

(i)   Collect account figures for resource requirements from a large number of different types and sizes of standard changes from a large number of system parts.

(ii) For the same cases, data or parameters describing the start and end of the standard change in question also have to be collected.

(iii) A resource requirement model then has to be formulated and quantified by analysis of data collected under (i) and (ii).

As a rule, it is also necessary to determine the way in which the resource requirements will vary with time in the future. In addition, the final depreciation value of each standard has to be determined, as well as how this value depends on the moment of change of the standard and its life range within the system part.

5.3.3 Resource Budgets

For each type of resource, forecasts for upper and lower budget limits have to be worked out. This has to be made from a macro-economic point of view and the distribution of resources between systems must be taken into account. The procedure should be similar to the procedure followed in traffic volume forecasts, i.e. observations of data collected from the present and the past, analysis of these data, and finally, calculations of future values have to be performed. The resource budgets, however, may be influenced to a great extent by the results of the priority rating calculations. For this reason, it will be worth while to work out several alternative forecasts for resource budgets and perform priority calculations for all the alternatives simultaneously, which process might give rise to planning on a higher level of the resource distribution among various systems.

5.3.4 Resource Requirements for the Operation of System Parts

The resources which are necessary for the operation of a system part in order to cover costs of maintenance, costs of accidents and passenger time, cargo time and other operating costs must be determined for each technical standard of each system part. These resource requirements should be specified as a function of the volume of different traffic categories. In order to solve such problems, data collection and analyses along the lines of the procedure mentioned in section 5.3.2, paragraphs (i), (ii) and (iii) are necessary.

5.3.5 Inter-Dependence Between System Parts

For systems with marked inter-dependence between the various parts of the system, methods have to be processed by which it will be possible to calculate the inter-dependent benefit of resource allocations. The way in which such inter-dependence appears varies strongly for different types of systems. It is not possible, therefore, to indicate a general procedure for the calculation of the inter-dependent benefit. Below, two different examples are given in order to illustrate the problem:

(i) In a road network, standard changes as "increase of strength" or "Improvement of alignment" in one part of the system may modify the distribution of the different traffic volume categories within the entire road network. According to this fact, the maintenance and operating costs of the roads as well as the traffic time costs, and thus the benefit of the parts of the road network where no standard change has been effected will also be influenced. In this case, the inter-dependent benefit will indirectly be determined by the distribution of traffic. Consequently, methods have to be worked out for the generation and distribution of traffic according to the composition of system part standards within the system. The method may then be applied as follows:

If the traffic assignment method mentioned above works sufficiently fast on the electronic computer, it might be built directly into the optimization method. The traffic assignment could then be made immediately after the set of development policies has been established. Thereafter, the inter-dependent benefit may be calculated.

If this procedure is not economically possible, the traffic assignment calculations may be performed in advance for a great number of combinations of system part standards. The result of these calculations may then be analyzed in order to produce a simplified model or a set of formulas for the determination of the traffic within each system part. These formulas may then be built directly into the optimization method. A research in this field is at present being carried out at the Institute of Transport Economy in Norway.

(ii) In port, ships go through several types of service, such as pilotage, towage, loading, unloading, bunkering, etc. The single ship may go through these processes contemporaneously or in series and, similarly, several ships may be served simultaneously or in series, one after the other. By change of standards in parts of the ports, the waiting time and service time for ships and cargo may be influenced, not only within the system parts where the standard change has taken place, but also in several other parts of the port. The inter-dependent benefit of a port may, as a rule, be expressed by the time spent by ships and cargo in the system. Such a problem has been solved by simulation in a research project carried out by the Institute of Transport Economy in Norway for the United National Conference on Trade and Development (UNCTAD) in Geneva. Cumulated values for time spent by ships and cargo in port have been tabulated for several combinations of system part standards by simulating the cases on electronic computer according to a comprehensive port simulation program. The results were subsequently analyzed and formulas describing the dependence between the time mentioned above, on the one side, and combinations of standards of the various system parts on the other side, have been worked out for the port in question. These formulas were then built into the calculation program for determination of optimal allocation of resources within the system.

6.   CLOSING REMARKS

For large systems, the research work necessary for production of a quantitative basis for the decision-making process has always been very time and money consuming. Previously, it has seldom been economically possible to present more than one main alternative.

The problems are so complicated that future work in this field will not be less expensive, but great progress in the field of electronic computers makes it possible to automize the data handling process to a great extent. Comprehensive calculation programs which have the possibility of taking into account a great number of factors are worked out and these will, in a relatively cheap and rapid manner, produce a data basis for the decision-making process in a concentrated form, making it possible to repeat the calculations with other input data. Several alternatives may then be presented. The following advantages are thus obtained: A large part of the factors which previously had to be evaluated directly by the decision-makers may now be determined quantitatively which combined with the greater number of alternatives, will give a higher degree of reliability to the decision process. However, evaluations of the not quantifiable part of the benefit and of the assumptions connected with the input data will always be needed.

Research work in several fields is required in order to establish a good basis for the decision-making process. Calculations of optimal priority rating of resource allocations within a system, as discussed in this paper, are only a part of this basis. This time consuming work is expensive, but the increase in benefit of the resource allocations will often be enormous and the research work itself may, as a consequence, give great benefit. The bottleneck of the research work is, however, the lack of qualified scientists but the interest in this field is growing fast and the prospects of the future seem good.

REFERENCES

(1)   Brooks, S.H. A comparison of maximum seeking methods *J. Oper. Res. Soc. Amer.* 7, No. 4, 1959.

(2)   Lingren, I., Carlsson, M. (Swedish language) Företagsekonomisk planering med Monte-Carlo-metod *Erhvervsekonomisk Tidsskrift*. Nr. 2 1966.

(3)   Bellmann, R.E., Dreyfus, S.E. *Applied Dynamic Programming* Princeton University Press, Princeton NJ 1962.

(4)   Gulbrandsen, O. Optimal Priority Rating of Resources—Allocation by Dynamic Programming (DYPRI) *Transportation Science*, ORSA, 1, No. 2, 1967

(5)   Skuland, K. (Norwegian language) Metode for prioritering av investeringer ved anvendelse av Monte-Carlo-teknikk (MOCAPRI) TOI, Oslo 1968

(6)   Johannessen, V. (Norwegian language) Prioriteringsmetodikk i Norsk Vegplan TOI, Oslo 1967

COST-BENEFIT ANALYSIS AND AIRPORT LOCATION

J.B.Heath

1. INTRODUCTION

The Commission on the Third London Airport, under the Chairmanship of Sir Eustace Roskill, has now reported. While this paper is based largely on earlier cost-benefit studies conducted within the Board of Trade on the optimum location of London's next and largest airport, inevitably it has been carried further because of the requirements of that commission, to which due acknowledgement is made*; however, because of these circumstances it is inappropriate to quote figures, and consequently the emphasis here is on methodology, not with the details of specific sites.

While most of this paper is about location decisions for civil airports, many of the same elements would arise in a cost-effectiveness analysis of the location of military aerodromes, and where important differences arise these are referred to in the paper.

An airport location project offers an ideal opportunity for the application of cost-benefit analysis (and for teaching purposes it is excellent, since it involves almost every type of problem in that technique). There may be many elements involved, each of a very different character, externalities are likely to be very important, and the analyst may be faced with a wide variety of problems of measurement and assessment.

However, this complexity makes for some difficulty in concise presentation, and this paper will concentrate on those elements which would seem to be most important and difficult.

2. PROJECT DEFINITION

The problem may be posed as "choose the optimum location for a new airport to serve the community at X", but this may not be its correct formulation. Where a locality is not at present served by an airport, it may be thought that at some set of prices and costs such an airport would earn an acceptable rate of return on the capital invested. Thus the problem may be "which airport location in the vicinity of X might be expected to give the highest positive net present value to the community, at some appropriate discount rate" (and the answer could be 'nowhere').

Or, where an airport already exists, basically the problem may have arisen because the forecasted number of aircraft movements beyond some future data (at the current—or expected future—landing fees) may be seen to exceed the expected capacity of that airport (or group of airports); again the true problem may be how to achieve the highest positive net present value to the community. There may be solutions to this situation other than building a new airport, including doing nothing (thereby causing congestion costs to rise) at least for a period, diverting traffic to other airports, with

---

* The views expressed here are, of course, entirely my own, and should not be taken in any way to represent those of either the Board of Trade or the Commission on the Third London Airport.

increasing diversion costs to the community as the demand for capacity builds up; other possible solutions might include manipulating traffic demand through the price mechanism, extending existing facilities, through building a new runway on the existing airport, improving air traffic control techniques, extending passenger handling facilities, etc. All of these possibilities may need to be explored initially.

If the question were indeed as simple as "choose an optimum location", one would seek to validate only a ranking of alternatives, based on measurements of differences between sites in which certain elements may be common, and could therefore be ignored (the size of the airport, its traffic and its rate of construction may or may not be common items, since the volume of traffic could be influenced by the chosen location). To demonstrate that a new airport would be a paying proposition for the community as a whole a rather more elaborate cost-benefit analysis would be required, embracing, for instance, landing fees, and the overall benefits to the relevant community of not turning traffic away or diverting it to other airports. Most of this extra information would be required, however, if the question were asked about the optimum *timing* for construction of the new airport, as well as its optimum *location*. While there may be good *prima facie* grounds for supposing that a new airport would be necessary, on the basis of traffic forecasts and the expected capacity of the existing facilities, it may be difficult to demonstrate the need convincingly until much work has been done on the costs and benefits of alternative locations.

Similar problems in defining the project and in ensuring that the right kind of cost-benefit study should be undertaken, may arise in the military field. The question may be where to locate a military airfield for a certain purpose, so as to achieve a certain minimum standard of military effectiveness with least cost to the relevant community . As in the civilian case, having correctly identified the problem alternative means of solving this problem would be sought.

3.   THE RELEVANT COMMUNITY

In any cost-benefit analysis, one has to decide early on *whose* costs and benefits would be relevant. It would not seem necessary to argue here that the relevant community should be wider than that covered by the commercial accounts of the authority responsible for operating the airport. An airport and its operations can affect the welfare of many individuals who could not feature in any way in the accounts of the airport authority (unless, of course, the authority were required, for instance, to provide an adequate surface transport system, to pay full compensation to all those whose welfare would be damaged, and if they were empowered to collect revenues from all those who benefit).

Assuming that the interests of residents in the country where the airport is to be located are thought to be paramount, a policy issue arises relating to the treatment of foreign passengers.

The treatment of foreigners in the analysis may arise in different ways in civil and in military projects. On the civil side, where the airport may be handling international traffic, the main issue would be whether to include foreign residents in the relevant community. One might say, for instance, that if foreign travellers are required to spend more time in travelling between the airport and their origin or destination in that country where the airport is to be located, such time would not be a relevant cost for the purpose of the project (assuming that the time occupied by domestic residents in travelling between the airport and their origin and destination was valued positively). Of course, foreigners themselves may value this time (as well as taking account of the paying out costs of surface travel), so that if total journey costs were raised for foreigners by locating the airport further from their (future) origins and destinations (which is likely to be primarily the centre of the principal city which the airport is designed to serve), then the *number* of foreign passengers who would travel would be reduced, if the price elasticity of demand for travel to that location was non-zero. This if one wished to exclude the surface transport user costs of foreigners, one would include any effects on the number of foreigners who would travel, because this would affect the welfare of citizens in the country where the airport is to be located. But in an increasingly international community, where many countries do include the welfare of foreigners in their own cost-benefit studies, the case for exclusion is weak. And if foreigners are included, logically their time costs should be based on their own welfare valuations, not ours.

Moreover, one might expect that the further away is the airport from the centre of gravity of surface origins and destinations of travelling passengers (which would entail higher surface transport costs) the lower would be the landing fees charged by the airport operating authority (since the landing fees would be reflected in the fare charged per passenger, and a profit maximising policy pursued by the airport authority would suggest this behaviour). Thus the landing fees charged by the airport would also influence the number of foreigner (as well as domestic resident) passengers who travelled, and the estimation of total user cost could not be determined in the absence of knowledge about the airport authority's pricing policy.

However, the inclusion of foreigners' welfare may give rise to political problems, as well as to difficult compensation problems, if the airport is located near to a city, which would simultaneously reduce the welfare costs of foreigners at the expense of increased noise costs on the local (perhaps lower income) community. Of course, agreement actually to pay compensation would affect air fares and hence the volume of traffic.

The relevant community for military airfield location decisions raises rather different issues. A NATO airfield which would be part of an international military arrangement would involve the military effectiveness both of the country in which the airfield is located and of other countries in the alliance. Thus it would be the *combined* military effectiveness which would seem to be relevant. Moreover, in this case presumably the welfare of foreigners not in the alliance—especially of a potential enemy—would not be included.

4.   THE GENERAL NATURE OF THE PROBLEM

On the assumption that the relevant community would be much wider than those covered by the commercial accounts of the airport operating authority, it may be convenient to enumerate the main elements which should be included—at least for initial consideration.

(i)   *Airport Construction Costs* (The capital costs of planning, designing and constructing the runways, terminal buildings and associated facilities);

(ii)   *Surface Transport Costs and Benefits* (Road and rail capital and current expenditures; the journey costs of airport traffic, allowing for the disutility of additional travelling time; and the indirect costs and benefits to other users of the transport system, taking account also of the large population that would be attracted to live in the proximity of the airport);

(iii) *Costs of Alternative Plans for Maintaining Military Effectiveness* (The costs of dislocation and/or subsequent reconstitution of military facilities which might be rendered unavailable by the air and/or land space required for a new civil airport, or the value of the loss of military effectiveness incurred);

(iv)   *Noise Nuisance and Amenity* (The costs to the segment of the existing community of a complete alteration in the *environment* over a large area surrounding the new airport, which would result from a change in land utilisation. These would include nuisance from noise, and the rendering of natural and man-made facilities unusable or of less value to the community than at present);

(v)   *Land Use* (The costs of a change in land use—avoiding double counting with the previous item—in particular the loss of agricultural or industrial output);

(vi)   *Air Traffic and Airport Operations* (The costs of having to re-locate air-lanes; restrictions on capacity due to interference with other airports or air operations in the same locality; greater or lesser flight distances for aircraft, according to the airport location and the origins and destinations of the aircraft; atmospheric and climatic conditions; operational restrictions due to noise; the extent to which airlines might have to duplicate ground facilities with other airports in the locality; restrictions on gliding and other flying activities in the general area);

(vii) *Labour* (Long term unemployment rates may vary in alternative locations, with differential benefits to the community of their reduction);

(viii) *Housing and New Town Considerations* (The costs and benefits of providing for the large population which will be attracted to the proximity of the airport; differential building costs in alternative locations);

(ix)   *Regional Planning Considerations* (The costs and benefits of inconsistency between an airport location and wider regional planning considerations for the area as a whole).

This is a formidable list, which contains within it a host of difficult problems for the cost-benefit analyst. All of these factors could be relevant, and there may be others which have not been included.

It may be remarked here that a cost-benefit analysis which involved all of the above elements would involve a major research effort, embracing the need for experts in many different fields of study, economists, systems analysts, computer programmers, geographers, engineers, town and regional planners. The inter-relationships between the various pieces of information which would be required, and the considerable resources that would be needed to obtain some of them, requires that the whole research effort would need to be planned using a critical path network analysis. This would assist with estimating the total resources required, and with phasing the work in the optimum manner. Thus a systems analysis approach would be essential.

It will be apparent that at almost every stage the analyst would be engaging in trade-offs between the various elements involved. What may be the best location from the point of view of air travellers may be the worst from the point of view of those living on the ground, and for air traffic control perhaps only sites that would incur very high surface transport costs would reduce interference with other airports to zero. Furthermore, a choice based on these considerations may conflict with the desire to use less good agricultural land, and to fit in with more general regional planning considerations. Thus essentially the analyst would be attempting to optimize for all these relevant factors, and this forces him to try to measure them all in the same units of account. It may be extremely unhelpful, for instance, to measure noise nuisance in decibels or in terms of the number of people who would be affected by certain noise intensities, if this has to be traded off against surface transport costs, air traffic control costs, and so on.

It is also obvious that there will be a need to formulate a number of sub-models within the overall network of relationships which would require separate development, and then to integrate them into the whole system. For limitations of space, all that can be done here is to indicate some major parameters which might be relevant, and to suggest the general nature of their inter-relationships.

One major resource problem, which raises a general issue of methodology, might arise if the initial site search, based upon minimum physical and operational criteria for the new airport, were to result in a large number of possible sites which would satisfy these criteria. To conduct a detailed comparison on the basis of the elements mentioned above for all sites which would satisfy the minimum physical and operational criteria might well prove to be beyond the resources which could be made available for such a cost-benefit study (or, given the resources available, the whole study might take far too long). The need, for example, to re-optimise the entire air traffic system surrounding a major conurbation for each of a large number of possible sites for the new airport may pose an impossible problem for the comparatively few experts in air traffic control systems who could be made available for such work.

In this event, there may be no alternative but to reduce the number of possible sites which would satisfy the minimum criteria to a comparatively small number on which it would be feasible to conduct a more detailed and rigorous analysis. The first problem, therefore, may concern the means of reducing the large number of possible sites to no more than a handful. There may be several ways of doing this. While a more formal type of decision tree procedure may seem to offer the best general approach, in practice a stage by stage process of elimination, as more details are obtained, may be the most practical. On the basis of the most important factors, in effect one would be conducting a crude cost-benefit analysis. But because at this early stage much detailed information could not be made available on every site, there may be no alternative but to estimate approximate extreme ranges of values for each of the elements in the analysis, and to test for the stability of the ranking of sites for the various possible combinations of these extreme values.

There is little doubt that initially one would be looking for site *areas* rather than closely defined plots of land which would constrain the runway alignment to a particular orientation. The precise runway alignment in a general location may affect a large number of elements in the analysis, ranging from air traffic control problems to noise and amenity considerations.

5.   SURFACE TRANSPORT

It may seem paradoxical that one of the major determinants of civil airport location—in most situations *the* major determinant—is the surface transport costs and benefits in alternative sites; but of course if travelling time has a positive value anywhere near average income levels, the aggregate passenger cost of travelling an extra mile is likely to be very large for all but the smaller airports. Moreover, airlines tend to charge the same fare to each of several airports serving the same conurbation (for the same class of passenger in the same circumstances), so that the air costs of flying longer distances where the airport is not in the optimum position with regard to the predominant air origins and destinations may be only partially reflected in the air fare charged (in any event this would be a comparatively small item).

As the basis for calculation, a surface origin and destination survey would be needed, although its projection into the future may cause problems. The determinants of population movement are imperfectly understood, and the location of the airport itself will influence the future geographical distribution of the local population. Moreover, different segments of the air transport market are growing at different rates (inclusive tours faster than business travel), and the origins and destinations of these market segments may not be identical. Nevertheless, with a suitable gravity model, and given adequate data, it should be technically possible to estimate the surface transport costs at each site.

The most difficult areas of analysis are likely to concern the following:

The determinants of the model split—the shares of traffic which will travel by road, rail and other means of surface transport which may be available or planned. This would depend upon the distance of the proposed airport sites from the surface origins and destinations of passengers, upon the frequency of service of the public (or airline) transport available, upon the relative cost of the various modes of transport, and upon the segment of the market being served (business, holiday etc.).

How the traffic will distribute itself between the available airports (if there is more than one serving the area), which would depend in part upon the range of air services offered at each of the airports and upon the air and surface origins and destinations of passengers.

How to determine the cost of time for the various segments of the air transport market (presumably a businessman's time in travelling to and from the airport would be valued more highly than a person on an inclusive tour holiday, or a child accompanying his parents—but how much more? And what if the businessman has a first class service which enables him to work efficiently during the journey, while the holiday maker regards his surface transport journey enjoyably as part of his holiday? Should the time of foreigners be valued more highly from rich than from poor nations?). In identifying the cost of time one should aim to isolate situations where passengers have a choice between higher cost and speed travel and lower cost and speed travel, and one should then analyse from such situations how much certain groups of people have in fact been prepared to pay for greater speed.

Non-airport users of a transport system improved for the primary use of air travellers would also benefit, while they may suffer extra congestion costs over unimproved parts of the system, and these may be difficult to estimate.

Whether it is worth the research resources to develop models and to generate the relevant data for solutions in all of these (and other) areas of analysis must depend upon the particular circumstances of the problem and upon the availability of suitable transport data for the areas under study. What has emerged from British work in this context, is that surface transport costs constitute an extremely important element in the overall structure of factors in a cost-benefit analysis of airport location, and that the research resources required to build the sub-models indicated would be very considerable.

6.   THE COST OF NOISE AND AMENITY LOSS

Noise may be regarded as one aspect of amenity, such that an increase in noise nuisance may reduce the value of amenity. (An increase in noise may not necessarily constitute a nuisance, and could even increase amenity in some circumstances, but here aircraft noise is regarded as a nuisance.) In any capital investment project there may be losses in amenity not associated with noise, involving the destruction of some features or facilities which would be regarded as having amenity value. Thus in an airport project the capital expenditure (construction) of the airport may involve a direct loss of amenity, while operating the airport system may involve a further loss of amenity due to noise nuisance, and possibly through increased dirt and air pollution.

6.1   The Cost of Noise

There is no space here to review the various methods of measuring the intensity of aircraft noise, and for present purposes the N.N.I. concept (Noise and Number Index, derived by the Wilson Committee on the Problem of Noise*) may be taken as a reasonable approximation. This was based on civil not military aircraft noise characteristics, however.

As stated earlier, because of the basic conflict between the needs of air passengers to have the airport close to the city which it serves, and the needs of the local residents to have the airport as far away as possible, there is a pressing need to evaluate noise nuisance in the same terms as the other elements in the analysis. The problem of costing noise (and other aspects of amenity) in money terms must therefore be faced.

From calculations of the shape of the various N.N.I. contours, showing the different levels of expected noise nuisance surrounding the airport at various dates in the future (according to the expected composition of traffic and the rate of growth of air traffic movements), the number of local residents could be identified at present living within the various noise contours, together with such facilities as hospitals and schools whose efficiency may be adversely affected by intense aircraft noise.

*   Committee on the Problem of Noise, Cmnd. 2056, July 1963.

While more research is needed into the costs of reduced efficiency (if any) in institutions such as hospitals and schools due to aircraft noise, the principles of cost evaluation if it were decided that such institutions would have to be moved elsewhere is quite straightforward (if, say, a hospital were planned to be rebuilt in any event, then the cost incurred may be solely the cost of bringing forward such expenditure by a certain number of years at the opportunity cost rate of interest). But housing and the local population at large create more difficult problems in evaluations.

Several approaches are possible, based upon the principle of compensation. Notional soundproofing costs, being the cost that local residents would be prepared to pay to avert part of the noise nuisance, offer one approach, but a more satisfactory principle—both methodologically more sound and perhaps easier to measure—may be based on the sum residents would be prepared to receive in order to tolerate the noise. Since noise is part of the environment, intensive noise would be a relevant consideration for many people in purchasing a house, and *ceteris paribus* intensive noise would be reflected in house prices. The *ceteris paribus* is important, since a major airport is a large employer of labour, and the desire for short journey-to-work distances may be expected to elevate house prices in the vicinity of an airport; moreover, supply conditions may also be important. The analytical problem, therefore, is the common one of isolating the partial effect of one variable in a multi-variate solution. Both the cross section approach, based perhaps on paired comparisons, and the time series approach (or a combination of the two) based on relating changes in aircraft noise over time with differential movements in house prices, with distance to the airport as an independent variable, may offer feasible approaches to measurement. Of course, values obtained from measurement at an existing airport could not simply be transferred to the housing density at each possible site since the population living near an existing airport may work there and physically be less sensitive to aircraft noise than residents in a quiet area.

6.2   The Cost of Amenity

In principle the damage to—or destruction of—some amenity asset due to the airport or its operations (excluding double counting with the previous item) could be measured in an analogous way. But instead of deriving a cost per house (or per capita) from an existing airport situation, because amenity assets, such as a park or a fine building, may be unique to the particular environment of the proposed airport site, a cost estimate based on each possible site would be necessary. While house prices may also reflect amenity assets, such as proximity to a park, users may be more diffuse and be located over a very wide area (the effects of supply may be more significant here). Thus the problems of measurement are likely to be more acute than for noise on its own. Several analytical approaches may be necessary, including replacement cost elsewhere of specific assets, the minimum cost being the relevant one.

7.   CONCLUDING COMMENTS

In a short space only the briefest insight into the problems of undertaking a cost-benefit study of airport location has been possible. Perhaps enough has been said to indicate the complexity of such a study, conducted properly and embracing all the factors mentioned.

SECTION 6

INVESTMENT PROBLEMS

Chairman: **M.G.Kendall**
Conference Director and
Chairman, Scientific Control Systems Ltd, U.K.

Speakers: B. Schwab
Department of Industrial Administration,
University of British Colombia, Canada.

J.-F. Boss
Société d'Informatique, de Conseils et de
Recherche Operationelle (SINCRO), France

CURRENT LIMITATIONS AND POSSIBLE EXTENSIONS OF SOME COMMON CRITERIA FOR INVESTMENT EVALUATION

Bernard Schwab

1. INTRODUCTION

In our competitive economy, the efficient use of productive resources, specifically of capital, becomes vital to the survival and success of a firm. Faced by allocation problems which grow in size and complexity, it is only natural that decision makers express an increasing interest in formal methods of investment evaluation. In designing any formal method of investment evaluation, a central problem is the choice of the proper criterion for measuring the economic desirability of investments. This problem is far from trivial, even if the results to be derived from an investment can be expressed purely in monetary terms, as we shall assume during most of our discussion. A number of different criteria have been proposed in the literature and are being used in practice. While these alternative criteria are often based on similar concepts, they are different enough to yield contradictory results in a number of situations. We shall start by discussing some of these criteria, such as various cost-benefit ratios and the net present value, and the implications of such contraditions for the economic evaluation of investments. In most instances, these criteria are presently used without explicit consideration of uncertainties. After giving a review of some of the techniques available to deal with uncertainties regarding the benefits and costs of the project to be evaluated, we shall explore some implications of uncertainty regarding alternate investment opportunities which may arise in the future. It is hoped that by pointing out the limitations inherent in some of the commonly used investment criteria and by suggesting possible extensions, the proper use of such criteria in evaluating investments will be promoted.

2. BENEFIT-COST RATIOS

Returns on investment or benefit-cost ratios are probably the most widely used criteria for evaluating business investments today. Let B and C be the present value of all benefits (income) and costs (outflows) generated by an investment project respectively, i.e.,

$$B = \sum_t b_t (1 + r)^{-t}$$

$$C = \sum_t c_t (1 + r)^{-t}$$

where

b_t all benefits generated in period t

c_t all costs, including operating costs, to be incurred in period t r   the discount rate which represents the time value of money to the firm.*

The benefit-cost ratio, R or profitability index as it has sometimes been called, is simply the ratio of the present value of cash inflows and outflows, i.e.,

$$R = \frac{B}{C}$$

Clearly, projects with ratios greater than one are acceptable, and the larger ratios are preferred.

In this context, the exact definition of cash inflows and outflows becomes important. Most investment propositions entail initial capital expenditures. Subsequently, cash inflows are generated which exceed the cash outflows required. Hence, such outflows can be met out of the benefits generated, with net inflows accruing to the investor. Thus, rather than aggregating all cash inflows and outflows, one may only consider the initial capital expenditure as a cash outlay, while benefits then become cash inflows net of current outlays. Accordingly, two different benefit-cost ratios which we may call the aggregate ratio and the netted ratio are presently in use.

Let the life of the investment be n periods, and assume that initial financing is required during the first m periods, while inflows, net of additional costs, accrue in each successive period. We may then define

$$C_1 = \sum_{t=1}^{m} c_t (1 + r)^{-t}$$

and $C_1 + C_2 = C$
$$C_2 = \sum_{t=m+1}^{n} c_t (1 + r)^{-t}$$

The aggregate benefit-cost ratio, R_A, is generally given as

$$R_A = \frac{B}{C}$$

with B and C as defined in (1). For the netted benefit-cost ratio, R_N, we have

$$R_N = \frac{B - C_2}{C_1} = \frac{P}{C_1}$$

where P is the present value of after-tax cash inflows net of operating expenditures.**

3.   ADVANTAGES OF THE NETTED RATIO OVER THE AGGREGATE RATIO

A variety of contradictory positions have been taken in the recent literature regarding the use and validity of these two ratios, often in a somewhat casual manner.† The formal relationships between these two ratios were analyzed in a recent paper by Schwab and Lusztig [11]. It is clear from (4) and (5) that for varying values of C_2 and

---

*   The proper determination of the discount rate is a separate problem to which we do not address ourselves in this paper. See, for instance [2, chapter 19] and [9, p. 36].

** P is also often called the net return. It is obviously not identical to profit, profit being equal to net return minus depreciations.

† See, for instance, [9, pp. 63–64; 1, pp. 310–320; 13, p. 6; 6, p. 179].

C_1, both criteria may yield contradictory preference rankings for an identical set of investments. In particular, it becomes clear that the aggregate ratio favors projects for which continuing operating expenditures are low in relation to initial investment costs—for instance projects which are capital intensive over those which are labor intensive.

In turning to the question as to which of these two ratios represents a more valid basis for sound decision making, we may look at the following example. Assume two investment propositions, both entailing an initial investment of say $10,000, one of which subsequently produces a stream of annual inflows of $3,000 and requires annual outlays of $1,000, the other one producing, *ceteris paribus*, annual inflows of $8,000 and requiring annual outlays of $6,000, and assume that these figures are given without uncertainty. Under conditions of certainty, it seems reasonable that an investor should be indifferent between both propositions, as the net inflows are equal and it is obviously the present value of net benefits which an investor values. That is, the absolute levels of benefits and of operating expenditures which are financed by such benefits are irrelevant; only their difference which represents net benefits is of concern. With such interpretation, the netted ratio R_N can be viewed as the "productivity" of the system, giving the level of valued output per unit of input.

The aggregate ratio, however, is not only determined by the levels of net benefits, but also by the absolute levels of total inflows and operating expenditures. Thus, we would obtain quite different values for the aggregate benefit-cost ratios of our two projects. From the above, it is obvious that such dependence is undesirable and misleading. Furthermore, by placing $C = C_1 + C_2$ in the denominator, the aggregate ratio does not recognize the essential difference between costs which the investor has to provide from his scarce capital resources as an input to the project (C_1), and costs which may be covered by benefits generated from the project (C_2). In effect, while the initial costs (C_1) are discretionary in the sense that the investor may initially well choose to allocate these resources to other projects, the later costs (C_2) are committed in the sense that this money is generated but also necessarily consumed by the project; it is not available to the investor for use in pursuing alternative investment purposes. Thus, of these two measures, the netted benefit-cost ratio is clearly the more rational one; the use of the aggregate benefit-cost ratio has to be condemned as violating some basic rules of sound economic analysis.

4.   SHORTCOMINGS OF THE NETTED RATIO AGAINST THE NET PRESENT VALUE

However, even the netted benefit-cost ratio is plagued by some shortcomings which are inherent in ratios. In particular, consider an investor who is faced with two mutually exclusive projects A and B, where project B entails a lower capital investment than project A. In order to obtain a valid comparison between the two projects, we have to consider how the investor would use the difference in investment capital $C_A - C_B$, if B is chosen; i.e., in order to compare B with A we will have to consider an investment portfolio containing B and some other investment(s) funded with the difference in capital, $C_A - C_B$. Thus, the relative desirability of B in relation to A will be influenced by the use which can be made of the funds which are freed by choosing B over A. It has been shown that if the marginal investment opportunity has a netted benefit cost ratio which is approximately equal to one,* the investment portfolio containing B and some other marginal investment funded with $C_A - C_B$ may become less desirable than A even if the netted ratio of B alone is higher than the netted ratio of A [11]. To illustrate with an extreme example, a firm operating under the above assumptions would clearly prefer to invest in a project A for which R_N = $120,000/$100,000 rather than in a project B for which R_N = $15,000/$10,000, thus in effect choosing the project with lower netted ratio but the higher net present value.

The net present value, PV, is usually defined as simply

$$PV = B - C$$

with B and C from (1). Obviously, with such definition the question of aggregating or netting does not arise. Again, the formal relationships between the net present value and the netted benefit-cost ratio have been analyzed elsewhere [11, 16]. Suffice it to say that while both yield equivalent results in evaluating investments in many instances, the net present value is the criterion of wider applicability in that it also yields valid results in the important case of mutually exclusive investment propositions with varying capital requirements, a case in which a mechanistic application of any ratio can become grossly misleading.

5.   THE MAXIMIZATION OF EXPECTED UTILITIES IN THE LIGHT OF UNCERTAIN FUTURE CASH FLOWS

In evaluating investment alternatives, use of the net present value has further advantages over ratios when including uncertainty and utility considerations into the analysis. Obviously, uncertainties are inherent in any assessment of the future. One source of uncertainty in investment evaluation lies in the forecasting of future cash flows, resulting in a probability distribution over the net present value. Whenever "risk" is of concern to the investor, it is not enough just to consider the expected value of such distribution, but the entire distribution becomes relevant. The probability distributions of cash flows in a given future period often become conditional on the past history of the investment, i.e., upon the values assumed by cash flows in previous periods. Under such conditions, it may be difficult or impossible to derive the resulting probability distribution of the net present value mathematically. However, computer simulation provides a powerful tool for deriving approximations of such distributions even in situations of considerable complexity [4]. Thus, if the investor can specify his subjective probability distributions of future cash flows—which in itself may be a formidable task—the resulting probability distribution of the net present value generally can be readily obtained.

---

* In a situation where we have no capital constraints, an investor should generally accept all projects which yield a netted ratio of greater than one and, conversely, reject all projects for which this ratio falls below one. Hence, we can expect that his marginal investment opportunity will have a netted benefit-cost ratio which is approximately equal to one. This argument is equally valid for the investor operating under capital constraints. For if in this case the discount rate is determined by the internal rate of return of the most attractive project foregone [9, chapter 3], the marginal investment opportunity will again be characterized by a netted benefit-cost ratio approaching one.

In order to evaluate propositions with varying probability distributions over net present values, a mapping has to be found which maps such distributions onto a one-dimensional utility scale. Cardinal utility theory presents us with the tools to accomplish such mapping in specifying that the decision maker ought to choose that alternative which maximizes his expected utility. The advantage of using the net present value rather than benefit-cost ratios as a basis for such analysis becomes apparent, since a utility of a benefit-cost ratio is a meaningless concept: One cannot place a value on a benefit-cost ratio without considering the absolute amounts entailed by the operation (for obviously, an investor would attach quite different values to two projects, both with an equal benefit-cost ratio of 2, but entailing investments of one dollar and $10,000 respectively).

While the powerful concepts of cardinal utility theory were developed by von Neumann and Morgenstern more than 20 years ago [15], a considerably lag exists between theoretical insights and widespread practical application. It is true that further research is needed, as pointed out in a recent article [14]. However, it is my belief that beneficial use can be made of the tools which are presently at our disposal. The recent successful implementation of a formal investment evaluation scheme including utility considerations by a diversified company, and the positive experiences resulting from this implementation lend support to this view [12].

6. INVESTMENT EVALUATION IN THE LIGHT OF UNCERTAIN FUTURE OPPORTUNITIES

While future cash-flows are one important source of uncertainty, it should be recognized that other factors may contribute to uncertainty or "risk" in a significant way. In particular, uncertainty regarding alternate future investment opportunities is of obvious importance in the capital budgeting context. Thus, an investor who made the best possible investment decision at a given point in time may deplore such a decision a short time afterwards simply because a better deal came along which he cannot exploit because of the previous commitment—often, just after having purchased a used car one hears from a friend of a much better car available at a lower price.

Consider an investor who at time $t_0 = 0$ accepted an investment proposition i_0 yielding a net present value of v_0. At some future time t, an alternative investment opportunity it yielding a net present value v_t may become available. The two investments are mutually exclusive. Assume also—for the time being—that if the investor has accepted the initial investment at t_0, he continues to be committed to such investment, i.e., we exclude the possibility of abandonment; for instance, this may be a reasonable approximation if we have high initial investments and low abandonment values. If at any future time we have

$$v_t \, e^{-rt} \; > \; v_0$$

i.e. if the present value of a new opportunity discounted back to time t_0 is larger than v_0, we will find ourselves in a position of regretting to have undertaken the initial investment. It would have been better to just have postponed the investment decision until the better opportunity for investment became available at time t.

Again, future investment opportunities are generally not known in advance; and the investor is faced with uncertainty. This source of uncertainty so far has received little attention in the literature. The one study which bears on this subject proposes to base such decisions on subjective assessments of the probabilities associated with relevant future events [10].

Let t_x be the time until an investment opportunity i_x with a present value of v of x or better arises, i.e., $v \geqslant x$, and let the probability density distribution which the investor assigns to t_x be $g(t_x)$. Assuming for simplicity a linear utility of money gains, the investor should postpone his initial investment decision if the expected value of the left hand side in (7) becomes larger than v_0, i.e., if

$$\int_{t_x=0}^{T} v'_x \cdot e^{-rt_x} \cdot g(t_x) \, dt_x > v_0$$

where v'_x is the expected value of v given that an investment opportunity of i_x of $v \geqslant x$ has occurred.

Explicit results have been derived for the case where the arrival of investment opportunities is random, with an arrival rate λ_x which is constant over time, which corresponds to a Poisson distribution of arrivals or to a negative exponential distribution of times between arrivals, so that

$$g(t_x) = \lambda_x \, e^{-\lambda_x \, t_x}$$

While the validity of such an assumption will have to be tested empirically, intuitively it seems a reasonable approximation for a good number of situations; e.g., arrival of new product ideas, of acquisition opportunities (in business as well as for the private individual searching for a house or a new car), etc. Based on (8), one can derive a cut-off value for the net present value which will generally be strictly greater than zero, and below which projects should not be accepted.

The analysis is further complicated if one considers the possibility of premature abandonment of a project: the machine which is presently in use may be sold or scrapped because acquisition of a new, better machine which advances in technology have suddenly made available on the market is considered.

An analysis of the economic consequences of abandonment of an investment proposition can probably best be obtained by plotting the net present value of that proposition as a function of time, V(t), under the assumption that the proposition will be abandoned at time t; i.e., the point for t = 1 year will give the net present value of the proposition assuming abandonment at the end of the first year, and so on.* Typically, because most investments entail initial capital outlays, one would expect an initial net present value which is negative for a very premature abandonment of the proposition, which then increases with t as net cash inflows gradually compensate for the initial investments, until finally it becomes positive, say at t°, at which point the

---

* With uncertain cash flows, each such point would obviously be characterized by a probability distribution; however, for simplicity we shall assume a utility function of money gains which is linear, and, hence, we are justified in just considering the expected values of such distribution.

proposition has proven itself economically even if abandonment should occur at any point in time thereafter.

Relating to our previous analysis, the investor should have undertaken an initial investment i_0 even if a new, better opportunity it arises at time t which fulfills (7) as long as the net present value of i_0, $V_0(t)$, given abandonment at time t, is positive. That is, if a new opportunity which is mutually exclusive with the original proposition only arises after t_0, i.e. for $t_0 > t$, the investor is better off by having undertaken such initial investment, in spite of premature abandonment. This point is well illustrated for what we may call "perfectly liquid investments" for which $V(t) \geqslant 0$ for all t, thus offering "complete flexibility". The simple holding of cash—which is often held for just this reason—is one example of such "investment"; and if we abstract from broker and transaction fees most short term papers equally fall within this category. In considering an investment which affords such liquidity, an investor need not take into consideration any expectation of alternate future opportunities; as new and better opportunities arise, he simply abandons existing propositions at no loss to him to take advantage of these better projects—he sells his ' liquid assets" to invest, e.g., in a new product idea. On the other side of the spectrum, we have seen that investments entailing a high initial investment and low values for premature abandonment imply continuing commitment by the investor, precluding him to change preconceived courses of action and, hence, they severely restrict his flexibility.*

Again it follows that the cut-off level for the acceptability of an investment proposition should not always be set at a terminal net present value of zero, as $V(t) = 0$ does not necessarily imply preference equivalence between the proposition and temporary inactivity. Generally, to evaluate the economic desirability of an investment, both the entire function $V(t)$ and the investor's expectations of future opportunities will have to be considered. For example, in searching to purchase a house, the acceptability of a particular house will be a function of the expectation to find a better house by continuing search [7]. Also, in light of the above said, one is likely to accept a house more readily if one only seeks to rent, as the economic penalty of premature abandonment decreases.

While explicit mathematical analysis to determine such cut-off levels is possible—at least in principle—as long as the bivariate probability density distributions expressing the investor's subjective expectations of new investment opportunities as a function of economic desirability and time is known, such analysis will seldom be feasible, mainly because of the difficulty of obtaining such input information. However, it is our contention that even a rough approximation to such analysis which is based conceptually on the dynamic nature of investment decisions will often yield better results than the tacit denial of such fundamental properties; for instance a rough but explicit graphical representation of abandonment functions may generally provide at

---

* For any t such that $V(t) < O$, the investor will only be able to abandon the original investment to pursue a new proposition if the net present value of that proposition at time t, say V_t, fulfills $V_t > [V(T) - V(t)] e^{rt}$. That is, the proposition not only has to be profitable in the sense of $V_t > 0$, it also has to make up for the loss which would be incurred in premature abandonment of the original investment as symbolized by the above formula. Hence, the larger the negative value of $V(t)$, the larger the right hand side of the above inequality and, hence, the more stringent the criterion for the acceptability of new opportunities.

least a first indication as to the economic consequences of an investment in a dynamic environment; if nothing else it will indicate to management where further analysis is warranted before reaching an inequivocal investment decision.

7.   SUMMARY

We have seen that the choice of an appropriate criterion for measuring the economic desirability of investments is far from trivial, even under the simplifying assumption that the results to be derived from investments are expressed purely in monetary terms. Yet, the specification of an objective function is obviously crucial in any formal approach to investment evaluation.

In reviewing various criteria which are presently in use, we found that use of the aggregate benefit-cost ratio should be rejected. The netted benefit-cost ratio, while often yielding results which are equivalent to the net present value, has limitations when considering mutually exclusive projects with varying capital requirements, and when including risk and utility considerations into the analysis. In situations where risk is of concern to the user, a probability distribution over the net present value should be derived to form the basis for an expected utility analysis. To incorporate explicit recognition of changes over time in the set of feasible investment opportunities, the proposed present value approach has to be further modified. In the light of such changes, the economic desirability of a proposition will not only depend on its projected (probabilistic) future cash flows, but also on the investor's probabilistic beliefs regarding the future composition of the set of feasible alternative opportunities. While an explicit mathematical analysis may operationally not be feasible—mainly because of the difficulty of obtaining probability density distributions regarding future events from decision makers—one may find that first estimates derived from various abstractions and approximations will provide a useful start. In any event, we can hope that awareness of the limitations of present tools for investment evaluation will aid in promoting a proper use of these tools and an adequate interpretation of any results.

REFERENCES

1.   Bain, J.S., May 1960, "Criteria for Undertaking Water-Resource Developments", *American Economic Review*

2.   Baumol, W.J., 1965, *Economic Theory and Operations Analysis,* Prentice-Hall, Englewood Cliffs.

3.   Fisher, I., 1930, *The Theory of Interest*, Macmillan, New York.

4.   Hertz, D. Jan.–Feb. 1964, "Risk Analysis in Capital Investment", *Harvard Business Review*.

5.   Hirshleifer, J., August 1958, "On The Theory of Optimal Investment Decision", *Journal of Political Economy*, LXVI, No. 4, reprinted in Ezra Solomon (ed.) 1959, *The Management of Corporate Capital*, Glencoe, The Free Press.

6.   Johnson, R.W., 1967, *Financial Management*, Allyn and Bacon, Boston.

7.   Kelly, R., August 29, 1968, "The Search Component of The Consumer Decision Process—A Theoretical Examination", paper presented at the Fall International Congress of the American Marketing Association, Denver, Colorado.

8.   Marschak, J., 1966, Decision Making, Working Paper 93, Western Management Science Institute, U.C.L.A., Los Angeles.

9.   Quirin, G.D., 1967, *The Capital Expenditure Decision*, R.D. Irwin, Homewood.

10. Schwab, B., November 7, 1968, 'Investment Evaluation in a Dynamic Environment: Some Notes on the Notion of Flexibility and the Role of Uncertain Future Opportunities", Working Paper No. 14, Faculty of Commerce, The University of British Columbia, presented at the National Meetings of the Operations Research Society of America, Philadelphia.

11. Schwab, B. and Lusztig, P., "A Comparative Analysis of the Net Present Value and the Benefit-Cost Ratio as Measures of the Economic Desirability of Investments", *Journal of Finance* (in press).

12. Schwab, B. and Schwab, H., May 1968, "Evaluation of Investment and Alternatives: A Sophisticated and Operational Approach for the Small and Medium-Size Firm", Working Paper No. 8, Faculty of Commerce, The University of British Columbia.

13. Sewell, W.R., Davis, J., Scott, A.D., Ross, D.W., 1962, *Guide to Benefit Cost Analysis*, Queen's Printer, Ottawa.

14. Swalm, R.O., November—December 1966, "Utility Theory—Insights into Risk Taking", *Harvard Business Review*.

15. von Neumann and Morgenstern, 1947, *Theory of Games and Economic Behavior*, Princeton University Press, Princeton.

16. Weingartner, H.M., Autumn 1963, "The Excess Present Value Index—A Theoretical Basis and Critique", *Journal of Accounting Research 1*, pp. 213-224.

L'APPLICATION DE L'ANALYSE DES COUTS ET RENDEMENT AU DEVELOPPEMENT ECONOMIQUE ET SOCIAL

J.-F. Boss

INTRODUCTION

En matière de développement économique et social, nous tirons d'une expérience limitée des conclusions pessimistes sur l'usage isolé de la méthode coût-bénéfice.

Alliée à la technique des graphes d'appui dans une analyse multicritères, elle offre au contraire de vastes possibilités qui font prévoir une fusion progressive des deux méthodes pour ces applications.

Nous rappelons ici les principes des choix en matière de D.E.S. global pour des économies développées, puis nous indiquons les particularités rencontrées dans le développement régional ou local de ces économies, et dans le développement global des économies en voie de développement.

1. ECONOMIE NATIONALE–PAYS DEVELOPPE

Nous évoquerons rapidement les critères de choix des investissements utilisés dans les pays développés de cadre libéral.

1.1 Raisonnements de Base en Matière de Choix des Investissements

Grâce à la notion d'actualisation, qui traduit par un taux la préférence pour le présent, et permet d'arbitrer entre celui-ci et le futur, on classera les projets concurrents indépendants compatibles ou liés, suivant la valeur de leur bénéfice actualisé. D'autres critères, comme la durée d'amortissement en avenir particulièrement incertain, ou le gain relatif en valeur actuelle, en régime de rareté des crédits, complètent le premier. La méthode pose les problèmes pratiques du choix du taux d'actualisation, de la période d'actualisation, de l'évolution du système de prix [Réf. 12]

L'utilisation de ces critères de rentabilité conduit à choisir les projets assurant un profit maximal à l'entreprise, en termes d'économie de marché.

1.2 Problème du Choix des Investissements Publics

Le choix des investissements ne se pose pas de la même manière aux pouvoirs publics. Dans la comptabilité d'une entreprise on néglige les phénomènes d'interactions ou d'interdépendances avec la collectivité, mais le choix des dépenses publiques implique de replacer l'investissement dans son contexte global d'influence sur la production et les consommations marchandes et non marchandes des autres agents économiques.

A la recherche d'un critère de choix spécifique pour l'économie globale, on a parfois voulu représenter l'intérêt de la collectivité par une fonction "d'utilité collective", liée aux satisfactions des individus, mesurées en termes de consommations de biens et de services, donc de revenus dans le cadre d'un système de prix. Pratiquement, on utilise le critère du "surplus", correspondant à une pondération égale de tous les individus, pour faire apparaître le bilan global d'une opération. On délimite avec peine le champ des effets, et les formes de l'information rendent encore plus difficile leur cadrage au niveau local ou régional. Pour la valorisation des biens collectifs, souvent gratuits et sans prix de marché, des effets externes d'entraînement et de nuisance, et des avantages non marchands, on rencontre des difficultés plus considérables encore, comme celles d'estimer le valeur de la vie humaine ou la valeur du temps.

1.3   Nouvelles Techniques de Préparation des Décisions

Si on reconnaît l'insuffisance d'un critère unique et, si on cherche à en formuler plusieurs systèmes correspondant à plusieurs classifications des projets, on est amené à regrouper ces classifications par souci de cohérence et d'homogénéité. On peut construire un graphe d'appui, qui regroupe les diverses décisions concurrentes, les ordonne, et précise les relations entre les éléments des diverses classifications. Destiné au dialogue avec les décideurs politiques et les analystes, les graphes vont des finalités de l'action politique en matière de développement économique et social aux modalités concrètes d'intervention.

Le dessin des graphes, qui recherche la compatibilité et la hiérarchie de plusieurs classifications, porte dans son parti et dans ses omissions une part d'arbitraire. Simplifiés nécessairement, toujours contestables, les arbres poursuivent à la fois une certaine neutralité politique et des arbitrages nets.

Nous fournissons à titre d'exemple un arbre général du développement économique et social, produit d'un "exercice" au Plan, et des extraits d'un graphe complet en matière de politique des transports [Réf. 1,2,3,4,15.]

On aboutit par approximations successives, dans le dialogue entre analystes et politiques, a une ébauche de fonction-objectif pour la collectivité. On pourrait être tentés, en attribuant des valeurs au progrès vers les finalités, de dresser des bilans actualisés pour classer les divers projets.

Cette approche théorique est irréaliste, et elle dissimule des arbitrages entre critères multiples. Nous ne savons pour le moment classer les décisions que dans la partie inférieure, technique, du graphe, où les analyses de coût et d'efficacité portent sur des programmes délimités et homogènes.

Pour remonter au coût du progrès vers les objectifs intermédiaires, puis combiner ces éléments en politiques complètes par appréciation de leurs efficacités au regard des finalités supérieures, ces méthodes n'ont pas encore dépassé la phase du dialogue et de la pédagogie.

2.   ECONOMIE REGIONALE

L'économie libérale suppose que par l'intermédiaire d'un système de prix arbitrés sur le marché, les décisions de développement économique atteignent le voisinage du rendement optimum. Nous avons vu que le choix des investissements publics n'est pas pour autant résolu.

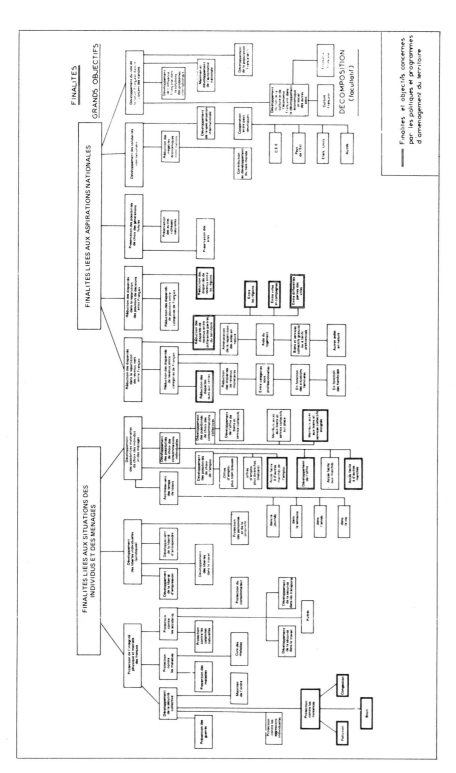

FINALITES DU DEVELOPPEMENT ECONOMIQUE ET SOCIAL

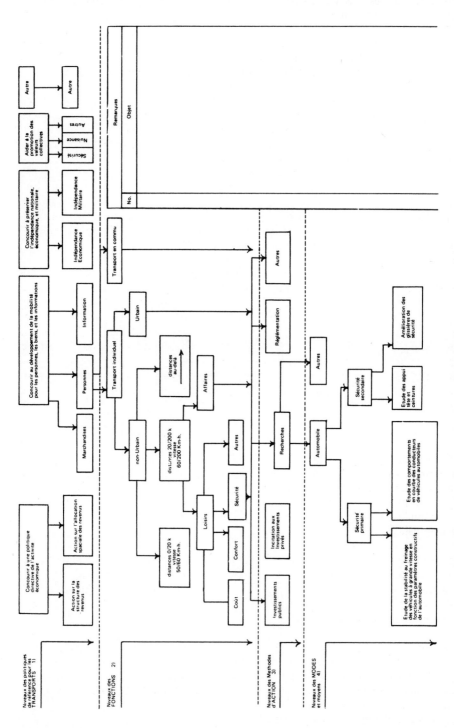

EXTRAIT D'UN GRAPHE DE TRANSPORTS (M. Rousselot et G. Gastaut)

Dans deux cas les lois du marché s'opposent au développement: pour l'économie régionale et pour l'économie des pays en voie de développement.

La tendance naturelle des entrepreneurs a choisir les implantations de leurs investissements sur la base d'une étude de rentabilité les amène au voisinage des sources de biens qu'ils transforment ou des marchés de leurs produits.

On observe alors le phénomène d'une concentration des moyens industriels autour de bassins historiques de main d'oeuvre ou de matières premières. Les services auxiliaires dont l'administration, la sous-traitance, les transports et les télécommunications y abondent plus volontiers. Le contraste entre ces zones de densité très forte et le désert environnant s'accentue par l'exode rural. Le sentiment qu'une telle concentration entraîne un coût élevé pour la communauté suggère des actions antagonistes.

Pour intégrer le coût collectif présumé dans les calculs de rentabilité des entrepreneurs l'administration dispose de deux moyens: surtaxer, voire interdire, les zones de concentration, détaxer les autres zones, qui présentent dans certains cas un véritable caractère de sous-développement.

Le premier moyen, dans un régime de concurrence internationale, a pour effet la fuite à l'étranger des installations les plus modernes des entreprises multinationales, ce qu'on peut sommairement considérer comme l'opposé du développement. Quant au second moyen, qui ne peut être raisonnablement envisagé que pour une durée limitée après l'implantation, il entraîne aussi des conséquences paradoxales. La subvention est recherchée par des sociétés en mal de trésorerie, dont les moyens ne permettent pas de dégager le financement des investissements. Pour les autres, si elle paraît toujours bonne à prendre, la subvention intervient faiblement dans le calcul économique, au regard des frais de fonctionnement en croisière, pour lesquels le coût des divers facteurs joue un rôle déterminant.

2.1 L'Intérêt de la Région

En économie de marché les responsables d'une région désirent sélectionner, puis promouvoir les investissements profitables à l'entité régionale et présentant un avantage pour les investisseurs par rapport aux autres localisations. Par nature, une telle étude impose un horizon assez long, de 5 à 15 ans, et suppose donc une prévision de l'ensemble des activités économiques, produits et marchés, à l'échelon national et international.

L'étude idéale se compose de deux volets principaux: le classement et le choix entre les diverses activités possibles pour la région, et la préparation de dossiers pour les investisseurs éventuels, mettant en évidence les avantages pour eux de l'implantation locale sous forme de comptes d'exploitation prévisionnels pour les diverses localisations concurrentes.

Les activités a priori intéressantes doivent présenter une forte croissance potentielle et un intérêt national ou international. Ces caractéristiques, indépendantes de la région, n'apparaissent qu'en conclusion d'études d'une ampleur démesurée avec les moyens locaux. Dans la région de Marseille, certains bureaux d'étude ont pourtant proposé l'étude de 3,000 activités différentes, tandis que le Plan n'étudie au niveau national que l'évolution à long terme de 28 branches.

Si on suppose ce problème résolu le classement et le choix des activités prendra en compte:

— des facteurs qui peuvent à eux seuls empêcher la localisation, dits "permissifs",
— des facteurs de prix de revient, agissant directement sur le compte d'exploitation,
— des facteurs d'environnement

Les critères ne se limitant pas à la simple rentabilité, on devra noter leur satisfaction par chacun des projets, leur accorder un poids, dans le cadre d'un scenario du futur, puisque certains facteurs sont appelés à évoluer au cours de la période envisagée, notamment la qualité et la richesse de l'environnement économique, industriel et tertiaire qui facilitent les relations intersectorielles, essentielles dans le phénomène du développement.

2.2   L'Intérêt de l'Investisseur

Sur un certain nombre d'activités choisies, on établit alors des dossiers d'implantation pour mettre en évidence l'intérêt d'une création d'établissement, et l'intérêt particulier de la création dans cette région, sous l'angle de l'investisseur. Le calcul de plusieurs comptes d'exploitation complets correspondant aux diverses localisations concurrentes, dépasse encore largement les moyens locaux. On se limitera donc en pratique aux éléments de rentabilité différentielle correspondant à la localisation.

Le coût de la main d'oeuvre et celui des transports des matières premières en provenance de leurs points de production et des produits finis vers leurs principaux marchés sont, sinon toujours les facteurs les plus importants, du moins les plus faciles à analyser comparativement.

Les trois tableaux montrent:

— des comptes d'exploitation résumés pour une région donnée et divers projets industriels suggérés,
— les éléments de classement de ces projets entre eux,
— le classement général des branches d'après la quote part de main d'oeuvre spécialisée et des coûts de transport pour une implantation.

3.   ECONOMIES EN VOIE DE DEVELOPPEMENT

Dans les pays en voie de développement, la rareté des facteurs domine l'étude de l'investissement: disponibilités en capitaux, disponibilités en hommes capables de réaliser un projet ou de produire, disponibilités en connaissances. L'absence d'infrastructure et la faiblesse des activités aggrave les interactions des projets. Si les contraintes sur le marché sont claires: absence de concurrence, protectionnisme douanier, tarifs de traite pour les importations, les prix du marché ne permettent pas d'analyser les priorités.

L'analyse coût-bénéfice achoppe sur les points suivants:

— l'échelle à laquelle elle conduit ne coincide pas avec *l'utilité* sociopsychologique
— l'évaluation des "bénéfices" de projets produisant des biens non marchands ou sur des marchés biaisés présente un caractère artificiel.
— les contraintes des économies en voie de croissance, notamment au dessous de décollage, échappent à sa description.

3.1 Arbre des Finalités

Une méthode permettant de dégager les priorités sociales, avec une idée nette de leurs coûts et de leurs rentabilités sous certaines réserves, puis de les hiérarchiser en fonction des contraintes externes, semble devoir d'entrée de jeu remplacer le critère de rendement par un critère d'utilité, multidimensionnel. La mise au point d'un arbre de

Tableau 1

Projets	Salaries (a)	Consommation Biens et Services (b)	Marges brutes (c)	Valeur nette de la production (d) = a + c
1	9,7	68,9	21,4	31,1
2	18,6	57,2	24,2	42,8
3	20,1	53,8	26,1	46,2
4	15,9	58,9	26,1	42,0
5	17,9	53,6	28,5	46,4
6	17,1	53,2	29,7	46,8
7	19,2	55,3	25,5	44,7
8	21,8	51,0	27,2	49,0
9	15,8	24,2	60,0	75,8
10	25,5	40,3	34,2	59,7
11	25,6	54,4	20,0	45,6
12	21,2	51,4	27,4	48,6
13	26,2	41,3	32,5	58,7

Comptes d'exploitation prévisionnels des projets (en % du C.A. de la production)

1 - Conserveries

2 - Confection

3 - Chaussures

4 - Papiers et Cartons

5 - Adhésifs

6 - Coulage de Matières plastiques

7 - Pièces mécaniques

(industries pétrolières, gazières, chimiques)

8 - Matériels électriques

9 - Circuits imprimés

10 - Matériel médico-chirurgical

11 - Produits pharmaceutiques

12 - Jouets

13 - Préfabriqués - Batiments - T P

Tableau 2

	Projets industriels, tableau récapitulatif									
Projets	C.A. annuel potentiel		Investissements		Nombre d'emplois créés (1)		V.A.		Rentabilité	I E (2)
	millions F.B	%	millions F.B	%	unités	%	millions F.B	%	Profit C.A	
1	1.120	7,84	250	4,25	620	1,86	348,0	4,87	21,4	0,42
2	600	4,20	60	0,85	1.500	4,50	256,8	3,60	24,2	0,03
3	1.600	11,20	1.410	23,97	4.000	12,00	739,2	10,30	26,1	0,35
4	1.100	7,70	440	7,48	4.100	12,3	462,0	6,47	26,1	0,11
5	700	4,90	350	5,95	875	2,63	324,8	4,55	28,5	0,86
6	1.530	10,70	750	12,75	1.500	4,50	716,0	10,02	29,7	0,50
7	1.000	7,00	868	14,75	1.400	4,20	447,0	6,26	25,5	0,62
8	1.220	8,54	915	15,55	1.600	4,8	597,8	8,37	27,2	0,57
9	500	3,50	100	1,70	350	1,05	379,0	5,31	60,0	0,29
10	500	3,50	300	5,10	1.000	3,00	298,5	4,19	34,2	0,30
11	500	3,50	90	1,53	210	0,63	228,0	3,19	20,0	0,004
12	540	3,80	135	2,30	1.200	3,60	261,4	3,65	27,4	0,11
13	3.600	25,20	213	3,62	3.500	10,50	2.113,2	29,59	32,5	0,06
Total	14.210	100,00	5.881	100,00	32.021	100,00	7,171,0	100,00		

(1)   Les chiffres incluent l'ensemble du Personnel : cadres, maitrise, employés et ouvriers participant à la production et à la gestion de la firme.

(2)   I = Investissements - E = Emplois

1 - Conserveries
2 - Confection
3 - Chaussures
4 - Papiers et Cartons
5 - Adhésifs
6 - Coulage de Matières Plastiques
7 - Pièces Mécaniques
      (industries pétrolières, gazières, chimiques)

8 – Matériels électriques
9 - Circuits imprimés
10 - Matériel médico chirurgical
11 - Produits pharmaceutiques
12 - Jouets
13 - Préfabriqués, Bâtiments, T.P.

pertinence cohérent et neutre représente là encore un travail considérable et arbitraire, et l'on ne trouvera ici qu'un exercice, tandis que les quelques cas cités indiquent la marche à suivre.

La méthode consiste alors à affecter chaque ligne de *critères* et à se demander dans quelle mesure les divers éléments de la ligne considérée satisfont aux critères correspondants. On attribue ainsi à chaque élément des *indices de pertinence*. Comme on a doté chaque critère d'un poids, un algorithme simple permet de traiter toutes les informations contenues dans les indices. L'ensemble critère-poids constitue l'essentiel de notre *vision* de l'importance relative des problèmes à résoudre, d'où le nom de *scénario du futur* qui lui est souvent donné.

Nous pouvons ainsi assurer la cohérence du classement final entre divers projets suivant le degré de satisfaction des objectifs qualitatifs et quantitatifs auxquels ils parviennent. On peut aussi étudier la structure de cette cohérence en faisant varier entre certaines limites les poids et les indices, on découvre comment les indices des lignes terminales sont affectés par ces variations et comment se modifie la *hiérarchie* de nos choix.

Tableau 3

Branches	moyenne des 2 rangs	main-d'oeuvre spécialisée		coûts de transport	
		Rangs	Coûts relatifs	Rangs	Coûts relatifs
23 - Caoutchoucs	2.5	2	10.02	3	0.25
44 - Trans. mat. plas.	6	4	6.25	8	0.53
40 - Céramiques	6	1	12.45	11	1.08
26 - Prod. papier-carton	7.5	5	5.57	10	1.02
14 - Tabacs	8	15	1.75	1	0.09
31 - Fila. coton	8	9	3.72	7	0.47
27 - Trans. papier-carton	8	7	4.67	9	0.83
20 - Savonneries	9	12	2.91	6	0.46
29 - Tanneries	9.5	14	2.11	5	0.27
33 - Fila. laine peignée	10	18	1.41	2	0.17
9 - Pâtes alimentaires	11	10	3.52	12	1.08
30 - Peignage de la laine	12	20	1.26	4	0.26
13 - Brasseries	12	3	7.52	21	2.44
10 - Chicorées	13.5	11	3.47	16	1.58
2 - Poissons	15	16	1.69	14	1.44
8 - Sucreries	15	8	4.39	22	2.67
42 - Cimenteries	15.5	6	5.45	25	35.08
38 - Agglo. houille	18.5	13	2.80	24	9.51
3 - Confitures	19	25	0	13	1.35
41 - Verreries	19	23	0.42	15	1.51
5 - Lait	20	22	0.85	18	2.09
15 - Huileries	20	21	0.90	19	2.23
12 - Alim. animaux	20	17	1.64	23	4.41
34 - Fibres dures	21.5	26	0	17	1.63
6 - Grains	22	24	0.15	20	2.39
17 - Raff. pétrole	22.5	19	1.34	26	35.61

Certaines priorités se maintiennent malgré de larges variations des estimations partielles, d'autres au contraire y sont très sensibles. Aux premières correspondent des choix très sûrs; les autres exigent des études complémentaires.

3.2 L'Analyse des Effets Croisés

En économie limitée, les projets d'investissement dépendent les uns des autres, leur calendrier modifie leur économie, on ne peut donc pas les évaluer indépendamment et le temps joue un très grand rôle. S'il paraît logique de commencer par l'infrastructure et les industries amont: barrage avant aluminium, pulpe avant carton, pour accélérer l'indépendance vis-à-vis des importations, la rareté des ressources pousse au contraire à la création d'industries légères, créatrices d'emplois et disposant déjà d'un marché:

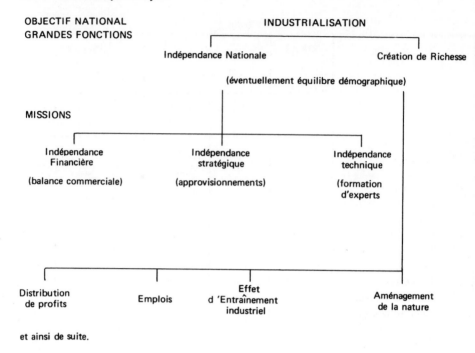

et ainsi de suite.

piles électriques, bière, peinture par exemple. Les effets d'entraînement se multiplient: un projet de conserverie valorisera le fer blanc des boîtes et le carton des caisses.

Le désir de ne mettre sur le marché international que des produits intermédiaires ou finis exige une prévision des débouchés et des technologies. La valeur potentielle des produits sont en effet trois phases; en *croissance*. La demande croît fortement, à une concurrence faible correspondant des profits élevés; en *maturité*, une concurrence vive se partage une forte demande et entraîne les prix à la baisse. Les pays en voie de développement se trouvent souvent contraints, en raison de leur retard technologique et de leur marché intérieur, à entamer des productions durant la phase de *déclin* du produit, où l'on assiste à leur remplacement par un autre produit en croissance.

On devra donc envisager les projets par systèmes, combinaisons de projets ordonnés; les versions les plus élaborées des méthodes à base d'arbre de pertinence, comme PATTERN, s'adaptent bien à l'étude des retombées entre projets (Cross-support) et de la non additivité des effets (force-mix).

3.3   Quelques Cas Concrets

(i)   Un cas de recherche technologique

Pour pomper de l'eau présente entre 8 et 40 m de profondeur dans un pays désertique et ensoleillé, on pense à l'énergie solaire et on en vient à comparer 3 solutions dont la dernière implique une recherche:

a) pompes classiques à moteur à explosion
b) pompes électriques alimentées par piles solaires
c) dispositif basé sur l'écart de température d'un fluide chauffé par le soleil et refroidi par l'eau profonde.

L'analyse économique initiale a montré a priori que b) était plus cher que a), mais que c) pouvait être compétitif. Le diagramme coût/probabilité de succès n'a cependant pas été fait, mais la recherche engagée sur des bases intuitives a abouti à un prototype satisfaisant.

Il faut produire en grandes séries pour que la solution c) soit compétitive avec a), bien que a) soit désavantagé par la consommation et le transport du fuel et les frais d'entretien. Mais on ne peut pas tenir compte de la probabilité de pannes et de dégâts dûs à la médiocre surveillance habituelle dans les pays en voie de développement sans généraliser l'analyse coût-bénéfice. Nous aurons à évaluer le coût de formation du personnel, de son entretien, dont une partie est proportionnelle au nombre d'hommes nécessaires, une autre largement indépendante. d'où la nécessité d'analyser le marché potentiel à différents coûts. Enfin, se pose le problème de l'évolution de la main d'oeuvre dans le temps, les hommes formés à l'entretien des postes de pompage dans le désert pouvant être attirés vers les zones industrilisées.

(ii)   Un cas de développement économique

Le bilan produit des pommes dont l'exportation est difficile. On envisage de valoriser les fruits en compotes, pâtes, jus, "sucre de pomme". L'opération comprend d'abord une recherche, puis l'acquisition ou le développement de technologies. Pour en calculer le coût et le rendement, on a besoin des prix des pommes. Le prix du marché en régime de m'évente n'a pas de sens, le prix de revient dépend de la production future. Puisqu'on ne peut pas isoler le problème pour l'analyse coût-bénéfice, on le situera dans un cadre plus vaste en utilisant diverses hypothèses sur le taux de production des pommes acheminées vers l'industrie de transformation.

On rencontre alors une difficulté propre à tout problème d'exportation pour un pays en voie de développement : il n'est pas équivalent de développer une production et un revenu interne, ou de toucher des devises, qui permettent l'achat de matériels autrement inaccessibles. Majorer arbitrairement d'un certain pourcentage la valeur des produits exportés traduit de façon sommaire la rentabilité des matériels importés, qui devrait à son tour faire l'objet d'une étude de coût-bénéfice.
Par ailleurs d'autres activités industrielles basées sur l'agriculture devraient rentrer en concurrence avec les pommes. On voit qu'on a besoin là aussi d'une méthode généralisée rejoignant les arbres de pertinence.

(iii)   Exemple de synthèse

Le bassin du fleuve Sénégal est sujet à des crues saisonnières considérables. On peut le mettre en valeur de trois façons :

a) faire des barrages de stockage et de régulation, et en tirer de *l'énergie* électrique.
b) faire des barrages permettant la *navigation*.
c) monter un dispositif *d'irrigation*.

En donnant la priorité à l'aspect énergétique, une étude de rentabilité a conduit à un plan de mise en place de barrages et d'usine pour un prix de l'énergie. En fait, le bénéfice sera plus complexe à cause de l'industrialisation, du développement de certaines régions, de l'emploi de la main d'oeuvre, d'exportations éventuelles. Pour situer le project dans l'économie nationale, il faudrait l'analyser dans toutes ces dimensions.

Le fleuve étant régularisé, on peut le rendre partiellement navigable. Les travaux supplémentaires augmentent le prix de l'énergie, mais ajoutent le bénéfice de l'équipement d'une voie navigable, et les deux aspects devraient être analysés globalement.

Cependant la régularisation du Fleuve rend impossible les *cultures de décrue*. Le coût de l'équipement agricole est alors beaucoup plus élevé. Pour trouver un compromis entre les usagers de l'eau, il faut aussi définir la nature des productions envisagées. La nature des aménagements dépend de ce choix, mais les bénéfices varient suivant les méthodes de culture, avec des écarts de rendement de 1 à 10 dans le cas du riz. L'analyse doit tenir compte de la propagation du progrès dans le milieu agricole, liée aux structures d'organisation agricole, dans lesquelles les coopératives jouent un rôle important.

On envisage d'autres cultures que le riz, et l'on dispose d'expériences concluantes de transformation de rizières en champs de canne à sucre. La structure du sol doit pour cela être modifiée, et on peut évaluer la différence des coûts d'équipement comme la différence des relevés. Mais l'évolution de l'Extreme Orient laisse à penser qu'il exportera de moins en moins son riz, ce qui ouvrira le marché à l'exportation. Une partie du sucre peut être exportée vers les populations nomades de Mauritanie et du Sahara. Nous retrouvons dans les deux cas des ressources possibles en devises, et l'on ne peut évaluer les solutions au simple prix du marché.

Enfin, si on choisit le sucre, il existe un risque très difficile à mesurer que la nappe d'eau salée ou saumâtre enfoncée grâce aux inondations fréquentes des rizières par de l'eau douce, remonte en entraînant une stérilisation progressive du potentiel agricole.

On voit les complexités de la mise en oeuvre de l'analyse coût-rendement dans un cas pourtant simple.

4.   CONCLUSION

Nous avons vu qu'en matière de développement économique et social, on devait dans tous les contextes dont nous avons pu avoir l'expérience adjoindre à la méthode coût-bénéfice une définition pluridimensionnelle de l'utilité qui l'amène progressivement à coïncider avec les techniques d'analyse des systèmes et de graphes d'appui.

Il ne faut cependant pas attendre de cette synthèse compliquée une efficacité immédiate. On n'a pas encore développé une technique globale satisfaisante, en régime de sous-développement les informations de base manquent le plus souvent, enfin l'expérience prouve que les résultats ne sont pas appliqués pour des raisons humaines : absence d'équipes de mise en place au sein des corps de fonctionnaires, identification des experts étrangers avec le gouvernement entraînant le refus des autres factions.

Au Congrès de Recherche Opérationnelle de Venise, le groupe de travail sur le développement présidé par le Professeur ACKOFF a d'abord pensé, qu'il fallait s'appliquer scientifiquement à obtenir les mêmes résultats que ceux d'une révolution sans la faire, puis au terme de sa réflexion, conclu qu'en l'état de nos connaissances, il valait mieux ne rien faire qui puisse empêcher cette révolution éventuelle.

SOURCES

1. *Exercice R.C.B. – Note sur l'analyse et la rationalisation des moyens de l'Etat,* Note 1 - Y.C. 8.1.69

2. *Note sur les finalités de l'Etat,* Note 2 - Y.C. 10.1.69

3. *Note sur les moyens et les conditions de réalisation des objectifs et des finalités de l'Etat,* Note 3 - Y.C. 19.1.69

4. *Note sur les finalités ultimes et intermédiaires de l'Etat,* Note 4 - Y.C. 14.3.69

   Commission R.C.B. du Commissariat Général du Plan - Notes de Travail

5. *Reflexions sur les activités des Pouvoirs Publics Methode et premières réalisations,* 23.1.69

   C.E.P.R.E.M.A.P. (Centre d'Etudes Prospectives d'Economie mathématiques appliquées à la Planification)

6. *Etude sur les coûts de transport et la main d'oeuvre salariale en Belgique,* Juillet 69

7. *Modèle pour l'étude économique de la Région de Hainaut,* Décembre 68

8. *Région du Hainaut Occidental: Programme d'action économique et régionale Projets industriels,* Décembre 68

9. Etude de projets industriels dans le Hainaut Occidental, Janvier 68

   C.I.M. Développement (pour l'Etat Belge)

10. *Direction privilégiées de développement de la Région Marseillaise au sein du développement économique national et international*

    Centre des Jeunes Dirigeants - Région de Marseille

11. LAMBERT, Hubert LEVY, "Les critères de choix des investissements publics, *Statistiques et études financières* - No 242, Février 69

12. "Appréciation de la rentabilité économique des investissements", *Statistiques et études financières* - Sup. No 239, Ministère de l'Economie et des Finances, Novembre 68

13. ENGLISH, J. MORLEY, *Cost Effectiveness* Wiley 68

14. PIGANIOL, P., *La prise de décision en matière de progrès économique et social,* UNESCO Paris, 1er Mai 68

15. ROUSSELOT et GASTAUD, G., "Techniques de préparation des décisions à caractère politique," *Conférence IFORS 1969*

16. "Introduction à la Méthode Pattern (Aide à la planification par l'évaluation technique d'indices de pertinence)," *Note interne SINCRO* Doc. 10.07.0469, Avril 69